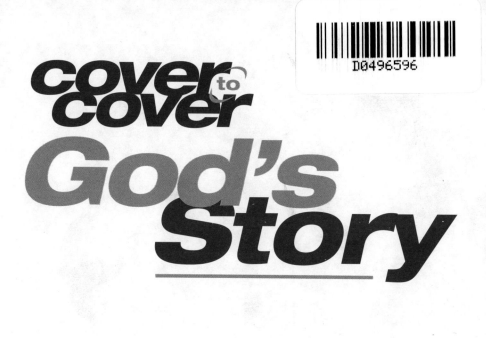

cover to cover
God's Story

Through the Bible **Promise by Promise**

365 daily readings

Philip Greenslade

WITH DEVOTIONAL NOTES BY **SELWYN HUGHES**

CWR, Waverley Abbey House, Waverley Lane, Farnham, Surrey GU9 8EP

Compiled by Philip Greenslade with devotional notes by Selwyn Hughes

Concept development, editing, design and production by CWR
Printed by: Litografia Rosés, SA Barcelona, Spain.
ISBN 1 85345 186 X

Photographic credits
All photographs (listed below) with the exception of the cover photo: jonarnoldimages, Jon Arnold, PO Box 455, Godalming, Surrey, GU7 3UD, England
Front cover: Water Droplet Creating a Whirlpool © Telegraph Colour Library, Getty Images Ltd., 101 Bayham Street, London NW1 0AG, UK

Pages		
	21	Sun over Dead Sea
	36	Amphoras, Bodrum Castle
	69	Desert, Petra, Jordan
	84	Banks of the Nile
	99	Via Dolarosa, Jerusalem
	123	Wadi Rum
	136	Evening Sky
	140	Well, Tel Ara, Israel
	156	Amphitheatre, El-Jem
	178	Treasury, Petra
	194	Steps to Mt. Sinai, Egypt
	215	Wadi Rum, Jordan
	233	Sea of Galilee
	238	Bath House, Masada
	253	Sinai Desert, Egypt
	269	The Treasury, Petra, Jordan
	285	Olive Tree, Turkey
	313	Stone Arches, Korazim
	337	Amphoras, Turkey
	370	Shepherd & Sheep, King's Highway, Jordan
	392	Shawbak Castle, King's Highway, Jordan
	421	Well, Judean Desert

Contents

FOREWORD

Nothing in my opinion is more spiritually rewarding and exciting than tracing God's story as it is unfolded for us in the Scriptures. Nor have I ever come across one as competent at presenting this concept as Phil Greenslade. He not only has a unique ability to delineate this most tremendous truth but does it with a passion that shows through in almost every sentence he writes.

How I wish that more Christians would take the point that Eugene Peterson makes, namely that the Bible comes to us as a story. "It does not come to us systematised into doctrine," he says, "or arranged as moral instruction. It is a story and the story form is as important as the truth it tells."

One of the greatest things we can do as believers is to open our ears to Scripture and one of the best ways we can develop our spiritual lives is by allowing ourselves to be drawn into the action of God through history, a story that began in the eternity past and will end in the eternity to come.

I shall never forget the moment when the concept first hit me, that God is not only writing a story but that I am in it also. It did more than anything I know to develop a sense of journeying and discipleship.

I suspect that the time you will spend going through this particular edition of *Cover to Cover* will turn out to be one of the highlights of your Christian life so far.

Be blessed.

Selwyn Hughes

Selwyn Hughes

Note to Reader

A DEVOTIONAL INTERLUDE

The purpose of the devotional interlude at the end of each day's commentary is to help you respond to the day's Scripture reading and teaching in a way that will apply the truth to both heart and mind. Sometimes it will be a prayer or a devotional thought arising out of the reading; at other times, a question, an affirmation, something to act upon or an issue for thanksgiving or praise. Note that the difference between a "thought" and "something to ponder" is this: the "thought" is something to think about immediately following the day's reading. Something to "ponder" might occupy your thoughts throughout the day and is deserving of deeper and further consideration.

INTRODUCTION

Welcome to this journey of discovery through the Bible. I trust you will be moved as I have been by following *God's Story* from cover to cover, from first creation to final creation.

Throughout this year, you will see how the familiar Bible stories fit into the larger, coherent story *of* the Bible which climaxes in the story of Jesus.

I hope you will marvel as I do at the covenantal commitments God has made to bring salvation to us and to the whole created order.

Let me explain how *Cover to Cover "God's Story"* works.

The first two sections show that Jesus taught us to "read" the Bible as God's story. This story centres on *Jesus* Himself, and encompasses the stories of the world, of Israel and of ourselves.

At the heart of this year-long programme are the major *covenants* by which God expresses His loving commitment to save the world He has made. The motif at the foot of each page represents the way these covenants sustain the progress of God's promise-plan through history.

In each of these central sections, *Cover to Cover* first looks at the key biblical passages where each covenant is described, and then shows how this works out from Genesis to Revelation.

Eventually, all the threads are pulled together in *Jesus* (as indicated in the diagram which prefaces each section) and are then elaborated through the voices of *Paul and John* who represent the New Testament witness.

As the year closes, we learn how we can respond to *God's story* and so find our personal narratives caught up in the large-scale adventure of what God is doing.

If you read in sequence, the effect is *cumulative*. So be patient and watch as each stage of the story gathers up clues from previous stages. Notice, especially, how particular themes re-occur with added significance. As you stay with the project, you will begin to make the connections which make the Bible so compelling.

The scope of the story is creation-wide. We start with Noah because covenant language is first explicitly used with him and because he marks the first major step on the recovery of Adam's position.

References supporting the biblical theology expressed here have not been included but may be found in my book *A Passion for God's Story* published by Paternoster Press.

So, we invite you to:

- experience the Bible as an enthralling narrative and learn of the five interlocking stories which help us interpret "God's master story" that points the way to Jesus.

- discover with Noah that God loves His creation so much that He pledges to preserve the planet in order to redeem it.

- join the adventure of faith with father Abraham as God sets in motion through him the promise-plan to bless all nations.

- stand with Moses at Sinai as God chooses Israel as His covenant partner for the sake of the world.

- sit awestruck with David as God entrusts to his "son-king" the "charter by which the whole of humanity's future is directed"

- feel the acute anguish and fierce hope of the prophets of the Exile as they forge out of "death" a new vision of God who so empowers His people as to make the covenant partnership with Him work

- meet Jesus again, as if for the first time, as He re-enacts all that Israel and her kings were meant to be and so brings God's promise-plan to strange but successful fulfilment.

- stagger with Paul as he unveils the amazing mystery of God's secret strategy to bring everything together under the lordship of Jesus, and glimpse with John the stunning glory of God's new creation.

Above all we invite you to make a sincere response of wonder, worship and faith – perhaps for the first time – perhaps for a fresh time.

Paul told Timothy that in the last days people would love themselves, their money and their pleasure and would become "allergic to God" (*The Message*).

Cover to Cover "God's Story" is our contribution to reversing that trend. It seeks to help you swim against the cultural tide by becoming a passionate lover of God.

So let's "roll up the sleeves of our minds" and ask the Holy Spirit to be our Teacher as we travel together through God's story.
Wishing you all joy on the journey,

Philip Greenslade.

Philip Greenslade July 2001

SECTION 1
JESUS' BURNING-HEART BIBLE SCHOOL

Jesus and the "Burning Heart Bible School" (Luke 24:13-49)

Noah and his ark, Joseph and his "technicolour dreamcoat", Moses "Prince of Egypt", David and Goliath, Daniel in the lions' den – these are some of the Bible stories that people of my generation grew up to be familiar with. But being familiar with Bible stories is one thing; *knowing the Bible story* is another thing altogether!

This, I believe, is what Jesus wanted His followers to grasp after His resurrection, as He makes clear to the two disciples on the road to Emmaus and to the rest of the disciple band back in Jerusalem: "And beginning with Moses and all the Prophets, he explained to them what was said in all the Scriptures concerning himself. ... Everything must be fulfilled that is written about me in the Law of Moses, the Prophets and the Psalms" (Luke 24:27,44).

It is unlikely that Jesus was merely listing certain proof-texts which in some way or other pointed to Him. More likely, He was seeking to show them how the whole of the earlier part of the story of Israel told in the Old Testament had come to a climax in Him. "So that the Scriptures might be fulfilled" cannot be reduced to those scattered predictions which land on target in Jesus. Jesus is, in effect, drawing the whole of the Old Testament story onto Himself. He is connecting up the well-loved Bible stories and showing how they add up to the one big story of what God is doing. This is the approach adopted in this study.

God's pledge to Noah to withhold further judgment on His first creation until His redemptive work is completed and He can bring in a new creation now converges with Christ's cross and resurrection. Here, in the cross, God absorbs and defeats the pain, sin, and mortality of the old fallen creation. Here, in Christ's resurrection, the one Creator God both endorses the goodness of His first creation and relaunches it as a new creation.

God's promise to Abraham to bless all the nations through him sets in motion the long story of faith that comes to fulfilment in Jesus, Abraham's true "seed", through whom the curse is turned to blessing for the world.

As Messiah and King, He assumes Israel's role as God's obedient Son, faithful covenant partner and servant who suffers for the sake of the world. What Israel's history was intended to achieve but left undone, He completes; what Israel was called to be but failed to do, He successfully re-enacts.

All God's dreams for kingship, first focused on David, by which Israel's King was destined to be Lord of the world – dreams turned to dust by five centuries of faithless monarchs – finally come good in Him!

What the prophets envisaged as salvation beyond the Exile when they saw God returning as King, and restoring His people on the other side of death and resurrection, is concentrated in Him. His blood is the blood of the new covenant shed for many, and His rising is the glory of His people Israel and the light of revelation to the Gentiles.

Every covenantal connection eventually leads to Him, every stream of truth flows into His river, every promise of God finds its "Yes" and "Amen" in Him, each aspect of God's overall strategy is filled-full in Him! This is what He wants them to grasp!

And the way He opens up the themes and traces the threads of God's purpose in Scriptures "warms the heart". Hearts which have iced up with despair or frozen over with false views of reality are thawed out with truth! And by opening up the Book in His own unique way He rekindles a lost passion. Later the apostle John would relive his first encounter when, with tears wiped from his eyes, he sees the slain Lamb standing, worthy to open the scroll of God's purposes for history.

For this *our eyes have to be opened, the Bible has to be opened, our minds need to be opened.*

It is quite possible, as some in Israel did, to follow Jesus on the road in admiration of His teaching right up to the cross. But if then we stop short of the cross we miss His whole reason for living since He enters into His real glory only through suffering.

It is perfectly possible to fall in with Jesus even after His resurrection but as though He were an unrecognised stranger who makes no difference to the direction our lives are taking.

It is even possible to have had a gloriously personal experience of Jesus as alive today and yet to remain in the dark about His central place in God's big story which alone explains Him.

Even then, though we have met the risen Christ and heard Him explain Himself from the big story, we will not know its truth until we join with other disciples in the community and learn to live out the story in our own lives in obedient joy.

So discover God's amazing story with us by enlisting in the Bible School of Jesus. And let's ask the Holy Spirit to be our teacher.

DAY 1

READ
Luke 24:1-14

When we lose hope it is as if we are relinquishing our hold on life itself. We feel we are closing the door on the future and reaching a dead end.

It was in just such a mood that two disciples of Jesus went back to their home village of Emmaus in the bitter aftermath of His crucifixion. Their personal correspondence with Jesus was now closed; the great adventure was over.

Emmaus is where we all tend to go at such times. Frederick Buechner puts it well: "Emmaus is whatever we do or wherever we go to make ourselves forget that the world holds nothing sacred; that even the wisest and bravest and loveliest decay and die; that even the noblest ideas that men have had – ideas about love and justice and freedom – have always in time been twisted out of shape by selfish men for selfish ends. Emmaus is where we go to forget."

Emmaus is the "comfort-zone" we retreat into as we attempt to piece together the shattered fragments of our own stories into something that makes sense.

A DEVOTIONAL INTERLUDE

Thought: Are you travelling along an Emmaus Road at this moment? Is your heart feeling dejected because God has not come through for you in the way you expected? Don't lose hope. Your own story (your plans and ambitions) may have to be shattered in order for God's big story to be acted out. Though it hurts to have one's own plans thwarted, always remember this: God's plans are not only the best for Him but also the best for us.

DAY **2**

READ
Luke 24:15-16

Dulled by despair and preoccupied with grief, the two disciples trudge home to Emmaus. Jesus had once assured them that there *was* a key even to death's door and they had believed that He held that key. But that glimmer of hope had been overtaken and buried by events.

They are so absorbed in their sad recriminations that they fail to recognise the Stranger who falls in alongside them on the road! They have lost the plot of whatever story it was that had held their lives together. Now they grope like bewildered characters in search of an author.

It is precisely in this context and mood that Easter is good news. There is a Stranger who falls in beside us on the uncertain road ahead to surprise us with hope. There is something that makes all the difference in the world; there is Someone who makes all the difference to the world!

The good news we celebrate is the resurrection of Jesus Christ from the dead!

A DEVOTIONAL INTERLUDE

Prayer: My Father and my God, forgive me that sometimes I allow myself to be so overcome by despair that my soul becomes oblivious of Your presence. Help me to understand that though I cannot feel Your presence, it is there nevertheless. One of the purposes of Your Son being raised from the dead was to be with me – always. I am so grateful that the message of the empty tomb is not just for Easter day but for every day. Thank you my Father. Amen.

DAY **3**

READ

Luke 24:17-21

Unable yet to appreciate His aliveness, the two disciples explain to Jesus their sense of despair. "We had hoped that he was the one who was going to redeem Israel" (v.21). "We *had* hoped ..." exactly sums up their disillusionment. Their dream was a proud one, kept alive in various forms within Israel for over five hundred years ever since the returning exiles had trudged back from Babylonian captivity.

These two, like so many before them, had hoped for someone to "redeem Israel" from its deeper exile in alienation from God and under His judgment. They had pinned their hopes on Jesus of Nazareth. They had joined those who thought they could get Him elected Messiah. They had thought this was their moment of destiny, the moment to engage with the cogs of history's big wheel. They had felt sure that "there is a life about to start when tomorrow comes". Only tomorrow never came, except as Good Friday.

Now death has slammed shut the door of their lives.

A DEVOTIONAL INTERLUDE

Thought: Faith, said someone, is "believing in the dark what you discovered in the light". If the two Emmaus disciples had done this do you think they would have been in such a sad state spiritually? Had not Christ told His disciples over and over again that He would die but would be raised from the dead? When you next find yourself in spiritual darkness cast your mind back to the things you saw when your path was bathed in light.

DAY 4

READ
Luke 24:22-24

It is important to realise that the resurrection is not some happy ending tacked on to the Jesus story. Without its final chapter, the gospel of Jesus Christ is no gospel at all. Now, as then, the resurrection of Jesus Christ opens the way into God's new creation and leaves a gaping hole in all failed, alternative versions of reality – be they scientific materialism, Marxism, or whatever.

Of course, nothing affronts modern sensibilities more than talk of resurrection from the dead! But we need not be deterred by those who say you cannot fit incredible happenings such as resurrection into the modern way of looking at the world. As Lesslie Newbigin said so well: "The resurrection cannot be accommodated in any way of understanding the world *except one of which it is the starting-point* ... the starting-point of a whole new way of understanding the cosmos and the human situation in the cosmos."

The resurrection of Jesus has to be the ultimate post-modern event! It opens up a completely new way of viewing the world around us, as the two Emmaus-bound travellers were soon to discover. A *resurrection-view-of-reality* is now about to break in and open everything up for them!

A DEVOTIONAL INTERLUDE

Prayer: Heavenly Father, help me to have a resurrection-view-of-reality and not allow myself to be brainwashed by an age which cannot conceive of Your miraculous interventions in the world. Help me understand that all alternative versions of reality are roads that lead nowhere. May the truth of Your resurrection fill and thrill my soul every moment of the day. In Jesus' Name I pray. Amen.

DAY **5**

READ
Luke 24:25-27

If we pause today to consider the situation in which Jesus speaks, we will marvel at His order of priorities. After all, what would any one of us have done immediately after being raised from the dead and vindicated as Messiah? What might He have been expected to do? Empty all the sick beds in Israel perhaps? Not so, it seems. Throw Himself off the pinnacle of the Temple to prove His divinity? No, He'd faced that one before! March to Rome to claim the world's throne? No, that was His for the asking!

His priority is different and very striking! He spends much of those precious forty days before His ascension in *Bible teaching*, explaining the Scriptures to them. Verses 25 to 27 give us a strong clue as to what He was up to: "And beginning with Moses and all the Prophets, *he explained to them what was said in all the Scriptures concerning himself*" (v.27).

This must mean that without the story of Jesus, the Old Testament makes no final sense. It also means that without the Old Testament we cannot understand Jesus, and that it takes the whole of the Old Testament story to explain who Jesus is.

To repeat what we have said before: this is not a matter of finding scattered proof-texts or predictions which somehow anticipate Jesus but of seeing how the whole Old Testament story reaches its climax in Him.

A DEVOTIONAL INTERLUDE

Thought: Imagine having an audio tape of that thrilling Scriptural exposition given by Jesus during the walk to Emmaus. How greatly do you think you would value it? The Holy Spirit has not seen fit to give us a record of it but we do know its central theme: "the things concerning himself". Never forget that the key to understanding both Old and New Testaments is *Jesus*. He is the hub of the Bible. Is He the hub of your heart and life?

DAY **6**

READ
Luke 24:28-31

Luke describes the impact of the resurrection by using three times in this chapter the verb "to open" – open eyes, open Book, open minds (vv.31,32,45). The opened tomb of Jesus truly works wonders.

Notice first how their eyes are opened. As evening approaches, He seems intent on moving on, but they urge Him: "'Stay with us ...' When he was at the table with them, he took bread, gave thanks, broke it and began to give it to them. Then *their eyes were opened* and they recognised him ..." (vv.29–31). This wonderful recognition scene grips the imagination – as it has done for many great artists, including Rembrandt! The fact of resurrection is brought home to them as they personally experience His risenness.

Such an experience will be different for each of us, of course, but every believer can testify to some moment of sudden or growing realisation that Jesus is truly alive and facing us, as it were, across the table! Those who have met Him in this way never forget the moment. And though called to walk by faith and not by sight, again and again – most likely in broken bread and poured-out wine – they meet Him afresh and know His presence as the living Christ.

A DEVOTIONAL INTERLUDE

Question: When were you last vividly aware of the closeness of the risen Christ? If your encounters with the Saviour are few and far between then ask yourself "Why?" Is it because your prayer times are rushed and you do not linger in His presence? Is there some unconfessed sin in your life? Throughout the centuries Christians have testified that prayer – unrushed prayer, that is – more than anything makes the risen Christ real.

DAY 7

READ
Luke 24:32-35

Such eye-opening encounters with Jesus can hardly fail to be life-changing experiences. All the more remarkable, then, when the Emmaus Two reflect upon it, is what stood out for them in such an experience: "Were not our hearts burning within us while he talked with us on the road and *opened the Scriptures to us*?" (v.32). This explains why, for me, Luke 24 is almost holy ground. I call this the "Burning Heart Bible School", and it is surely the one we would all like to attend!

The sequence of events is striking and very revealing. First, Jesus *opens the Scriptures* to them (v.32c) and sets their hearts on fire with the breathtaking purposes of the big picture from Scripture! Then, while breaking bread over supper, their eyes are opened to recognise Him.

In our day it is cause for great rejoicing that more and more eyes are being opened by the Holy Spirit to the truth of the gospel and to the reality of the risen Jesus. The narrative strongly suggests that such a meeting with Jesus sets us on a lifetime of learning. It is precisely those *whose eyes are being opened* to His aliveness and personal presence who are the prime candidates for enrolment in His "Burning Heart Bible School" and who, in turn, see Jesus in a fresh way.

A DEVOTIONAL INTERLUDE

Action: Many have never had the opportunity to attend a Bible School. But everyone can be a student in the "Burning Heart Bible School". All you have to do each time you open your Bible is to make this your prayer: "Open my eyes that I may see wonderful things in your law" (Psa. 119:18). Realise, as you read, that through the written Word you are meeting up with the living Word – the Word who is bigger than men's words.

DAY **8**

READ
Luke 24:44

"Everything must be fulfilled that is *written about me* in the Law of Moses, the Prophets and the Psalms."

Once more, it is important to emphasise what Jesus is asserting here. Without Him the Old Testament revelation of God is incomplete. Conversely, we cannot understand who Jesus is and why He has come without understanding something of God's story in the first half of our Bible. Again, it is vital to realise that it is not a matter of finding isolated prophetic predictions that somehow land on target in Him. Something much grander is afoot! The very language used – "must" and "be fulfilled" – implies, as we shall find later, a coherent thread of divine purpose.

As I see it, what Jesus is doing is connecting up the familiar Bible stories and showing how they form the one big story told in the Bible of what God is doing. He is, in effect, gathering to Himself the whole of the story the Old Testament tells. He brings the long-range strategy of God to its successful conclusion. He is showing these disciples the larger story of God's strategic plan.

A DEVOTIONAL INTERLUDE

Thought: So many believers in this busy modern age neglect or ignore the reading of the Old Testament. You can be sure of this: no true or complete picture of Jesus or of God's story can be built up if the Old Testament is disregarded. While enjoying the little stories of the Bible, be careful that you don't get so caught up in them that you miss the big story of what God is doing. That's like not seeing the wood for the trees.

DAY **9**

READ
Luke 24:45-46

What happens now in Jerusalem is similar to what happened at Emmaus. After appearing before the disciples and convincing them of His aliveness, Luke tells us, *"he opened their minds so they could understand the Scriptures"* (v.45).

As was stressed in the introduction, it was – and is – vital that everyone, with heart on fire and eyes wide open to His risenness, should have their *minds opened so they can understand the Scriptures*. Our modern minds are often shut by the limits set by materialism and unbelief. The resurrection breaks into the rationalist's closed system and opens it up to new possibilities.

But what were the disciples slow of heart to believe? Where are the obvious prophecies of suffering leading to glory? How is this connected to the story of Israel told in the law, the psalms and prophets?

Like the first disciples, we are slow of heart to believe the paradoxical message of the prophets that Israel's rejection and vindication is a pattern of suffering and glory which has settled on her anointed King and Messiah. Only slowly does it dawn on us that losing our life is the way to find it, that dying is the way to live again! Our minds certainly need to be opened to see all this otherwise we will mistakenly believe the path of discipleship is too hard for us and step off the narrow way that leads to life.

A DEVOTIONAL INTERLUDE

Prayer: Lord Jesus Christ, I acknowledge that while I enjoy the emotional side of Christian experience, that is never enough. I long to have a heart that feels like Yours but a mind that thinks like Yours. Enable me, dear Lord, to think Christianly about all of life's issues. Help me to keep my mind open to the truth of God as it is found in the Scriptures, especially to the idea of God's big story. In Jesus' Name. Amen.

DAY **10**

READ
Luke 24:47-48

Not only do we need our minds opened to the wonder of God's big story in Christ, but we need to have our minds stretched if we are to take in the worldwide implications of what God has done in Jesus and commissions us to tell. We have been caught up in a story that reaches beyond private faith and personal experience into the realm of *public truth*. "And repentance and forgiveness of sins will be preached in his name to all nations, beginning at Jerusalem" (v.47). The gospel is a call to the nations to forego their nationalist agendas, to rally to the flag of the Lord of the nations, and to lay their tribute at His feet. It challenges every one of us, whatever our race, skin colour or social status, to tear up the script of our own self-made stories and to enlist with a clean start in God's big drama of redemption.

This is a bold claim to make in a pluralistic world, one regarded as arrogant. But the uniqueness of Jesus is the only way to the whole world's salvation. Only by being exclusive to Him can the story be inclusive of all. His unprecedented suffering and unheard-of resurrection form the unique centre-piece of all the stories He redeems.

This is His story, this is our song. And it is the world's story. If we Christians could only stay together, we might even teach the world to sing this song in perfect harmony!

A DEVOTIONAL INTERLUDE

Thought: One Christian leader has said that the biggest challenge facing the Church in the twenty-first century is remaining true to the uniqueness and exclusivity of Jesus. This means holding fast to Jesus' own claim that He is the only way to God. Christianity not one religion among others but in a category all by itself. Are you strong on this issue? You may be tested on this matter sooner than you think.

DAY 11

READ
Luke 24:48-53

As with the Emmaus Two, our personal stories are redeemed from insignificance and futility by being reattached to God's big story of salvation for the world! Because "the End of the story" has already lived among us, we can be sure we are included in a story which had a good beginning and will have a satisfactory conclusion.

Since this is wholly God's work, we must rely utterly on being empowered by His Holy Spirit (vv.48–49). God creates and redeems. God appoints and assigns and works out His long-term covenantal purposes through the painfully human story of Israel. Having brought that stage of the story to its intended destination in the cross of His Son Jesus, God raises Him from the dead, so vindicating Him as Messiah and Lord. As the head of a great family invested blessing in his sons, or as a priest pronounced a lasting benediction on the worshippers, so the risen Lord blesses His witnessing disciples with all the creative potential of resurrection-life. No wonder they are overwhelmed with joy and overflow with praise. Who could ask for a better story to be part of than this?

A DEVOTIONAL INTERLUDE

Prayer: O Father, what a thought this is to carry into my day. My little personal story, when caught up into Your big story, is invested with a dignity and a meaning that almost blows my mind. I am part of a story that has a good beginning and a perfect ending because I belong to You. There is no story in the world I would rather be a part of than this. Thank You my Father. Hallelujah! All honour and glory be to Your peerless Name. Amen.

SECTION 2
THE BIBLE AS GOD'S STORY

The Bible as God's story

In approaching the Bible, we must keep in mind that it has been given to us largely in the form of a *narrative*, or *story*. This should drastically affect the way we handle the Bible.

In fact, as Eugene Peterson has reminded us: "The *way* the Bible is written is every bit as important as *what* is written in it: Narrative – this huge, capacious story that pulls us into its plot and shows us our place in its development from beginning to ending. It takes the whole Bible to read any part of the Bible." Of course, not every part of the Bible is "narrative" in a literary sense. It includes laws and songs and words of wisdom. "Sometimes," says Peterson again, "we are told that the Bible is a library made up of many kinds of writing: poems and hymns, sermons and letters, visions and dreams, genealogical lists and historical chronicles, moral teaching and admonition and proverbs. And, of course, story. But that is not so. It is all story."

In one sense, then, even the non-narrative parts of the Bible – the wisdom literature, for instance – take for granted the particular story-line we are following of the one Creator God and His people, Israel, among whom such literature was treasured and preserved.

The Bible exhibits the features common to all gripping narratives. There is a *vivid opening*, acting like the rousing overture to a stirring symphony, which determines the shape of the plot. Every great drama has its *catastrophe*, disaster or fall which, in turn, calls forth a *rescue mission*. It has depth of *character development* which usually determines the quality of the story and distinguishes a classic novel from a "pot-boiler" paperback bought at an airport bookstall to help time fly! And the best stories don't leave the plot hanging in the air but have a *satisfactory ending*. They are – to use the theologian's jargon – "eschatological"; that is, they end well.

God's story

The starting-point, then, for this Cover2Cover journey of discovery is the fresh realisation that *the Bible is essentially God's story*. As Stanley Hauerwas and William Willimon note: "We are forever getting confused into thinking that Scripture is mainly about what we are supposed to do, rather than a picture of who God is." God is the chief actor in the drama that unfolds through the Bible. God reveals Himself to us by participating with us in the story.

The word "God" refers simply to a deity whose character is not known before we start the story. Only by reading His story will we discover who the real "God" is and find out, through interaction with events and people, what He says and feels and plans and does.

In *The Sacred Romance* Brent Curtis and John Eldredge ask: "What if? Just what if we saw God not as Author, the cosmic mastermind behind all human experience, but as the central character in the larger story? What could we learn about his heart?"

Plot-line

But, if the Bible tells the story of God, our next move is to ask: Is there a plot? Is God, in fact, working to a purpose or is He simply seen as reacting to events in a random way? Does God merely have a "devotional" relationship with believers or has He a plan for human history and for His creation?

The whole Bible presupposes that He has, and psalmists, prophets and apostles celebrate it (Psa. 33:10–11; Isa. 46:10–11; Eph. 1:9–10).

Promise-plan

We can gain more purchase on what this plan entails by adopting Old Testament scholar Walter Kaiser's designation of it as the *"promise-plan of God"* – referred to in over forty passages in the New Testament simply as the *"promise"* (e.g., Acts 26:6).

Kingdom and covenant

We can bring the promise-plan of God into even sharper focus by employing two key categories: *the kingdom of God* and *the concept of covenant.*

The kingdom of God is the overarching theme, viewed as God's lordly rule over creation and demonstrated partially in

Israel's calling and kingship. It can be seen as decisively established in Jesus, especially in His cross, resurrection and exaltation to be Lord and Christ. God's kingdom is anticipated in the Church by the ruling presence of the Holy Spirit, and looked for as the eventual outcome of Christ's second coming. In other words, we enjoy the presence of God's kingdom and yet still pray "your kingdom come".

The concept of covenant

Covenant spells relationship and mutual agreement. William Dyrness defines covenant as "a solemn promise made binding by an oath", often accompanied by signs, whether verbal or symbolic. In O. Palmer Robertson's words, "a covenant is a bond-in-blood sovereignly administered."

Covenants were made in the ancient world between individuals – as in the biblical case of David and Saul's son Jonathan – but our aim will be to trace the covenantal arrangements God makes.

The biblical story, then, can be seen in the broadest way as the implementing of *God's kingdom rule* in history through a series of *covenantal arrangements*: God's covenants with Noah, Abraham, Israel, David, and the new covenant promised by the prophets – all in pursuit of that coherent goal.

The approach adopted here can be pictured as a viaduct supported by five major Old Testament covenants across which the promise-plan of God makes its way to Christ.

He takes the weight of all the previous covenant commitments of God, launching the worldwide promised blessings and inaugurating the still future kingdom.

"The promise-plan of God" .... JESUS

Covenant with
Noah > Abraham > Israel/Moses > David > New Covenant

This feature appears at the bottom of each day page.

At the heart of God's promise-plan, as we shall see, is undoubtedly the promises and *covenant made with Abraham*. Genesis 12:1–3 is the launching pad for the redemptive story in Scripture.

Before we look at this, we first need to embrace the fact that *the Bible is our story too*.

To accept the gift of life is to acknowledge the call to participate in the flawed but glorious human story. To accept the call of grace is to accept the call to join the divine story, the redemptive, covenantal story of the kingdom of God, and to gain the recovery of our true humanness.

Abraham's faith was not that of a man seeking to fit God into his world, to make God useful to his success or family or even retirement. Abraham – whose faith-footsteps we all follow in – was enticed away from his culture by the glimpse of God's glory, lifted out of his world to be fitted amazingly and riskily into God's world and into God's adventure story.

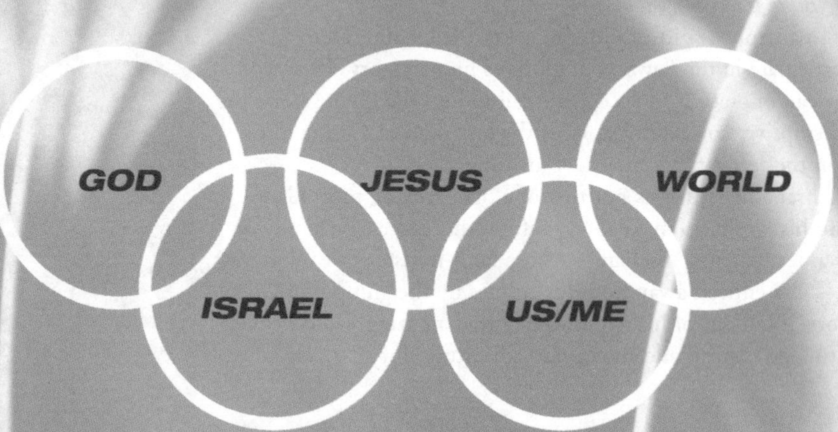
GOD
ISRAEL
JESUS
US/ME
WORLD

DAY 12

READ
Romans 15:7-9

The daily readings which start today invite you to view human history as the unfolding of a great drama in which God is the chief actor.

I have found it helpful to view it as five overlapping, interlocking stories, which can be compared to the Olympic rings: the story of *God*; the story of God's *world*; the story of *Israel* in the Old Testament; the central story of *Jesus* as gathering in all the other stories; *our story* as the people of God, including your story and mine as we personally by faith participate in God's big story.

(See diagram opposite)

As an example of how these stories interact we can take Paul's brilliant summary statement in Romans 15:8–9, which encapsulates the whole biblical story. Here the *Jesus story* is viewed as the culmination of the *story of Israel*, among whom He comes as the Jewish Messiah (Christ) to bring to fruition God's promises to Abraham and the patriarchs. The result is that blessing reaches the whole *Gentile world* and, in this way, the *story is told of a God* who is both truthful and merciful.

At conversion, this story became the Roman Christian's story, and by grace it becomes *our* story too. Like Paul's original readers, we too are called to be characters in this story and invited to live it out by accepting one another in the Church and glorifying God together.

A DEVOTIONAL INTERLUDE

Question: How secure are you in your relationship with the Lord? One of the characteristics of the human soul, say many psychologists, is the need to "belong". Those who do not feel they belong tend to be deeply insecure. This sense of belonging is extremely important in our relationship with the Lord. If it doesn't exist to a high degree then talk to your minister or a counsellor. And do so without delay.

DAY 13

READ
2 Corinthians 13:14

The form taken by the biblical narrative makes it clear that only by tracing the unfolding *story of God* in His interaction with history can we know who God really is.

"Story" – in the sense in which we are using the term – is therefore not inferior to "doctrine", as if the matter could be better told in theological concepts. In fact, doctrines are essentially only shorthand ways of defining the terms in which we retell the story. The Christian doctrine of God as Trinity is a case in point, for it was an inevitable outcome of the story told in the New Testament. The apostles, who were heirs to the Jewish Old Testament relationship with the one Creator God, encountered Jesus, who reintroduced them to God as His Father and theirs. Through experiencing God's Spirit as the personal Spirit of Jesus they were pressed, post-resurrection, to include Jesus in the same categories normally reserved for the one Creator God – and this without dissolving the unique "oneness" of God! The story they lived was the raw material for the finished doctrine.

Through hearing God's story we encounter the real God, get to know His character, and find out what He's really like. In worship and through discipleship we relive God's story with Him, and in so doing find our true selves shaped by it.

A DEVOTIONAL INTERLUDE

Thought: Do you realise that the story which the Trinity summarises is at its core a romantic one? The three Persons who form the Trinity enjoy a loving relationship in which there is perfect harmony. In this atmosphere a plan was devised to draw you into that inner circle. God thought it, Christ bought it, the Holy Spirit wrought it, and now, through grace, you've got it. No wonder it has been called "The Greatest Story Ever Told".

DAY **14**

READ
Romans 8:18-21

In telling the *world's story*, the Bible moves from *first creation* to *new creation*, addressing the concerns of the whole earth and all humankind. The story of Adam, of Israel – called to renew humanity – and Jesus – the Last Adam – are directly linked.

If we bear this in mind, we will not limit the Bible to private devotional exercises, but relish its power to speak truthfully across the whole range of human affairs. This will not provide us with all the answers to every question we decide to put on our agenda, but we will gain a wholly new and true vantage-point on reality. This *creational* approach will save us from devaluing the material and physical realm in favour of the "spiritual" realm. Hopefully, it will incite our thinking to a *world-view* and our mission to *world-vision*.

In his stunning prophetic vision, Paul sees the destiny of believers and the future of creation mysteriously intertwined. As we know, our sin dragged creation down into fallenness and frustration. Now, strangely, our redemption offers hope to a groaning world. "The creation is on tiptoe to see the wonderful sight of the sons of God coming into their own" (v.19, Phillips).

A DEVOTIONAL INTERLUDE

For praise: Creation plays a great part in God's story. The old creation, because of sin, groans under the burden. Who can doubt it? Everything that lives is subject to disease. Life seems strangely poisoned at the fount. But hear with wonder the promise that the power released through the new creation will one day affect the old creation. The last word in the universe will not be a groan but Joy! Joy! Joy!

DAY **15**

READ
John 4:1-42

To read the Bible well we must take history seriously and pay close attention to the *story of Israel* told in the Old Testament.

"Salvation is from the Jews" (v.22). This teaches us not only that the Messiah is a Jew but that the previous revelation, which God gave to Israel, is the birthplace of the world's salvation. In other words, Israel's story encapsulates the world's story. Israel was made the steward of our human vocation to reflect God's image by being "holy as God is holy". Israel was the nation entrusted with the revelation of the one Creator God which she was to pass on to the world so that none should live by bread alone. Israel was fated to bear the strange burden of the world's hopes.

The paradox of the Bible story is that only by being exclusively Jewish can it ever transcend all cultures. The specifically Jewish Messiah comes to slake the thirst of all so that we no longer need drink at Jacob's well or any other. This very Jewish Messiah leads all lost worshippers home to the Father to worship God neither at Samaritan shrines nor the Jerusalem Temple but "in spirit and in truth" (v.24) to which He alone gives access.

Salvation is truly "from the Jews" for from them and their history comes the *"Saviour of the world"* (v.42).

A DEVOTIONAL INTERLUDE

For action: The Samaritan woman represents all who are thirsty everywhere. Like her, many have tried every sensual experience and remained unsatisfied. True soul satisfaction is found only in God, who offers us living water in Jesus. But in order to receive it, all must bow the knee to Him. When we humble ourselves and drink from the source of a Jewish Messiah, we find Him to be the Saviour of the world. Nothing satisfies like Jesus.

DAY **16**

READ
John 5:31-40

As we have seen in the first part of our introduction, the *story of Jesus* is the key that unlocks the whole Bible. To miss this is to miss everything. The Pharisees were diligent in their Bible study. But keen Bible students though they were, they refused to acknowledge Jesus and so deprived themselves of the life-changing impartation of the truth of God's Word. This Cover2Cover programme takes an unashamedly Christ-centred approach to the Bible. Not that we read Jesus back into Old Testament in an artificial or contrived way. We do, however, see the Lord Jesus Christ as the central figure in God's plans. Into His safe keeping is entrusted the fulfilment of all previous Old Testament types and patterns. We repeat once more: we will not understand Jesus without understanding the Old Testament which leads up to Him; nor, on the other hand, will we understand the Old Testament without seeing it in the light of its completion in Him.

As the Samaritan woman said to Jesus: "I do know that the Messiah is coming. When he arrives, we'll get the whole story" (4:25, *The Message*). In Him, the final Word made flesh, the *story of Israel* is successfully rewritten, the *story of God* is fully revealed, and the *story of the world* redeemingly redrawn.

A DEVOTIONAL INTERLUDE

Thought: In the British Isles schoolchildren are often told that from every village, town and city there is a road that leads to the capital – London. Something similar can be said about the Bible. Wherever you start in Scripture there is a road that leads to Jesus. Every time you open up your Bible remember this: it wasn't Jesus who came out of the Bible, it was the Bible that came out of Jesus. To understand it you have to know Him.

DAY **17**

READ
Romans 15:1-4

"Even if it was written in Scripture long ago, you can be sure it's written for *us*" (v.4, *The Message*). So the Bible is telling *our* story too.

We can take the Word "personally" and "corporately".

When you and I believingly receive the biblical story we are drawn into the action and find ourselves caught up in the saving movement of God. As the late Lesslie Newbigin taught us well, we will learn to *indwell* the story so that we begin to look out *from within* the biblical world with new eyes onto the world in which we live.

Rather than striving to make the Bible relevant to our lives, it might be better to begin to allow our lives to be made relevant to the Bible! By faith, we can trade in the dog-eared, self-written script of our own self-directed lives in order to be written into the larger script of God's big story. When this happens, "my" story becomes "our" story as we are joined to a community of faith, the one covenant family of God. We gain, at once, a new history, and in the Church we become new chapters written by the Spirit into the script of the ongoing story.

A DEVOTIONAL INTERLUDE

Prayer: My Father and my God, help me to grasp more clearly this concept of the bigger story – and to live in wonder of the fact that I am part of it. Help me also to understand that without demeaning my family attachments or depriving my loved ones of my affection, I can relate to my Christian brothers and sisters with a deeper sense of kinship than it is possible to experience with my blood family. Amen.

DAY 18

READ
Ruth 4

A notable feature of the biblical story is that seemingly minor stories gain their significance from the part they play in the overall narrative of God. This warns us against using Bible characters solely to draw moral or even spiritual lessons unless at the same time we take the trouble to place these characters in the story and to show how integral they are to it. In fact, many biblical characters make decidedly shaky moral examples! Far better to see them as stories about how unlikely people can, by grace, be grafted onto God's story. Ruth is a shining example. This simple story of a young widow and the redemptive friendships which change her life gains its significance from the way the book is placed in the canon. There it is a beacon of light in the darkest days of the judges (1:1). Even more strikingly, it forges another link by joining the ancient patriarchs with the future King David (4:13–22). In short, Ruth serves both to offset the terrible "Bethlehem" stories of Judges 18–21 and to carry forward the promise-plan of God to the model Davidic king and eventually to the Messianic Davidic King who shared the same birthplace.

Ruth says to each of us: "You can make a difference. Your small-scale domestic story – if lived faithfully before God – can be of strategic importance to God!"

A DEVOTIONAL INTERLUDE

Question: Does the phrase "You can make a difference" fall flat on your ears? Maybe you feel your life is humdrum and you struggle to see how it can be of strategic importance to God. Though it may be hard for you to see the truth we are presenting here be assured of this: faithfulness in small things – a character quality – has a part in God's story that is equal to the exploits of the renowned and the great. It really does.

DAY **19**

READ
Psalm 33

Even if we accept that the Bible is God's story, we do need to ask: Is there a plot? Does God merely react randomly to events by stage-managing an occasional show of force to indicate His existence? Or does he, perhaps, have a personal relationship with believers and nothing more?

No, the Bible, including this psalm, assures us that God has *plans*. These plans are implemented by His *covenant word* which forges a reliable covenant partnership with His people (v.4), just as His *creative word* well ordered everything at the beginning (vv.6–9). So the *plans of the Lord* shape the way the world is going. Despite appearances to the contrary, it is not military hardware that determines the outcome of history (vv.16–17). And the *eyes of the Lord* oversee His purpose (vv.18–19). The righteous are not promised success and wealth but – even in famine and death – a covenant love that will not let them go (v.19).

The power which made the world, the plans that steer it to its intended goal, the providential care that watches over the process – all are symptoms of that unfailing love of God which we dare to hope will be the last word in the universe.

To ponder: It may be hard to believe as one looks at the world that a providential God is working out all things according to His purpose. But He is. Scripture may not tell us all we would like to know about why God allows bad things to happen to good people, but the psalmists shed some light on the darkened way by telling us, as in this psalm, that despite the God-denying look of things, He is in control. Ours is not to trace but to trust.

DAY 20

READ
Isaiah 46

As we prepare to trace the unfolding story of God in the Bible we note that Isaiah, too, is confident that God has a *plan and purpose* (vv.10–11). The prophet is seeking to raise the spirits and sights of the exiles in Babylon, swamped as they are with Babylonian propaganda and values. But God's plans are sovereign and *rooted in a long history* of sustaining His people from birth to "old age and grey hairs" (v.4). Our memory of God's "proven track record" plays no tricks, for God's actions are based not on whim but on the forethought of *long-term plans* (vv.9–10). Yet God "moves in mysterious ways His wonders to perform", summoning "a bird of prey" from the East – the Medo-Persian Emperor, Cyrus – who will conquer Babylon and let God's people go (v.11). This is a strange way to effect a new exodus, but all God's plans are *saving plans* to those who believe (v.13). Not that knowing God's plans makes us party to privileged, "insider" information which we can proudly use to control events or people. Rather, it evokes a deep, daring *trust*.

In the end, there is all the difference in the world between a god you carry and *a God who carries you* – between a god you include in your plans and a God who includes you in His!

A DEVOTIONAL INTERLUDE

Question: An elderly Christian talking to a group of young believers told them how his life had changed since he resigned as "Director of the Universe". One day he had awakened to the truth that he had been carrying God rather than letting God carry him. Here's the question: Are you trying to hold God up or is He holding you? Relax. Let God carry you. He has been holding up the world for aeons and is hardly likely to let you slip.

DAY **21**

READ
Ephesians 1:1-14

In a marvellous movement of grace, the Father's eternal love reaches out to draw us back into His covenant family, sweeps into history in the incarnate love of His Son Jesus to forgive us our sins, and is vividly brought home to our experience through the impact of His Spirit by whom we are sealed as God's own possession.

Just as Israel was entrusted with the wisdom of God in the form of the law, so now, "in Christ", and through the Spirit, Christian believers are privileged to share God's secret wisdom. We are initiated into "the mystery of his will", the strategic plan of God to redeem His creation (vv.9–10).

The scope of this is breathtaking. God intends to reunite everything, to restore the original harmony to a fractured world, and to reconcile people to each other and to Himself. "Everything will again be united in Him," wrote Dr Martyn Lloyd-Jones. "That is the message and that is God's plan. This is the mystery which has been revealed to us. Do you know that these things are so marvellous that you will never hear anything greater, either in this world or in the world to come?" And everything in the working out of this plan by the Father, Son and Holy Spirit tends to the praise of the glory of God's grace (vv.6,12,14).

A DEVOTIONAL INTERLUDE

Prayer: O Father, thank You that You have given me the gift of Your Holy Spirit, who seals me as Your possession and continues to reveal to me Your redemptive plans. I am so thankful, too, that in Jesus You bring together all the divided strands of history. Surely there can be nothing greater in earth or heaven than that Jesus my Saviour will bring all things to a glorious conclusion. Everlasting praise be to Your holy Name. Amen.

JESUS

NEW COVENANT

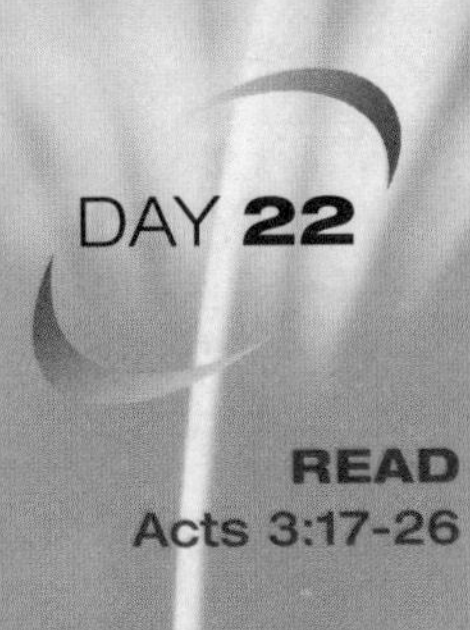

DAY 22

READ
Acts 3:17-26

This stirring narrative reinforces what we have discovered so far. In the dramatic aftermath of the day of Pentecost, Peter preaches Jesus as the One who fulfils all Israel's long-held prophetic hopes (v.18).

In the mystery of His ways, God achieves this despite – even because of – the ignorant rejection of Jesus by the people He had prepared to receive Him! And just as Jesus, by dying and rising, validates all God's dealings in the *past*, so His second coming is the guarantee of God's *future* plans for the restoration of all things (vv.20–21). Whether past, present or future, Jesus is clearly the crux of all God's purposes. All the prophets spoke of these days and they related them to Jesus (v.24).

The privileged natural heirs of a covenant which promises blessing for "all peoples on earth" should have known this better than anyone. To them the Christ makes His first appeal. But for all of us, Jesus is the *one* prophet who embodies what all the prophets announced. We cannot pick and mix here; He is all or nothing! To listen to Him in obedient faith is to embrace God's vision of worldwide blessing. To refuse to hear Him is to miss the plot entirely.

A DEVOTIONAL INTERLUDE

Thought: When Peter, James and John saw Jesus transfigured before them, we read that Moses and Elijah were present also (Matt. 17:1-13). Moses was the one who gave the law to the people of Israel; Elijah was the one who called them back to it. You can be sure of this: had Jesus not come and paid our debt to the law on Calvary, Moses and Elijah would never have been accorded a place in heaven. We are all what we are because Jesus is what He is.

DAY 23

READ
Acts 26

We have already noted that in the Bible there is *one* promise, his single plan of salvation. Paul's defence before Agrippa illustrates the point: "And now I am standing trial for the hope of *the promise* made by God to our fathers" (v.6 NASB). "Paul's confidence then," says Walter Kaiser, "rested on a single promise, not a prediction, nor a number of scattered prognostications. It was a definite singular plan of God to benefit one man and through him to bless the whole world."

Meeting the risen Jesus on the Damascus Road transformed Paul's view of the promise-plan of God. Nothing but the resurrection could have convinced the arch-Pharisee that the dead and discredited Messianic pretender, Jesus of Nazareth, was, in fact, the long-hoped-for Messiah and the key to our hopes and all God's dreams. Clearly, Paul did not convert to a new religion; all he now experiences "in Christ" and understands of God's plan is the résumé of all the previous stages of the story. This remains the Jewish hope (v.7) until the light of Christ dawns (v.23).

Paul risks his life to tell this story because he knows it "was not done in a corner" so as to become merely a matter of private religion but is "public truth" to be proclaimed on the world stage to Jew and Gentile alike as the light of freedom and grace (vv.17–18, 23–26).

A DEVOTIONAL INTERLUDE

Question: Has someone broken a promise to you lately? There is hardly a human being on earth who has not had this experience. One saying goes like this: "Promises are made to be broken." Not God's promises, however. It has been calculated that there are 365 promises in the Bible, one for every day of the year. And every promise of God can be banked on. Hold fast to this: others may break their promises but the Almighty – never.

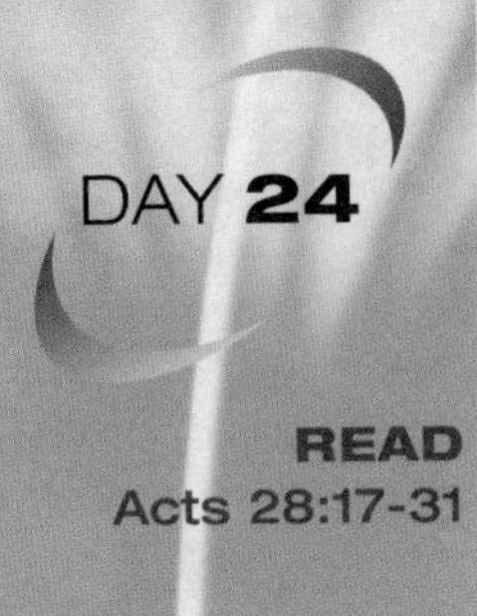

DAY **24**

READ
Acts 28:17-31

Luke's final view of Paul shows him under some kind of house arrest, still taken up with "the hope of Israel" for the coming of God's kingdom. Connected by the prophets to the arrival of the eagerly awaited Messiah, this stream of hope, Paul argues, had flowed into Jesus, and he worked tirelessly to convince others about this (v.23).

Again we notice that the apostles viewed the gospel not as an innovation, a brand new religion that had popped up without precedent, but as the fulfilment of texts and teaching, promises and prophecies deeply embedded in the Jewish Scriptures. But, in a tragic and ironic twist to the story, those whom God had prepared to receive their Messiah repeated their own history and closed their ears to His truth. In God's sovereignty, however, even this is turned to good. Since it was God's intention all along that Israel should bear His gospel to the world, He achieves this not through their co-operation but despite it – so sending the message to the Gentiles who, Paul asserts, "will listen" (vv.26–28).

How persistent God is in His plans to bless the world! In the Greek text, Luke's very last word here is the word "unhindered" (v.31). How apt, for the story of God's kingdom and its King, the Lord Jesus Christ, is an ongoing story in which we are challenged to take part.

A DEVOTIONAL INTERLUDE

Thought: How persistent God is in His plans to bless the world. He will let nothing hinder or deter Him. Persistency has been defined as the ability to keep going no matter what obstacles are in the way. The good news is that God is able to help us develop that same characteristic in our own hearts but it won't happen automatically. It comes by spending time with Him. There is no other way.

DAY **25**

READ
2 Corinthians 1:12-22

In defending himself against the charge of being inconsistent, Paul offers us this gem: "For no matter how many promises God has made, they are 'Yes' in Christ" (v.20). That all the promises of God find their "Yes" in Jesus does not mean He randomly rubber stamps these promises but rather that they *all converge on Him* as the focal point of a coherent plan that occasions them all.

It is my conviction that nothing from the Old Testament bypasses Jesus. Every promise and prophecy goes through Jesus and in the process is fulfilled and transformed. Every covenantal connection connects with Him, every tributary of truth flows into His river, each aspect of God's strategy focuses and is filled-full in Him! All the prophetic affirmations God has ever given add up to one mighty "Yes" which is Jesus! He is truly the final Word.

No wonder in Him we are established, empowered, owned as belonging to God, and guaranteed a future by the Spirit of God (vv.21–22). What would all our "Amens" amount to if they were not responses to His resounding "Yes"?

A DEVOTIONAL INTERLUDE

To ponder: A great Bible translator of the early twentieth century was a man called James Moffatt. He translated 2 Corinthians 1:20 in this way: "The divine 'yes' has at last sounded in him [Jesus], for in him is the 'yes' that affirms all the promises of God." Many think Christianity is a "No" religion – "No" to this, "No" to that. Instead it says "Yes" to life – life more abundant. And Jesus is that life. Aren't you glad you have said "Yes" to God's "Yes"?

READ
Ephesians 2:11-22

Paul talks intriguingly of the *"covenants of the promise"*. In other words, there are several covenants – in the plural – which all serve the one singular promise-plan of God.

The approach being followed in Cover2Cover has been pictured as a viaduct supported by five major Old Testament covenants across which the promise-plan of God makes its way to Christ (as illustrated in the diagram at the bottom of most pages).

Such a diagram, of course, conceals the uneven progress of God's plan. It masks the many occasions when God makes Himself strangely vulnerable to rebuff, or when He enters into risky intercessory negotiations with them.

But what it does show is that all the covenantal commitments God makes are intended to further the progress of His promise-plan on its way through history to its crucial goal in Jesus and its ultimate goal in the renewal of His whole creation. What a plan! What a prospect!

At the heart of God's promise-plan, as we shall see, is undoubtedly the promise and the covenant made with Abraham in Genesis 12:1–3 where Abraham is promised *descendants*, a *land*, and a *relationship with God characterised by blessing*. And the bottom line of His promise – later guaranteed by covenant – is God's intention to bring *blessing to all the nations of the world*. The exclusive relationship with Abraham and his descendants, in other words, tokens the commitment of the one Creator God to redeem the whole of His creation, which is why our story will begin with Noah.

A DEVOTIONAL INTERLUDE

Prayer: My Father and my God, I pause before moving on into whatever lies before me to once again give You praise and thanks that I am on the pathway of faith because of Your commitment to redeem Your creation. Drive this truth deeper into my spirit, dear Lord, so that I shall see, and see even more clearly, that salvation is mine not because of my merit but because of Your mercy. All honour and glory be to Your Name. Amen.

NOAH
ALL CREATION

ABRAHAM
all nations

ISRAEL
one nation

DAVID
representative king

NEW COVENANT
faithful covenant partner

JESUS
faithful covenant partner

JESUS
Davidic King Messiah

JESUS
the New Israel

JESUS
the world's Lord

JESUS
the truly Human One crowned with glory and honour

JESUS
cosmic Ruler in God's new creation new heavens and new earth

SECTION 3
GOD'S COVENANT WITH NOAH

God is committed to preserving the world for future redemption - God's covenant with Noah

This dramatic story starts with the pain God feels at the tragedy that has overcome His world.

Noah's story puts us in touch with the turbulent emotions of a God who is grief-stricken over the way evil has spoilt His "good" creation. But Noah finds grace in the eyes of the Lord and is burdened with the terrible secret of what God plans to do to judge the world and to save it.

God's judgment in unleashing the floodwaters represents an undoing of the act of creation. The waters out of which the world was formed – according to Genesis 1 – and which were set within bounds, now return unchecked to overwhelm Noah's world in judgment. It becomes clear, however, that judgment changes nothing. Despite the flood of God's judgment, our propensity to evil and wickedness remains the same.

Remarkably, it is God who freely chooses to change! He resolves "never again" to destroy His creation in this way, by flood. Instead of cancelling His creation experiment, God renews His determination to uphold and eventually to redeem His world. He opts for patience and forbearance in His long-term dealings with His world.

To mark this, God makes a startling *covenant with Noah, with the animals, and even with the earth itself* (Gen. 9:12–13). To signify His enduring commitment, God hangs His war-bow in the sky as the rainbow-reminder of His pledge of grace.

Although we are far distant from Noah, we are, like him, "saved through water" (1 Pet. 3:21). Drawn by faith-baptism "into Christ" – and into His dying and rising – we pass through the waters of judgment, leaving behind our old selves and world, to emerge as part of the "new creation" (2 Cor. 5:17). As Noah did, we can stake everything on the covenant faithfulness of this tough and tender God.

Through faith, we too may prove to be the firstfruits of a new human race. Like Noah, we can be preachers of righteousness, not a self-righteousness that condemns, but a saving righteousness that through the cross offers hope of redemption. In this hope, we refuse to call down floods of wrath upon the heads of sinners and can instead bend to wash their dusty feet.

When Noah stepped into the ark he saved himself and his family; when he stepped out of the ark he saved the world! By God's grace we, too, can take those small steps of faith and obedience which may truly make a difference to our world beyond our wildest dreams as we wait for the world to come.

Let's look more closely at how one small step for Noah was one giant leap for mankind!

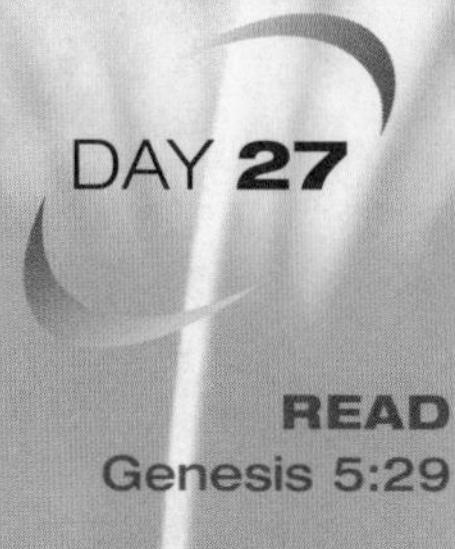

DAY **27**

READ
Genesis 5:29

As we consider the heart of Noah's story, we soon begin to realise that what makes Noah significant is that he is the pioneer of God's intention to renew His creation and redeem His world. *Noah's role, in effect, is to be a new Adam,* as the many echoes of Genesis chapters 1 to 3 indicate.

The first point to notice is that Noah's role as a new Adam is anticipated in the name given to him by his father, Lamech: "He named him 'Noah' saying: 'Out of the *ground* that the Lord has *cursed* this one will bring us *comfort* from our painful toil'" (Gen. 5:29, NRSV, adapted). Noah's name is said to be derived not from the Hebrew word for "rest" (*nwh*) but, by a bit of word-play, from the word (*nhm*) which means "comfort". Noah is a gift to the world from the "God of all comfort". Lamech prophetically announces an antidote to the judgment of Genesis 3:17 where the earth is "cursed" and made the scene of Adam's "painful toil". And there is almost a hint of something incarnational in the statement that it will be out of the very ground cursed that the comforter will come!

A DEVOTIONAL INTERLUDE

For action: Noah was a gift to the world from the God of all comfort. His preaching and teaching was largely rejected, but despite that he remained faithful. In a sense everyone who is a Christian is a gift to the world from this same God of comfort. With appropriate humility keep this thought ever before you: I am God's gift to the world. He has blessed you so that you might bless others. Go out and in His Name bless someone today.

DAY **28**

READ
Genesis 6:5

What we need to notice here, particularly, is that Noah has been drawn so deeply into the drama only because of God's own deeper interest in the fate of His creation. The text highlights *what God saw, what God felt,* and *what God decided.* first, "The Lord saw ..." What the Lord sees is how evil and wicked the earth has become since the Fall. He sees how His untrusting human partners have succumbed to demonic seduction. He sees them accusing and blaming one another in an early exercise in scapegoating. He has watched as their mounting anger eventually turns to blood feuds and murder, culminating in a strange and illicit involvement with angelic beings. And God looks not only on the outward appearances but deep into the human heart out of which, Jesus was to say, comes all manner of evils. Fantasies relished in the hotel bedroom conjure up the pornography and adultery that follow. Radical dreams of social engineering darkly imagined by Pol Pot and his fellow Paris-educated comrades spawn the "killing fields" of Cambodia. Ideas always have consequences. And the Lord sees it all.

A DEVOTIONAL INTERLUDE

Prayer: Gracious and loving heavenly Father, help me see as You see, feel as You feel, and make only those decisions that fit in with Your plans. I am so prone to take my way in everything. Forgive me for my self interest and self-centredness, and dwell so deeply in me that self will become marginal and You will become central. This I ask in Christ's precious Name. Amen.

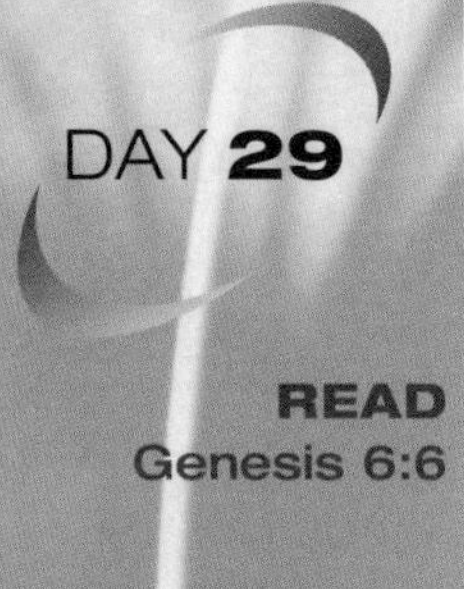

DAY **29**

READ
Genesis 6:6

Our attention is now rivetted on *what God felt!* The Lord sees the serious betrayal of His trust. And seeing this: *"The Lord was grieved ... and his heart was filled with pain."* These strong words show the emotions of someone who loves deeply and is deeply hurt. They invite us to feel the fierce pain in the heart of God.

The Bible tells us that God cannot change, in the sense that external pressures cannot control Him. He is always unthwarted in His sovereignty. But that understanding must not cancel out for us this equally biblical insight into a God who is not detached or unfeeling, but who is deeply moved by the world's tragedy. We are being given a glimpse into the deep pathos in God. God is emotionally affected by our human condition. The narrative does not focus on the Flood, as if to highlight only the severe judgment of God, but on the profound feelings of God, as if to emphasise His depth of mercy and grace.

Looking through this window into God's heart, we may perhaps begin to see that when He finally defeats the evil that plagues His fallen creation, it will involve Him in becoming vulnerable to its pain and wickedness, and in some strange way taking it upon Himself.

A DEVOTIONAL INTERLUDE

To ponder: How glad we should be that God *feels*. Some theologians believe in the "impassibility of God" – the idea that God does not feel. However, where there is love there must, inevitably, be vulnerability to the pain of rejection. How our rejection of the Almighty must have pained His heart. But now how much pleasure it must give Him to have us on His side. Let's live in such a way that our lives will bring Him pleasure, not pain.

DAY **30**

READ
Genesis 6:7

Having glimpsed what God saw and having been made aware of God's feelings, we now learn *what God has decided:* "So the Lord said, 'I will wipe mankind, whom I have created, from the face of the earth ...'"

God decides for justice. Whereas before He had looked on His creation and seen that it was "good" (1:31), now He sees only corruption and violence. He resolves to judge the world by bringing everything to a watery end (6:13,17). The Flood, it is important to notice, will soon be portrayed as the unravelling of God's creative work. The fountains of the deep are about to burst forth and the windows of the heavens to open to drown the world in judgment (7:11) – language which harks back directly to Genesis 1 verses 2 and 7. In other words, the Flood will seem to be an undoing of God's original creation, as though He is going to press the rewind button and allow His created order to return to the watery chaos out of which it had been formed.

So God decides on the Flood. He calls "time" on His grand creation experiment. The final curtain falls. Or does it?

A DEVOTIONAL INTERLUDE

For Praise: Do you know this song: "Ascribe greatness to our God, the Rock; His work is perfect and all His ways are just"? If you do then sing it now. If you don't then make up your own song of praise in words that glorify God for His sense of justice. "Justice," commented C.S. Lewis, "is an old name for what we now call fairness ... it includes honesty, give-and-take, truthfulness and keeping promises." Praise God in your heart for that.

DAY **31**

READ
Genesis 6:8

Suddenly the text strikes a new note: *"But Noah found grace in the eyes of the Lord"* (AV). Suddenly Noah emerges from the gloom as a significant figure. Noah finds favour from God, and when he does the whole human race finds itself a future.

But what strange grace it is! It is a strange grace that makes you the sole survivor of an environmental disaster of cosmic proportions! It is a tough grace that lifts Noah fearfully into the larger drama of God. When anyone receives such grace they cannot help but look at the world through God's eyes and see what He sees and inevitably – though the text does not explicitly say so of Noah – begin to feel what God feels.

And the grace which relieves our fears lets us in on God's awesome secrets and daring dreams. All who live under this grace submit their lives to the overruling providence of God's redemptive activity. This is what grace does to you! In this way, we gain a strange new vantage-point from which to see that *judgment is not God's final word.* We begin to discern that plans are afoot that provide hope.

A DEVOTIONAL INTERLUDE

Prayer: A Scottish preacher used to pray a prayer that stressed the pre-eminence of grace. Why not pray it today? "Lord Jesus, from whom all grace is given and from whom all blessings flow, give me grace to feel my need of grace, and give me grace to ask for grace, then give me grace to receive grace. And when grace is given to me give me grace to use that grace and, above all, give me grace to be grateful for the grace I am given. Amen."

DAY 32

READ
Genesis 6:11-22

As we begin to trace the threads of God's redemptive purpose, it is helpful to distinguish two overall strands to this purpose which involve Noah.

First, what God is doing here is *saving one family for the sake of the whole world!* The narrative explaining this in several ways.

The first point to notice is that *God confides in Noah* (6:13,17) about the judgment about to be let loose. As with Abraham later in the story (18:16–33), God acts as if He would rather not bear the burden alone but seeks to take Noah into His confidence. When Noah is instructed to make the ark, everything depends, not for the last time, on one man's obedience. And not for the last time, when the storm winds of divine judgment beat upon the house and rain pours down, the man whose house survives is the one who hears the word of God and does it. It seems that Noah obeyed at every turn (6:22; 7:5).

We come now to another turning-point in the story. As part of His plan to save a family for the world's sake, *God promises to establish His covenant with Noah* (6:18). In contrast to the threat of verse 17 we read: "But I will establish my covenant with you." God is now building a bridge across which all His plans will pass into fulfilment in the future. On this God stakes His redemptive dreams.

A DEVOTIONAL INTERLUDE

For action: To quote C.S. Lewis again, he once said: "Obedience is the key to all doors in the Christian life; feelings come and go." Do you know the hymn that begins: "When we walk with the Lord, in the light of His Word"? The chorus goes like this: "Trust and obey! For there's no other way, to be happy in Jesus, but to trust and obey." Lift your heart in a hymn of prayer and praise right now and affirm your decision to obey Him in all things.

READ
Genesis 7:11-12

In the meantime, judgment has to be done and seen to be done. The Flood, as we have said, is pictured as the dismantling of God's creative work. The waters that burst forth from the great deep and from the windows of the heavens (v.11) undo the process of creation as recorded in Genesis 1. *The Flood is an act of decreation!*

This is a key point to grasp. From here on, throughout the Bible, God's acts of judgment within history are often described, figuratively, in the *language of decreation* (e.g., Isa. 9:1–10:34; Jer. 4:23–28). In this way, language which sounds as if it is describing the end of the world is used to give ultimate significance and theological weight to historical events which might otherwise be regarded as accidental. With this use of language, events within history become parables of, and portents of, the final end of history.

Jesus spoke like this to show how important was the imminent destruction of Jerusalem and the Temple which would, paradoxically, vindicate Him in glory as the Son of Man (Matt. 24:29–31). Conversely, God's salvation is characteristically described as an act of *new creation* (eg., Isa. 41:17–20; 43:18–21; 65:17; 2 Cor. 5:17). There is life beyond judgment, it seems.

A DEVOTIONAL INTERLUDE

Prayer: O Father, how can I express the gratitude that begins to well up in my soul as I realise I am part of a new creation – a creation that is more marvellous and wondrous than anything that was part of Your first creation? The old will pass away, but the new – the salvation You have given through Jesus, Your Son – will last eternally. Life of my life, Being of my being, my heart belongs to You for ever. Amen.

DAY **34**

READ
Genesis 7:13-8:1

So Noah finds himself shut inside this strange vessel by the Lord and therefore shut in to God's grace as his only hope (7:16). Noah and his entourage sit out the Flood as the sole survivors (7:23).

What were Noah's feelings as he entered the ark facing the prospect of sharing living space with a volatile assortment of animals! And who can possibly imagine how Mrs Noah coped with domestic management inside that gloomy and increasingly smelly ark? Above all, what did it feel like to be in a tiny boat – the only hope of life afloat on a sea of death and destruction? Presumably the Noah clan found grace for all this too! But the text offers us not one word from Noah through the entire episode!

What matters above everything else to the narrator is *what God is thinking and doing: "But God remembered Noah ..."* (8:1). Remembering Noah, God remembers mercy, and causes the Flood to recede and the earth to dry out.

A DEVOTIONAL INTERLUDE

For thanksgiving: Consider where you would be today were it not for God's mercy. It will not be difficult for you, no doubt, to enter into these words of the psalmist with a true sense of understanding. Repeat them out loud and don't forget to say "Amen" at the end. "Oh, give thanks to the Lord, for He is good! For His mercy endures forever. Let the redeemed of the Lord say so, whom He has redeemed from the hand of the enemy" (Psa. 107:1–2, NKJV).

DAY **35**

READ
Genesis 8:15-22

When Noah disembarks (v.15), he is recommissioned to the calling of Adam and Eve to be fruitful and multiply, and, in worshipful response, builds an altar. But God's response is even more striking: *"Never again will I curse the ground because of man,* even though every inclination of his heart is evil from childhood. ..." (v.21). What is extraordinary here is that despite the judgment which has taken place, human wickedness continues. The floodwaters of judgment have abated but the tide of evil has not! Remarkably, it is God who freely chooses to change: "Never again will I ..."!

In the face of continuing human rebellion, God deepens His commitment to His creation. It seems that He intends, whatever it costs Him, to persist with His creation purposes until they come to fruition. In judging the world He reduced it to temporary disorder; now He pledges to maintain the regularity of the seasons, and to uphold the stability of the created order (v.22). Great is His faithfulness – it stabilises the natural world, and so makes life livable and makes it possible to do science.

At almost any time in the future God will have ample reason to destroy the earth and its inhabitants. But His "never again" changes the picture to one where grace reigns.

A DEVOTIONAL INTERLUDE

For action: You will be familiar, no doubt, with the hymn "Great is Thy faithfulness". One line goes like this: "Morning by morning new mercies I see!" Besides lifting up your heart in grateful adoration as you sing it yourself (or with someone else), once again make a list of all God's mercies you can recall over the past few days. Here is one to get you started: you awoke this morning to face a new day. That's the first; now add some more.

DAY 36

READ
Genesis 9:1-6

Long before Neil Armstrong stepped onto the moon, Noah had stepped onto the post-Flood world and taken a giant leap for mankind. As if he were a new Adam on a new earth, Noah is blessed as at the beginning (v.1).

Nothing, of course, can turn the clock back completely. The way back is already barred; there is only a way forward towards the cross and resurrection. God is not reinstating the old creation just as it was; He has His sights already on a new creation. We can never regain "paradise", and our relationship with the animal world is now shadowed with fear. Our human calling to exercise dominion over nature becomes fraught with risk and demands we do so with delicate skill if we are not to ruin our earthly environment.

After the Flood, God lays down three new ground rules – all of which aim to preserve and dignify human life. First, perhaps as a concession, the eating of meat is now allowed (v.3), though we might hear a warning against ranking animal rights higher than human life. Second, the command to reverence all "lifeblood" encourages respect for all forms of life, but chiefly puts a premium on human life so that murder is construed as an attack on God in whose image humans are made (vv.4–6).

A DEVOTIONAL INTERLUDE

For praise: Give praise to God as you repeat this prayer and reflect on the glory of God that fills both earth and heaven: "Almighty God, whose glory the heavens are telling and whose skies proclaim the work of Your hands, we give You thanks that by Your Spirit You renew the face of the earth and give breath to every living creature. We will give You praise, Lord God, for as long as we live, as creatures who are made in Your image and who have been redeemed and restored by Jesus Christ, Our Lord and Saviour. Amen."

DAY **37**

READ
Genesis 9:7

In continuing to portray Noah as a new Adam, the narrative now tells us of the third directive which is to govern human life after the Fall and Flood. God reiterates His desire to see the world populated: "Be fruitful and multiply ..." (9:7 NKJ).

This is a striking statement in view of the fact that human sinfulness has outlived the Flood (8:21b). Here, the text is probably refuting those Mesopotamian flood stories in which the gods grow increasingly annoyed by the number of babies and the amount of noise humans make, and act to cull the human race by officially promoting infanticide and childlessness. By contrast, the one Creator God apparently loves making people too much to abort His creative experiment for ever!

Even modern research grudgingly admits that our world's greatest problem is not so much overpopulation as the unequal distribution of resources. Nor must we be resigned to exhausting our sources of supply in the light of God's commitment: "I now give you everything" (9:3c). From now on, it will certainly be harder to be truly human, but Noah's God refuses to hand in His resignation and entrusts Noah with the future of His creation.

In picturing Noah as a representative head of a new human family, standing on new ground, we can see that God *has preserved a family for the sake of the world.*

A DEVOTIONAL INTERLUDE

To ponder: Take a moment to respond to today's reading by turning to Psalm 65 and linking your heart with that of the psalmist. There is hardly a psalm or passage in the whole of Scripture that surpasses this in terms of giving thanks to God for the way He sustains the earth. We take the blessings of God for granted so often, but change all that today by deciding in future to take them with gratitude.

THE PROMISE-PLAN OF GOD

COVENANT WITH: **NOAH** **ABRAHAM**

DAY **38**

READ
Genesis 9:8-13

Today we tease out the second major strand in God's strategic plan and say: *God preserves the world for the sake of His future – and that future is redemption.*

In inviting us to see Noah as a new Adam, the text shows us the post-Flood world as a renewed creation. If, as we have noted before, the judgment of the Flood represented an act of *decreation,* then the receding of the Flood signals a new beginning. Just as before, the creative Spirit-wind of God – His *ruach* – blows over the waters to dry out the earth (8:1). And just as His life-giving word once was "Let there be ..." so now the earth resonates with God's gracious vow: "Never again ..." (8:21).

In this way, this stage of the story reaches its climax. "*I now establish my covenant with you and with your descendants ...*" (9:9), *"and with every living creature ..."* (9:10), and – this is remarkable – *even with the earth itself* (9:13). In this staggering covenantal promise, God commits Himself to keeping Planet Earth in existence, sustaining its fruitfulness and the regularity of the seasons. God pledges to maintain life on Planet Earth by continuing to breathe into it His life-giving Spirit to replenish its resources.

A DEVOTIONAL INTERLUDE

For thanksgiving: Do you ever pause to thank God for the fruitful earth? If so, good. But do so again now. God did not set us on the earth to have food merely by wishing for it. It is produced by toil and sweat and foresight. However, sweat and toil would be useless without the added blessing of God. Think of the fruitful earth, the predictability of the seasons, the framework of a universe shaped in love and given to men and women. Think and give thanks.

DAY 39

READ
2 Peter 3:3-13

If we ask *why* God pledges to the human and animal family that He will keep this old earth going, we have to turn to the New Testament and to the apostle Peter for the clue.

Writing to Christians who are being mocked by unbelievers for the seeming delay in the return of Jesus, Peter reminds them of the creation and the Flood (vv.4–6). When this present creation is brought to an end, it will not be by water, says Peter. God's "never again" sees to that. Next time it will be fire that will reconstitute the elements of this old order (v.7). What will emerge are "a new heaven and a new earth, the home of righteousness" (v.13). Until then, do we conclude that God is slow or forgetful? No; He is patient because He does *not want "anyone to perish, but everyone to come to repentance"* (v.9). Here is the clue we are looking for as to why God chooses to sustain this old world still, even in its sin. It is because, under the terms of this Noahic covenant, God has pledged to preserve the earth until His redemptive purposes are completed. He is committed to the upkeep of this first, old, creation until the fruition of His plans to bring in a new creation.

A DEVOTIONAL INTERLUDE

Prayer: My Father and my God, I am in awe of the fact that in Your patient commitment to Your redemptive purposes You waited for me to come to repentance and become part of Your new creation. I ask myself: What if You had not been patient? And what if I had missed hearing of Your redemption? But all is well. I am Yours and You are mine. Our paths have crossed – and how! I am so grateful. Thank You dear Father. Amen.

DAY **40**

READ
Genesis 9:14-17

We noted that God's covenant with Noah and the earth was not merely an ecological pronouncement, important as that is for us today, but a statement of redemptive intent.

The permanent sign God has given of His intention is the *the rainbow* (v.13). God's later covenant with Abraham will be marked with the sign of circumcision, and with Israel by the Sabbath, but now, with Noah, it is the rainbow in the clouds. The rainbow is God's "preservation order" on this decaying but still beautiful old "house" of creation. Having used His arrows of judgment, God can now hang His "war-bow" in the sky as a sign of peace. Just as God's original Sabbath-rest showed that He has completed His *creation* work, so the war-bow at rest is the sign that He has ended His *decreation* work.

What is wonderful is that the bow is there not so much to remind *us* as to *remind God* (vv.15–16)! God continues to look down on human sin, but when He does, He sees too His rainbow-sign in the sky and remembers His covenant! For God to remember His covenant in this way spells salvation for us (Psa. 105:8–9), just as, in its own way, His forgetting does too (Jer. 31:34; Isa. 43:25)! This shows how determined God is to preserve this present world as the stage on which the future acts in His drama of redemption can be played out.

A DEVOTIONAL INTERLUDE

A Litany: We praise You for the creation of the world and all living creatures in it. Thank You, Lord. We especially praise You that each time we see a rainbow, we can realise afresh Your commitment to Your covenant with the earth itself. Thank You, Lord. We praise You for the vision of a future Kingdom in which all living creatures dwell in peace and security. Thank You, Lord. Hasten the coming of this glorious Kingdom, we pray. Through Jesus Christ our Lord. Amen.

READ
Genesis 1:1-25

As we trace the implications of God's covenant with Noah and the earth, we first of all look back to the picture painted in the opening chapters of Genesis. From this dramatic opening to its end in the book of Revelation, the whole Bible story sweeps majestically *from creation to new creation.* But we soon realise that progress is going to be neither smooth nor inevitable. The story moves through Fall and Flood, Exodus and Exile, death and resurrection, to secure its outcome.

This section – Genesis chapters 1 to 9 – describes a dramatic sequence of events in which God, who creates in love, decreates in judgment, and recreates in grace.

This chapter affirms the uniqueness of the one Creator God over against all possible rivals. It celebrates the God-given beauty, light, and order of creation. Like a peal of bells, it seven times affirms the essential goodness in God's eyes of all that He has made.

Our starting-point is God, not ourselves or our experience – a God who took the responsibility of creating because He knew He had the power to redeem.

A DEVOTIONAL INTERLUDE

Affirmation: In the light of today's reading use these words of St Francis of Assisi to affirm the uniqueness of God: "You are holy, Lord, You are the only God, and all Your works are wondrous. You are strong, You are great, You are the Most High, You are the Almighty King! You are the mystery of Three in One, the Lord above all gods. You are good, You are *all* good."

DAY **42**

READ
Genesis
1:26-2:16

It arouses an almost unbearable heartache and awakens a deep longing to be told that our human story was birthed in unconditional blessing (1:28). We have already seen that when God blessed Noah after the Flood, He was reaffirming His original blessing on Adam and Eve. "Blessing" in the Bible is never an empty word or casual wish, but the imparting of life and prosperity. Blessing was an act of empowerment and destiny. We are truly human only when we live by the blessing of God.

Blessing, and its opposite, curse, become in time the semi-legal language of covenant arrangements. This led earlier Christians to posit an original covenant between God and Adam. Be that as it may, what we see here is a powerful combination of God's word (1:26) and God's Spirit (*ruach*, wind, breath, 2:7) which, in wonderful harmony, continue to be God's creative agents in shaping the unique dignity of men and women. Men and women are equal bearers of God's image, partners with God in ruling His world wisely. They are called to populate the planet to the glory of God (1:26–28). Our role as workers is a worthy one, which is dignified by the fact that God adopts a six-day working week! Yet we are more than workers; we are worshippers, invited to enjoy with God the Sabbath-rest of His creative accomplishment.

A DEVOTIONAL INTERLUDE

Blessing: Think of someone you would like God to bless especially today. Picture that person in your mind's eye and pronounce this blessing on them: "The Lord bless you and keep you; the Lord make His face shine upon you, and be gracious to you; the Lord lift up His countenance upon you, and give you peace" (Num. 6:24–26, NKJV). Now expect God to do what you have asked, and give Him thanks for the blessing that person will receive.

DAY **43**

READ
Genesis 2:15-25

Today, we face the *realism* of the creation narrative. While a God-given environment, the Garden of Eden is not a paradise in some Utopian sense.

The human condition in Eden even before the Fall is marked by *challenge* (2:15), *limitation* (2:16–17), *loneliness* (2:18), and *temptation* (3:1ff.).

For a start, there is challlenging work to be done! Called to subdue the earth, men and women must exercise skill, energy and sensitivity in managing the natural world, without exploiting or despoiling it. As we care for and nurture, God's creation, we find ample scope for every legitimate human art, from ground-level cultivation to high culture.

And God sets boundaries not to cramp our style but to keep us humble and to stimulate our respect for others. Our essential aloneness stirs us to reach out for loving relationship. The possibility of temptation creates space for obedient choices that make a difference.

Adam's privilege of naming other creatures, shows how, uniquely, human beings share God's authority to define the world (2:19; cf. 1:5, etc.). Adam's outburst of joy (2:23) is the first song in the Bible. It celebrates intimacy with one who is part of oneself yet truly other. Inevitably, same-gender sex can never be truly complementary but remains a distorted form of self-love.

A DEVOTIONAL INTERLUDE

For action: God has given us a great deal of freedom in life, but with that freedom comes responsibility. Adam and Eve in the Garden of Eden chose wrong rather than right and thus used their freedom in a way that violated the divine commands. Ask God today, in your own words, to enable you to choose good and not evil, life and not death, truth and not lies. Your choices make a difference, either for right or wrong. Let it always be for right.

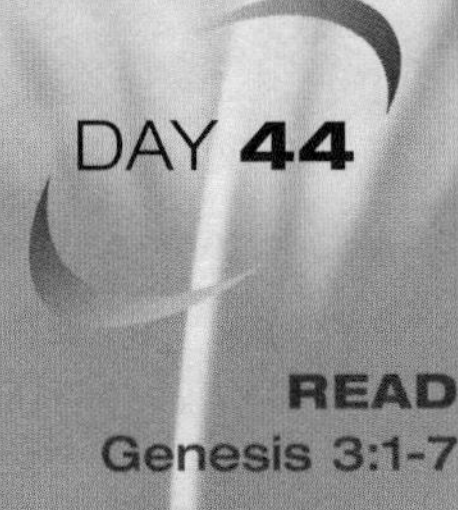

DAY **44**

READ
Genesis 3:1-7

Now the shadows lengthen over the lovely land of God's creation as the darkening reality of our human sinfulness unfolds. Later, but not here, the serpent is associated with the devil. Here, the text will not allow us to off-load any responsibility for our mistrust and rebellion. The insidious voice comes from *within* creation, not from outside.

What the serpent says constitutes a *threefold attack*: on God's word (v.1), on God's authority (v.4), and on God's goodness (v.5). The last thrust is to insinuate to the couple that God is not really out for their best interests but is keeping something from them that would advantage them! What the woman perceives has a *threefold attraction*: it is good for food, delights the eyes, and is desirable for gaining wisdom (v.6). This triple attraction, characterised later by the apostle John as "the lust of the flesh, the lust of the eyes, and the pride of life" (1 John 2:16, NKJV) is crucially mirrored and mastered in the victory of Jesus in the Judean desert (Matthew 4:1–11; Luke 4:1–13).

A DEVOTIONAL INTERLUDE

To ponder: Spend a few moments meditating on Jesus' victory during His temptation in the wilderness (Luke 4:1–13). What was the secret of His triumph over Satan? His trust in God and His knowledge of the Word. His rebuttal of Satan was based on texts all drawn from the book of Deuteronomy. If you were faced with a powerful attack of Satan would you know what Scripture to use against him? Worth thinking about isn't it?

DAY **45**

READ
Genesis
3:8-4:16

Here our human story starts on its terrible slide into that degeneration which will culminate with the Flood. The Fall leads to embarrassment and shame (cf. 2:25; 3:7); to escape from God in fear (3:8); and to evasion of responsibility – either by confessing symptoms rather than sin (3:10) or by shifting the blame to someone else (3:12).

God's initial response to His sinful creatures is to ask a series of penetrating questions (3:9,11,13; 4:6,9)! And each question is intended to rouse them to *take responsibility* again for their lives.

The divine judgmental curse signifies that the spiritual battle has been joined (3:14–15), but carries with it a hint of promised salvation and victory on the human battlefield. The battle of the sexes also follows (3:16), as does our estrangement from the natural world (3:17–19).

Eden is barred for ever (3:24); there is no going back to lost innocence. The only way is forward to atonement and reconciliation. Behind us is the first Adam who sinned, but ahead of us is the Last Adam whose "agony in the garden [of Gethsemane] heals all the agony of the race" (P.T. Forsyth). As we have seen, God's dealings with Noah constituted the first major step on that journey.

A DEVOTIONAL INTERLUDE

Prayer: Gracious and loving heavenly Father, how grateful I am for the fact that although the first Adam failed in a garden of beauty, You triumphed in the midst of the most humiliating conditions. As I think of Your agony in the Garden of Gethsemane and Your sufferings on the cross my heart cries out: Thank You dear Lord. Your agony has healed my agony. Amen.

DAY **46**

READ
Exodus 25:1-9; 31:1-17

In continuing to explore the creational dimension to the redemptive story, we move beyond Noah and the patriarchs to the nation of Israel. God selected Israel to be His covenant partner in bringing blessing to the whole world. To that end, God redeemed his people from slavery in Egypt so that they might embody what a truly human race might look like which lived by God's grace and for God's glory. The book of Exodus is shaped throughout by a theology of creation, not least in the parallels between Exodus and Genesis. The plagues on Egypt, like the Flood, are ecological judgments; deliverance is through water (15:1ff.); and chapters 25 to 40, like Genesis 1 to 9, may be seen as a sequence of creation-decreation-recreation.

In particular, the building of the tabernacle in chapters 35 to 40 can be seen in terms of recreation. The parallels are intriguing. The creative Spirit is again at work (31:1–11; cf. Gen. 1:2); seven speeches in chapters 25 to 31 mirror the seven days of creation, climaxing, like them, in the Sabbath (31:16–17) which, as the sign of God's special covenant with Israel, reminds His people also of its role in His wider purposes for His creation. In this portable worship-centre then, and with His pilgrim people, the mobile God is on His way to the new creation!

A DEVOTIONAL INTERLUDE

To ponder: A key passage to focus on is Deuteronomy 26:16-19. Note particularly verse 17: "You have declared this day that the Lord is your God and that you will walk in his ways, that you will keep his decrees, commands and laws, and that you will obey him." God selected the Israelites to be His covenant partner. How sad that so often they failed. We too are God's covenant partners – let's draw daily on God's grace to ensure we do not fail.

THE PROMISE-PLAN OF GOD

COVENANT WITH: NOAH ABRAHAM

DAY 47

READ
Exodus
39:43-40:38

Still pursuing our creation theme we note that, in building the tabernacle, Moses draws together materials and skills which God has invested in His creation. It is as if the whole material world and all human craftsmanship is being redirected to its original goal of glorifying God. The sanctuary itself exhibits beauty, order, design and colour – just those features most evident in God's original "good" world.

As in Genesis 1, so here the work is finished, evaluated as satisfactory, and blessed (39:43). The tabernacle is dedicated on the first day of the first month, corresponding liturgically to the first day of creation (40:2,17). In other words, the tabernacle symbolically celebrates, within a disordered world, the beauty and order of God's creation.

This makes worship hugely significant. Worship becomes, for us, the one spot in the midst of a fractured world where we declare God's redemptive reordering of the world. In worship we exult in God's promise of a new creation. We take the holy time and make holy space which God can fill with His glorious presence (40:34).

A DEVOTIONAL INTERLUDE

Thought: Worship, it has been said, is "inner health made audible". What is meant by this? We are made for worship, and when we engage in true worship our souls are drawn to health. Those who do not worship may have physical health but not spiritual health. The worship of God is the way to achieve spiritual health. But remember, there can be no true worship where there is no trust. You cannot worship someone you do not trust.

DAY **48**

READ
Job 38:1-42:7

Our story now takes us to a mini-drama all its own; a series of tense dialogues between a suffering man and his so-called friends and spurious theological experts, and, lastly, his encounter with the Creator God in person! Job's "advisers" finally grind to a halt. Having stubbornly refused to deny his own integrity, Job, too, falls silent. When at last God speaks, He overwhelms Job with a dazzling recital of His power as Creator. Is God browbeating Job into submission? Or is he, perhaps, taking drastic measures to break through Job's defences? In his pain, Job has often complained that he hates being human (7:17–21; cf. Psa. 8). But we do not glorify God by loathing ourselves.

God's rebuke is not meant to cut Job down to size, but to rouse him to measure up as a worthy conversation partner and co-worker. On one possible reading of the text of 42:6, Job repents *of*, not *in*, "dust and ashes". That is, he repudiates his low sense of self-worth, turning from his own self-hatred to re-engage with the One in whose image he is made. God summons Job to stand on his feet "like a man", to look Him in the eye (38:3; 40:6–7).

One glimpse of this majestic God cleanses and clarifies as no judgmental friends or self-condemnation can ever do (42:5). This is the wisdom Job finds in the end, albeit through suffering.

A DEVOTIONAL INTERLUDE

Prayer: Gracious and loving Father, forgive me if I tell You what I think *You* should do rather than listening to You to learn what *I* should do. How I pray that the drastic steps You took to silence Job may not be necessary with me. If I have been focusing more on speaking than listening, then help me through this problem. In Jesus' Name. Amen.

DAY 49

READ
Psalm 8

In the moonlight, under a star-studded sky, how big and majestic God seems; how tiny and insignificant I feel! When I glimpse the big picture, it seems to dwarf my little domestic story.

Undeterred, the singer celebrates by setting Genesis 1:26–28 to music. "Made a little lower than God" (v.5) helps us find our bearings. We neither *deify* human beings as gods nor *denigrate them* as junk! In the vastness of the universe we may seem fragile and insignificant. But God *considers us*, and what we are in His eyes is what counts! Not, as the famous philosopher said: "I think, therefore I am." But rather: "God thinks of me, therefore I am"! Neither the planets nor the apes determine who we are! *It is our relationship with God that defines us most accurately.*

"Crowned with glory and honour ... and given dominion" (vv.5–6), we have a calling that ennobles us. Although sin and suffering can make it seem an oppressive burden (Job 7:17–21), being human is a royal vocation.

Our text awaits the victory of the truly human One who, conquering evil and death, emerges with everything – even death – successfully "under his feet" (1 Cor. 15:20–28; Eph. 1:16–23; Heb. 2:5–8). "The head that once was crowned with thorns is crowned with glory now."

A DEVOTIONAL INTERLUDE

To ponder: Someone has commented: "I am not what I think I am. I am not what you think I am. I am what I think you think I am." In other words, the way we think about ourselves is not the way others think of us but the way we think they think of us. How do you think God thinks about you? He thinks you are special, someone in whom He delights. Now think that way about yourself. Remember: "It is our relationship with God that defines us most accurately."

DAY **50**

READ
Psalm 19

God speaks in both the *sky* (vv.1–6) and the *Scriptures* (vv.7–14). In the *sky* the "voice" of His creation declares His glory and proclaims His handiwork in morning lectures and evening classes. As joyfully as a bridegroom is meant for his bride, and an athlete is meant for the finishing tape, so the sun, by rising and setting, adds its witness to the glorious purpose of things.

In the *Scriptures* (vv.7–14) God speaks firsthand in the words of the law. The psalmist exults in what the law *is* – God's testimony and precepts – and also in what the law is *like* – perfect, sure, radiant, pure, sweet. Above all he relishes what the law *does*: it revives the soul, makes wise the simple, gives joy to the heart and light to the eyes! The fear of God this evokes does not deter but attracts (v.10), enabling us to breathe moral fresh air (vv.11–13). In the end we fear to mar such beauty, deny such truth, grieve such love.

This remarkable song joins what God reveals in creation (general revelation) with what He reveals through the story told in Israel's Scriptures (special revelation). Both invite *saving* revelation. God is the Rock which His creation reveals Him to be and becomes the Redeemer His law needs Him to be. But to tell *that* story and declare *that* glory we must follow another star.

A DEVOTIONAL INTERLUDE

For Thanksgiving: Two thrilling verses that join creation and redemption are found in the book of Revelation: "You are worthy, our Lord and God, to receive glory and honour and power, for you created all things" (Rev. 4:11). "You have made them to be a kingdom and priests to serve our God, and they will reign on the earth" (Rev. 5:10). How wonderful God is in creation, but how much more wonderful is He in redemption.

THE PROMISE-PLAN OF GOD

COVENANT WITH: NOAH ABRAHAM

DAY **51**

READ
Psalm 104

We pause to reflect further on how the prophetic singers of Israel praised the one Creator God, and celebrated His works of creation.

Dramatically, in the first stanza, the psalmist pictures God clothed majestically in a cloak of light, striding through His world, painting the world in glorious colours, sparking into life everything He touches. Here is no distant God, locked outside His world. This is the biblical God, pouring out His creative energies and love all the time from *inside* His world.

Echoing what we have seen of God's commitment to Noah and the earth, the song relishes the way God's faithfulness guarantees the world's *stability* (vv.5–9), His creativity funds its *fruitfulness* (vv.10–18), His design shapes its *orderliness* (vv.19–23), and His multifaceted wisdom is prodigal in its *variety* (vv.24–26). Unless we act irresponsibly and ransack the earth, we can be sure its resources will never run out! God's Spirit "renews the face of the earth" (v.30).

Feasting, working, researching, praising – it's a wonderful world!

A DEVOTIONAL INTERLUDE

For Praise: "Jesus is Lord, creation's voice proclaims it, sun, moon and stars in heaven cry Jesus is Lord." Echo these words of this song and think about the fact that throughout the whole of creation there are evidences of His creative hand. It is the same in the Christian life. His resources – grace, love, joy, peace, and so on – will never be exhausted. For that also gives Him praise.

DAY **52**

READ
Proverbs 8

This remarkable flight of prophetic imagination pictures the wisdom of God as God's creative partner in making the world, dancing beside Him in the sheer joy of creativity (vv.30–31).

Scholars argue over whether or not this is strictly a personification of wisdom. Be that as it may, we can find the wisdom of God at street level (v.2). Following the Maker's instructions, we learn the life-skills to raise a family, run a business, rule our tongues or rule a nation! When moral choices must be made we can find God's wisdom along the paths of righteousness (v.20). And this wisdom, we discover, is nothing less than the very wisdom with which God made the world (vv.22–31)!

From Proverbs 8 the trajectory of wisdom travelled through the Jewish writings *The Wisdom of Solomon* and *Ecclesiasticus* until it lodged in the mind-set of the apostles. There it provided the key categories which enabled them to speak of the divinity of Jesus without compromising the oneness of God (see Col. 1:15ff.; cf. 1 Cor. 1:18–2:4; 8:4–6). For the apostles and for us, the wisdom of God finally came down to earth *in Person* in the words and work of Jesus of Nazareth.

A DEVOTIONAL INTERLUDE

To ponder: The difference between knowledge and wisdom, it has been said, is this: knowledge is what one knows, wisdom is knowing how best to use that knowledge. Jesus is described as the "power of God and the wisdom of God" (1 Cor. 1:24). What an apt description. Not only does He have all the information He needs to run the universe but He also knows the best way to use it. And that wisdom is available to you and me – any time (see James 1:5).

THE PROMISE-PLAN OF GOD

COVENANT WITH: NOAH ABRAHAM

DAY **53**

READ
Isaiah 54

The experience of the Babylonian Exile was so traumatic that the prophets who lived through it harked back to the old Flood story to define it! It was Jeremiah who pictured the impending Babylonian invasion of Judah as a catastrophe on a scale which could only be described as an act of decreation (Jer. 4:19–28). The great "Israel adventure" seemed to have come to an end with the people of God engulfed in a "flood" of judgment. So severe is the crisis that not even Noah, Ezekiel said, could have made a difference (Ezek. 14:12–20)!

But it was just at this point that talk of Noah gives hope. For Isaiah, God's commitment to Noah in covenant not only guarantees creation but becomes a pattern and a promise of God's renewing work after the Exile (Isa. 54:5–10). We recall that after the deluge of water and destruction, God swore that the Flood of His judgment would never happen again. Now, says Isaiah, the God of all the earth swears never again to desert His people or loosen the grip of His covenant love upon them. This pledge of reconciliation Isaiah calls "a covenant of peace" (54:10). The Creator resolves to be Redeemer, ultimately on an unprecedented scale (Isa. 65:17–25).

A DEVOTIONAL INTERLUDE

Prayer: My Father and my God, how my heart rejoices at this truth that You have sworn never to desert Your people or loosen the grip of Your covenant love upon them. How secure it makes me feel that as one of Your covenant people my name is written on Your hands. This means I cannot be forgotten. My name is before You for eternity. How can I ever sufficiently thank You for that tremendous fact? My heart is Yours for ever. Amen.

DAY 54

READ
John 1

John here recalls Genesis 1, introducing Jesus as both one with the eternal Creator God and as head of a new creation. John calls Him "the Word" (*logos*), a term known in Greek thought, but, more importantly, with Old Testament roots. There, God's word is world-making, powerful and effective (e.g., Gen. 1:2ff.; Psa. 33:6ff.; Isa. 55:10–11). This "word" is now concentrated in a person, Jesus Christ.

John draws on two other sources. First, is the Old Testament and Jewish concept of "personified" wisdom as God's agent in creation (Prov. 8:22ff.). Secondly, John is, no doubt, echoing the early Christians' experience of the gospel as the powerful "Word" that saves (e.g., Rom. 1:16; 10:17; Col. 1:5). John celebrates this Word as eternal, as personal, as light and life, and, above all, as truly human (v.14). God's openly spoken word and God's deep, underlying wisdom come into sharp focus in the face of Jesus. God's grace and truth have taken on flesh-and-blood reality (cf. 1 John 1:1ff.). His glory fulfils and eclipses all that's come before, even through Moses. The incarnate Word is the "exegesis" or "narration" of God (v.18). *The story of Jesus is the story of God.*

Reading His script and singing His song, we, too, behold God's glory in Jesus Christ.

A DEVOTIONAL INTERLUDE

For thanksgiving: Dr E. Stanley Jones told of a little boy who stood in front of a picture of his absent father and then said wistfully to his mother: "How I wish Father would step out of the picture." Throughout the Old Testament we can almost hear the same cry: "If only the Father would step out of the picture." Well, He has. He did so at Bethlehem. It shouldn't be only at Christmas time that we thank Him for stepping out of the picture. Do so now.

DAY **55**

READ
Romans 1:16-32

In this devastating analysis of sin, Paul argues that creation displays unmistakable evidence of God's power and personality; enough, at least, to damn us if not enough to save us (v.20)! Failure in *worship* is the root sin (1:21). Our inbuilt drive to worship is then diverted into idolatry. Rejecting the Creator, we make a threefold "exchange": God for idols, the truth for a lie, the natural for the unnatural (1:23,25,26).

Of persistent rebels, God is said, in judicial language, to "give them up" to experience the inevitable consequences of rebellion (1:24,26,28). Sexual perversions are seen here not so much as acts which incur God's wrath but as *signs of a society already under God's wrath*. Homosexuality is highlighted, of course, not because it is more heinous a sin than gossip or envy (1:29ff.), rather, it graphically illustrates how sin destroys God's creation order, and how society has lost its way. Homosexuality is vivid idolatry, the ultimate form of self-love. But this passage is a devastating indictment of *all* human sin and leaves no one in a position to judge others (2:1).

Thankfully, the gospel is more than adequate to redeem the human condition even in cities such as Rome (1:15–17).

A DEVOTIONAL INTERLUDE

Response: What better response could we give to today's reading than to reflect on the words of the well known hymn by Isaac Watts. Say it or sing it now: "When I survey the wondrous cross, on which the Prince of glory died, my richest gain I count but loss, and pour contempt on all my pride."

DAY **56**

READ
Colossians
1:1-2:7

It is exciting to make the biblical connections and to see how the whole story hangs together. So it is with this stunning "hymn" (1:15–20) which celebrates the supremacy of Jesus and is the hub around which the whole letter to the Colossians revolves.

This breathtaking vision is couched in language employed in the Old Testament and in Jewish writings to describe the creative wisdom of God. *In relation to God,* Jesus is the image (*icon*). *In relation to the cosmos,* He is the "firstborn" of all creation (1:19), which does not imply that He ranks merely as a created being (the next verse precludes this). The likely background here is the inheritance rights of the eldest son in Old Testament families. Paul is stressing that *Jesus has priority, precedence, and stands to inherit the whole world.*

This is in line with the King's destiny as "Son of God" (Psa. 2). Amazingly, He is also the "glue" that holds all things together (1:17). *In relation to the Church,* He is its Head (1:18). Applied to someone who had been crucified as a false prophet only some thirty years earlier, Paul's description is truly staggering! This is Jesus who, by virtue of His death and resurrection, is the climax of the old creation and the starting-point of the new creation where all things are reconciled to God's loving will.

A DEVOTIONAL INTERLUDE

For action: Though many "hymns to Christ" have been developed over the centuries, nothing comes near to the inspired words of the apostle Paul in the passage we have read today. Consider composing your own "hymn to Christ". List all the things He has done for you – saving you, delivering you, and so on. Remember that the law of expression deepens impression. The more you express something the deeper it penetrates. You'll see.

DAY 57

READ
Hebrews
1:1-2:18

It seems a long journey from Noah, but the trajectories being traced are now converging again and again on Jesus. Here, the majestic opening statement (1:1–4), and the seven Old Testament references that support it (1:5–14), magnificently declare once more that Jesus is God's "last word" to His old creation and the "first word" on the new creation. From this we learn that Jesus can be explained only as One who comes out of God, from outside creation.

Chapter 2 then claims that He comes, at the same time, from our human side of things, from within the created order! The writer builds his case on Psalm 8 (Day 49, Psa. 8) to show that the transcendent Son of God made the human condition fully His own. In His real humanity He became like us, liable to temptation, suffering, and even death, in order to restore us to the glory of our God-given human destiny (2:9). As the truly human One Jesus has lived our life, died our death, and now wears our crown. This is the guarantee that, in Him, we shall make it back to the glory from which we so tragically fell (2:10).

We see now only glimpses of this future but we do see *Jesus crowned* ... and holding to His cross, we trust in His achievement.

A DEVOTIONAL INTERLUDE

For Praise: There is but one response we can make to today's reading; it is to say or sing these words:

Crown Him with many crowns,
The Lamb upon His throne;
Hark! how the heavenly anthem drowns
All music but its own.
Awake, my soul, and sing
Of Him who died for thee,
And hail Him as thy matchless King through all eternity.

DAY **58**

READ
Romans 8

As we round off the implications of God's covenant with Noah, we reach this exalted vantage-point from which we see laid out before us the breathtaking panorama of God's saving plans. Fresh from the Exodus, Israel was claimed as "God's son" and pointed towards the Promised Land (Exod. 4:22–23).

But it was Jesus alone, centuries later, who succeeded, through suffering as the obedient "Son of God", in the role created for Israel and her anointed king (2 Sam. 7:12–14). For us who are now "in Christ" to fulfil our destiny as God's sons is both an incomparable privilege and a bracing challenge (vv.15–18).

Since our sinful failure mysteriously dragged creation down with us into frustration, so, by a miracle of grace, our faithfulness raises hopes of creation's renewal (v.19). We too wait in hope for the redemption of our bodies. Meanwhile, with those who love God, the Spirit works all things together for God's good. This Spirit takes the dumb sighs of nature for release, the uttered cries of human beings for liberty, joins them to the groaning prayers of believers, and makes mysterious intercession that this decaying world may one day find its redemption and come to share in the glorious freedom of the sons of God. To this end Love has spared no expense (v.32) and suffers no separation (vv.38–39).

A DEVOTIONAL INTERLUDE

Question: How astonishing – a groan in the heart of God. The *Spirit* groans. And what for? That sin and its effects will at the right time be removed from the universe for ever. One preacher has said: "All progress in this world is by the echo of the groan of God in the heart of man." Here's a question to consider today: Can I hear the echo of God's groan over creation in my own heart? Little progress will be made in prayer unless you do.

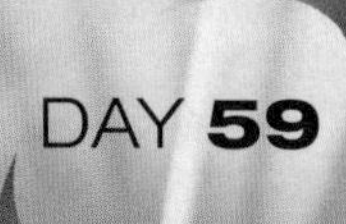

DAY **59**

READ
Matthew
24:36-44

Jesus mentioned Noah's name only once but, when He did, He issued two urgent warnings: *"stay awake"* and *"don't speculate"!* "Spiritual sleeping sickness" can afflict any of us. As in the days of Noah, we can become so preoccupied with everyday affairs that we forget the larger drama we are meant to take part in. Unlike Rip Van Winkle we Christians cannot sleep through the revolution but must *stay awake*.

An opposite danger is the fevered *speculation* of armchair experts on the end times. One brand of pop-prophecy harks back to verse 31 to support its theories about the "rapture". It assumes that those "taken" (in verses 40 to 41) are believers, and those "left behind" are unbelievers. In fact, in context, the exact opposite is likely to be the case. Those "taken" are those who, as in the Flood (v.39), are taken away by judgment, while those left behind are God's vindicated people!

Jesus says plainly about the present: don't fix dates. The timing and exact sequence of future events can safely be left in the Father's hands. Staying awake (being spiritually aware) is evidently not something to lose sleep over (make a worrying obsession)!

In passionate trust, faith walks with God into an unknown but not uncertain future, looking for the light of His Son's coming? And that leads us to reflect on Abraham's part in the story!

A DEVOTIONAL INTERLUDE

Prayer: Gracious and loving Father, help me not to become preoccupied with dates and seasons but to remain spiritually awake, knowing that the future is in Your safe hands. Watch over my spirit and keep me free of all speculation, content in the knowledge that in the end everything is going to work out as You have planned it. Drive that conviction deeper and deeper into my spirit. In Jesus' Name I pray. Amen.

NOAH
all creation

ABRAHAM
ALL NATIONS

ISRAEL
one nation

DAVID
representative king

NEW COVENANT
faithful covenant partner

JESUS
faithful covenant partner

JESUS
Davidic King Messiah

JESUS
the New Israel

JESUS
the world's Lord

JESUS
the truly Human One crowned with glory and honour

JESUS
cosmic Ruler in God's new creation new heavens and new earth

SECTION 4
ABRAHAM'S ADVENTURE

God is committed to blessing all nations on earth - God's covenant with Abraham.

Abraham surprised himself, late in life, by becoming an adventurer. When the great Polar explorer, Sir Ernest Shackleton, planned his ambitious and ultimately unsuccessful trans-Antarctic expedition of 1914, which turned into an epic survival story, he reputedly advertised for recruits with this notice: "Men wanted for hazardous journey. Small wages, bitter cold, long months of complete darkness, constant danger, safe return doubtful. Honour and recognition in case of success." Five thousand men are said to have answered the call.

When Abraham responded to God's call, the hazards ahead were different, but, in its own way, the challenge he faced was every bit as daunting.

Abram – as he was known then – is called to exchange a settled and reasonably comfortable lifestyle in what, by ancient standards, was a sophisticated society, for a nomadic existence trekking to and through foreign, and for him, unexplored territory. Abram chooses to break the close ties of clan and kinship, to leave the "comfort-zone" of social standing and acceptance, to forsake the traditional gods of his fathers, for the sake of this risky journey into the unknown.

Glimpsing God's glory is evidently enough to disenchant Abram of anything Babylon had to offer. God's lordly command clearly overrides all Babylonian claims upon him (Acts 7:2–3; Gen. 12:1). Childless and dispossessed, Abram is promised multiplied descendants, and a land for them to inherit (Gen. 12:7) – a famous name and great nation and, eventually, an extended family beyond his wildest dreams, too numerous to count. This new God promises to bless him and his descendants, and make him the pivotal figure through whom He can bring blessing to all the nations on the earth (Gen. 12:2–3).

Abram's role is global. He has been lifted out of his domestic story and made part of God's big story. Abram obeyed and left.

As the years drag by, however, without children, and Abram begins to question God's promise, God steps in again with the staggering new promise that Abram's descendants will be as numerous as the stars in the night sky. Abram responds by trusting God utterly and "he credited it to him as righteousness" (Gen. 15:6), so establishing the abiding scriptural principle that faith alone brings us into a righteous relationship with God. To reinforce His commitment, God then makes a covenant in a ritual which sounds bizarre to us but which, in the ancient world, meant that the parties to the agreement swore to their own death should either break it (Gen. 15).

Even when Abram's patience runs so thin that he takes matters into his own hand, and he has a son, Ishmael, by Hagar, Sarah's maidservant (Gen. 16), God does not write him off.

Just as the covenant of chapter 15 reassured Abram about the descendants and the land, so now God makes a covenant again to reassure Abraham about the third strand to the promise – "blessing for all nations on the earth" – this time in a challenging mutual exchange of vows (Gen. 17). His name is now changed to "Abraham", meaning "father of many nations" (Gen. 17:5). The patriarch is later tested by God, who asked for the sacrifice of his beloved son, Isaac (Gen. 22:1–18). Though Isaac is spared, the oath this elicits from God commits God, in effect, to matching Abraham's offering of his son in order to maintain the integrity of His long-term plans for redemption.

With the promises made to Abraham, sealed in covenant, God has laid down His permanent intentions to redeem His world. Nothing less than the establishment of His kingdom on a global scale, and the blessing of all nations with salvation, is the goal of the Abrahamic covenant.

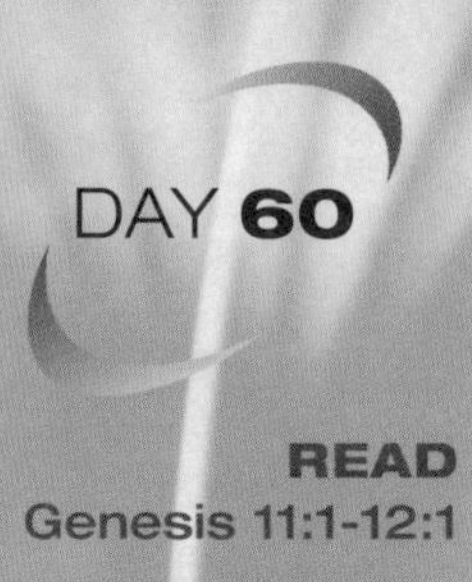

DAY 60

READ
Genesis 11:1-12:1

The Bible can be viewed as the "tale of two cities": Babylon and Jerusalem. City-building reveals our best and worst. On the one hand, God-given creativity worked out in community; on the other, the arrogant pursuit of the glory of man.

The tower of Babel, perhaps an ancient ziggurat reaching to the heavens, seems construed by the text as an attempt to displace God or the gods. The resolve "not to be scattered over the face of the whole earth" (11:4) directly contradicts the Creator's original command to fill the earth (1:26). In short, we have a vivid cameo of a God-defying civilisation. With delicious irony, the text tells us that the Lord had to "come down" to inspect the tower, so infinitesimal was it! The repeated "come, *let us* ..." parodies the original divine "*let us make*" (1:26), only to be matched by a further divine *"let us"* (11:7). God scrambles human languages to a "babble" – "Babel" – the root of "Babylon"!

We glimpse two cities, then, which will reappear in the Bible's final vision: one that man is building for his own short-lived fame, the other which God is building for His eternal glory. Abraham left the one for the other in the service of God's promise-plan of salvation. For the same reason, you and I rise each morning to trust and travel with God in pursuit of His dreams.

A DEVOTIONAL INTERLUDE

To ponder: When you awoke this morning did you consider yourself as a modern-day Abraham led by God to pursue His dreams? Probably not. But consider now: whose dreams are you pursuing? Yours or His? Are your working for the "city" or are your eyes focused on the one to come? We must not ignore our responsibilities on earth, but they must always be balanced by the recognition that this world is not our home – we are just passing through.

DAY **61**

READ
Acts 7

Abraham – we shall call him by the longer form of his name throughout these notes – left Ur. But why? What made him do it?

When the first Christian martyr, Stephen, reviewed Israel's history, he said that "The God of glory appeared to our father Abraham while he was still in Mesopotamia ..." (v.2). Was this the vision that impelled Abraham to uproot from his own country and journey to the land of promise? Did the glimpse of God's glory outshine the splendour of Babylonia?

Stephen's speech goes on to suggest that Abraham's decision to leave embraced his father, Terah, too – no small thing in such a patriarchal society. Stephen's whole prophetic review of the Old Testament story strongly implies that God's people have been most in touch with Him when they lived outside the land rather than in it. If so, then again it was Abraham who pioneered a relationship with God which did not depend on territory or Temple but followed in faith a God on the move who was going places.

Merely to glimpse His dazzling glory is to be spoiled for the attractions of Babylon. It makes living as a nomad in a foreign land bearable and even – as Stephen immediately discovered – dying as a martyr meaningful (v.55)!

A DEVOTIONAL INTERLUDE

Thought: Paul reminds us in 2 Corinthians 5:20 that we are ambassadors for Christ. An ambassador, as you know, represents his country in a foreign land. Think of it: you are a personal representative of a heavenly King! What is more, an ambassador has direct access to the ruler of his native country. And so do you! Make sure you maintain daily communication with your heavenly King. A vision of His glory makes every other vision dim.

DAY **62**

READ
Genesis 12:1

If seeing God's glory unsettles Abraham, causing his disenchantment with Babylonian culture, then it is hearing God's word which cuts him loose from it, launching him on the flowing tide of faith in search of an alternative.

That God has spoken His word to us is the foundation of all biblical faith. Abraham, however, has long been exposed exclusively to Babylonian versions of truth. All Abraham has heard are Babylonian promises and propaganda, information and misinformation. But when God speaks, Abraham hears a voice he's never heard before. God speaks a piercing word which cuts through all settled convictions, all unexamined dogmas and ideological slogans, all undisturbed assumptions about the way things are and must be. God speaks like a crystal clear stream in a desert, like blissfully cool water to a parched throat, like a clear trumpet call above the confused cacophony of human opinions.

So Abraham obeys and goes. And so must we, not in the old pietistic and passive sense of "Let go and let God" but in the more bracing and adventurous Abrahamic sense of "Let God and let's go"!

A DEVOTIONAL INTERLUDE

Question: When in prayer, do you take time to listen for God's voice? The art of listening is the product of long practice. Those who would cultivate the ability must set time aside specifically for the purpose, and set it aside every day. Be quiet before God. At first you will not be able to disentangle His voice from your thoughts. But be patient. Eventually you will hear His voice, and when you do it will be well worth the wait.

DAY 63

READ
Genesis 12:1

God's promise to Abraham has three vital elements. First, God promises Abraham *land* (12:1,7) or, at least, a sight of the land of Canaan which his descendants will possess as the land of promise, *the Promised Land.* But to receive it Abraham must leave and let go of his old securities.

The tension between promise and fulfilment which is a recurring pattern in the story, is heightened as we see Abraham, a stranger wandering through the land but not settling in it! Even when he returns from Egypt where famine has driven him (12:10), Abraham is a "resident alien", pacing out the length and breadth of the land as if to lay claim to it, but oddly never taking root in it (13:17). And by his death, he owns nothing of the land except the burial place he has paid good money for in which to bury his beloved Sarah (23:4–20)!

In this way Abraham pioneers what it means to live by God's grace: to have nothing yet possess all things, to be gifted a homeland but to sit light to it and to continue to live a semi-nomadic existence. There was a clear lesson here for Abraham's descendants when they eventually possessed the land if only they could have heard it: never take the land for granted, it is pure gift; respect the gift and the Giver or it will be lost; and never stake everything on occupying the land at all costs.

A DEVOTIONAL INTERLUDE

Prayer: O Father, help me I pray to understand that I am not a proprietor but a steward. You are the true Owner of everything. May I therefore hang to things lightly, knowing that one day I shall leave them all behind to be with You. Give me the wisdom to use the resources that are in my hands wisely so that when I face You I will hear the words: "Well done, good and faithful servant ... enter into the joy of your Lord." Amen.

DAY **64**

READ
Genesis 12:2

Second, God promises Abraham's *descendants* (12:2). "I will make you a great nation" is bold talk to a childless man whose wife is barren (11:30) and beyond the age of child-bearing.

Once more dramatic tension is built into the narrative. The tension mounts as God speaks of offspring like the dust of the ground and the stars in the sky (13:16; 15:5) while the reality of Abraham and Sarah's condition becomes laughable (17:17). For over twenty-five years the question hangs in the air: Will there be any son at all? Even when the miracle child arrives, the suspense is maintained as the reader wonders whether or not he will survive the sacrificial knife. Will the sons survive each other's jealousy? The later chapters also seem to show the promise under threat since not only Sarah but then both Rebekah (25:21) and Rachel (29:31) are said to be barren.

These stories will in time remind the "great nation", Israel, that she does not exist on her own merit but solely from God's grace. Israel is an impossibility which exists only because God wills and works miracles of grace.

A DEVOTIONAL INTERLUDE

Question: Do you long for a miracle at this present time? Then reflect on these words: "Is anything too hard for the Lord? I will return to you at the appointed time next year and Sarah will have a son" (Gen. 18:14). God's Word is written for our admonition and encouragement. Let this verse encourage you today to ask God for the miracle you desire. However, first make sure that the miracle is what you *need*, not merely something you want.

DAY **65**

READ
Genesis 12:2

God promises Abraham, thirdly, a relationship with Him which is characterised by *blessing* (12:2–3). In the Old Testament, to bless someone is not to make a merely formal gesture of goodwill but to speak a life-changing word. This word not only transmits happiness and material success – which Abraham certainly enjoyed in abundance (e.g., 24:1,35) – but, at an even deeper level, connects the recipient with God's original empowerment of humankind.

God's "I will bless you" is therefore doubly significant, not only aligning Abraham with future prosperity but connecting him back through Noah to Adam and God's original creation-blessing and mandate (Gen. 9:1; 1:26).

So Abraham is presented to us, like Noah before him, as a "new Adam", the forerunner of a new humanity, though with an added vital dimension. Where God's covenant with Noah was largely preservative, maintaining the earth as a settled environment for human beings in general, His promise to Abraham launches His specific redemptive programme for blessing the human race.

Significantly, the fivefold mention of blessing here seems to mirror the fivefold curse of Genesis chapters 1 to 11 (3:14,17; 4:11; 5:29; 9:25). Evidently, Abraham's call is crucial if worldwide curse is to be turned into a worldwide blessing.

A DEVOTIONAL INTERLUDE

For action: One of the greatest joys in life is to have God's blessing. But there are conditions to receiving God's blessing. Read again the first verses of Matthew chapter 5 to see those conditions. You will see that the scope of God's blessings is endless but the conditions have to be obeyed. Do you want to be blessed? Then take the eight Beatitudes and work out how many apply in your life and how many are missing.

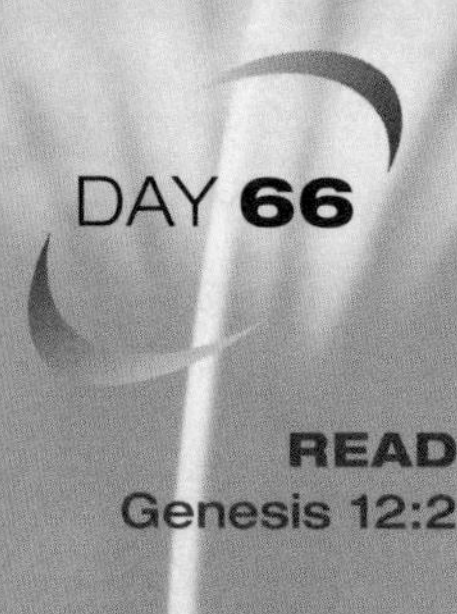

DAY **66**

READ
Genesis 12:2

Every phrase in these texts is important for understanding God's plan of salvation, so we must linger another day on this verse.

God's promise, "I will make your name great," almost certainly implies royal status, as is soon confirmed by the explicit anticipation that "kings will come from you" (17:6,16). This connects Abraham to Israel's future kings, especially David, of whose line the same promise is made (2 Sam. 7:9). Abraham's God-shaped royal future also sets him in sharp contrast to the inhabitants of Babel whose stated objective was to make a name for themselves (11:4). Abraham will owe his fame and place in history to God alone! Furthermore, he will make his reputation by being made the means of blessing to others. And there is an astonishing scope to this.

God decides that Abraham and his seed, insignificant players though they seem to be on the world-stage, will become the touchstone by which all nations are measured (12:3). The destiny of all nations is mysteriously and critically bound up with the future of Abraham's descendants!

As we shall see all along our route, what makes people great – or sometimes famous – is the extent to which their faith is not self-serving but makes them willing participants in God's plan to bless the whole world.

A DEVOTIONAL INTERLUDE

To ponder: "Life," said Dr Martyn Lloyd-Jones, "is all about service." That being so, we have to decide: Do we serve ourselves or others? Our Lord put the needs of others before His own, eventually giving up His life on a cross. Has this mark of the Saviour been written into your life? To live effectively you must serve somebody. Ask yourself now: How well do I serve others? "Whatever He says to you, do it" (John 2:5, NKJV).

DAY **67**

READ
Genesis 12:3

God's ultimate intention, the bottom line of His promise-plan, is that "all peoples on earth will be blessed through you" (v.3b). By staying close to these Abraham stories, Israel could embrace the challenge to remain sharply different from other nations yet without becoming exclusive or self-serving.

But throughout the story, Abraham's "great nation", Israel, betrays its calling by allowing its special nation status to degenerate into an inward-looking nationalism. Just such a situation confronted Jesus and faced the Jewish-Christian apostles as they battled to get the gospel to the Gentile world in the teeth of often fierce Jewish opposition.

Tragically, Israel, entrusted with blessing for the world, would be unready to receive the blessing for herself when offered it *first* through her own Messiah and then through His apostles, as Peter did in the immediate aftermath of Pentecost when he pleaded with the people of God not to disown their ancient destiny (Acts 3:25).

Paul, for his part, strove to convince his fellow-countrymen, both inside and outside the Church, that Gentile acceptance of God's blessing of salvation in Christ was exactly what God always intended in the promise-plan announced to Abraham as the "gospel in advance" (Gal. 3:8).

A DEVOTIONAL INTERLUDE

For thanksgiving: How grateful we should be that the gospel is being spread throughout the whole earth. Have you ever thought how many people have been involved over the centuries in making known the gospel? Preachers, missionaries, evangelists, open-air speakers, tract distributors, and many others. Some have given their lives to spread the gospel. Give God thanks today for this great army of men and women.

DAY **68**

READ
Genesis 15:1

We come now to the next major move God makes and Abraham's reaction to it. First, we find Abraham evidently afraid, and after the crises reported in chapter 14, he might well have felt physically and emotionally exhausted and so fallen prey to anxiety. A 150-mile route march and a night battle against superior forces are taxing enough for an old man. But, in addition, Abraham has had a close encounter of a strange kind with a mysterious, almost supernatural, royal figure called Melchizedek, and has turned down the King of Sodom's offer to make him a rich man!

In the anticlimax, following momentous events, the human spirit is often vulnerable to fear and self-doubt. "Will my enemies return to seek revenge? What was a shrewd business operator like me doing rejecting such a generous financial package? Can God be trusted in the end?"

Sensing Abraham's mood, God reassures him through a prophetic vision. Abraham sees what looks like a covenant ceremony in which the king rewards the conquering hero with his royal weaponry and pledge of royal protection. It is as if God were saying to him: "Everything I have is at your disposal. I am committed to being at your side to protect you. Your battles are My battles, My victories are your victories." Already, it seems, there's a covenantal gleam in God's eye.

A DEVOTIONAL INTERLUDE

Prayer: O Father, how reassuring it is when I am troubled by doubts and fears to know that You are present at my side. When next I am called to deal with something that causes me concern, or I face an overwhelming test, then may I realise that Your promise holds firm – You will never leave me nor forsake me. But let this be more than mere theory, dear Lord. Help me to really *feel* Your presence – to *sense* that You are near. Amen.

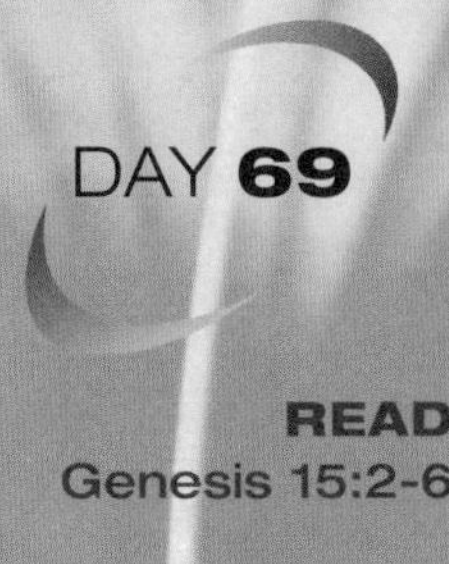

DAY 69

READ
Genesis 15:2-6

The reassurance God gives now encourages Abraham to question Him about the promised descendants (15:2–3) and the promised land (15:7–8).

First, Abraham takes God up on the promise of children. This is Abraham "in God's face": "You can be my benefactor, Lord, but of all that You can give me, what I want above everything else is the promised child!" Abraham even offers to help God out of a fix by adopting Eliezer, his servant, as his legal heir, but God emphatically rules this out: "a son coming from your own body will be your heir" (15:4).

Given Abraham and Sarah's condition, nothing short of a miracle will do, and God seems committed to acting supernaturally to make good His promise. Under the night sky, God reaffirms His pledge to give descendants as numerous as the "dust of the earth" (13:16) who will be as countless as the "stars in the sky" (15:5)! Abraham is being forced to turn away from looking down or at himself for any half-baked alternative solution. He is being encouraged to look up to the God who made the stars, a promise-keeping, miracle-working God.

Abraham's response is striking and crucial to the unfolding story in the rest of the Bible: *"Abram believed the Lord, and he credited it to him as righteousness"* (15:6). Abraham takes God at His word in a moment of faith.

A DEVOTIONAL INTERLUDE

Question: Many years ago a little boy in Sunday school, when asked to define "faith", took the letters F.A.I.T.H. and gave this as his reply: "Forsaking All I Trust Him." Here's a question to consider as you make your way into the day: How strong is your faith in God? Can you trust Him when all ahead is dark and confusing? It's so easy to trust when the road ahead is clear, but what about when a fog descends? You will never know how strong your trust is until you are called upon to exercise it.

DAY **70**

READ
Genesis 15:6

Abraham's declaration of faith and God's endorsement of it are among the most important elements in the whole scriptural story. On the basis of his faith, God credits Abraham with righteousness.

"Righteousness" in the Old Testament is primarily a relational term, so that what Abraham is granted is a "right relationship with God" – one shortly to be sealed by the covenant. This is not reckoned to Abraham because he keeps religious observances or matches up to ethical demands, and Abraham does not immediately become noticeably more ethical as a result of this. The key point is that righteousness is counted to him on the basis of his *faith alone*! This is a revolutionary move. Just as blessing is more original than sin, so, long before the law was given, even before circumcision was enjoined, Abraham is credited with a covenant relationship.

No statement proves more foundational to the apostolic understanding of God's grace in the gospel (see Rom. 4:3; Gal. 3:6). "Justification" or "righteousness" (synonymous translations of the same word in Greek) is by faith alone! Paul can argue that this has been the case right from the beginning so that it is not the "works" of the Law but the "faith story" of Abraham told in the Law that provides the key to a true relationship with God.

A DEVOTIONAL INTERLUDE

For praise: In response to today's reading make this a special day of praise, and reflect on the fact that through the grace of God you are saved, made righteous, and put into a covenant relationship with the God of Abraham. Ask God also to deepen your understanding of this fact. To grasp it, and grasp it clearly, will cause a spirit of praise to burst inside you like an artesian well. So once again – think and praise.

DAY 71

READ
Genesis 15:7-21

Having been reminded of God's promise, Abraham asks about the land (v.8). How God responds is crucial for Abraham and for the outworking of His redemptive purposes for the rest of history!

At God's command, Abraham kills three animals, and arranges the split carcasses in two parallel lines, with a bird at the end of each line. After a day in the sun, Abraham falls into a deep and dreadful stupor, during which he is shown his people's future slavery and release.

In ancient covenant ritual, as far as we can tell, each party walked between the pieces in a figure-of-eight manner to settle their agreement. The shedding of the substitute blood probably invoked a "maledictory oath", so that each party swore death to itself if it defaulted on the arrangement. Significantly, in this ceremony only God, in the form of fire, passes between the pieces to "make covenant with Abraham" (v.18). Here is no negotiated settlement but an amazingly one-sided commitment on God's part, which puts the sleeping Abraham on the receiving end of the sovereign grace of a God who is acting unilaterally.

God pledges unconditionally to bless Abraham and the nation that comes from him as the means of blessing all the nations of the world! No wonder this covenant with Abraham has been called the "very backbone of the Bible".

A DEVOTIONAL INTERLUDE

Prayer: Father, the ancient ceremonies sound strange to me but I thank You that they are recorded to show Your unconditional love and Your commitment to us. Every one of Your covenant moves and gracious initiatives is so wonderful that they stretch the natural mind. But I thank You that You have given the Holy Spirit to be my teacher. Continue to enlighten me by Your Spirit as I read on. In Jesus' Name. Amen.

DAY **72**

READ
Genesis 17:1

Today's text confirms that God's promise-plan sealed in covenant with Abraham determines the future of God's dealings with His world. Whereas chapter 15 revolved around the issues of descendants and land – affecting domestic family and future nationhood – here the focus is on the *third*, international strand of God's promise in Genesis 12:1–3: "blessing for all nations". Once more Abraham needs God's reassurance.

Years before, Abraham has finally lost patience with this dilatory God who keeps making "promises, promises", and has slept with Sarah's maid, Hagar, and fathered Ishmael, now thirteen years old! Of course, Ishmael's presence is a standing indictment of every attempt to force God's hand, to speed up His workings by taking things into our own hands! Abraham had made a terrible mistake and stepped outside of God's will for his life. But had he blown his chances for good?

Again God's reassurance is covenantal – announced with a *new name for God*: "I am El Shaddai, God Almighty". Is this comfort or rebuke? Perhaps both. "I am the Almighty". I am full of resources, I can cope with impossible situations, and I can do this on My own, thank you very much; I don't need your misguided efforts to help me out; I can make this promise-plan and covenant work!"

A DEVOTIONAL INTERLUDE

Thought: One translation of the great Hebrew name for God, El Shaddai, is *God the Enough*. Have you grasped the implication of this? There is only one way the human heart can have enough, or, to be more exact, only one Being who can satisfy it, and that is God. Only He is sufficient for us. Only He can really satisfy our souls. You may think you do not have enough of many things, but when you have God, He is *Enough*. Worth thinking about?

DAY **73**

READ
Genesis 17:2-5

God issues Abraham with the new challenge of walking blamelessly before Him. This obligation, however, also sounds like an invitation to experience God's ongoing presence!

Then God gives him new hope of the promised increase in numbers (v.2). Embarrassed by grace, Abraham prostrates himself before the Lord.

God reassures Abraham, but this time spells out the mutual obligations of the covenant. In doing so, God deepens relationship into partnership by an exchange of vows: "As for me" (v.4) ... "As for you" (v.9; cf. vv.15,20). For His part, God re-emphasises the strategic role Abraham plays on the world scene by giving him a *new name*, endorsing him as the father of many nations (v.4) – a significant upgrading of the original promise that Abraham would produce a great nation.

Unlike the men of Babel, Abraham had foregone the right to make a name for himself, trusting God to do it for him, and God rewards that faith by changing his name from Abram (which means "exalted father") to Abraham, "father of many" (v.5).

A DEVOTIONAL INTERLUDE

Prayer: O Father, from the bottom of my heart I want to tell You that my greatest longing is to walk blamelessly before You. Yet I fail so often. Forgive me dear Father. The fault is never Yours, but mine. You have promised me grace, yet frequently I spurn it and rely on my own resources. Help me from now on to turn to You in utter dependence and rely on Your strength, not my own. All this I ask in the precious Name of Jesus. Amen.

DAY **74**

READ
Genesis 17:6-22

By mentioning Abraham's promised fruitfulness, the text connects Abraham *back* to the earlier story of Noah and Adam, and *forward* to Abraham's descendants in Egypt (Exod. 1:6), and – with the promise of kingship – even further forward to the Davidic kingship (2 Samuel 7) in which Sarah is included (vv.15–16). For his part, Abraham must walk blamelessly before the Lord and must commit himself to circumcision (vv.9–14); and he does. A year later, with the birth of Isaac, God has the last laugh on Abraham and Sarah!

Ishmael, too, is to be blessed but, crucially, is not in the line of covenant purpose. In the redemptive future neither circumcision nor uncircumcision will count for anything, neither ethnic roots nor genealogical status will matter, but only grace and promise and faith (Romans 4).

All this the God who is "El Shaddai" will do for Abraham and for you, making His resources available, time and time again. Our God is Abraham's God and He is not a puny, under-achieving God. Right from the start of the story we are invited to be joined to a God who, as creator of the universe, is well able to redeem it. This is God's story. God is the prime mover at every stage of it. We will always fall back on this grace; He is "the author and finisher of our faith" (Heb. 12:2, NKJV).

A DEVOTIONAL INTERLUDE

Question: At this stage in the journey how clear is the concept of God's story to you? Can you see how God has been pursuing a theme from all eternity which has taken in priests, prophets, the whole nation of Israel, and that you have a part in it too? Consider the words: "He is 'the author and finisher of our faith'." He started it and He will finish it. Be assured of this: the more the thought of story grips you, the more exciting the Christian faith becomes.

DAY **75**

READ
Genesis
17:23-27

We pause in this chapter to comment on Abraham's commitment to circumcision. Circumcision, which was widely practised in the ancient world, was set to become the key identity marker for Israel. By commanding it God was saying three things:

"I want your whole body, Abraham. Marked 'in the flesh' (v.13) you henceforth belong to Me."

"I want your whole family, Abraham. By the mark in your reproductive organ I lay claim to your seed, your descendants, your children."

"I want your whole heart, Abraham."

Circumcision, of course, is intended to be the sign not of outward conformity but of inner covenant loyalty. So, in Deuteronomy and the prophets, circumcision becomes a metaphor for that inner "cutting" of the heart that marks the repentant, humbled member of God's covenant people. Paul picks this up when he writes to the Romans that "it's not the cut of the knife that makes a Jew" but the "mark of God on your heart" (Rom. 2:29, *The Message*).

A DEVOTIONAL INTERLUDE

To ponder: Reflect on these great verses from Paul's letter to the Thessalonians: "May God himself, the God of peace, sanctify you through and through. May your whole spirit, soul and body be kept blameless at the coming of our Lord Jesus Christ" (1 Thess. 5:23–24). Do these verses come alive to you now in the light of today's reading? Whatever else they mean they mean at least this: God wants the whole of us, not just a part.

DAY **76**

READ
Genesis 18

This strange scene in which the Lord appears in the form of the three mysterious visitors has long inspired reflection, notably expressed in Andrei Rublev's famous and much imitated icon of "The Trinity". It first shows us God talking to Himself, reminding Himself of Abraham's strategic importance, and so resolving to take Abraham into His confidence (vv.17–19). The cry that arises from Sodom is voiced presumably by those being sexually violated and economically oppressed (cf. Ezek. 16:49–50). God is moved (cf. Exod. 2:23–25) to go down and inspect the city (cf. Gen 11:7). But if God has already decided what to do, why tell Abraham?

Abraham discovers that to know God's secrets is a mixed blessing! To share the long-term redemptive plan of God is also to be burdened with the short-term pain of God.

What follows is Abraham's extraordinary intercessory negotiation as the "friend of God" (cf. 2 Chron. 20:7). It is almost as if Abraham's "far be it from you" (v.25) is helping a sovereign God decide what kind of God to be! This is a remarkable tribute to the potential of covenant partnership. Out of it comes a new revelation of God, and even Sodom is blessed!

A DEVOTIONAL INTERLUDE

For action: A ministry of intercession is probably the crowning ministry of the Christian life. Today why not ask God to give you the name of someone or something to intercede for. Then plead for them. Hold them there in your heart before God for as long as you feel it is right. Pray passionately for their needs. There is no ministry greater than the ministry of intercession. With that statement the whole Church must surely agree.

DAY 77

READ
Genesis 22:1-14

Our final move in this stage of the story is to watch as God tests His covenant partner, Abraham, in a way that sounds incomprehensible to modern ears. Challenged perhaps to match the devotion of the pagan child-sacrificers to their gods, Abraham is asked to offer up the miracle child on whom the promise-plan hangs!

The text is sparse and poignant in its details. "Take your son [does God really mean the miracle child of promise?], your only son, Isaac, ['only', but what about Ishmael?] whom you love [what an understatement since in the East to sacrifice oneself was less than to sacrifice one's son and therefore one's lineage and future]."

To his credit, Abraham doesn't dismiss this as a bad dream but seems able to discern the voice of God. Rising early, in prompt obedience, Abraham makes three great faith statements on the way: *we will worship* (v.5), for Yahweh is worthy to receive back His best gifts; *we will return* (v.5), which the writer to the Hebrews interprets as faith in resurrection (see Heb. 11:17–19); *God will provide* (v.8). So it proves. God does provide and Isaac is spared.

Of course, Abraham is a test case; we are not asked to sacrifice our children in just this way. But his kind of faith has passed its fiercest test; and to those with Abraham-like faith, the promise is certain (see Rom. 4:16).

A DEVOTIONAL INTERLUDE

For Praise: As you consider Abraham's great faith give praise to his God and yours – the God who delights in responding to a believing heart.

The God of Abraham praise, who reigns enthroned above,
Ancient of everlasting days, and God of love.
Jehovah! Great I AM! By earth and heaven confessed;
We bow and bless the sacred Name, for ever blessed.

DAY **78**

READ
Genesis
22:15-18

In a remarkable response to Abraham's act of obedient faith, God swears an oath which confirms the international aspects of the original promise-plan (vv.17–18). Abraham will have a multitude of descendants that no one can number; they will be triumphant over their enemies; through them the nations of the world will know God's blessing. God makes this commitment on oath because Abraham has not withheld his only son.

Is God here demonstrating His willingness to match Abraham in offering up His only beloved Son? This is the theological time bomb buried in the Abraham narrative. At the point where God seems to demand most He gives most. He will not be outdone in sacrifice by any of His creatures. Here is a hint of the gospel "in advance", telling us that God is not a God who demands sacrifice but a God who makes sacrifice. Our salvation lies not in the sacrifices we make but in the sacrifice we trust. "Bring me a thirty-three-year-old man; cut Him to the heart; let His blood be shed."

In the deep darkness, the all-consuming fire of God's holy love "passes between the pieces". And the covenant is sealed by blood. Whenever we break bread and drink blood-red wine we remind ourselves that God will provide; that where Isaac was spared, Jesus was not (Rom. 8:32).

A DEVOTIONAL INTERLUDE

Thought: "The God who demands most gives most." God has a perfect right to ask sacrifice of us because He has given His own Son as a sacrifice for our sin on the cross. He does not ask of us what He is not prepared to do Himself. A poet has put this same thought in these words: "By all that God requires of me, I know that He Himself must be." "He will not be outdone in sacrifice by any of His creatures."

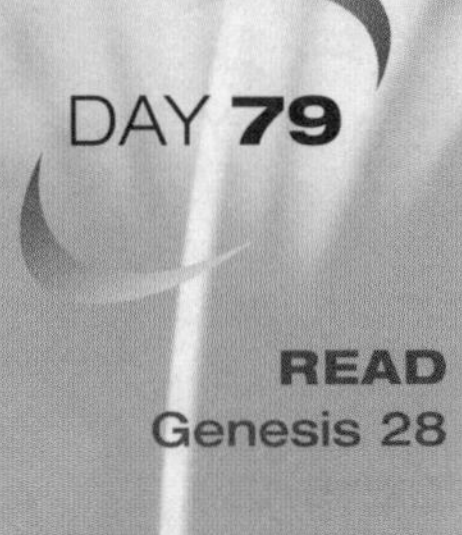

DAY 79

READ
Genesis 28

Today we see how God's promise-plan is carried a stage further by being reiterated to Jacob, as it had been to Isaac (26:3–5). Like his father and grandfather before him, Jacob is made party to the covenant purposes of God for the world, becoming for a symbolic moment the meeting-point between heaven and earth (28:2,17).

Surely the Lord is in the most surprising places and with the most surprising people! The text is frank about Jacob's character, showing that God enlists the most unlikely people in His story. That God should be the *God of Jacob* the con man, from whom you wouldn't buy a used camel, is the scandal of grace.

Jacob, intent on survival, is promised salvation. Alone and in exile, Jacob feels heaven to be remote, but heaven comes down to earth with one man at one particular spot on the earth. The seeds of incarnation are sown that will one day see some surprising people surprised by grace by a man from an unlikely place (John 1:51)! Only through brokenness will this happen, as Genesis 32 affirms.

Crippled in a strange wrestling match with God, Jacob limps off into the sunrise of a new day to give his new name to the nation that would treasure both his story and God's story.

A DEVOTIONAL INTERLUDE

To ponder: Have you ever wrestled with God over some issue you were reluctant to surrender? At such a time, as with Jacob, He will ask your name. What is it? Pride, ego, self-sufficiency? Confess it and God will change your name and your nature too, just as He did with Jacob. Instead of "Inferiority" it will be "Confidence", instead of "Self-pity" it will be "Faith", and so on. But remember: no new name until you confess the old one.

DAY **80**

READ
Psalm 105

In worship, Israel regularly celebrated its history as a record of the mighty acts of God. No reference is made here to the Sinai covenant as the basis of Israel's identity, suggesting that this song came out of the experience of the Babylonian Exile. In exile, without land or Temple or kingship, only God's *word* remains to define who Israel is (vv.5,19). Specifically, Israel praises God for His *covenant word* to Abraham (vv.8–11, 42).

The psalm celebrates the power of the promise to generate energy and faithfulness across the generations and to shape the course of history. Israel's whole history – from the patriarchal wanderings (vv.12–15) and Joseph's sojourn in Egypt (vv.16–25) to the exodus under Moses (vv.26–43) and the conquest (vv.44) – is brought under the one original covenant promise (vv.8,42).

The good news is always that *God remembers His covenant with Abraham,* and this turns out to be not a mere episode but the start of an epic story running through all of time in which every believer in every generation is caught up. This is our story, this is our song!

A DEVOTIONAL INTERLUDE

For action: Just as in Old Testament times worship involved thinking about and focusing on the record of God's mighty acts so we too should look back over our own lives and recollect what God has done for us in times past. Make a list of all the great things you can recollect that God has done for you. Do you know the advantage of this? John Newton put it in these words: "His love in time past forbids me to think He'll leave me at last in trouble to sink."

DAY 81

READ
Isaiah 41

When world events are in turmoil, as they are here, we grope for a reason. The idol factories go into over-production to secure the tottering faith of their adherents (v.7). But to the prophet, God's ways are traceable even in the most turbulent times. Behind the tumult of nations, the movements of armies, the rise and fall of empires – such as that of the Medo-Persian ruler, Cyrus, here – the prophet detects the sovereign authority and even initiative of the one Creator God.

Israel, can be confident, as God's servant nation, of being at the disposal of these larger plans and purposes, though only, like Abraham, through being God's "friend" (v.8).

We sometimes loosely say that God "uses" people. He certainly overrules His enemies and commandeers godless warlords such as Cyrus for His purpose. But He does not "use" His own people. Such a term is too mechanical, too utilitarian to describe the relationship God desires with them. God works "in", "through", and "with" His own people; but He never "uses" them. Rather, they are called in love to intimate friendship. Burdened with God's dreams, entrusted with His painful secrets – as Abraham was over Sodom's fate – they hold their heads high with the privilege of being friends of this humbly sovereign God!

A DEVOTIONAL INTERLUDE

Question: Do you doubt that God can use you? Are you held back by feelings of inadequacy? Then focus on your Abrahamic roots. God is the God of the impossible. The One who worked a miracle for Abraham and Sarah is just the same today. God's covenant with Abraham stretches through time to encircle you too. Rise up and face whatever is your need at this hour. Exercise faith and see that the God of Abraham is your God also.

DAY **82**

READ
Isaiah 51

The prophet urges those exiles whose hearts are set on covenant integrity ("righteousness", cf. v.7), to look to the Lord and to be inspired by the early chapters of their story. The Lord is the rock from which His people have been hewn (cf. Deut. 32:18) – in particular His miraculous and covenantal beginnings with Abraham and Sarah. To live out of these Abrahamic roots is to live by faith in the impossibilities of divine grace and power.

Abraham felt hopeless and helpless – one man among many – when God called and blessed him; the exiles, feeling a beleaguered minority, should take heart from this. Abraham was as good as dead, and Sarah was dead in her womb, when God acted; so, out of the womb of the "death" of exile, God will bring His people into fruitful new life (cf. Isa. 54:1ff.).

The memory of the Creator God's conquest of chaotic forces at the exodus (vv.9–10) inspires hope that God will comfort and save His people once more.

For, if God can carve a people out of the rock of barrenness or exile, making somebodies out of nobodies, then His people should avoid presumption or complacency and "awake" to seize the opportunities for faith presented by the hour (vv.17ff.). Then they will see God's covenant faithfulness acting in salvation (vv.5–6, 8).

A DEVOTIONAL INTERLUDE

For action: Read through Isaiah 51 once more. Consider what God says and give your response. For example, God says, "Listen to me ..." Respond by saying, "Yes, Lord, I will listen." Again He says, "Look." Respond by saying, "Yes, Lord, I will look." Go through the whole chapter, making your response to each of God's challenges. God challenges us in order to change us. But there can be no change without a positive response.

READ
Luke 1:39-80

Luke here describes just the kind of faithful, covenant-keeping remnant, envisaged by Isaiah, now forming the "welcoming committee" for Jesus. Christmas, for all its wonderful freshness, does not come out of the blue but is the decisive turning-point in the age-old story which began with Abraham. This remnant has kept alive the dream of what God promised Abraham, interpreting what happens now, as Mary does, as "God remembering His covenant to Abraham" (vv.54–55).

Zechariah, filled with the Spirit, is singing from the same hymn-book, interpreting events within his own family as the stirrings of a great move of God prompted by His remembrance of the oath and covenant He long ago swore to Abraham (vv.72–73).

In this way Luke highlights the historic significance of the babies born to Elizabeth and Mary. Already we begin to see that Jesus is the fulfilment, the climactic chapter of the much older story of Israel and her patriarchs. Sarah's barrenness, Abraham's childlessness, and the details of their story, are mirrored in the miracles of grace of Elizabeth and Zechariah and Mary. Zechariah hails the dawning of the age of forgiveness and mercy. Mary, stirred by the recreative energies of God within her, celebrates a new exodus when tyranny is overthrown and the oppressed are given freedom.

A DEVOTIONAL INTERLUDE

Prayer: My Father and my God, I see more clearly day by day the wonder of Your covenant-keeping abilities. Help me, I pray, to increase my understanding of this concept of covenant. I sense that the more I can comprehend it, the more secure I will be and feel as a Christian. You are a God who keeps His covenant and allows into my life only that which will work for my highest good. Blessed be Your wonderful Name for ever. Amen.

DAY **84**

READ
Acts 3:11-26

By staying close to the old Abraham stories, the Israel that first cherished them might have remained sharply different from other nations without becoming exclusive or nationalistically self-seeking. Israel's failure in this mission and her attendant suffering were – as her prophets anticipated – brought mysteriously to concentrated fulfilment in her suffering Messiah, the Servant-Son of God, the final Moses-like prophet who must be listened to (vv.18, 22–23; cf. Deut. 18:15). In Him and through Him the ancient patriarchal promise of blessing for the world, paradoxically entrusted to one nation, was now seen to be redeemable. So the apostle Peter, pleads with the heirs of the prophets and the descendants of Abraham not to renege on their God-given destiny and so miss their hour of decision (vv.18ff.; cf. Joel 2:1–3:21).

The dramatic healing of one lame man symbolised the healing of a broken nation, guaranteed further times of refreshing, and heralded the restoration of all things. Meanwhile, Abraham's promised inheritance of blessing for all the nations was gloriously available through the gospel. This was something – and still is – to make a song and dance about!

A DEVOTIONAL INTERLUDE

To ponder: Christians are called to weep with those who weep and rejoice with those who rejoice. And frequently the two emotions are expressed within a short space of time, for instance, when we rejoice for those who see the Abrahamic covenant in Jesus, and then weep for those who have not yet entered into it. Today, while rejoicing for those of your loved ones who know Christ, spend a little time praying for those who do not yet know Him.

DAY **85**

READ
Romans 4

Richard Hays paraphrases Paul's question: "'Have we found Abraham to be our forefather according to the flesh'?" (4:1). In expecting the answer "No" Paul is able to advance the argument of 3:27–31. Jews have never relied for their status only on physical descent from Abraham. The gospel of grace, therefore, does not contradict the Law but upholds it (3:31) – that is, if we view the Torah rightly as embracing the narratives of Abraham in Genesis. God has always intended a worldwide family of faith. So Abraham is set to inherit not merely the land of Canaan but the entire world (4:13). And what kind of faith is Abraham-faith? It is faith which, as with Isaac, believes in a God who can raise the dead, for even a "dead" Israel is "resurrectible" (cf. Ezek. 37). It is a faith which believes in a God who, as at creation, can call into existence the things that do not exist so that even Gentiles who, in terms of the covenant, are non-existent "no-people" (cf. Rom. 9:25–26) are included through Christ in the people of God.

Covenant status (what Paul calls "righteousness" or "justification") comes by grace to those who believe in Him who raised His own "Isaac", Jesus, from the dead (4:25). No wonder Abraham's faith was so pivotal or that Paul describes him as the father of all who believe (4:16).

A DEVOTIONAL INTERLUDE

For praise: The movement of God that has taken those of us who were outside the covenants of promise and has put us on the inside deserves endless praise. To be "in Christ" is, in a sense, to be "in Abraham" by believing in the resurrection. Lift your heart now in praise that we who were "excluded from citizenship in Israel and foreigners to the covenants of the promise ... have been brought near through the blood of Christ" (Eph. 2:12–13).

DAY **86**

READ
Galatians 3:1-9

The question Paul pursues here is: Who are the true sons of Abraham? He concludes that all who believe in Christ – whether Jew or Gentile – are sons of God and offspring of Abraham (vv.26–29). This global faith community was in view in God's original promise to Abraham that "all the nations will be blessed through you" (v.8), the gospel in advance. Just as "Abram believed the Lord, and it was credited to him as righteousness," so, Paul argues, with us all.

As we have seen from Genesis 15, Abraham's relationship was soon defined in covenantal terms so that thereafter in the Old Testament to be righteous was not so much an indication of moral character as of covenant status and identity. Similarly, to refer to the "righteousness of God" – as the Psalms and Isaiah do particularly – will be to speak primarily of God's own *covenant faithfulness* which prompts Him to *saving action.*

Paul seizes on Genesis 15:6 not as a quick proof-text but because he is tracing the trajectory of faith right back to its Abrahamic launching pad. He is not merely illustrating faith but is convinced that Christian believers stand in unbroken continuity with God's covenant people stretching back to the patriarch Abraham, the father all who believe. To be "in Christ" is to be "in Abraham".

A DEVOTIONAL INTERLUDE

Thought: Think about this truth a little more: to be in Christ is to be in Abraham. We come to Christ by faith, we live by faith (as did Abraham), and we will receive the promised reward by faith. Abraham's life was characterised by faith. His name is recorded in the "Heroes of Faith" chapter – Hebrews 11. No higher commendation will be given to any Christian in heaven than the commendation given for having lived by faith.

DAY **87**

READ
Colossians 2

Covenantal language, though not prominent in Colossians, is never far from the surface of Paul's mind.

"The circumcision of Christ" (v.11) could, grammatically, be taken as referring to what Christ does *to us* in order to bring about that "circumcision of the heart" which marks the new covenant transformation of believers. More likely it refers to something done *to Jesus* – most probably to His death on the cross, so that "circumcision" is a gruesome metaphor for crucifixion. Not the neat and swift surgical removal of the foreskin by a skilled rabbi, but the tearing apart of Jesus' body by ruthless executioners – *this* is what brings us into covenant membership. As we put our faith in this circumcised-by-crucifixion and raised-from-the-dead Jesus, expressed in the "baptismal burial" of our old life, we are joined to God's covenant community.

So Jesus proves entirely sufficient for our salvation and covenant membership; we need no extra qualifications provided by the "dos" and "don'ts" of legalism, the fantasies of mysticism, or the lashings of asceticism – whether of a Greek or Jewish or hybrid variety! His cross is our new identity-marker as God's people in Christ – not worn as an outward badge or decoration but written on our hearts and worked out in our lives in self-giving.

A DEVOTIONAL INTERLUDE

To ponder: One of the biggest threats to Christianity, said C.S. Lewis, is "Christianity and". The truth is that Jesus is entirely sufficient for our salvation and no add-ons are needed. Some think that living out the Beatitudes is what saves us. However, Jesus is not saying, "Live like this and you will be saved," but, "Be saved and you will live like this." Good works cannot save us. Salvation is through Christ – and Christ alone.

DAY **88**

READ
Hebrews 6:13-20

Conventional Christianity has been described as "an initial spasm followed by chronic inertia"! Unconventional Christianity imitates the patriarchs in overcoming sluggishness (v.12) and pressing on to inherit the promises.

God is so committed to His redemptive plan that He guarantees His promise to Abraham by swearing an oath – swearing "by himself" (v.13) – putting His own reputation as a God who does what He says, on the line. These two unalterable things – God's promise and His sworn oath – encourage us, on our leg of the journey, to travel with endurance and hope. Christian hope is no wishful thinking or mere optimism, but is pinned on Jesus who has pioneered the way into God's vivid presence and eternal future. This anchors hope in the permanent realities of the kingdom of God. A hymn I learned as a child poses the question: "Will your anchor hold in the storms of life?" Hebrews answers "Yes".

Whether in the flux of a first-century or a post-modern world, this is the fixed point faith can rely on. We are not anchored "downward to the sea-bed" so that we stay immovable, victims of chronic inertia, but "upward to the Trailblazer on the summit" so that we keep climbing. This anchor takes the strain even when the ledges are narrow, the grip is weak, and our hold on the rockface is precarious.

A DEVOTIONAL INTERLUDE

Question: Could your Christianity be described as "an initial spasm followed by chronic inertia"? The Christian life is kept alive by many things, not the least *hope*. The common assessment of hope is that it is a poor, vain, deceptive thing. Cowley said: "Hope is the most hopeless thing of all." In worldly terms that may be so, but not in biblical terms. Christian hope has a specific object – Jesus. Joined to Him, despair is impossible.

DAY 89

READ
Hebrews 7:1-28

Tracing the path of God's covenant with Abraham has brought us to the priesthood of Jesus! As the High Priest in Israel entered the Holiest Place, symbolically bearing the people into the presence of the Most Holy God, so, even more and in reality, Jesus has secured permanent access to God for us by His atoning death and continuing life of intercession.

His priesthood, however, is not based on that of Aaron but on that of Melchizedek, the strangely superior priest-king to whom Abraham paid tithes. Since the seeds of the later Levitical priests were in his body when he did this, Abraham, symbolically, ranked the Levitical priesthood beneath that of Melchizedek! Melchizedek appears in Genesis out of the blue, with no mention of ancestors or successors. Hebrews exploits this literary gap to present Melchizedek as prefiguring Jesus, who has eternal roots and who continues His priestly activity, uninterrupted by death, in the power of an endless resurrection life (v.16)! Psalm 110 confirms this, linking the Abrahamic experience to a prophetic oracle made to the Davidic king which was also backed by an oath (7:17–21).

Who would have guessed that following in the footsteps of our faith-father Abraham would have taken us this far – to the very High King and High Priest of heaven Himself!

A DEVOTIONAL INTERLUDE

For Praise: You will undoubtedly know this hymn. Sing it to yourself as you reflect on the reading today:

Be Thou my vision, O Lord of my heart,
Naught be all else to me, save that Thou art,
Be Thou my best thought in the day and the night,
Both waking and sleeping, Thy presence my light.

READ
Hebrews 11:1-12

The writer's pastoral urgency is obvious as he warns and encourages his Christian friends not to shrink back from full-blooded commitment to Jesus Christ in face of the type of harassment that is the prelude to full-scale persecution (10:32–39). He has already made unfavourable reference to Israel's unbelief (4:2) but that isn't the whole story; there are also outstanding stories of faith to be told. But these are not simply held up before us as examples of how to believe from *another* story but presented to us as *earlier* chapters in the *same* story. What we have here is not simply a borrowed vocabulary but a common vocation. "They" remain incomplete without "us", and we without them (11:40)! Their story is our story, the story of decision-making faith.

For the builders of the Tower of Babel, "Come, let us build ourselves a city ..." (Gen.11:4) set the limit of their horizon. Abraham makes a radical counter-cultural statement by turning his back on the city that man is building – visible and tangible to all – for the sake of the city that God is building, which is still invisible except to faith. He refuses to sink his roots into that man-made city because, in the words of Hebrews again, "he was looking forward to the city with foundations, whose architect and builder is God" (Heb. 11:10).

A DEVOTIONAL INTERLUDE

To ponder: Some consider that keeping the vision of heaven in view hinders us from fulfilling our responsibilities here on earth. Such is not the case, however. Throughout time great Christians (such as General Booth of the Salvation Army) have claimed that the prospect of heaven nerved them on to do remarkable work here on earth. Thinking about heaven can give us the incentive to leave earth a better place than we found it.

DAY **91**

READ
Hebrews
11:13–12:3

These heroes show us just how radically counter-cultural faith is! In an age obsessed with self-fulfilment, we recall that Abraham was not moved to sacrifice Isaac in order to satisfy personal needs. In fact, as Heschel again reminds us, "To believe in God is to fight for him, to fight whatever is against him within ourselves, including our interests when they collide with his will."

For faith, what gives significance to our lives lies beyond the visible satisfaction.

The negatives say it all: not seen, not visible, not knowing where he was going. This last is hardest for modern people who value self-determination above all. But beyond the ability to manage our own lives, faith marches to a louder drumbeat! A glory beckons.

This is a high-risk strategy, that stakes all on a "better country" (v.16), an abiding city (13:14)! "Otherworldly" is too tepid a word for such earthy faith.

The supreme example and the climax of the covenantal story of faith is Jesus Himself (12:2f). The story goes on but His is the crucial chapter. In His Name our resolve is stiffened; we go on, we risk and obey, we endure and overcome, we forego pleasure and face pain, we fight to the finish and run the race. Our prize is to share in that same joy that was set before Him.

A DEVOTIONAL INTERLUDE

For action: The apostle Paul resolved to run the race set before him with an enthusiasm and determination that echoes the commitment of Jesus Himself. Read Philippians 3:12–14 and ask yourself: Am I willing to risk and obey, endure and overcome, forego everything necessary, face any pain, to win the prize – the joy that C.S. Lewis says "is the business of heaven"? Now prayerfully renew your commitment to the Lord.

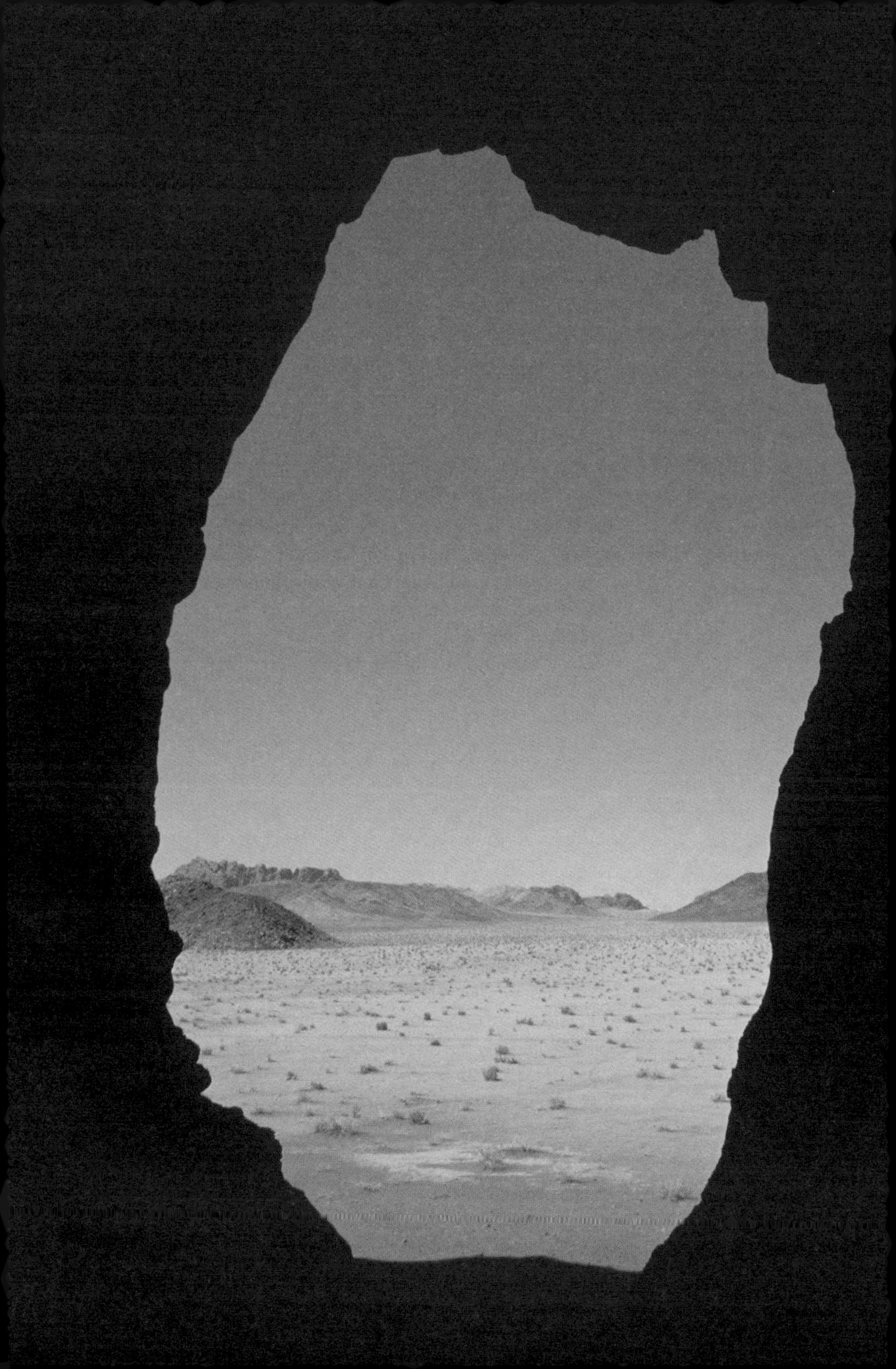

DAY 92

READ
James 2:14–26

We have surely seen enough of Abraham's story and the reverberations of it down the centuries to know one thing: faith is action and adventure. Faith has too often in modern Christianity become reduced either to an intellectual assent to certain dogmas or to a vague God-dependency characterised by a particularly religious state of mind.

Real faith of Abraham dimensions, takes risks, feeds the hungry, takes in the orphans. Faith like this goes beyond words into heroic deeds that authenticate the commitment.

The apostle James – like Paul – hears the contemporary power of the ancient text (Gen. 15:6) in which Abraham is declared righteous on the basis of his faith (v.23). Faith without its "Isaacs" is dead: faith which offers up its "Isaac" is alive with resurrection life. Faith-doers are God's friends. This is the challenge of Abraham to us: to participate in God's story. "I happen to believe," said A.W. Tozer, "that Abraham's encounters with the living God nearly 4,000 years ago leave modern men and women without excuse."

Abraham, you've a lot to answer for!

This is the faith adventure: to have something to die for is to have something to live for.

A DEVOTIONAL INTERLUDE

Prayer: My Father and my God, if I have been blocking Your power in my life by my lack of faith let this day be a day of release and deliverance. Help me take the steps that will lead me on a new adventure – one that goes beyond mere words and issues forth in actions. Show me what I can do to authenticate my commitment – some new task or project, a loving deed for someone. Help me my Saviour. No more words. It's time for action. Amen.

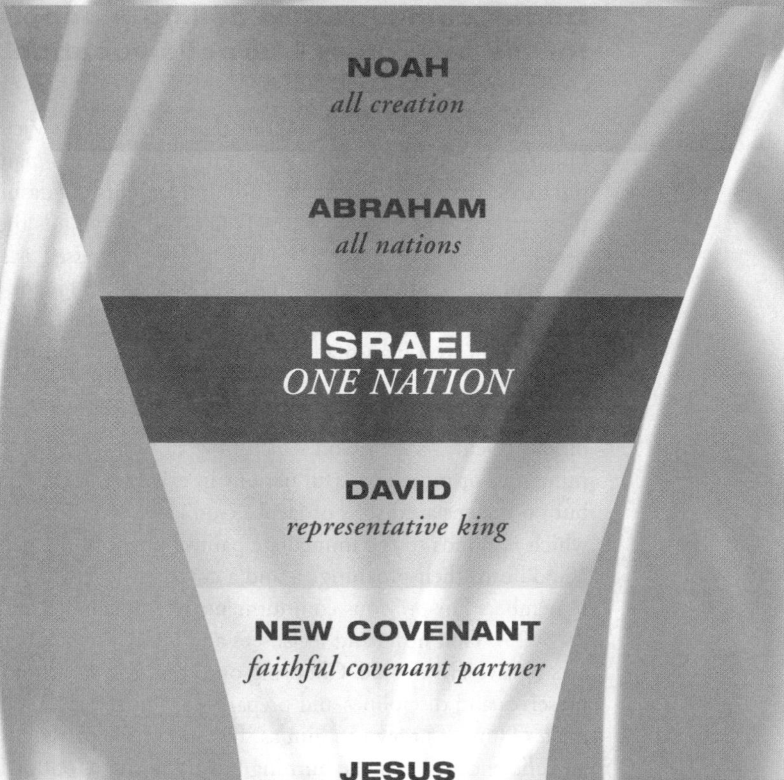

NOAH
all creation

ABRAHAM
all nations

ISRAEL
ONE NATION

DAVID
representative king

NEW COVENANT
faithful covenant partner

JESUS
faithful covenant partner

JESUS
Davidic King Messiah

JESUS
the New Israel

JESUS
the world's Lord

JESUS
the truly Human One crowned with glory and honour

JESUS
cosmic Ruler in God's new creation new heavens and new earth

SECTION 5
ISRAEL'S CALLING

God is committed to calling a people for his own glory – Israel's vocation.

Les Miserables, the world-famous musical, based on Victor Hugo's novel, celebrates the optimism of the students manning the barricades in revolutionary Paris and laments the dashing of their dreams. The origins of Israel's national story finds the people of Israel also among "les miserables", oppressed as slaves in Egypt and clamouring for freedom. But, unlike Hugo's tragic heroes, their longing for liberation was realised, and realised, not by a man-made revolution, but by a God-wrought redemption.

Why God chose Israel is explained by the text as the mystery of love (Deut. 7:7–9). God set His love not on the more numerous or more powerful nations in existence at the time but on the enslaved sons of Jacob. God's love is a caring love which responds to the immediate painful plight of the people – "God heard their groaning" – and a covenant-love which remembers His previous commitments to Abraham (Exod. 2:23–25). God hears and feels, sees and knows, remembers and acts to save His people. Choosing one man, Moses, whom He preserves and disciplines and prepares for His service, God makes Himself known to him as the God of the patriarchs in an eerie encounter at the burning bush. Pressing God for His real name, Moses soon learns that God is not only the God of the known past who made promises to Abraham but He is the God of the unknown future. To know God's future, Israel must trust and travel with Him, experiencing along the way that God "will be what he will be" as and when they need him (Exod. 3:1–22)! Suitably emboldened, Moses is told to demand that Pharaoh let God's "firstborn son" go. God protects the Israelites – as the judgment of death "passes over" the blood-marked homes of the Israelites – and then, even more dramatically, rescues them from Pharaoh's army by opening the Red Sea. This saving "Exodus" is forever commemorated in the Passover Feast and the Song of Moses (Exod. 14–15).

Brought to Mount Sinai, Israel is made party to the covenant God had already made with Abraham to bring blessing to the world. There Israel is honoured as God's own treasured possession, called to be a holy nation, a kingdom of priests to represent God before the watching nations (Exod. 19:1–6). The Torah is given to show Israel how to live as covenant people. Israel is intended to be a showcase nation, her mandate to "be holy as God is holy" aimed at taking up the discarded human mantle of being image-bearers of God in the world.

But before the "ink is dry", as it were, Israel falls from grace in the golden calf incident, so proving to be as much part of the problem as the answer. But it remains Israel's privilege both to keep the Sabbath which sanctifies time so that God and his people can renew relationship, and to erect the tabernacle which sanctifies space where God can dwell in concentrated holiness with his people.

On the verge of entry to the promised land, Moses warns that covenant unfaithfulness will eventually incur the ultimate curse of judgment – exile from the land, so repeating the Adam and Eve pattern.

What a turbulent story it was – and remains. Israel, said Abraham Heschel is "God's stake in history", a people burdened with "dreaming the dreams of God". In her proneness to suffer, Israel is, said Arthur Koestler, "the exposed nerve of the human race". This history is unusual in being history from the "underside". History is usually told by the "winners" as the top-down record of conquest and domination, enshrined in the annals of the superpowers from Egypt to Rome. But Israel's is the story of ex-slaves and former exiles who are God's gift to the world and through whom God will gives Himself to and for the world.

The whole Old Testament story of Israel revolves around the twin poles of Exodus and Exile, ironically from slavery to slavery again! Hopes beyond Exile look to a New Israel, a true son and covenant partner, who will bring salvation by faithfully acting out the story of Israel and her God by re-enacting the one and embodying the other.

DAY **93**

READ
Exodus 2:23–25

Israel's key role in the great story starts with a Great Escape. Abraham's descendants, Jacob's sons, have been enslaved in Egypt under a Pharaoh no longer favourable to them as his predecessor had been to Joseph and his kinsmen. But their cries for help and groaning under repression and injustice do not go unheard by God. In noting this, our text highlights the twin aspects of God's love that make Him concerned for the plight of the Israelites. First, God cares and is moved to respond to the immediate cries of His people. God is also stirred to remember His long-term commitment to the patriarchs, Abraham, Isaac and Jacob in the earlier stages of the story. Already we see the kind of God disclosed by the story. This is a God who is passionately aroused by injustice, and plunges into emotional involvement with His people. Yet, at the same time, His love is not a fleeting pang of sympathy but a tough, enduring, steadfast love, grounded in covenant making and keeping.

As with Noah, and as in significant future situations, salvation will depend on God remembering His covenant promises as much as it does on God forgiving and forgetting sins! God "remembers" not as if He suffers from occasional amnesia, but in the sense of acting to implement his previous commitments.

A DEVOTIONAL INTERLUDE

To ponder: The point, "God 'remembers' not as if He suffers from occasional amnesia" ought to be a tremendous personal encouragement to us. In other words God simply cannot forget us, and all our interests, even the tiniest detail, are ever before Him. Meditate on this text as you go through the day: "The Lord remembers us and will bless us: He will bless the house of Israel, he will bless the house of Aaron" (Psa. 115:12).

DAY **94**

READ
Exodus 3:1–10

Typically, in reaching out to rescue His people, God starts with one man, selecting Moses to be the agent of deliverance. Already God has sovereignly preserved Moses' life through the shrewd enterprise of his mother and sister, aided and abetted by Pharaoh's own daughter (2:1–10). Ironically, Moses is educated, all expenses paid, by the very regime he is called to undermine! God sets Himself against arrogant and God-defying powers. But Moses' first attempt to assert God's justice by taking matters into his own hands fails miserably and he has to flee the country (2:11–22). God will deal with the Egyptians in His time and in His way. Now, shepherding in the desert, Moses' attention is rivetted by a burning bush which does not burn up and from which a voice speaks. Moses concedes to being on holy ground by taking off his sandals. This occurs in the shadow of Horeb, the mountain of God. Not that Horeb is special – it becomes special only because God appears there. "Any old bush will do" for God to incite your curiosity and so draw you deeper into His self-revelation. But when you do glimpse Him or hear Him, it will not be to enrich your stockpile of spiritual sensations but to implicate you further in the ongoing story of God's plans to bless and save the world.

A DEVOTIONAL INTERLUDE

Question: God called Moses and he answered, "Here am I!" God called Samuel and he answered, "Here am I'. God called Isaiah and he answered, "Here am I!" What a blessing they were there! Dr Alexander Whyte of Scotland once said in a sermon that God often calls but His children are not always listening. If God were to call you to do something for Him today are you there – listening, eager, willing and ready to do His bidding?

DAY 95

READ
Exodus 3:7–22

Having first reassured the awestruck Moses that He is none other than the God of Abraham, God shares with Moses His determination to immerse Himself in His people's troubles and to act to redeem them.

So far so good. All this is music to Moses' ears until the words "So now, go. I am sending you". Moses then demonstrates how to have cold feet while hopping barefoot around a blazing fire! What God has in mind sounds to Moses like "mission impossible". With his "Who am I?" Moses heads a long line of reluctant biblical heroes. We can understand his reaction; after all in view of what God has promised to do, why should He need Moses' help? God promises to be with him but offers no guarantees about the future. Moses' initial "Who am I?" dissolves into a bigger question: "Who are you? . . . What is your name? Who is authorising me to act in this way?" God's reply – a virtually untranslatable version of the verb "to be" – has provoked philosophical speculation. But in context the accent is less on God's self-sufficiency, true as that is, than on His passion to be intimately involved with His people: "I will be what I will be" to you and for you whenever and wherever you need Me.

A DEVOTIONAL INTERLUDE

Prayer: Father strengthen me I pray for those times when You call me to do something for which I feel utterly inadequate. Help me know that when Your finger points the way, Your hand provides the resources I need. Drive this truth deeply into my spirit that the task ahead, whatever it may be, is never as great as the power that lies behind me. Teach me how to rely less on my sufficiency and more on Yours. In Jesus' Name. Amen.

DAY **96**

READ
Exodus 4:18–23

Moses is told to call on Pharaoh to release Israel – God's "firstborn son". This crucial statement connects with the death of the firstborn in Egypt (v.23) and the later consecration of the Israelite firstborn to the Lord. Beyond this it shapes the role of the king in Israel who is called God's "son" because he represents both God and the nation. It takes final form in the Sonship of Jesus who perfectly embodies Israel's destiny and fully incarnates her God. Suffice it to say here that God's fatherly image is not in conflict with the tough sovereign decisions He takes against the Egyptian regime. The Exodus story all along shows the absolute power of God over the opposition of despotic earthly rulers like Pharaoh. God's harsh threat to him is in the cause of justice and aims at unseating a cruel tyrant. God is clearly not a tame God as is shown by the way He threatens to kill Moses, who is saved, not for the first time, by a woman's wit. The incident serves to highlight the significance of the key covenant sign of circumcision which Moses has evidently neglected. Certainly when the people learn that God is concerned about their plight, they bow to worship this fatherly God whom they may not fully know but are beginning to trust.

A DEVOTIONAL INTERLUDE

For praise: How diverse and wondrous are the ways of God. The more we read Scripture the more of the facets of His character we see. Lift your heart in praise as you sing or read this song:

Give to our God immortal praise,
Mercy and truth are all his ways
Wonders of grace to Him belong,
Repeat His mercies in your song

DAY **97**

READ
Exodus 12

Pharaoh's reluctance to let the Israelites go elicits a series of plague-judgments, culminating in the death of all the firstborn. But God aims to preserve the Israelites, instructing them to daub their doorposts with lamb's blood so that judgment will "pass over" their homes. Notice that God's controversy is not with things Egyptian, nor even with Pharaoh himself as an individual, but with the gods of Egypt (12:12). Since the cross, we now know that we do not fight flesh-and-blood people. But from the outset, the conflict has always been a spiritual battle between the true God and all false rivals to His unique glory. Pharaoh is a front for false gods but he tragically represents his people who suffer with him.

By the feast of Passover, which commemorates Israel's deliverance, Israel renewed its identity as God's redeemed people. Later sharers in the feast, through remembering, "relived" the Exodus experience. So Israel escapes, clutching the unleavened bread as God has commanded and now weighed down with the treasures the panic-stricken Egyptians have pressed upon them. Pharaoh has been paid in full for his genocidal policy and cruel repression. Israel leaves, as it were, by the "front door", heads held high and dressed no longer as slaves.

A DEVOTIONAL INTERLUDE

For action: Paul in Ephesians 6:12 says: "For we do not wrestle against flesh and blood, but against principalities, against powers, against the rulers of the darkness of this age" (NKJ). A preacher suggested that many Christian lives could be summed up in the first five words of that text. Are you a wrestling or a resting Christian? Begin to use the power that you have been given against the forces of darkness. Don't just nestle, wrestle.

DAY **98**

READ
Exodus 15

Pursued to the sea, hemmed in by Pharaoh's army, Israel has been miraculously delivered by the parting of the waters. Redemption – release from the slave-market which was Egypt – is something now to be celebrated in song. To be saved and delivered is to be reinstated in the chorus of praise of a redeeming God. So, awestruck and relieved, the people stand on the banks of the Red Sea. And relief soon bursts into song as Moses and then Miriam lead them in celebrating their mighty warrior-God who has fought His people's battles and won a stunning victory over their enemies. Here is a pointer to true biblical praise. There is a better reason for praise than our fluctuating feelings. True praise is a thankful, joyful, recital of God's character and saving deeds. And nobody sings about this God more than freed slaves. "Les miserables" learn to sing "the music of a people who will not be slaves again". All the more sad then to see Israel, almost immediately in the following chapters of the story, descend into grumbling and complaining! Undeterred, God works wonders of bread and water to sustain His people in their risky new freedom. The "eagles' wings" of a merciful God who is determined not let His people go, picks them up and carries them forward to the next stage of the story.

A DEVOTIONAL INTERLUDE

To ponder: Today consider the number of deliverances God has wrought in your life. Use biblical language to express your gratitude to God. For example: I will praise You O Lord for You have triumphed gloriously in my life, saving me from destruction, keeping me from sin. I will bless You O Lord for You have become my salvation . . . and so on. Using Bible language to express your thanks to God does something to your soul. Try it and see!

DAY **99**

READ
Exodus 19:1–4

Today we arrive at Mount Sinai and the momentous events that made Israel into a nation. Here a bunch of ex-slaves were forged into God's covenant partner and entrusted with His redemptive plans for the world. Israel has truly been carried here "on eagles' wings". God has heard their cry for help, raised up Moses to lead them to freedom, performed signs to break Pharaoh's resistance, protected them from judgment, brought them through the Red Sea, provided food and water for them in the desert and brought them to His holy mountain. This is a record of grace! Sometimes we make the serious mistake of offsetting the Old Testament God of law against the New Testament God of grace. But Israel was never intended to "work her passage" into God's favour and covenant by doing good works. Rather, as we shall see, the Law was given to a people already delivered and assured of a relationship with God. "'Tis grace has brought them safe thus far" and it will be "grace that leads them home" to the promised land. Now grace is set to turn relationship into covenant partnership and give them the law.

A DEVOTIONAL INTERLUDE

For praise: The more we ponder Israel's deliverance the more it seems right to focus on the theme of gratitude, thanks and praise. And how better than to sing the following song. Thousands will be singing it with you today.

Amazing grace, how sweet the sound,
That saved a wretch like me
I once was lost, but now I'm found,
Was blind but now I see.

DAY 100

READ
Exodus 19:5

As we saw yesterday, it makes a great difference if the God who commands us is the same God who carries us. But that He does command us is a fact we must face squarely.

Obedience, of course, is almost a dirty word in our modern world, for we have been taught to believe that the self is autonomous, that is, answerable to no one and nothing outside itself.

But in the story we are following, willing obedience is the true pathway to fulfilment and human wholeness. Whereas, "I feel therefore I am" is the order of our day, the true essence of being a human being, said the great Jewish scholar, Abraham Heschel, can be summed up as: "I am commanded, therefore I am".

The Israelites who had gone into Egypt to find bread ended up making bricks under very harsh commands! God's promised freedom was not meant to be a self-serving independence but a new kind of servitude under God's "tender" commandments. A God who has extricated his people from a tyrannical, authoritarian regime in Egypt, is hardly likely to want to initiate them into an even more repressive rule. In fact, God loves freedom more than we do! To obey the One Creator God who makes covenant is to pave the way for a just and free society where neighbours and aliens work and worship Him together.

A DEVOTIONAL INTERLUDE

A Collect:

Almighty and everlasting God,
increase in us Your gift of faith;
that, forsaking what lies behind
and reaching out to that which is before,
we may run the way of Your commandments
and win the crown of everlasting joy through
Jesus Christ our Lord.

DAY 101

READ
Exodus 19:5-6

God now graciously states his intention to make this bunch of ex-slaves partners in what God calls "my covenant". By calling it "my covenant", God is emphasising that He is entering into a covenant relationship with Israel in order to take a stage further His original covenant promise to bless Abraham and through him bless all the nations of the earth. To this end, Israel will be His "treasured possession" – his personal property which is what the Hebrew word "*segullah*" basically means. The idea of value may be present too. Many of you reading this may have a jewellery box or precious stone collection. As God's "treasured possession", God's people are infinitely precious to him (cf. Mal. 3:17).

But in case Israel should ever misconstrue this special place in God's heart as an exclusive, self-centred or nationalistic relationship, the text adds the telling comment: "all the earth is mine". God has still got His sights firmly fixed on all the nations, even at the precise moment when He chooses one nation to serve Him in the world! What could be clearer? Israel is, undoubtedly, the jewel in God's crown, but the crown God wears is not that of a tribal or even a national god, but the One Creator God of all the world.

A DEVOTIONAL INTERLUDE

Prayer: Gracious and loving God I thank You from the depths of my heart that though Israel were Your chosen people, they were not Your exclusive people. Your love spilled over to the other nations of the world, and through the sufferings of Your Son on the cross I am now in the fold. There is no way I could be closer to You. I am Yours and You are mine. And we are going to spend eternity together. I am so deeply thankful. Amen.

DAY **102**

READ
Exodus 19:5–6

Pondering these words, we note that Israel is called "a kingdom of priests" who will enjoy living under God's direct kingly rule. But they do so as priestly mediators between God and his world! As a priestly kingdom, Israel is entrusted with God's Word so that others might come to know Him. The temptation for God's people – as it was for Israel – is to forget this challenging vocation and turn God into our exclusive possession or make religion into a private, self-serving experience. But we are chosen for mission. And the priestly calling inevitably works the other way too – not only from God to the world but from the world to God. Here we are on the edge of a mystery: that Israel is called in some strange way to intercede for the world, to echo its groaning for redemption, and, in an even stranger way, to embody the world's sin and suffering on God's behalf. In the end, of course, only one true Israelite, the final priestly King, was up to doing this job.

And Israel is called to be God's holy nation, devoted to God, a showcase nation, showing God to the world. "Be holy as I am holy" becomes Israel's national charter as a prototype new humanity, reflecting God's image to the world as Adam and Eve had been intended to do. Again, only in Jesus has God begun to achieve this, but this has always been His aim.

A DEVOTIONAL INTERLUDE

Thought: Years ago a saying that was very popular in evangelistic churches was this: "We are saved to serve." New converts were told, now you are a Christian your job is to win others to Christ. This emphasis is missing in many of today's churches. How deep is the passion to tell others about Jesus in your heart? In 1 Corinthians 9 Paul appears to be saying that he would do anything short of sinning to bring people to Christ. Would you?

DAY 103

READ
Exodus
19:16–20:2

Spectacular as the natural phenomena at Sinai were, what was crucial was what Israel heard God say, directly in the "ten words", and indirectly through Moses in the rest of the laws.

To maintain Israel as God's holy nation, for the world's sake, God gives the law. The "law", we recall, does not precede God's grace, but is given to a people already redeemed.

So, as Ron Mehl calls them, these are truly "ten(der) commandments", that reflect God's loving desire that Israel should stay free. They are given to ensure Israel's freedom in a just and equal society – the very opposite of the oppressive, slave-driven regime in Egypt.

Our modern world mistakenly believes that we become free by rebelling against God. Ours, it is rightly said, is not so much a permissive society as a transgressive one!

Not that the "ten words" are meant merely to produce good citizens in a conventional society. Rather, they are the means by which the Creator God's ordering of chaos at creation is re-established at the social level so that heaven's will is done on earth. Rather than being relics of an outmoded social system, therefore, the "ten words" are signposts to the renewal of human community in Christ. They come from the One Creator God as the "maker's instructions" for a better world, as an act of re-creation.

A DEVOTIONAL INTERLUDE

For action: Spend a few moments now reading through the Ten Commandments and after each one use this responsive prayer which is based on the *Baptist Hymn Book* (UK Edition): "Lord have mercy on me and incline my heart to keep this law." In reading these commandments you may think God lifts the standards to almost unbelievable heights, but never forget that He also provides the power by which we reach up to them.

DAY 104

READ
Exodus 20:3-21

It is because God is Israel's Saviour that Israel is to have no rivals to Him.

Strictly speaking, what is commanded here is not "monotheism" – "you must worship only one God" – but that among rivals, "there is only One God who has lifted you on eagles' wings, who is worthy of your love, just Me and no one else!"

Likewise, the ban on idols is meant to safeguard not so much God's transcendence as His ability to relate to us. Idols are pilloried by Isarel's prophets for being inanimate objects, unable to communicate with their devotees. But Yahweh is the Living God who speaks.

His "jealousy" – a term taken from close relationships like marriage – does not mean that God is spiteful or capricious but that He cares passionately about His involvement with His people so that He alone deserves their undivided loyalty.

From the first four commands which guard Israel's bond with God, flow the last six – governing Israel's relationships within the covenant community, and beyond. That free, just and loving society God wants His people to enjoy, depends entirely on their maintaining a right relationship with Him. The "ten words" thus show us not only "what we must do" but what God is like.

Israel is entrusted with the sacred task of embodying that God-likeness for the rest of the world.

A DEVOTIONAL INTERLUDE

For praise: In *Songs of Fellowship* (Kingsway Music, UK) there is a song that suggests an appropriate response to what has been said today: Its title is "No One but You Lord". If you know the tune sing it. If not, say it:

Only You can fill my deepest longing,
Only You can breathe in me new life,
Only You can fill my heart with laughter,
Only You can answer my heart's cry

DAY **105**

READ
Exodus 24:1–18

As God's covenant with Israel is ratified, two features in the ritual involved merit our attention: the book and the blood. Moses reads from the Book of the Covenant and gains the people's assent to what is said in God's Word. He sprinkles the blood over the people and on the altar, thus confirming the bond-in-blood between God and His people. The mention of "burnt offerings and fellowship offerings" reminds us that the sacrificial principle was at the heart of Israel's worship. This doubtless echoed the earlier substitutionary blood-shedding of the Passover Lamb and became institutionalised in Leviticus as the regular means of grace by which a sinful people could repair and sustain the covenant relationship. What follows in our text is that Moses and the group with him "see" God – or rather they see only what looked like a sapphire pavement beneath His feet. Their gaze is down and what they see is beyond words to describe. But "seeing" what cannot be seen or uttered, they eat and drink before God's face. As we gaze on "things unseen" and words fail us for joy, we too can re-affirm the bond-in-blood between us and the Lord. As we eat bread and drink wine in our never-to-be-forgotten covenant meal, we renew our participation in God's story.

A DEVOTIONAL INTERLUDE

To ponder: Whenever you attend the Table of Communion (The Lord's Supper, Eucharist, etc) what are the thoughts that go through your mind? Many no doubt. Our main thought in our minds, however, ought to be this – Lord Jesus You have given Yourself for me, in a fresh act of commitment I now give myself to You.

"Take our bread we ask you; take our hearts we love You
Take our lives O Father, we are Yours, we are Yours."

READ
Exodus 25–27

No part of Scripture has suffered more from over-eager students in the search for spiritual analogies to the Christian life than this description of the tabernacle. But if the writer to the Hebrews is our guide, we must not overpress the details of our interpretation but rather ask: "What does this tell us about God and His intentions towards His people?"

Firstly, in line with his stated aim (Exod. 15:17), the tabernacle is a portable sanctuary for God so that He can dwell among His people (25:8) during their wilderness wanderings. From walking in the Garden of Eden conversing with Adam and Eve in the cool of the day, to the pillar of cloud and fire, God has already shown His intense desire to be present with His human partners.

Secondly, Moses was to build the tabernacle "according to the plan shown you on the mountain" (26:30). This implies that the earthly structure is a symbol of a heavenly reality. Because God is King over Israel, the tabernacle, and later the Temple, are not only His earthly address but His royal palace. The ark of the covenant – the chief article of furniture in the sanctuary – is later described as the footstool of His throne; that is, the earthly footstool of God's heavenly throne. When God's people worship, they know the King is among them.

A DEVOTIONAL INTERLUDE

Prayer: My Father and my God I am so grateful that You are not only transcendent, far above all, but also imminent, close at hand. I do not have to go up to You; You are here in my heart. What love you must have, to come to earth in the person of Your Son to live amongst us and die for our sins. You are so big that You fill the heavens yet so small that You can fill my heart. How can this be? Yet I know it to be so. Thank You dear Father. Amen.

DAY 107

READ
Exodus 31:12–18

If it is clear from Genesis that human beings are the crown of God's creation, then it is equally clear that the Sabbath is the goal of creation.

God's human creatures are indeed the peak of His work, with exalted responsibility over everything else He has made. But Sabbath represents what all creation – including humans – are moving towards. For Israel, God's immediate Sabbath rest was the promised land, but this in turn becomes a symbol of the ultimate rest of God's salvation in the coming kingdom when God "rests" from His new creation labours. Israel was to keep this memory and hope alive in the world by keeping Sabbath. Israel kept Sabbath as a badge of its covenant identity as the steward of the world's future. The practical benefits of Sabbath were obvious, too, with animals and fields given regular respite from being worked. For ex-slaves above all, Sabbath was a treasured gift, reminding them of the grace that had rescued them from the round-the-clock production lines of Egypt's slave economy. Sabbath was not meant to rob life of fun or encourage the work-shy but to enable God's people to know God better (v.13). Just as God's seven-day working week dignifies the work we do, so God's Sabbath-rest reminds us weekly that we are called to be worshippers not workaholics.

A DEVOTIONAL INTERLUDE

Thought: David Adam once wrote a prayer on the theme of "Work". Today you may like to pray the following words based on that prayer:

In the quiet of the morning, In the new day that is dawning
Thy Kingdom come
In my tasks and my employment, In my leisure and enjoyment
Thy Kingdom come
All day, until its very ending, Praise to You I shall be sending
Thy Kingdom come.

DAY **108**

READ
Exodus 32:1-6, 15-29

Today's reading comes as a shock after what we have been reading of Israel's redemption and covenant with God and God's desire to dwell among His people. It puts the whole Exodus experiment at risk. Barely is the "ink dry" on the precious bond between them than Israel falls from grace and lapses into idolatry. It is not so much that the people want another god, as that – unsettled perhaps by Moses' absence – they hanker after a visible symbol of God's presence. Whatever the reason, they now seek to honour God in an illegitimate way. Coming down the mountain, Joshua hears what he takes to be the noise of war in the camp. But Moses hears otherwise, hearing not the sound of heroes exulting, nor the sound of the vanquished lamenting but merely the sound of random singing! Such idolatrous worship is a sad parody of the praise of Exodus 15. Celebration without victory, rejoicing without reality, neither high praise or deep lament, just a meaningless round of songs to make people feel good about themselves.

Aaron's excuse is that he was going with the flow of popular demand and giving the people what they want! That's where idolatry starts and immorality isn't far behind.

A DEVOTIONAL INTERLUDE

To ponder: Is it possible that we can engage in singing "the songs of Zion" in an effort to feel good about ourselves rather than focusing on how our singing can bring honour and glory to the Lord? How careful we should be that we enter into worship not for our own sake or to give ourselves a spiritual "lift" but to glorify the Lord. In the glorifying of God the "lift" comes, but we ought not to do it for our own sake but for His.

DAY 109

READ
Exodus 32:7–14, 30–35.

This tragic incident with the "golden calf", as we have seen, threatens to bring the Exodus story to an abrupt end and to unravel all God's future plans. God's reaction shows Him in a mood to disown Israel, because, as He insists to Moses, "Your people whom you brought out of Egypt have become corrupt" (v.7). As if to forestall any possible intervention from Moses, God then tells him, "Now leave me alone so that my anger may burn against them" (v.10), even offering to start all over again with Moses as His new Abraham by making him into a "great nation"!

Moses' intercession saves the day. He pleads God's previous saving power, argues that God's reputation is at stake – what will the neighbour-nations think? – and then reminds God of His long-standing covenant promises made to the patriarchs. As a result the Lord relents. What a prayer. Boldly Moses holds God to His own integrity of word and action and offers his own life in Israel's stead. Prayer urges God to be God and to act in Godlike ways, true to His own nature. What an amazing God too who is willing to be entreated in ways that change the course of history. Even more amazingly, one day, this same God would offer His own life to make atonement for our sins.

A DEVOTIONAL INTERLUDE

For praise: Do you know the first verse of the hymn that follows? Sing it to the Lord. Let it be your response to the reading today.

Great God of wonders, all Thy ways
Display Thine attributes divine
But countless acts of pardoning grace
Beyond Thine other words shine
Who is a pardoning God like Thee?
Or who has grace so rich and free?

DAY 110

READ
Exodus 33:1–23

That Israel's "fall" has not aborted the story of redemption is due to Moses' timely intervention. But the situation is still serious as God refuses to travel any further with His stubborn people in case He destroys them en route. Has Moses' intercession changed nothing? If so then to build the tabernacle is pointless since God will not come and occupy it, and the first 31 chapters of Exodus are undone. Everything hangs in the balance. Moses again steps into the gap and presses his case like a faithful friend, in a "face to face" meeting with God: "You want me to lead, Lord, but who will follow me? I may have found favour with you but what about the people, do they have a future?" "My Presence will go with you Moses."

But Moses persists. Without Your ongoing presence we have an unenviable future (v.15), uncertain of Your favour (v.16). Without Your presence we will lose our distinctive identity in the world and who else will be Your witnesses? This is powerful persuasion encouraged by God's grace and matched by God's response. Emboldened further, Moses asks to see God's glory but is allowed a glimpse of God's back not His face. This was the closest Moses got to the glory until, on another day and mountain, he found himself talking with Jesus who was transfigured before his very eyes.

A DEVOTIONAL INTERLUDE

Prayer: O Lord that is my prayer also. If your Presence does not go with me into the day and every day that is ahead then I just don't want to go. The thought of You not being at my side is something I do not want to contemplate. You designed me to function best when I am dependent on You. You are my hope, my strength, my light, my way. I do not want to take one step into the future without You. Stay with me dear Father. Always. In Jesus' Name. Amen.

DAY **111**

READ
Exodus 34:1–35

These verses represent the closest Israel came to God's autobiography.

The Lord is "compassionate and gracious", tender towards sufferers and full of unmerited favour. When a partner has a short fuse, life is tense, but thankfully, God is "slow to anger, abounding in love and faithfulness" (v.6). God is full of "*hesed*" – that tough, covenant-love which matches his tenderness and guarantees the continuance of the covenant bond. The outflow of this is God's "faithfulness" – a consistency of purpose and commitment that reflects His own integrity. And this faithful loving "abounds" so that God is not grudging or frugal but is as quick to love as He is slow to anger. His reservoir of patience is no more depleted than is His readiness to be forgiving.

But the text reminds us sharply that God is not complacent about sin, that sin incurs judgment, and that seeds sown in one generation are often tragically reaped in another.

Moses, seeking reassurance about Israel's future, confesses the people's stubborn sinfulness, and is granted a renewal of the covenant (vv.10–28). Moses is personally reaffirmed in his mediatorial role by the radiance that streams from his face when he has spoken with the Lord. So awesome is this speech and sight that Moses has to veil his face whenever he speaks to the people on God's behalf (vv.33–35).

A DEVOTIONAL INTERLUDE

Thought: How balanced are the qualities of compassion and judgment in the heart of our heavenly Father. Verses 6 and 7 are "the closest Israel came to God's autobiography". Think about your own life for a moment; are you slow to anger, abounding in love and faithfulness, but not complacent about sin? These are qualities that all of us ought to possess – and they ought to be reflected in our autobiography too.

DAY **112**

READ
Exodus 35–40

If, as we noted a day or two ago, we stand back from over-elaborate attempts to interpret the details of the tabernacle, we see a big picture. In fact, the tabernacle is less a coded model of salvation and more a wonderful microcosm of creation. It represents a creation-in-miniature, marked by all the features found in the first chapter of Genesis. Notice the following: the seven times the Lord spoke to Moses, ending with the Sabbath; the bringing of all the rich resources of God's world into order and beauty; the action of the creative Spirit of God; the way the work is said to be completed; the way Moses inspects the work, pronounces himself satisfied and blesses it; the commencement date on the first day of the first month . . . all of these features echo the Genesis 1 account.

In other words just as the Sabbath sanctifies time, so the tabernacle sanctifies space. In the midst of a fallen, disordered, rebellious world, there is one place where the original beauty and design and purpose of creation as a vehicle for God's glorious presence can be seen! Where God dwells with Israel, on this small scale it is "just as it was at the beginning".

The tabernacle also points forwards, a prophetic parable of "what will be at the end" in the final splendour of God's new creation where He will dwell with His people for ever.

A DEVOTIONAL INTERLUDE

To ponder: How grateful we should be that God's presence is everywhere. Let these words rest on your heart: "How lovely is your dwelling-place, O Lord Almighty! My soul yearns, even faints, for the courts of the Lord; my heart and my flesh cry out for the living God. Even the sparrow has found a home, and the swallow a nest for herself . . . a place near your altar, O Lord Almighty, my King and my God" (Psa. 84:1–4).

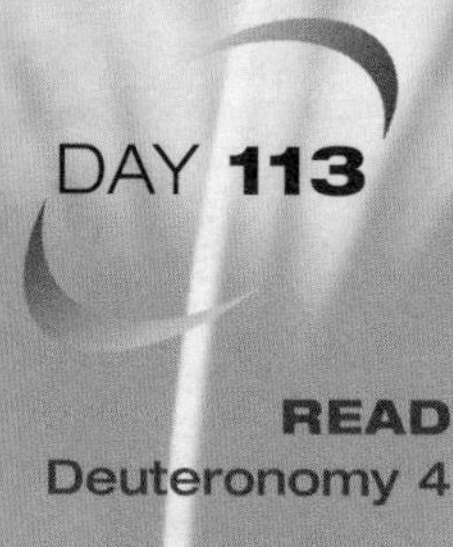

DAY **113**

READ
Deuteronomy 4

Forty years of disobedient wandering have elapsed since the Exodus and Sinai, and now, on the verge of the promised land, Moses gives a second reading of the law ("*deutero-nomos*") climaxed by a renewal and expansion of the original covenant.

Today's text urges Israel to live up to her unique story by remembering the Exodus (vv.15–20) and Sinai (vv.10–14) as they cross over into the land (vv.21–24), warning that failure will bring exile (vv.25–30).

Israel must not forget the covenant because God never will (vv.23,31).

Israel is distinctive because her God is unique.

No other nation has ever heard the Creator God speak out of the fire or been singled out for redemptive help, only Israel (vv.32–34). The world that watches and waits for Israel's story to unfold for its salvation depends upon a faithful Israel (v.6)! That God chooses to save the world through one particular nation has to many always been a scandal. Old Testament scholar, Chris Wright, brilliantly draws out the implications of this when he says: "The uniqueness of Jesus as the Messiah of Israel and thereby as Saviour of the world, is grounded in the uniqueness of Israel itself and of Yahweh as God, for according to the New Testament Jesus embodied the one and incarnated the other."

A DEVOTIONAL INTERLUDE

For praise: Turn right now to Psalm 147, and join your heart with the psalmist who furnishes us with one of the most delightful frameworks for praise found in the Bible. Note especially verse 20 where he says: "He has done this for no other nation; they do not know his laws. Praise the Lord." How grateful we should be that we have come to know His laws. And not only know them, but live by them. Blessed be His Name for ever.

DAY **114**

READ
Deuteronomy
7–9

Israel is here reminded of her special vocation as God's holy people and is dared to be different (7:1–6).

Israel exists only as a miracle of grace and choice of love (7:7–8) by a Lord who is faithful and keeps covenant (7:9).

God's people had been urged to love Him with all their heart in the Shema (6:4–5) but other voices would seek to seduce Israel from the path of whole-hearted trust. The thrice-repeated phrase: "If you should say in your heart" (NKJV), highlights the three key temptations Israel will face in the land. Intimidated by larger nations, Israel will be tempted by militarism to put her faith in military power rather than trust in Yahweh (7:17). Forgetful of where the good things of the land come from, Israel will be tempted to listen to the voice of materialism and bow down to the god of self-sufficiency (8:17). When the voice of moralism is heeded Israel will forget the grace which saved her and exalt the god of national self-righteousness and communal pride (9:4).

The wilderness years were meant as discipline to show that a true son does not live by bread alone but by the ever-spoken word of a fatherly God. From here we might readily trace a trajectory to the One true Son in the wilderness who absorbed His people's failure in His own faithful compliance with this Deuteronomic covenant charter.

A DEVOTIONAL INTERLUDE

Thought: If the Israelities were tempted to think that they were favoured by God because of some special characteristics they possessed, then here they learned differently. They were loved not because of what was in them but what was in God – eternal boundless Love. It is the same with us. We are what we are because God is who He is. As the hymn writer put it:

He has loved, He has loved us
We cannot tell why

DAY **115**

READ
Deuteronomy
27–30

Moses here lists the blessings of covenantal obedience and the judgmental curses that fall on disobedience. Moses anticipates that Israel's future covenantal unfaithfulness will incur God's ultimate judgmental curse of ejection from the promised land (28:63). Sadly, Israel's story replicates the human story. Israel's exile from Canaan – a place often portrayed in Scripture in Edenic language – mirrors the expulsion of Adam and Eve from the Garden of Eden. And Moses issues this warning before Israel has even entered the land!

Tragically, what Moses anticipated became grim reality 800 years later in the Babylonian Exile so that when the Torah takes final shape as Scripture, his warning is already in the past tense (29:28 "as it is now"). Even more remarkably, Moses points to a hope beyond exile that is not based on the sacrificial system, Israel's conventional means of grace. Rather, pre-empting Jeremiah and Ezekiel, Moses looks to when God will create radically new covenant hearts in God's people. We can glimpse this hope by comparing Deuteronomy 10:16 – where God commands, "Circumcise your hearts" – with 30:6 where God does it. When commanded human action turns into promised divine action, the new covenant is on the horizon. The law is grace in the end.

A DEVOTIONAL INTERLUDE

Prayer: My Father and my God, once again I lift my heart to You in deepest gratitude that Your law drove me to the place where my heart opened to grace. I shall never cease to praise You that You not only commanded righteousness but provided it through the innocent sufferings of Your Son on Calvary. The more I learn of Your Story, the more amazed I am that I am part of it – and grateful to the depths of my heart. Thank You Father. Amen.

DAY 116

READ
Amos 3

Today we dip briefly into Israel's long-running love–hate relationship with the prophets whom God sent as prosecutors to hold Israel and her kings accountable to the covenant bond.

The prophetic oracles brought by prophets like Amos constitute "covenant lawsuits" in which God indicts His people for turning away from Him and for failing to live covenantally. The outcome of God's plans told by the prophets is inescapable (vv.3–7).

Amos' own lion-like roar especially exposes the injustice at the heart of the nation's life – the poor exploited by corrupt economic practices, and all masked by hypocritical religion. Israel's unique privilege –"You only have I chosen of all the families of the earth" – automatically entails ("therefore") solemn responsibility and, in the case of failure, judgment – "therefore I will punish you for all your sins" (v.2). Even hardened international observers, well-versed in the black arts of oppression and injustice, will look askance at Israel (vv.9–12). If God's people are to be saved it will only be as a remnant, unflatteringly described here as the tattered leftovers of a lion's dinner! (v.12). Not much left for God to work with! But, as so often with God, these pitiful scraps are just enough for Him to begin to write a new chapter in the story.

A DEVOTIONAL INTERLUDE

For action: How grateful we ought to be for those who in Old Testament times spoke the Word of the Lord to the people – and for those now who faithfully preach His Word. Willard F Jabusch has taken an Israeli folk melody and put these words to it. Give God thanks for the fact that He spoke through His Word and that He speaks through it still.

God has spoken to His people; Hallelujah!
And His words are words of wisdom; Hallelujah!

DAY 117

READ
Hosea 11

This is rightly regarded as one of the most moving chapters in the Bible. God's relationship to Israel is likened to that between parent and child and it yields an astonishing view of God's tenderness. "Out of Egypt I called my son" (v.1) echoes the claim made by Moses to Pharaoh at the Exodus (Exod. 4:22). Israel is pictured as a toddler nation unaware of being taught to walk by a patient and gentle God (v.3). For a moment the image fades into that of a good farmer sensitive to how young animals need to be nurtured and not over-driven (v.4). But again Israel fails to respond and turns away from God (v.7).

Should God repudiate His people? As we overhear His own self-questioning, we gain a remarkable insight into the agony of indecision in the heart of God. God is emotionally involved with Israel. He feels with and for His people.

But these human-like emotions, paradoxically, show God to be God not man (v.9)! Human patience would have been exhausted long ago but divine love will not let His people go. The God of our story is not woodenly acting out a pre-determined script, He is living out a passion for His people and for the world's redemption that will one day cost Him if He's not more careful! His prodigal sons will return home when the prodigal Father opens wide His arms of love.

A DEVOTIONAL INTERLUDE

Thought: One of the greatest aspects of the love of God is not just that He loves, but it is a love that will never let us go. Let your response to today's reading be expressed in the words of one of the verses of the well known hymn:

O Love, that wilt not let me go,
I rest my weary soul in Thee;
I give Thee back the life I owe,
That in Thine ocean depths its flow
May richer, fuller be.

DAY 118

READ
2 Kings 17:7–23
2 Chronicles 36

We trace the fate of the divided kingdom down to the demise of the northern kingdom of Israel whose capital, Samaria, fell to the invading Assyrians in 720 BC, and to the exile of Judah to Babylonia, climaxing with the fall of Jersualem in 586 BC.

In both cases, tragic judgment finally overtook God's people due to their covenant unfaithfulness and treatment of the prophets. In Israel's case, records the historian, they failed to trust God but "worshipped other gods . . . and rejected . . . the covenant . . . and the warnings he had given them" through the prophets (2 Kings 17:7,15). Reneging on their unique calling to be a holy nation, believing and behaving no differently from the surrounding cultures, they "imitated the nations around them" (2 Kings 17:15).

As for the people of Judah, surviving for another 120 years or so, they eventually succumbed to the Babylonians and were taken into exile because "they mocked God's messengers . . . until the wrath of the Lord was aroused against his people and there was no remedy" (2 Chron. 36:16)! Or was there? In the marvellous paradox of grace, the prophetic word which, when rejected, sealed Judah's fate, also offered a glimmer of hope for future restoration. If the old covenant people could not be patched up, perhaps a new covenant people might be created, raised to life out of the "death" of exile!

A DEVOTIONAL INTERLUDE

To ponder: The thing that has puzzled the people of God through the ages is why some who have been delivered from so many things by the good hand of God can then turn against Him. Our natural minds might reason thus: if God foresees that some people He delivers would not stay faithful to Him then why deliver them in the first place? The answer must surely be this: God blesses us not for what we will be tomorrow but for who we are today.

DAY **119**

READ
Romans 9:1–5

With breaking heart, Paul faces the mystery of Israel's unbelief. He sadly recalls the unique privileges Israel enjoyed, above all being the race that produced the Messiah (vv.1–5). So why has Israel rejected him? Paul's answer starts from one rock-bottom conviction: that whoever or whatever has failed, it is not God or God's covenant faithfulness (v.6).

Paul reviews Israel's entire history from Abraham to the Exile (vv.6–29) and discerns that from the start there has been a selectivity of God at work. Always, Paul sees, there has been an Israel within Israel, for covenant relationship has rested on faith and obedience not on mere biological descent from Abraham. Grace not race explains God's workings.

And if a remnant exists – Jews who like Paul believe in Jesus as Messiah – then just as Isaiah saw, there is hope for the future (vv.27–29). Wonderfully, Paul expands Hosea's promised restoration of disowned Israelites, to explain the adoption of Gentiles into God's enlarged family (vv.25–26).

And if it had long been true that Israel could not be affirmed as she stood but needed to undergo renewal through judgment and mercy, exile and restoration, then was Israel's failure perhaps mysteriously built into the plan from the start? The mystery of Israel continues as the scandal of grace.

A DEVOTIONAL INTERLUDE

Thought: Consider this – no one can ever bring a justifiable complaint against God. Whatever the Almighty does is always good. At times it may not seem so to us, but in the bigger scheme of things His goodness is at the heart of everything. When you find yourself doubting God's goodness, remind yourself of this – a God who gave His Son to die for us on a cross has got to be good. This you will find will help put things in proper perspective.

DAY **120**

READ
1 Peter 2:1-12

So crucial is Jesus to us that Peter, using Isaiah's words, sees Him as either the stepping-stone to salvation or the stumbling-block of judgment (vv.6–7). To highlight this, Peter applies to the Church, the classic descriptions of Israel's status, titles and role, culled from Exodus 19 and Isaiah 43 (v.7).

Like Paul, Peter extends Hosea's promised reinstatement of Israel to include Gentile believers in Christ (v.10). In Christ, "nobodies" become "somebodies", even alienated, "non-people" are now by grace in God's covenant family!

The "Church" then is not meant to be a Gentile innovation which replaces Israel in a simplistic way. Rather, it exists as a remade and enlarged Israel on a world scale. Isn't this just what God promised Abraham? All believers in Jesus Christ inherit those promises. But with the privileges come the obligations. God's aim has never been to save random individuals for a privatised heaven but to create a people out of all nations for his own glory. Jesus is the one foundation that can bear the weight of such a vast and living Temple from which, whether in evangelism, worship or God-glorifying living, flows a stream of endless praise. The story we have been tracking from Noah to Abraham to Israel now narrows down to one individual – the king. To this we now turn.

A DEVOTIONAL INTERLUDE

Prayer: My Father and my God how grateful I am for the fact that the foundation which has been laid in the Church is Jesus. Because He is the Eternal Rock, I am standing safe and secure on something that can never be moved. There are times when I may tremble on the Rock, but I am more grateful than words can convey for the fact that the Rock never trembles under me. All honour and glory be unto Your peerless and precious Name for ever. Amen.

COVENANT WITH: NOAH ABRAHAM

NOAH
all creation

ABRAHAM
all nations

ISRAEL
one nation

DAVID
REPRESENTATIVE KING

NEW COVENANT
faithful covenant partner

JESUS
faithful covenant partner

JESUS
Davidic King Messiah

JESUS
the New Israel

JESUS
the world's Lord

JESUS
the truly Human One crowned with glory and honour

JESUS
cosmic Ruler in God's new creation new heavens and new earth

SECTION 6
DAVID'S DESTINY

God is committed to crowning His Son King – David's destiny

The second book of Samuel, chapter 7, has been called a "mountain peak in redemptive history". It dramatises the frustration of David's plans to build a house or temple for God and the announcement by God through the prophet Nathan of God's intention to build a house for David! Even without this chapter, it would be hard to overestimate the importance of kingship to Israel. We recall that the promise of kings was part of the original covenantal promise to Abraham (Gen. 17:6) and prescriptions for kingship were written into the law (Deut. 17:14–20). Following the false start with Saul, David is seen to be the "man after his own heart" (1 Sam. 13:14), who will shepherd God's people. But the commitment God makes to David and his kingly line goes beyond national interests. David is promised a dynasty, a throne, a kingdom that will last for ever, and a special father–son relationship with God.

This astonishing commitment which leaves David dumbfounded and humbled is celebrated as the Davidic "covenant" in Psalm 89. One implication was that, in line with the ancient concept of "sacral kingship", each subsequent king in Israel was regarded as God's representative on earth to whom was applied the privileged affirmation "You are my Son, today I have become your Father". Psalm 2 from which these words come was probably a song sung at the king's coronation in which the prophetic singer declares that Israel's king in Zion is destined to become Lord of the whole world!

Not only does the king represent God but he represents the people. His subjects are so bound up with his interests and fate that what happens to him happens to them. This is one reason why, with the rise of kingship – the Old Testament narrative about the children of Israel becomes the "chronicles" of the kings of Israel.

So, as the ancient historian saw, God's covenant commitment to David remained as a lamp that would never go out even in the darkest days of the most evil kings (2 Kings 8:19).

In the unfolding of revelation, it was, no doubt, the failure of the kings to live up to the ideals of kingship that, in part, prompted hopes for the coming of an ideal ruler who would restore God's people and implement God's kingly rule. This vision, first glimpsed by Isaiah and Micah in the middle of the eighth century BC, comes into more urgent and clearer focus in the Exilic prophets, Jeremiah and Ezekiel. It is left to Isaiah to put a wholly new spin on the notion of kingship by unveiling the mysterious figure of God's anointed servant who will suffer as God's agent of salvation. Isaiah, at the same time, envisages the coming of God Himself as King to establish His kingdom of justice and peace. Only the New Testament will resolve these paradoxes. Suffice it to say that all this background of kingship – especially Psalm 2 – informs the language of the Evangelists when they describe Jesus at His baptism being anointed by the Spirit and singled out by the divine voice as God's royal "Son". This Sonship which begins as a national epithet and a royal vocation – reaffirmed at Jesus' transfiguration – blossoms into full-scale divine Sonship in the wake of the resurrection which acclaims Him as God's Messiah and therefore Lord of the world (Acts 2:13).

So with the Davidic covenant, God narrows down His redemptive purpose, not in the sense of restricting its scope, but in the sense of concentrating on one representative figure. Where the covenant with Noah concerns the whole creation; the covenant with Abraham potentially effects all nations; and the covenant with Israel channels that purpose into the stewardship of just one nation – so now the plan of God is focused on a representative individual. To the king and his dynasty who represent God and the people is entrusted the plan of God. On the future ideal King rests the hopes of the people for national renewal and new covenant blessings, and in turn the hopes of the nations of being blessed through Abraham's seed. Kingship was always the truly human vocation. By recovering Adam's lost dominion, retrieving Israel's kingdom calling, and redeeming the office of kingship, Jesus, the Truly Human One, now wears the crown of honour and glory which alone guarantees us glory and offers creation hope of renewal.

DAY 121

READ
2 Samuel 7:1–17

The event described here is one of the supreme moments in Scripture.

Safely settled in his own palace in Jerusalem, David's thoughts turn to more grandiose schemes. Like a typical ancient king, David's ambition is to erect a palace for the god who sponsors his regime. He shares with his key advisors this desire to build a house for God.

No doubt anxious to please, his court-prophet, Nathan, readily rubber-stamps the proposal. But prophets are expected to be "open all hours" and during the night Nathan is woken by God and told that God forbids the king from building him a house. Instead, God will build a house for David and with it, a throne and a kingdom that will last for ever. Above all, the king is promised a special father–son relationship with God! With what trepidation, I wonder, did Nathan enter David's quarters the next morning with his bitter-sweet news? "No, you are not to build a house for God . . . but God will build a house for you!" The death of David's dream makes way for the bigger dreams of God who always does far more than we can ask or imagine.

Though the word does not appear in this text, God's commitment here to David is rightly recalled by later writers as God's "covenant" with David. As such it is unconditional. Even though individual kings will fail, God's covenant love for the Davidic line will remain. On this hangs the success of God's plan.

A DEVOTIONAL INTERLUDE

Quote: Following today's reading consider this powerful quotation from Dr Larry Crabb: "Shattered dreams are never random. They are always a piece in a larger puzzle, a chapter in a larger story. The Holy Spirit uses the pain of shattered dreams to help us discover our desire for God, to help us begin dreaming the highest dream. They are ordained opportunities for the Spirit first to awaken, then to satisfy our highest dream."

DAY **122**

READ
2 Samuel
7:18–29

Deeply disappointed yet dumbstruck with wonder, the king tries to come to terms with the night's events. David has tried to fit God into his programme, but God refuses to be accommodated in this way and instead makes a place for David in the divine scheme of things. David is suitably humbled and awed – and asks, literally, "Is this the law of man?" This is variously translated, with the NIV taking the minimal reading: "Is this your usual way of dealing with man?"(v.19). But other Old Testament scholars see weightier issues here, noting that in some ancient languages the phrase "the law of man" concerns human fate and destiny. So one scholar translates it, "Is this the charter for humanity?" This is surely to be preferred. In the prophetic oracle Nathan has delivered to him, David rightly sees beyond the domestic or royal honour done to him and senses that the future of the whole human race is involved.

We know only too well that life does not conform to our expectations or desires and that control evades us. Only with time do we come to appreciate the strange grace that denies us our requests in the interests of God's bigger visions.

If God sometimes thwarts even our godliest plans it is only so as to include us in His larger, long-term plans.

In this case, David's disappointment is the world's destiny.

A DEVOTIONAL INTERLUDE

To ponder: Have your plans been thwarted in some way? Then hold on to this – the Almighty dismantles our plans in order to build bigger and better ones – plans that fit into the story He is telling. It is disappointing when the things we want to do or accomplish do not have the divine approval, but learn to change the first letter of the word disappointment from "d" to "h". Then rejoice in the change of perspective.

DAY 123

READ
Psalm 89

The psalmist here reflects ruefully on the humiliating and shameful demise of kingship at the time of the Babylonian exile. The unthinkable appears to have happened; God seems to have repudiated His covenant promises to the Davidic monarchy (vv.38–45).

Yet still the psalmist's faith reaches out to grasp the faithfulness of God guaranteed by His covenant with David. "O Lord, where is your former great love, which in your faithfulness you swore to David?" (v.49). Israel's hope for the future lies in recalling God's commitment to David which He said was inviolable (vv.19–37).

For the king to call God his "Father" and to be called "God's son" is an intensified form of the relationship Israel enjoyed with God (Exod. 4:22–23). This reaffirms the view that the king – in effect – assumes the role and responsibilities of the whole people. As a representative figure, when he fails, they are deemed to have failed. So the people's future is still bound up with that of God's promises to the king.

The world role of Israel's king is remembered, too (v.27). He is destined to be ruler of the world, lord of lords and king of kings. Now what will happen?

The answer told in Psalms 90 onwards is that God will re-assert His saving kingship in the world in His own way and person. What a prospect!

A DEVOTIONAL INTERLUDE

Thought: How our hearts rejoice that one day the Saviour who first came to this world as a baby is going to return as King. But we must not forget that He is King now (Heb. 2:9). Join with thousands today in expressing praise and renewed dedication through the following verse:

Rise up O men of God
Have done with lesser things,
Give heart and soul and mind and strength
To serve the King of kings!

DAY **124**

READ
Psalm 2

This psalm was probably first sung at a king's coronation in Israel.

The prophetic singer sings a vision of the nations in uproar, their leaders in fierce debate as if at a world-summit conference. For all their differences, they are perceived by the psalmist as conspiring together "against the Lord and his Anointed" (v.2). Beneath their well-spun political manifestos, the men of power intend to run God's world without Him.

But what our visionary singer sees and hears is very different: he sees God's throne and hears God laugh! It's not a cruel laughter but a divine derision which pricks the bubble of human arrogance. Now one voice rises authoritatively above the rest to declare that the decision about who rules the world is not open for discussion but has already been taken! "I have installed my King on Zion, my holy hill" (v.6).

How incongruous it sounds to the world's empire-builders, to be supplanted by this King in Zion, a puny hill in the capital of an obscure, uninfluential, out-of-the-way nation.

But let the King speak: "He said to me, 'You are my Son; today I have become your Father. Ask of me, and I will make the nations your inheritance, the ends of the earth your possession' " (vv.7–8).

Next time we hear this we will be with two men, standing dripping wet on a river bank on the verge of the kingdom of God.

A DEVOTIONAL INTERLUDE

For praise: Have you ever considered how many times the Old Testament prophets were sustained by a vision of the throne – a place of power and authority? When things looked bad on earth they lifted their eyes to heaven and drew inspiration from the fact that ultimately God was in control. Earthly thrones may be toppled, but as the writer to the Hebrews says, "Thy throne O God is for ever and ever". Give God praise for that glorious fact.

ISRAEL / MOSES

DAY **125**

READ
Judges 21

We pause for a moment to acknowledge that God's commitment to the royal office is remarkable in the light of its inauspicious beginnings in Israel. Today's passage makes for sorry reading!

In pre-monarchical days, in the period of the Judges, Israel was meant to model social salvation by experiencing the blessings of living under a theocracy – that is, under the direct rule and government of God. Tragically, by the end of the Judges period, the divine experiment of Israel as a "holy nation" in the promised land had degenerated into moral and social anarchy. The ancient historian sounds a society's epitaph like the dull tolling of a funeral bell: "There was no king in Israel; everyone did what was right in his own eyes" (Judg. 21:25 NKJV). This repeated "There was no king in Israel" is intended to alert the reader of the text to the deadly spiritual vacuum that preceded the rise of kingship in Israel. In Germany in the 1930s, social, moral and national disarray prompted a groundswell for a strong and authoritarian leader who would "make the trains run on time". The German people, resentful of its treatment by the Allies after World War I, and facing economic and social meltdown, got the Nazis and Adolf Hitler! Israel got Saul!

A DEVOTIONAL INTERLUDE

Prayer: O Father I am aware that deep down in my heart I have longed all my life for someone to rule and reign over the forces and energies within me that are too strong for my feeble will to control. Now I have made You the King of my life – things are so different. You have filled this "deadly spiritual vacuum" that was in my heart. And how! Help me to give You sway over every part of my being. In Jesus' Name I pray. Amen.

DAY **126**

READ
1 Samuel 8

The moral and spiritual vacuum left by the period of the Judges stirs up popular clamour for a king and a deputation comes to Samuel to demand one. Sadly, the people ask for a king for the wrong reason and end up with the wrong man!

They ask for the wrong reason, demanding a king so as to be like every other nation – thus, directly repudiating Israel's destiny which was to be *unlike* any other nation.

Coming from a people meant to live "theocratically" – that is, directly under God's rule – it is tantamount to rejecting God Himself as King.

Furthermore, the "wrong man", Saul, is installed, whose obvious "head and shoulders" suitability, will soon compare poorly with David, the man "after God's own heart", and His choice.

God through Samuel concedes to their demand, perhaps because, since Abraham and Sarah's time, kingship has always been within His plan for Israel. But Samuel warns the people of the dire consequences of humanly contrived monarchy, foreseeing just how oppressive and self-serving the kings would become.

But if bad and power-hungry kings – and with few exceptions they were bad – misused kingship for their own ends, God remained capable of using the royal category for His own purpose and glory. In God's hands, the office of kingship was redeemable and might become redemptive.

A DEVOTIONAL INTERLUDE

To ponder: You take a certain risk when you ask God for something that you think is right for you, but does not conform to His will. He may give it to you, and you may not like it. Israel demanded a king but the one they got ended up ruining much of Israel and his life ended in tragedy. Be careful when you pray for something, to always add the phrase "but only if it be Your will". Remember, God always gives the best to those who leave the choice to Him.

DAY 127

READ
2 Samuel
19:39–20:2

In the disruption that follows Absalom's rebellion, David flees for his life across the Jordan. After Absalom's death which grieves David deeply, a coalition of troops from David's own tribe of Judah and from Israel, escort him back across the river. When the men of Israel complain at being upstaged by the men of Judah, they are told that such a course of action was obvious since David was a close kinsman of theirs. But, the men of Israel retort: "We have ten shares in the king . . .!" When this appeal cuts no ice, the Israelites are induced by a troublemaker to renounce their claim on the king and desert him by saying: "We have no share in David." And it's this language of having "shares in David" which is intriguing. It suggests that the king is an incorporative person, one who embodies his people, so that allegiance to him gives them an interest in him and makes the follower a part of his people. It's not too fanciful to see here the germ of an idea which will blossom again with telling effect in gospel times when those who follow Jesus Christ, the true Messianic King, are said to be "in Christ". Once more we see how crucial the right king is to the ongoing plan of God.

A DEVOTIONAL INTERLUDE

Thought: Dr Deismann, the German scholar, said that the phrase "in Christ" and its equivalent occurs no less than 164 times in Paul's writings. How much that concept must have meant to the apostle. How it sustained him in the work that he did for the Master. Let that same thought lie on your heart today. Meditate on it. Say to yourself "I am in Christ . . . and Christ is in me. I am safe from all that Satan would do to destroy me."

DAY **128**

READ
Psalm 72

True kingship is here celebrated for its justice, righteousness and concern for the poor, the afflicted and the weak. The lovely image of rain falling on mown grass (v.6) – briefly scented in David's rule (2 Sam. 23:4), suggests how deeply satisfying such a kingdom might be. To such a kingdom, all kings will be drawn as to a magnet (v.11). Through it will flow blessing for all nations as promised to Abraham (v.17).

This vision has inspired some of the greatest Christian hymns. In "Jesus shall reign where'er the sun" Isaac Watts shrewdly notes that this ideal King will not merely return things to their original state but will bring to fruition all the unfulfilled potential in God's creation:

Where He displays His healing power
Death and the curse are known no more
In Him the tribes of Adam boast
More blessings than their father lost.

The "more blessings" reminds us that redemption is an advance on creation, a decisive change for the better. And in "Hail to the Lord's Anointed", James Montgomery glories in the one constant factor:

The tide of time shall never
His covenant remove;
His name shall stand for ever,
His changeless name of love.

On this empire of God's true King, the sun will never set, and for us and our needy world, it can't come quickly enough!

A DEVOTIONAL INTERLUDE

Prayer: Father, my heart awaits the dawning of that great day when Jesus the King will return to establish His rule of righteousness in the earth. And I see that Your coming will not only return things to their original condition but will bring out the potential that because of sin was never fully realised. How wonderful. For me and for my brothers and sisters in Christ, it can't come quickly enough. Even so come Lord Jesus!

DAY **129**

READ
Psalm 110

This royal song became the most quoted psalm in the New Testament, applied to the Messiah.

First, the Lord – that is Yahweh – is heard by a subject of the king, addressing his royal "Lord". The king is promised an elevated place alongside God as His co-regent who will share in God's victory over His enemies. His troops will not be conscripts but willing volunteers in the fight. Verse 3b may be read literally as, "on the holy mountains, from the womb of the dawn, I have begotten you", so harking back to Psalm 2:7's picture of the king's coronation day. The dew at dawn imagery symbolises the life-giving hope offered by the king in a land noted for its parched summers.

The prophetic singer's second oracle singles out a priestly figure – modelled uniquely on the strange priest-king of Salem who met Abraham – who will triumph militarily, in the cause of God's just judgment. The picture in verse 7 may reflect a ritual which accompanied coronation (cf. 1 Kings 1:38–39). If this second declaration, like the first, was addressed to the Davidic king, then it is an unprecedented joining of the roles of priest and king – previously kept rigidly separate – in one person. The writer to the Hebrews, as we shall see, was not slow to exploit this prophetic song to glorify Jesus as the Son–Priest–King of God!

A DEVOTIONAL INTERLUDE

For praise: Give thanks to God today for the ministry of our Lord, which encompasses the role of Priest and King. Realise and rejoice in all that this means. As our great High Priest He represents us before God, prays for us and pleads for our deliverance from Satan's bondage. As King He rules and reigns over sin, self and the world. Now in your own words give God thanks for all the implications of this great truth in your life.

DAY **130**

READ
Psalm 132

The "ark of the covenant" was that wooden chest surmounted by cherubim which was the key piece of sacred furniture in the Temple. It acted as the earthly footstool of God's heavenly throne where God's holy presence was concentrated.

The entrance of the ark into the tabernacle in Jerusalem had sparked wild rejoicing (2 Sam. 6:1–15) and continued to inspire sublime songs like today's well-crafted psalm.

This old "ark song", once sung at the dedication of the Temple, would have stirred the faith of later pilgrims to the feasts (Psa. 132:8).

In it, four prayers of David (vv.1–10) are then perfectly matched by God's fourfold prophetic answer (vv.11–18).

When David asks that his oath of allegiance to the Lord be remembered, the Lord reminds him of the divine oath that guarantees the Davidic covenant promises!

When David leads the pleas that God would arise and come to His resting place, the Lord reassures king and people that Zion is indeed His chosen resting place.

The prayer for the priest to be clothed with righteousness is answered by the Lord's promise.

Finally, when David asks not to be rejected, he is overwhelmed by lavish pledges of future glory.

Marvellously, the fears, doubts, questions and prayers, even of the anointed king, are met and matched by God's unswerving covenant commitment!

A DEVOTIONAL INTERLUDE

For action: We see in today's reading that the entrance of the ark into the tabernacle sparked off wild rejoicing and inspired songs of praise and gratitude to God. Think of this: our Lord Jesus Christ died on a cross, was buried in a tomb, rose from the dead and has returned to His rightful place in heaven. Is not that a cause for "wild rejoicing"? Compose your own psalm of praise. Try it and see what it will do for your soul.

JESUS

ISRAEL / MOSES

DAVID

NEW COVENANT

DAY **131**

READ
Micah 3:5–5:4

The history of kingship after Solomon in the divided kingdom of Israel and Judah is the sad but not unfamiliar story of how power corrupts and absolute power corrupts absolutely. The prophets voiced God's passionate protest at this trend as they sought to recall both kings and people to covenantal standards. Where false prophets defended the status quo with a false sense of security, the true prophets, like Micah, shattered such complacency for the sake of a deeper peace (3:5–12).

God can start again if necessary with the most unlikely material – such as the bruised and homeless – in order to build a new people for Himself. He will make the "lame the nucleus of a nation" (4:6 Moffatt). They will be "a showcase exhibit of God's rule in action" (*The Message*) to which the nations will stream (4:2–5), no longer tearing each other apart but secure and at rest in the king's greatness (5:4–5). "He will stand and shepherd his flock in the strength of the Lord, in the majesty of the name of the Lord his God" (5:4). This ideal king holds the key to Israel's hope and the whole world's peace (5:3,5). God's plans are safe in his hands. And where else could this ideal king originate but in David's birthplace? (5:2). As Micah says, when it comes to the future, it's back to Bethlehem!

A DEVOTIONAL INTERLUDE

Prayer: O Father, I am so grateful that the plans You devise are guaranteed not to fail. They are in safe hands. I rejoice even more that my life is in Your hands. Scripture tells me that my life is hid with Christ in God. You have been holding up the universe for aeons and it is still intact, still runs with amazing mathematical precision. In Your hands I am safe and secure. Deepen that assurance within me. In Jesus' Name. Amen.

DAY 132

READ
Isaiah 8:16–9:7

As we said yesterday, the prophets clashed with the kings, holding them accountable to the covenant. This was particularly true of Isaiah, fighting for faith with a mistrustful king, Ahaz.

In response to total lack of faith, God is hiding His face from the king (8:17). As dawn light fails, unbelief turns from the light of the Torah and gropes for occult meaning in the darkness that descends (8:19–20)! Over all, death casts its long shadow (9:2).

But those who rally to the prophet's word of truth and become his disciples are shown the shining vision of another kingdom, the birth of another king (9:1–7). This Prince with the four names – will take the government back from fallible rulers onto His own broad shoulders.

Humiliation gives way to honour, darkness to light, despair to joy.

And the joy is even sweeter than over a bumper harvest, a victory in battle or freedom from oppression! There is no decline and fall of His empire, only continuous increase! The Davidic covenant comes good in and through this Prince of Peace (v.7). And if our zeal for God's work ever cools, we can be sure that God's never does (v.7). God remains infinitely more enthusiastic for His work and plans than we ever do. His passionate commitments will see this through!

A DEVOTIONAL INTERLUDE

Thought: How comforting to know that though sometimes our enthusiasm wanes and our love cools God's does not. Do you know someone whose love is consistent and whose enthusiasm for life (and perhaps for you) never changes? Multiply those qualities a billion times and you come near to understanding something of the passion for the Big Story to which God is committed. He is going to see this thing through – right to the end.

DAY **133**

READ
Isaiah 9:2–7

Let's relish again this stunning prophetic vision of the Prince with the fourfold name.

Here is the Wonderful Counsellor in a darkened world where so many have lost the light of God's truth and grope for answers in the twilight realm of their own opinions or the murky underworld of occultism and pseudo-science.

His wisdom is wonderful. He is the bearer of supernatural counsel.

Entrusted with the grand strategy of God, He can surely be trusted for the details of your life and mine.

Mighty God or – better – Mighty Warrior, this almighty little One, is a child born to us, who tips the balance of power in God's favour and therefore in ours, our champion in the battle for faith.

And the Son is also the Everlasting Father! Given to us is a royal child who becomes the source of eternal life to those who embrace His rule and find Him to be the Prince of Peace. And this is not peace at any price, but peace as the costly foundation of His kingdom.

If your faith seems a flickering candle in the wind, rekindle it at the great flame of this vision – a vision which was one day enacted in a life on fire for God, a bush that burned but was not consumed by crucifixion, that burst forth from the shadow of death in a blaze of resurrection light which will one day flood the earth in glory.

A DEVOTIONAL INTERLUDE

To ponder: One Bible teacher claims that "Wonderful Counsellor" can be translated: "As a counsellor he is a wonder". Jesus Christ is the only counsellor who doesn't need counselling Himself. The two main resources of a counsellor are knowledge (how problems arise) and wisdom (how to rightly apply that knowledge). Jesus is the fount of all knowledge and wisdom. And it's all available – free of charge – for you and me.

DAY **134**

READ
Isaiah 11

Isaiah now speaks of impossibilities happening, a new shoot from the root of Jesse, David's father.

All along, Isaiah has been convinced that God cuts down only to start again, that from the decimated stump of judgment, grace can flow into new life (6:13). The Assyrian oppressors of God's people will themselves be cut down never to rise again (10:34) but from the stump and root of David's line, amazingly new life will sprout and grow into a Branch (11:1) to be the leader, judge and standard-bearer of the nations.

His humble beginnings (v.1) only highlight the fact that He qualifies to rule (vv.1–3) only by His endowment with God's Spirit. This reminds us of the wild "wind of God" ("*ruach*") which had invaded David, marking him as God's appointee. The Spirit heightens our awareness of the solemn joys of living with the awesome majesty of God. He will draw breath in the fear of the Lord as if the very atmosphere is charged with grandeur. To fear God in this way is to know that rush of spiritual adrenaline in the presence of holiness.

With such a ruler comes a vision of a transformed earth (vv.6–9). Creation's unrest is pacified by an Adamic dominion cleansed of unrighteousness. Noah take note! The earth will be brimful of knowing God! The nations – Abraham are you watching? – will rally to His banner!

A DEVOTIONAL INTERLUDE

Thought: Humble beginnings can be of great significance when God is in them. An unknown poet wrote this:

I said Master, where shall I work today,
And my love flowed warm and free
And he pointed to a little plot and said,
There, tend that for me.
But Lord, I said, not that, not that little place for me.
And his voice when it spoke was soft and warm,
Bethlehem was just a little place – and so was Galilee.

DAY 135

READ
Jeremiah
22–23:8

Being a King during Jeremiah's time was often a very uncomfortable experience. The prophet gives the kings a hard time.

Chapter 22 is a savage indictment of the kings in Judah for their injustice, ostentation and self-seeking – a sadly familiar litany of abuses of power. In contrast to his father, Josiah, Shallum is upbraided for failing to defend the poor (22:11–17). Knowing the Lord is not a matter of having exalted religious experiences of God but of practising social justice. If you don't do justly, you don't "know" God.

From this sorry scene, Jeremiah turns in a burst of prophetic hope to depict the grace that will emerge triumphant out of judgment. Uncaring, false shepherds who have misled and scattered God's sheep will be supplanted by God Himself who will regather and grow the flock (23:1–4). God will raise up a righteous Branch in David's line (v.5). This King will reign wisely and be known as "The Lord Our Righteousness" (v.6). This is an ironic twist in the story. The name of Judah's last, disgraced king, Zedekiah, means "Yahweh is righteous". But where he failed to live up to his name, the future King will embody God's righteousness.

Through this King God will not only bring social stability and well-being (vv.4–6) but will bring His people home in a radical new exodus which will eclipse the memory of the first (vv.7–8)!

A DEVOTIONAL INTERLUDE

Hymn: What better response can we give to today's reading than to sing with all the enthusiasm possible:

Rejoice the Lord is King,
Your lord and King adore
Mortals give thanks and sing,
And triumph evermore,
Lift up your voice, lift up your voice;
Rejoice, again I say, Rejoice.

DAY **136**

READ
Ezekiel 34

In trying to stay on the track of the promise given to David, we have already seen how the kings who followed him both in Israel and Judah, proved, almost without exception, to be both unworthy recipients of the magnificent promises God had made to him, and unfaithful stewards of God's long-term plan to bless the world through them.

Nowhere are these royal failings more ruthlessly exposed than in this prophecy of Ezekiel.

Because the king carries within himself the whole nation's destiny, his disloyalty brings ruin to the people. So God holds the royal shepherds accountable and acts to remove them from office. But as is typical of the prophets, judgment is not God's final word. The demise of kingship in Judah at the Babylonian Exile, clears the way for a renewed appreciation of God as the only true King and Shepherd of His people.

And Ezekiel speaks a strangely ambiguous hope of the coming of a true Shepherd who, at one and the same time, is God Himself – come to do the shepherding job that has been so badly neglected – and a Prince of the house of David sent to restore His people. A good shepherd who is both God and the Davidic king? We haven't heard the last of this, that's for sure. And what is unambiguous is that He will usher in the long-awaited day of covenant fulfilment and salvation!

A DEVOTIONAL INTERLUDE

Prayer: O Father, I pray today for those who are shepherding Your flock – Your precious under-shepherds – that You will keep them and protect them from evil. They are the special targets of the devil's strategies and they can easily get discouraged, become dysfunctional. Bind Satan's power in their lives and anoint them afresh to preach and teach Your Word. I ask this in and through the precious Name of Jesus. Amen.

DAY **137**

READ
Isaiah 55

In a bustling market-place, street-traders shout out their special offers to grab the attention of passers-by. In the Exile, as now, cultural airwaves are jammed with conflicting ideas and opinions.

Into this babble of competing truth-claims, God speaks the word which is above all words, an invitation of pure grace.

We are rightly suspicious of free offers but this one, while free, will cost us "nothing less than everything" (vv.6–7)! But it invites us to satisfy our hunger and quench our thirst at the only source of true satisfaction for our souls.

Above all, God offers us a part in an alternative story to the one peddled by the Babylonian media, the true story of God's redemptive plans. Everyone is promised a role in making history with God. God's covenant with David – that "charter for all humanity" through the Davidic king – is here democratised and opened up to all who repent and believe (vv.3–5)! David's "sure mercies" are here extended to all who rally to the true King.

Like the earlier covenants, this "everlasting covenant" (v.3) will have a sign attached to it – unlike before, an everlasting sign which is nothing less than a resplendently transformed creation (v.13).

God's final covenant will not cancel out all the previous ones – reviewed in chapter 54 – but will fulfil and perfect them. What a God!

A DEVOTIONAL INTERLUDE

To ponder: What a God indeed! Have you ever considered that the way our personality works is like this: what we think about affects the way we feel and how we feel affects the way we act. Throughout the day ponder this truth: "Everyone is promised a role in making history with God." The more you think on that, the more it should affect your emotions and move you to deeper dedication. The best way to prove that theory is to put it to the test.

JESUS

ISRAEL / MOSES

DAVID

NEW COVENANT

DAY **138**

READ
Luke 1:26-56

We have traced the trajectory of the covenant made with David through the rise and fall of kingship in Israel and now to its fulfilment, a thousand years later, in a baby born to a young up-country girl in Nazareth. Betrothed but not yet married to Joseph, Mary knew that any son born to her would be a dim-distant descendant of David. But what kind of son and descendant was pure revelation to her.

Gabriel tells Mary that her child is set to inherit the enduring throne and never-ending kingdom promised to David.

As for the special father–son relationship with God this would be assured from conception by God's creative Spirit who will "overshadow" her as God's glory cloud "overshadowed" the tabernacle. This royal Son's birth truly marks the dawn of a new creation, and a new start for God's people.

Through Mary's son, the Davidic covenant will find its climax and be fulfilled (v.32), Israel will be remembered by the Lord and mercifully restored (v.54), and the Abrahamic promises will be honoured (v.55)! Favoured by God, she joyfully responds with obedient co-operation – the very model of what it meant to be a true Israelite.

But what she had learned about her son remained a treasured secret for over thirty years until the joy she felt at his being part of her body was eclipsed by her being part of His body!

A DEVOTIONAL INTERLUDE

Question: In some sections of the Church Mary's role is overplayed while in others it is underplayed. What a choice young woman she must have been to be selected as the mother of Jesus. Consider the way in which she responded to the announcement that she had been impregnated by the Holy Spirit: "May it be to me as you have said." When God asks you to do something for Him is your response as quick and decisive?

DAY **139**

READ
Luke 2:1–15

In his opening chapters, Luke is painting with broad brush strokes, writing what amounts to a remake of the story of kingship in Israel, especially its beginnings. So in Luke's parallelism, John the Baptist is acting as Samuel to Jesus' David. And this is set on the even larger canvas of the Roman Empire and its Caesars to make an immediate point. Jesus is Israel's true King, come at last to take His place on the throne of Israel and the world. Just as Samuel spelt judgment for the house of Saul and the priesthood of Eli, so the birth of John and the advent of Jesus spell judgment on King Herod and the current house of Israel. And the map of international power must be redrawn.

Where Rome issued a "*euangellion*" or "gospel" to announce the emperor's birthday or success in battle, the angel declares the real good news in this baby's birth (2:10–11). The child born in Bethlehem is Israel's long-awaited Messiah who will reclaim from Caesar the self-appointed title of "Saviour of the world". And this Christ, as Psalm 2 had announced so long before, was destined to usurp the Caesars – and any other claimants – as the rightful Lord of God's world! His peace, unlike Rome's peace (the "*pax Romana*") would be founded not on the crosses of its victims but on the cross on which He would suffer.

A DEVOTIONAL INTERLUDE

Prayer: Lord Jesus Christ, I have thanked You time and time again for dying for me on the cross but I realise that I can never thank you enough! I am touched to the depth of my soul that You would give Your life for me, a sordid sinner, but even more for the fact that, in reclaiming this world for Yourself, you have included me in Your Story. It's almost too good to be true. But too good not to be true. Amen.

DAY 140

READ
Luke 3:21–4:13

As Jesus was baptised, the voice from heaven said: "You are my Son."

We last heard these words in Psalm 2 and 2 Samuel 7. There God promised the Davidic dynasty a unique father–son relationship with Him in which the king could call God his Father and God would look on the king as His son. So, as we fast forward to two men, standing, soaked through, on the bank of the River Jordan, we see the Holy Spirit single out one of them, and alight upon Him. At which the heavens open and God points out Jesus as His Son.

So, whatever else we come to know about Jesus of Nazareth, at least we know for sure that He is Israel's anointed King who inherits the Davidic mantle and promises. Luke underlines this by giving Jesus' family tree and tracing His ancestry back to David. Not only back to David, however, but through David right back to Adam, "son of God". Jesus, the Messiah, takes up the human mantle and inherits the vocation to have dominion.

It is precisely in His royal human vocation as Son of God that Jesus is then tested. But, like David before Him striding out to meet and defeat Goliath, Jesus meets and routs out the age-old enemy of humanity.

Where the first Adam failed, the second Adam succeeds and comes to our fight and rescue.

A DEVOTIONAL INTERLUDE

Thought: The story is told of Greig, the composer, who, sitting in a hotel in Oslo, heard one of his songs being sung by a woman in the next room. Unable to contain himself, he went to her door and said to her, "That is how my songs should be sung!" God does something like this at our Lord's baptism. He breaks in, so to speak, on the life of Jesus and shouts: That is how My life should be lived. What a life! What a death! What a Saviour.

DAY **141**

READ
Mark 1:1–18

After His investiture at the Jordan River, Jesus proclaims the good news of God. The word "gospel" needs serious attention. It is not a blank cheque to be filled in at our discretion. As Jesus uses it, it has two reference points: one that establishes its content; one that points up a contrast.

Its content stems from its Old Testament usage, particularly in Isaiah (Isa. 40:9; 52:7) who identifies the "good news" as the announcement of God's return as King. The contrast is with the use of the concept by the Roman emperor who applied the term "good news" to a public proclamation of his birthday or military victory.

The time for God's kingdom to come is here, says Jesus. The time for the Caesars to be upstaged and threatened by the world's real Lord is now! God's kingdom is not so much a realm or territory as His saving reign, His active rule in the affairs of this world. Because of its upside-down nature, God's kingdom is brought home to us in parable and metaphor. But its effects are felt in the miracles and healing and exorcisms Jesus performs. When Jesus forgives sins and welcomes sinners to eat with Him, then the kingdom has come.

It is to serve the cause of God's kingdom that Jesus commands recruits to His disciple band (vv.16–17). It's high time to repent, believe, come and follow!

A DEVOTIONAL INTERLUDE

To ponder: The biblical equivalent of "ponder" is meditate. And meditation has been described as "holding a thought like a sweet on the tip of your tongue and sucking every precious drop from it". Take the thought suggested that God's kingdom is upside down and suck every precious drop from it. Here are a few starters: We lose to gain, we die in order to live, we become slaves in order to be free. Now over to you.

DAY **142**

READ
Matthew 21:1–11

When Jesus eventually enters Jerusalem after three years of ministry, He causes great excitement.

He comes there for a final showdown. And there is a certain inevitability about His arrival.

After all, where else would a king in Israel come to be crowned?

The crowds certainly greet Him as a Messianic claimant, with their cries of "Hosanna to the Son of David!"

But His manner of entering the city is strange and disturbing, reminiscent of David's own disconcerting entry a thousand years before (2 Sam. 6).

Clearly the procession Jesus is leading is purely a symbolic one. No heavily armed troops accompany Him. He is not making a serious attempt at a coup d'etat or palace revolution. In the crowded city, Jesus causes a stir by enacting a piece of political street-theatre to symbolise what kind of kingdom He is bringing. He rides in on a donkey, the least militaristic animal available, in conscious echo of Zechariah's poignant prophecy. By this odd, almost eccentric action, He subverts current expectations of how kings act, and in particular, how Israel's king might act at a time when armed revolution against the occupying Romans was in the air. At the same time it is a winsome appeal to Israel to change before disaster strikes.

A DEVOTIONAL INTERLUDE

Thought: There is nothing dignified about a donkey – from any angle it lacks what we call "presence". Whoever heard of a conqueror riding on an ass? Yet we read that the Lord needed him. There is a parable in this. No matter how ordinary, ill educated, disabled, ill born, talented or obscure a man or woman may be Christ has use for them. The world may not know your name, but rejoice that it is written in the Lamb's book of life.

DAY **143**

READ
Matthew 21:12–17

The Temple had been David's original idea, his son Solomon built it, and two of Israel's better kings, Hezekiah and Josiah, had cleansed and restored it. It was the king's role to be the Temple builder.

But, like His entry on a donkey, Jesus' so-called cleansing of the Temple is, in effect, an acted parable of judgment

It is not simply a critique of economic corruption, since, in any case, it is doubtful if there was anything intrinsically wrong with changing common currency into Temple coinage in order to buy the requisite sacrifices. But, the Temple was meant to be a "house of prayer for all nations" (Isa. 56:7), and its current role as a focus of nationalism threatens to deny the Gentiles their intended blessings. And as if to dramatise how drastically different God's kingdom is, Jesus opens the Temple courts to the sick and ritually excluded. When David originally attacked Jerusalem, its Jebusite defenders mocked him, saying, "Even the blind and lame can ward you off" (2 Sam. 5:6). Afterwards, David turned the taunt back on the lame and blind who are David's enemies (2 Sam. 5:8). This, says the ancient historian, explains the proverb: "The blind and lame shall not enter the palace!" But no proverbial saying is going to stop King Jesus opening His doors to the lame and blind and healing them!

A DEVOTIONAL INTERLUDE

For praise: What other response can we give to today's reading than to sing out in praise to God a verse taken from the hymn: "O for a thousand tongues to sing".

Hear Him, ye deaf; His praise, ye dumb,
Your loosened tongues employ;
Ye blind, behold your Saviour come,
And leap, ye lame, for joy.

DAY 144

READ
Acts 2:22–36

If this scripture teaches us anything it is that there is nothing superficial about events or people but that a deeper design is discernible beneath the surface. To all appearances, Jesus of Nazareth was a discredited Messianic pretender. But in reality He is the centre-piece of God's age-old plan to bring salvation to the world. The cross which looks like a defeat turns out to be the victorious crux of all God's aims. The worst that men can do, turns out to be the best that God can do! Such deep paradox at the heart of God's workings requires the resurrection to overturn the verdict of God's enemies and stand scepticism on its head. Similarly, when Peter quotes David's life and words, he is not simply finding useful analogies to Jesus but bringing to the surface the deep underlying connections in Scripture. So David is a prophetic person whose part in the plan of God carries the seeds of its greater fulfilment in Jesus. David both spoke and lived "more than he knew" when he anticipated a triumph over death only realisable by the Messiah's resurrection from the dead (Psa. 16) and subsequent enthronement (Psa. 110).

God's tough and persistent determination – shown in Psalm 2 – to make His Anointed King in Israel, Lord of the world, comes good in Jesus, whom Peter proclaims as Lord and Christ.

A DEVOTIONAL INTERLUDE

Prayer: O Father how grateful I am that I am in the hands of a God who can take the worst that men can do and turn it into the best You can do. The things I call stumbling blocks are really stepping-stones, the setbacks are really springboards. All things serve me when I serve You. Whatever happens turns out through You to my advantage. I am so thankful. Amen.

DAY **145**

READ
Acts 4

Psalm 2 again comes into its own to help explain the deeper issue at stake in the seemingly random crucifixion of a Galilean preacher.

Just as God's salvation comes to its climax in the events of Easter, so does the long battle with evil. By referring to Psalm 2, the apostles are not merely comforting themselves with an apt scripture, but rising to the conviction that they are part of God's bigger and better story.

Herod and Pilate are unlikely bedfellows, showing that sin dupes us all into being unwitting conspirators against God and his Anointed King. But Herod and Pilate, of course, are really mere stooges, the front men for darker forces.

Pit your puny pragmatism against God's mighty eternal plans and you find yourself outwitted and outdone at every turn.

Congratulating themselves on a job well done, His enemies might roll down their sleeves, having washed their hands of this troublesome young prophet. But He just won't go away. Their lasting frustration will be to discover just how much they have contributed to their own defeat and His own triumph!

If this is the case then the persecuted disciples of such a sovereign Lord and servant-King, rebound from setbacks as irrepressible people, praying irresistible prayers, and proclaiming an unstoppable gospel.

A DEVOTIONAL INTERLUDE

For praise: Thank God that through His Word you have learned one of life's deepest secrets – namely that in Him nothing can work successfully against you. The wind can blow from any direction but it will only drive you towards the goal of making you more like Jesus Christ. Everything can be used by those who are in Christ. You may be knocked down but you cannot be kept down and when you come up you will come up smiling. All because of Him.

DAY **146**

READ
Acts 13:13–52

This powerful sermon preached by Paul to the synagogue in Antioch is rich in Davidic allusions and echoes. Sweeping from Abraham through Moses and Israel's election down to the days of Samuel and Saul, Paul's survey of the earlier stages of God's story, focuses on the link between Jesus and David. Scriptures that we have already recognised as significant – Psalm 2, Isaiah 55, Psalm 16 – feature in Paul's gripping account of how God's dealings with the patriarchs and chosen people have channelled down through David to Jesus. The framework which enables Paul to discern the coherence of God's plan in the Scriptures is that of "promise and fulfilment".

For Paul, God's over-arching promise-plan has reached its intended goal in Jesus (v.32). To preach the gospel is precisely to declare the good news that everything God promised to the fathers has now come to fruition in Jesus Christ. The raising of Jesus from the dead is His coronation as Son–King, in line with Psalm 2, the "sure mercies" promised to David's people in Isaiah, and the protection from decay for which the royal psalmist hopefully sang.

The enormous emphasis on the resurrection in the proclamation of the good news may come as a surprise to us modern Christians. But to the apostles it was the beating heart of their message of hope.

A DEVOTIONAL INTERLUDE

Thought: When did you last hear a sermon on Christ's resurrection? Today's Church tends to emphasise it only at Easter. The early disciples made much of the cross but seemed to make more of the resurrection. Consider this: had there been no resurrection there would be no salvation. The cross was a wonderful event, but had He not risen from the dead we would not be saved. Think about that today.

DAY **147**

READ
Acts 15

The synod in Jerusalem, attended by apostles and elders, marks a crucial turning point in the early history of the Church. Under James's wise, Spirit-directed leadership, it resolved any doubts about the terms on which Gentiles could be included in God's covenant family. The prophets had said that God would first restore His people Israel and then the Gentiles would come in. Only this sequence, perhaps, explains why the apostles had strangely held back from obeying the great commission in order to concentrate on the Jewish mission. Events, however, had taken a seemingly different tack. How could they square a largely hostile Jewish reaction to Jesus with the eager response shown by the Gentiles now flocking into the kingdom? There could be only one answer: in some mysterious way, Israel must have already been restored in and through Jesus! For scriptural support for the conclusion of the council, James fastens on the prophet Amos' vision of a restored Davidic house. In David's unique tabernacle in Jerusalem, the psalms were sung that summoned the nations to praise the one true God (1 Chron. 16). It was a foretaste of worship in the Spirit in God's kingdom. Now, both Jew and Gentile in Christ call gladly and joyfully on the Name of the Lord.

A DEVOTIONAL INTERLUDE

Praise: Do you know this well-known hymn? If so lift your heart in praise and give thanks to God for the promise of His glorious return:

Sing we the King who is coming to reign,
Glory to Jesus, the Lamb that was slain;
Life and salvation His empire shall bring,
Joy to the nations when Jesus is King.

DAY **148**

READ
Romans 1:1–5

The gospel recalls God's promises, and evokes God's initiatives.

God's promises, which stretch back to Abraham, explode with colour in the visions of Israel's great prophets. They see a kingdom coming, a new era of forgiveness and justice, of exile ended and homecoming to God's gracious rule. The gospel is the public declaration that God has kept His word!

Central to it is God's Son, Jesus. At one level, His Sonship is a royal and Jewish sonship as befits a descendant of King David. This Sonship was lived out on the level of our normal fleshly human existence, marked by weakness and limitation. But this same Jesus has been declared to be the "Son-of-God-with-power" Son of God! Raised from the dead, He eclipses everything David was and fulfils everything David stood for. His resurrection has launched Him into a new sphere of human existence characterised by the unlimited power and possibilities of God's creative Spirit. The resurrection happened in history but came from beyond history as the mighty inrush of God's coming kingdom. This Jesus is truly Israel's Messiah and the world's true Lord, claiming the allegiance of everyone, everywhere, and commissioning heralds, like Paul, to go through the Roman Empire and beyond to announce His accession to the world's throne!

A DEVOTIONAL INTERLUDE

To ponder: Let this powerful and weighty text lie upon your mind throughout the day and draw from it the inspiration you need to face whatever are the difficulties confronting you at this moment:

> And if the Spirit of him who raised Jesus from the dead is living in you, he who raised Christ from the dead will also give life to your mortal bodies through his Spirit, who lives in you. (Romans 8:11)

READ
Hebrews 1

God's previous revelation, varied and fragmented as it was, is now gathered up in completed form and offered to us in Jesus.

When I was young, a board stood outside our local newsagent on which was scrawled the breaking news only briefly covered in the midday editions of the newspapers but with the added promise of the "full story in the final edition".

This is exactly what Jesus is to the Old Testament stage of God's plan. What was only partially said before is now fully said in Jesus. What was provisional is now final in Him. Whereas, before, God spoke through God's servants, now He has spoken through His Son. Jesus, God's Son, is the full and final edition of all God wants to say to us.

God's story has already entered its "last days" – not as the end of the space–time world as we know it – but as the culmination of the long progress of God's promise-plan.

Not surprisingly, the flood of Old Testament truth comes in like a tidal wave.

Seven quotations from the Old Testament in verses 5–14 rush to the spot like iron filings drawn to a magnet to confirm the vision of Jesus given in verses 1–3, of Jesus as royal heir apparent, as mediator of creation, as enjoying eternal glory, and as exalted to God's right hand.

It's all come together in God's time and God's Son! Who can say more or afford to neglect this? (2:1–4).

A DEVOTIONAL INTERLUDE

Thought: People unread in comparative religions say one religion is as good as another, which is actually a judgement of ignorance. Certainly there are fine things in other faiths. But Christianity is not one religion amongst others, it is in a category all by itself. Christ is the Light of the world. We are not unmindful of other lamps but He is the only One who illuminates the world with the truth about God. For He is God.

DAY 150

READ
Revelation 1:4–7

When John wants to comfort and encourage the churches he pastors, his top priority is a fresh vision of Jesus. In his pastoral letter, top billing is given to Jesus, the faithful witness, answering any doubt about His reliability. In Him is true and trustworthy testimony to the reality of who God is. Intriguingly, the book of Revelation, while never explicitly quoting the Old Testament, is soaked through with allusions to it. Jesus is the climax to the Scriptures, the conclusive witness to all that God has said. That He is the firstborn from the dead answers any worries about his being still alive. Jesus inherits the ascription to which the Messianic King was entitled (Psa. 89:26f), giving him priority in His Father's affairs. Because He has won this right through dying and rising, He is the pioneer of many who will follow Him in resurrection glory. He is the ruler of the kings of the earth, assuming the messianic mantle (Psa. 2:7; Psa. 89:27), so answering any fears as to who is ultimately in charge of our world. All this John's readers needed to know, oppressed as they were by a pervasive Roman Imperial power. And they need be in no doubt that this faithful firstborn, ever-living Jesus – whose death frees them from their sins – loves them still. He couldn't love us less; He can't love us more!

A DEVOTIONAL INTERLUDE

To ponder: How different is the love of God from human love! Our love changes with circumstances. Consider as you go through the day that "Jesus could not love us less nor love us more". Nothing in us gave rise to it, and nothing in us can extinguish it. "There is no greater security in life," said someone, "than knowing that we are loved with a love that will never be taken away." That's the kind of love that fills our hearts.

DAY **151**

READ
Revelation 5

We have come a long way from the image of David with his dreams dashed. But the outcome of God's promise-plan is still sufficiently uncertain as to reduce John to tears, that no one seems qualified to effect God's final will for the world's redemption. Then, in the Spirit, he sees the Lion-King silhouetted on the skyline of history. Here is David's descendant, custodian of the scroll of God's covenant purposes for all mankind, the only one worthy to implement God's plans. He has reclaimed, for His Father on the throne, the praise of "every creature in heaven and on earth" (v.13) of which Noah was a lonely pioneer. He is the Lord of the world and the King of kings, head over an international multitude no more capable of being counted than Abraham could count the stars in the night sky. And it all began with David's disappointment at the dashing of his dreams! But God can do "far more than you could ever imagine or guess or request in your wildest dreams" (Eph. 3:20 *The Message*).

The evidence is Jesus, the High King of heaven, and heaven's bright sun; the keeper of the keys of David (Rev. 3:7) that open the door to God's eternal kingdom. Beyond this door, there are no tears or broken dreams, no disappointment or regret. Beyond this door, there is no night: it's always bright and sun-drenched morning.

A DEVOTIONAL INTERLUDE

Quotation: "Shattered dreams are never random," Dr Larry Crabb says. "They are always a piece in a larger puzzle, a chapter in a larger story. The Holy Spirit uses the pain of shattered dreams to help us discover our desire for God, to help us begin dreaming the highest dream which when realised will release a new song, sing with tears until God wipes them away and we sing with nothing but joy in our hearts."

NOAH
all creation

ABRAHAM
all nations

ISRAEL
one nation

DAVID
representative king

NEW COVENANT
FAITHFUL COVENANT PARTNER

JESUS
faithful covenant partner

JESUS
Davidic King Messiah

JESUS
the New Israel

JESUS
the world's Lord

JESUS
the truly Human One crowned with glory and honour

JESUS
cosmic Ruler in God's new creation new heavens and new earth

SECTION 7
THE PROPHETIC VISION

God is committed to changing his people from the inside out – the prophetic vision

When the Babylonians over-ran Judah and started deportations to Babylonia around 606 BC, there began the most traumatic period in Israel's history since the Exodus.

Three pictures from Scripture vividly highlight for us both the reasons for the Exile and the reactions to it.

Firstly, in memorable imagery, Jeremiah lamented the persistent disobedience of kings and people and their deep-seated inability to alter their uncovenantal patterns of behaviour: "Can the Ethiopian change his skin or the leopard its spots? Neither can you do good who are accustomed to doing evil" (Jer. 13:23).

This is the reason why God has judged His people and sent them into exile (cf. 2 Chron. 15–21).

Secondly, the reaction to Exile when it happened is poignantly expressed in Psalm 137 with its vivid echoes of the "day the music died" by the rivers of Babylon when harps were hung, discarded, on the willow trees and the plaintive question hung in the air: "How can we sing the songs of the Lord while in a foreign land?" (v.4).

The book of Lamentations is a great outpouring of grief which graphically captures the sense of national bereavement. Loss of kingship, Temple and land must have seemed terminal, ending Israel's unique identity and destiny – even perhaps spelling the death of God Himself.

So, in a third vivid metaphor, the prophet, Ezekiel, himself one of the first to be taken to Babylon, pictured the state of Israel as a valley full of bleached and dry bones – one vast graveyard – and he too left a question hanging in the air: "Can these bones live?" (37:3).

But buried deep in the pain was a glimmer of hope: "Because of the Lord's great love we are not consumed, for his compassions never fail. They are new every morning; great is your faithfulness" (Lam. 3:22–23).

There is hope because God is faithful to His covenant.

Jeremiah's response is twofold.

With life in Babylonia an accomplished fact, Jeremiah urges the exiles to accept their situation in Exile with realism not wishful thinking (Jer. 23). But he also urges them by a flight of imagination to envisage salvation beyond Exile in the promise of a new covenant (Jer. 31:31–34).

God will make the covenant effective with His people by working on both sides of the covenant relationship. He will give His people a new disposition to obey Him, a fresh reassurance of belonging to Him, an unprecedented knowledge of God that works social justice, and a deep and lasting forgiveness of sins!

Ezekiel added to this hope with his vision of a transformed people, washed and cleansed, with an entirely new heart empowered by the very Spirit of God to live in covenant loyalty with God! (Ezek. 36).

The question too, "Can the dead bones live?" God answers with a vision of "resurrection from the dead" (Ezek. 37).

But, of course, not only the people but the kings have consistently failed and so the prophets of Exile, as we have seen, begin to project hopes of a new kingship.

God would raise up a new David (Jer. 23:5), accompanied by or identical with the coming of God Himself to be the Shepherd–Ruler of His people (Ezek. 34).

Isaiah proclaims the "good news" of God's kingdom as God Himself leads the Exiles home across the desert, returning as King in Zion, at the centre of His people's life again to establish justice and peace and salvation (Isa. 40:9–10; 52:7f).

But Isaiah's unique contribution is to show that none of this will take effect except through the shameful suffering and ignominious death of a mysterious servant of God.

We have noted the tragic irony before, that Exodus and Exile – are the two poles around which the Old Testament story of Israel revolves. From slavery in Egypt – so the story runs – to slavery in Babylonia – where Abraham had come from to begin the faith journey over 1,000 years earlier! But the hopes of the Exilic prophets are even more remarkable.

Exodus gave birth to a nation for God out of slavery through deliverance and redemption. Exile yields promise of a new people of God redeemed this time out of the deeper slavery of sin through "death and resurrection".

Here then is the prophetic vision: the new covenant community – a community newly motivated to obey God, deeply secure in belonging to God and being His people, with an all-pervading God-consciousness – a grateful community of forgiven-forgivers; a community empowered by the creative Spirit of God, under the Lordship of God through His appointed Messiah, the foretaste of a brand new creation!

This depiction of new covenant realities begins to sound very much like a description of vibrant Christian experience – like that described in Acts 2! And, praise God, that's exactly what it is!

DAY 152

READ
Psalm 137
Lamentations 3

Psalm 137 poignantly captures emotions felt by the Exiles beside the "rivers of Babylon" in shoulder-shrugging mood.

"There on the poplars we hung our harps" sums up the futility induced by despair. Pain has paralysed praise. Mockery mercilessly picks at their emotional wound (v.3). How can we sing the Lord's song in a strange land? Unwilling to forget Jerusalem, the exiles struggle with the bitter-sweet burden of memory. In the end, the dark violence of the victimised spirit, erupts in a raging resentment from which we recoil (vv.8–9). But better that such anger is heaped on God in prayer than hurled at people in vengeance!

This emotional intensity caused by Exile is matched only in the book of Lamentations – the most "tear-stained book" in the Old Testament" – a grief-stricken litany of national bereavement.

From the first deportation in 606 BC down to the demise of Jerusalem in around 586, the protracted Babylonian conquest of Judah brought the long slow death of a nation.

But, although God's heart "breaks" over His people's failure and disgrace, His heart does not "fail" (3:19–25). His covenant faithfulness proves greater than our failure. A new day of His mercy dawns on the long night of our shame. Fresh hopes are pinned on this God who "turns all our sunsets into sunrise".

A DEVOTIONAL INTERLUDE

Prayer: My Father and my God, whenever I feel in exile help me let You be my home as well as bringing me home. Help me not only understand that You are my Hiding Place, my Shelter in the time of storm, my Rock and my Fortress, but show me how to lean on You, to trust You and give myself to You in such a way that the theory becomes fact. I want this to be my experience – always. Grant it Father in Jesus' Name. Amen.

DAY 153

READ
Ezekiel 37

To many of the exiles taken to Babylonia, the loss of kingship, Temple and land must have seemed the virtual end of everything, the end of Israel's unique identity and destiny – even perhaps the death of God Himself.

The prophet, Ezekiel, himself one of the first deportees, saw the state of Israel, in prophetic vision, as a valley full of bleached and dry bones – one vast cemetery with the dead humiliatingly left unburied, for the vultures to strip the carcasses, and the elements to dismember the skeletons! But there is hope.

Challenged as to how these bones can live again, the prophet – shrewdly enough – puts the onus back on the Lord: "O Sovereign Lord, only you know!"

Commanded to prophesy to the bones, he does so and the bones come together again and flesh re-forms. Told to prophesy to the "*ruach*" or "breath" or "wind", the prophet obeys and the very breath or Spirit of God enters into the bodies and they stand on their feet – a living army of God – raised, as it were, from the dead!

This establishes a crucial pattern or model for God's work.

Salvation and restoration, it appears, lie on the other side of Exile, that is, on the other side of "death and resurrection" and by the Spirit's empowerment.

A DEVOTIONAL INTERLUDE

Thought: Dwell for a few moments before you go out into the day on the glorious fact that you have been re-born through the power of the Holy Spirit and have become part of a people empowered by the Holy Spirit. Think of it – the same Holy Spirit who rested on Jesus and filled His life with power and joy is resting on you and is in you. Could there be anything more wonderful in earth or in heaven? If so then we have still to hear of it.

DAY **154**

READ
Isaiah 43

As we look back on the extraordinary start which Israel had as a nation, it would seem hard to improve on its dramatic evidence of God's power at work to save. From the plagues which tested Pharaoh's resolve, through the miraculous protection from death on Passover night, to the parting of the Red Sea, the Exodus seems unsurpassable as an intervention of God. But the first Exodus from enslavement in Egypt is destined to be eclipsed in a new and greater Exodus – this time from slavery in Babylon (vv.16–21)!

In fact so remarkably will God act to bring His people back from captivity that He urges them to forget the former things and not to dwell on the past (v.18)! Whereas, once, He made a dry way through the sea; now He proposes to make streams flow in the desert (vv.16,20). Either way, nothing is impossible to God when He acts to bring salvation to His people. The first Exodus is but a parable of a future, final Exodus. Israel's God is the One Creator God. He is not bound by His past, nor exhausted by His past achievements. Only our persistent sin and lack of trust in Him weary Him (v.24). But even our past cannot cripple God (v.25). He has a reputation to maintain for making new starts and so He forgives! And the forgiven – and only the forgiven – have a future

---

A DEVOTIONAL INTERLUDE

For action: If it is true (and it is) that only the forgiven have a great and glorious future then it follows that the unforgiven face an eternity where all is gloom and sadness. Ought not this stir our hearts to pray more passionately and persistently for those in our circle of loved ones and friends who do not yet know Christ? Put a fence around fifteen minutes of your day and intercede for them.

DAY **155**

READ
Jeremiah
31:31–34

As a key feature of the new and greater Exodus coming to His people, God will create a new and better covenant arrangement with them. The covenant promised now will not be like the covenant which bound Israel to God at Sinai but which has broken down (v.32). Not that there was anything wrong with that "old" covenant.

The prophet makes clear that the fault lay not on the "divine side" of the covenant relationship but on the human side, with Israel's persistent inability and unwillingness to keep covenant: "they broke my covenant" (32b).

Four elements of this wonderful new covenant promise are spelt out: first of all, God promises to give to His people what we might call "a new disposition to obey Him" – He promises to "put my law in their minds and write it on their hearts" (v.33).

This is not so much a change of law as a change in the way the covenant is administered. The law – previously external to the people, written on tablets of stone – is now to be internalised and imprinted on the hearts of God's covenant partners.

God's people will receive a new, inner motivation, empowering them to do God's will from the "inside out"!

This in turn, can be expected to produce what Jeremiah later calls a "singleness of heart and action" (32:39). God seems determined to have a people who will share His story with Him and live out that story to His glory.

A DEVOTIONAL INTERLUDE

Prayer: O Father the more I read of Your determination and resolve to have a people with whom You will share Your story the more amazed I am that I am part of this great epic. How I praise You too for the fact that Your law is not outside me but inside me. I have a new disposition to obey and share Your glory through the power of Your Holy Spirit. Thank You my Father. Thank You. In Jesus' Name. Amen.

DAY **156**

READ
Deuteronomy 30

We pause to note that the first of the new covenant's blessings, as outlined by Jeremiah, recall words spoken long before which we have previously touched on. Jeremiah's prophecy echoes a speech given by Moses at the end of the forty-year wilderness wanderings to the new generation poised to enter the promised land.

Even before Israel has entered to possess the land, Moses anticipates a tragic end of the story when by her persistent disobedience Israel will incur the ultimate covenantal judgment of forfeiting the land!

But in an extraordinary move, Moses offers the people hope.

Intriguingly – and prophetically – Moses does not refer for hope to the system of animal sacrifices, the appointed way of dealing with sin. No mention is made of this as part of the long-term solution. It is, as if, in the end, sin will prove so deep-seated and stubborn a problem as to require an act of God beyond what the Torah provides. What Moses does say is that God will bring His people back from Exile to the land. God pledges then to turn His demand: "Circumcise your hearts" (Deut. 10:16) into a promise "The Lord your God will circumcise your hearts ... so that you may love him with all your heart and with all your soul, and live" (30:6). God, it seems, is intent on having a covenant partnership that works, come what may!

A DEVOTIONAL INTERLUDE

Thought: Sin (both Adam's sin and our own) has produced a stain on the soul that nothing could erase – except the blood of Christ. The old covenant, based on law, worked from the outside in but the new covenant based on grace reaches deep into our lives and changes us from the inside out. The law said; do this and you will live. Grace says I will do it for you. Pause to give God praise for this great and glorious fact before moving out into the day.

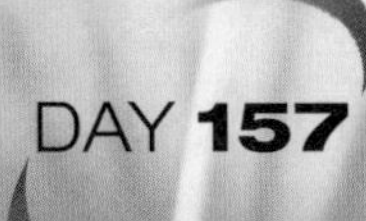

DAY **157**

READ
Jeremiah
31:31–34

The second promise of the new covenant is the promise of a fresh sense of security in belonging to God.

God re-affirms the heart of the covenant: "I will be their God and they will be my people" (v.33). These words crystalise as a formula, the bond of mutual commitment that was meant to characterise God's special relationship with Israel.

Despite failure, and defeat, the bond is now to be intensified and renewed. God's people are to be re-established as His own possession.

The repercussions of this promise would prove be truly amazing. Hosea – some two centuries earlier – had already held out the hope that God would one day say "to those called 'Not my people', 'You are my people'; and they will say, 'You are my God' " (Hosea 2:23). But even such far-seeing prophets as Hosea and Jeremiah could scarcely have envisaged the day when those alien to God's original vow – the Gentiles scattered across the wider world – would lay hold of this promise for their own salvation and inclusion in God's covenant family (Rom. 9:25; 10:19; 2 Cor. 6:16)! The apostle Peter would, one day, be in a position to encourage the new covenant communities, in time-honoured terms, by reminding them – especially, no doubt, the Gentile believers among them – "Once you were not a people, but now you are the people of God" (1 Pet. 2:10).

A DEVOTIONAL INTERLUDE

To ponder: How secure do you feel in your relationship with Jesus Christ? Psychologists tell us that there is no greater security that realising that one belongs. Children who never feel they belong show evidences of deep insecurity. A sense of belonging it seems is essential to a secure personality. You belong to Jesus Christ; you are an heir of God and a joint heir with Jesus Christ. Dwell on that fact but more – rejoice in it.

DAY **158**

READ
Jeremiah
31:31–34

Today, we relish the next great promise of the new covenant: an unprecedented assurance of knowing God personally. No longer will "knowing God" be second-hand, inherited or merely mediated, but first-hand and immediate. The emphasis on the word "all" (v.34) implies what has been termed the "democratisation of the knowledge of God". No longer confined to priests or prophets, knowledge of God is accessible to everyone.

But knowing God is not a matter of having some mystical or private religious experience. In fact the words "from the least of them to the greatest" (v.34) alert us to the profound social implications of the new covenant. "Knowing God" – especially in Jeremiah – always involves knowing what kind of God God is, namely that he is a God of justice (see 9:23–24).

As Jeremiah challenged King Jehoahaz, son of the godly Josiah: " 'Did not your father have food and drink? He did what was right and just, so all went well with him. He defended the cause of the poor and needy, and so all went well. Is that not what it means to know me?' declares the Lord" (22:15–17)

Knowing God means loving your neighbour through loving God and loving God through loving your neighbour. Not to "know" your neighbour in this way is not to know God – something on which the apostle John would later have much to say (cf. 1 John 2:4ff.)!

A DEVOTIONAL INTERLUDE

Question: Ask yourself this important personal question: How well do I know God? Knowing *about* Him is one thing but knowing Him intimately as a friend and confidante is another. The way to get to know someone is to spend time with them. How much time do you spend with the Lord in personal prayer? Psalm 46:10 says: "Be still, and know that I am God." If you are too busy to develop intimacy with God then you are busier than God intends you to be.

DAY 159

READ
Jeremiah 31:34

Undergirding all the other promises of the new covenant is that of a radical forgiveness of sins.

God pledges a permanent solution to the deep-seated problem of human sin and covenant unfaithfulness: "For I will forgive their wickedness and will remember their sins no more."

In one sense, this is nothing new. Forgiveness was always available under the old covenant arrangement, through repentant use of the sacrificial system.

Clearly, Old Testament sacrifices were effective, but only temporarily and needed to be constantly repeated – a point, which as we shall see, the writer to the Hebrews exploits in expounding the blessings of being in the new covenant (Heb. 8–10). As we have noted, neither here nor in Deuteronomy 30 which anticipates restoration beyond Exile, is the sacrificial system deemed adequate to deal with the deep-rooted sinfulness that has led to the judgment and "death" of Exile!

God will need to do a "new thing" to atone for such sin that will bring lasting forgiveness and a permanent state of non-condemnation where sins are remembered no more. But how He will do this Jeremiah is not told. At this stage in the story God is simply pledging to exercise His amazing grace, working on both sides of the relationship to make covenant work! Watch this space and watch this God!

A DEVOTIONAL INTERLUDE

Prayer: O Father what a joy it is to live in a permanent state of non condemnation. The thought has never gripped me in this way before. I can sing with Wesley: "No condemnation now I dread, Jesus and all in him is mine." What a blessed sense of freedom this gives me. Help me never to forget that to bring me into this place it cost Your Son His precious blood. My heart is grateful more than words can ever convey. Thank You Father. Amen.

DAY 160

READ
Ezekiel 36

As befits a man who was trained as a priest, Ezekiel uses cultic or sacrificial language. He talks of the "washing and cleansing" by which God will effect a complete change of heart in His covenant people. God will give a new heart – one which is soft and responsive to God – to replace an obdurate and unresponsive one.

Furthermore, God's very life-breath will pour into us to invigorate our covenant instincts, an action which matches the original in-breathing of Adam to make him a living being (Gen. 2:7).

As in Jeremiah's version, so in Ezekiel's; God's own creative Spirit will empower God's covenant people to faithful covenant behaviour and practice.

This, says Ezekiel, will happen in the midst of Israel in the very land where unfaithfulness had led to Exile. So God's name will be hallowed which is His first concern and, according to Jesus, our first priority in prayer. By new covenant people, filled with His Spirit, God aims to redeem His reputation and to have the covenant people He has always set His heart on. As we have seen this will amount to a "resurrection" of God's people from the dead, achieved by the prophetic word and powerful Spirit of God (Ezek. 37). The Spirit of life animates the new covenant community.

A DEVOTIONAL INTERLUDE

Thought: To be part of the new covenant community means we are told that God "aims to redeem his reputation". The people of the old covenant acted shamefully at times and brought the Name of God into disrepute. It is our task now, aided by the Holy Spirit, to show the world that it is possible to live the life He wants us to live and to keep His commandments. The challenge is tremendous but then so is the power available to us.

DAY **161**

READ
Joel 2

This is perhaps an appropriate point to consider the undated prophecy of Joel with its vision of a Spirit-drenched future.

But the prophet warns the people against complacently assuming that this future "Day of the Lord" will be like a good-natured school prizegiving! When the day comes it will bring judgment as well as grace and will be as terrible as it is wonderful (v.11).

Joel warns God's people not to presume on God's grace but to be morally and spiritually ready for God's day. His message is a trumpet-call to Israel to reckon with the sobering reality of the coming Day and to return repentantly to the Lord.

Joel echoes the new covenant language of Jeremiah when he urges his hearers to "Rend your hearts and not your garments" – in short, to change their habits not just their habit (v.13)! In a moving call, young and old, newly-weds and priests at worship, are urged to drop everything else in order to implore God with tears to remove His people's reproach and to silence the pagans' sneering, "Where is your God?"

Some of the greatest prophetic promises are at stake here: "I will make up for the years the locusts have eaten" (v.25 *The Message*). "I will pour out my Spirit on all people . . . everyone who calls on the name of the Lord will be saved" (vv.28,32).

A DEVOTIONAL INTERLUDE

To ponder: How wonderful to be alive in a day that is "Spirit-drenched". In Old Testament times the Holy Spirit seemed to come upon people for temporary purposes. His visitations were special and occasional. Since Pentecost, however, His presence is continuous and perpetual, bringing us to repentant praise and restoring to us the years which the locusts have eaten. Let the wonder of that fill your mind this day.

DAY 162

READ
Jeremiah 33

In tracing the trajectory of the Davidic covenant, we noted that it was not only the people but the kings who failed and needed renewal. From the emergence of kingship in Israel (1 Sam. 9:9), it seems that one of the most important roles a prophet had to play was to act as a standing reminder to the kings that they held their kingship in trust as stewards of God's sovereign rule.

Wherever kings abused their power, the prophets boldly threatened their continued claim to the privileges of the Davidic covenant. But when the dismal failure of the kings became evident, the prophets of Exile – as we have seen – begin to project hopes of a new kingship.

God would raise up a new David, "a righteous Branch [a king who] will do what is just and right in the land" (vv.15–16).

Jeremiah envisages what seems a two-fold office, blending the roles of Davidic king and Levitical priest, backed by God's covenant commitment (vv.19–21). Significantly, he links the emergence of this fascinating priest-king with God's foundational promise to Abraham of descendants as "countless as the stars of the sky and as measureless as the sand on the seashore" (v.22 cf. Gen. 15). In the thread of God's great strategic plan of redemption, the stories of Jacob and David are joined to the future hope of one faithful Israelite (v.26)!

A DEVOTIONAL INTERLUDE

For praise: God's plan to have a worldwide family of faith has threaded its way through history until this very moment – and that great plan includes you. It is as if a great river runs down to water one little daisy. Let your heart overflow in praise right now as once again you dwell on the fact that God's story includes you. "Praise," said C.S. Lewis "is always the right response to the discovery of God's mercies."

DAY **163**

READ
Isaiah 40

Isaiah chapters 40–55 constitute the high point of Old Testament revelation. By portraying, in vivid imagery, the future stages of God's story, these chapters are the seedbed from which springs the Evangelists' understanding of Jesus and the apostolic understanding of the gospel. It is to Isaiah that we owe the very meaning of the concept of "gospel".

For Isaiah, the gospel which the herald announces is, "Here is your God" (v.9). God Himself, in grace and for glory, will return as King to Zion – leading the homecoming exiles on the road across the desert. This God who comes as strong soldier and sensitive shepherd (10–11), is no less a deliverer than the One Creator God, the mastermind behind the whole teeming, multi-coloured creation project (12–14). This God both grasps the big picture and notices the detail of a falling star. This is the independent, all-sufficient, incomparable, Holy One of Israel, who never suffers compassion-fatigue or brain-drain (v.28)! The Creator is the Redeemer who aims at nothing less than a renewal of His whole creation.

Today we can replenish our supply from His strength and resume our homeward journey with the buoyancy of soaring eagles, the energy of relentless runners and the dogged persistence of tireless walkers.

A DEVOTIONAL INTERLUDE

Question: Are you feeling tired and weary? Do you feel you are running out of spiritual or physical resources? Then hold on to the thought, "we can replenish our supply from His strength". Let your weakness lie limp on God's shoulder. Draw from His endless resources which so immeasurably exceed our demands. Lift your heart in believing prayer at this moment and take God at His word. He will not fail you.

DAY 164

READ
2 Chronicles 36:15–23
Isaiah 41:2–4; 44:24–45:7

So far we have traced God's promise-plan as it makes its way through history, implemented by God's covenant commitments: with Noah and the earth, with Abraham for the nations, through Moses for Israel, and with David for the sake of the future. Now has come Exile and the judgment and grace God speaks through His prophets of the time.

From a wider perspective we can see that Exodus and Exile are the two poles around which the Old Testament story of Israel revolves. Ironically, Israel's story which began in slavery in Egypt, effectively ends in captivity in Babylonia from where Abraham had come over a millennium earlier!

But the hopes of the Exilic prophets are remarkable.

If, in the first Exodus, Egypt gave birth to a nation for God out of slavery through deliverance, so, now, Exile yields promise of a new people of God, redeemed this time in a greater exodus, out of the deeper slavery of sin through "death and resurrection".

So two problems need to be addressed.

To get God's people physically back to the land, God raises up Cyrus, who does not know Yahweh.

But to restore God's people to Himself, cleansed, forgiven and reconstituted, is an issue way beyond the scope of political warlords like Cyrus. For that God will need another, altogether different kind of "servant"!

A DEVOTIONAL INTERLUDE

Thought: We have seen that it was one thing for God to bring His people back to the land He had given them, but it was quite another thing to bring them back to Himself. The men God used in Old Testament times to achieve this were flawed, but now God's servant, who because He is both human and divine joins us to the Father and journeys with us, helping us day by day to develop a deeper intimacy with God. To Him be eternal praise.

DAY **165**

READ
Isaiah 42

It is given to the prophet Isaiah movingly to unveil the figure of this mysterious servant who alone will achieve God's greatest work. He does so particularly in what have been called the "servant songs".

In the first of these songs, we learn that God will select and endorse this servant. The servant will know God's approval and anointing and will nourish His true self-identity in God's delight in Him. His manner of ministry will run counter to worldly methods by showing self-restraint, neither raucously promoting Himself nor blusteringly protecting Himself. He will win people's allegiance but not by trampling over them. When He meets the weak He does not overpower or crush them. His own strength of purpose will remain uncrushed and undimmed. And His mission will be the establishment of God's justice in the earth (vv.1,3,4). As Creator, God guarantees the success of the servant's cause.

As covenant-maker, God will cause the servant to embody the covenant, so that He becomes the means by which people enter into a covenant relationship with God (v.6). His light shines not only in Israel but to the world of nations, working wonders of healing and freedom that demonstrate the unrivalled glory and unprecedented newness of God, and spark riots of rejoicing and praise (vv.6–13).

A DEVOTIONAL INTERLUDE

For praise: Embarking upon the theme of the "servant songs" brings to mind the chorus from Graham Kendrick's wonderful hymn: "The Servant King". Sing it with praise and gratitude in your heart for the One who stooped to serve.

This is our God, the Servant King
He calls us now to follow Him
To bring our lives as a daily offering
Of worship to the Servant King

DAY 166

READ
Isaiah 49

In this "servant song", the mystery deepens as to who or what this strange agent of God can be. There is a puzzling ambiguity about the prophet's description of Him. It seems that, on the one hand, the servant is to be identified with Israel (v.3) but that, on the other, He will have a ministry to Israel and will thus fulfil Israel's vocation of being a saving light to the Gentiles. How can this be? We are reminded, perhaps, of the way in which the king, as a representative figure, carries the nation in himself. Perhaps this is our clue here. It helps to remember that "Israel" was a name first given to an individual, the father of the nation, Jacob. This servant then, by living out Israel's covenant faithfulness, will, as it were, "father" a new people of God.

He will be both the glory of His people Israel and the light for the Gentile nations. Again, God's own faithfulness guarantees the servant's mission, once more by making Him an embodiment of the covenant (vv.7–8). It is as if all the covenant promises and dreams will converge on Him so that everyone must come to Him to receive the blessings of salvation.

When that day comes it will be a day of favour and opportunity none can afford to miss (v.8) and none would want to. From dark dungeons captives will step out in the fresh air and daylight of God's freedom.

A DEVOTIONAL INTERLUDE

Prayer: O Father how can I ever thank You enough for reaching down into the dungeon of my life, shattering the chains of sin that bound me, and delivering me from the bondage I was in. In Wesley's words; "My chains fell off, my heart was free, I rose went forth and followed Thee". Now I want to be Your willing slave for ever. All honour and glory be to Your peerless and precious Name. Amen.

DAY **167**

READ
Isaiah 50

Through the prophet, God once more gently chides His people that He has not divorced them nor has He settled a debt by selling them off. God's people have been "sent away" into Exile not because God has failed but because they refused to recognise His presence and power. One exception stands out – a servant of God who speaks for himself in this third "servant song" (vv.4–9). When God came and called no one responded except God's servant who is "all ears", listening for the voice of the Lord as a true disciple of the Lord. He hears "morning by morning", giving priority to God's Word, as prophets did (cf. Jer. 7:25).

Daily He will speak words that sustain the weary, offering an easy yoke to replace a burdensome law – only to be beaten and spat upon for His pains. The servant's vigilance makes Him vulnerable to humiliation ("pulled out my beard . . . mocking and spitting") and violence ("beat me"). Undaunted, he endures with flint-like determination, trusting to God to vindicate Him (vv.6–9). As a result, He forces everyone else to make a life-or-death decision whether to walk by faith though in the dark or to walk by the light of their own self-lit fires. God's long redemptive story seems to comes down in the end to the trust of this one faithful Israelite. Who on earth is He? And when on earth will He appear?

A DEVOTIONAL INTERLUDE

Question: When God calls you to walk in the darkness of confusion and wait for His answers, what do you do? Cling to Him in deep trust or seek to illuminate your surroundings by lighting your own fire? (See again vv 10–11). There is nothing like confusion to erode our sense of competence, but it is in such situations that the muscles of faith and trust are exercised. How good are you at trusting God when you cannot see the way ahead?

DAY 168

READ
Isaiah 52

As we have said, no other prophet so vividly anticipates the gospel as Isaiah does. He heralds the return of God as King to be at the centre of His people's life again (40:3–10); declares the joyous prospect of forgiveness for the nation's sin (43:25ff.; 44:22ff.) and envisages the establishment of this kingdom of grace paradoxically through the suffering of God's servant. Here in 52:7–12, particularly, we find promises which become "thematic for the whole work of Jesus" (Tom Wright).

Isaiah presents powerful images and hopes about how life might look on the other side of Exile.

Watchmen on the ruined ramparts of Jerusalem will shout for joy as they glimpse a distant runner with "beautiful feet" that convey good news of God's kingdom. God is always King over creation and history but, as we have learned, His redemptive plan is to implement His rule in a dynamic, active sense that changes conditions on earth and ultimately renews His created world. The herald's gospel proclamation announces "peace" and "salvation", where and when "the Lord reigns".

From the outset, as we have seen, Abraham's inheritance and Israel's hope were always meant to spell hope for the whole world, so that, when salvation finally comes to God's people, the ends of the earth hear of it (v.10).

A DEVOTIONAL INTERLUDE

For praise: It seems appropriate to respond once again in a song of praise. Join in with the thousands who sing these lines:

You watchmen lift your voices joyfully as one
Shout for your king, your king,
See eye to eye, the Lord restoring Zion
Your God reigns, your God reigns.

He does. Blessed be His name for ever!

DAY **169**

READ
Isaiah 53

God's servant suffers as a free and willing partner who submits to the consequence of doing the Lord's will.

He at last will be despised, rejected and crushed – cut off from the land of the living – cast forth into the land of Exile and forsakenness. He achieves the salvation which could not be achieved by either animal sacrifices offered in the appointed way at the Temple or repeated prophetic calls to repentance. Only beyond Exile, as Israel attaches itself to this strange figure and goes down into death with Him, is there hope for the future.

Mysteriously God's suffering servant will atone for the sins of the people. His solo work will achieve the vindication of the justified many, and, as a result, He will be raised and lifted up and highly exalted (52:13–53:12)

This exaltation unveils the strangest form of kingship ever seen. Stooping to conquer, suffering in order to save, He is the wise fool, the wounded Healer, the Servant King!

Who is this servant? Did Isaiah know?

Probably not, is the answer to the second question.

As G.B. Caird said of the prophet, "It was as though he was publishing an advertisement: 'Wanted: Servant of the Lord: all applications welcome' accompanied by a job description."

As we now know there was only one applicant for the job who fitted the description!

Thought: How privileged we are to look back to the cross and see the suffering servant, the one whom Old Testament saints saw as just a vague figure in the future. Now we know this suffering servant is none other than the second person of the Trinity – our Lord Jesus Christ Himself;

With what rapture, with what rapture
Gaze we on those glorious scars!

A DEVOTIONAL INTERLUDE

DAY **170**

READ
Isaiah 35, 65:17–19; 66:1

From the covenant with Noah, God has made clear His intention to reclaim His once-good creation.

Isaiah picks up this divine ambition and sees further into its future than any prophet before him. He sees that the triumphant outcome of all the servant's labours will be not only the restoration of God's people to include the Gentiles, but the eventual renewal of all God's works – the re-creation of new heavens and a new earth (65:17; 66:22)!

Isaiah's visions of hope had, from the beginning, been cast in extravagant creational language.

"The wilderness will rejoice and blossom. Like the crocus, it will burst into bloom" (35:1). God will provide water in the desert, streams in the wasteland (35:6); "mountains and hills will burst into song . . . and all the trees of the field will clap their hands" (55:12). In contrast to the fallen, sin-cursed old world, the new world will be a thornless world.

Isaiah consistently links creation and redemption. Just as God pledges to redeem what He has created, so the power by which He creates guarantees His ability to redeem. Isaiah, for one, is convinced that the God who created is the same God who redeems. "No half God could redeem a world it took a whole God to create" (P.T. Forsyth).

Final salvation will be a new act of creation, as the apostles Paul and John will one day celebrate even more confidently in the light of Christ.

A DEVOTIONAL INTERLUDE

For praise: Such a revelation of creative power deserves to be responded to by an abundant outpouring of praise. Praise God in your own way and in your own words as you consider once more the fact that the same God who created the world is the One who redeemed it. Let the thought from P.T. Forsyth "No half God could redeem a world it took a whole God to create", stir you to express your deepest gratitude to God for dying for you on Calvary.

READ
Daniel 9
Nehemiah 9

Exile as a physical separation from the land lasted barely 70 years as Jeremiah had promised. But "Exile" as a state or condition of being under judgment and awaiting the fulfilment of promises of restoration and new covenant – that was an entirely different matter.

Both Daniel and Ezra in words written after the physical return to the land, pray as if Israel were still slaves in Exile (Dan. 9:3–19; Ezra 9:8–9; Neh. 9:36).

For the next four centuries, while Israel – except for a brief period with the Maccabees – remained under foreign domination, there were perceptive Jewish writers who considered Israel to be still under God's judgment "in Exile".

Right up to the time of Jesus, no Jew that we know of seriously imagined that the new covenant promises had been fulfilled – except, that is, for the small Qumran monastic sect, emerging a century and a half before Jesus, who called themselves the "Covenanters" and who, later, after the fall of Jerusalem in AD 70 when threatened by the Roman armies, buried their precious scrolls in the caves beside the Dead Sea!

The prophetic vision awaited the arrival of God's servant who in Isaiah's words was Himself to be "a covenant for the people" (Isa. 42:6; 49:8) as if embodying all God's covenantal investment.

A DEVOTIONAL INTERLUDE

To ponder: "Exile" we have learned is something more than a physical separation – it is also spiritual. Even after the Israelites were back in the land given to them by God their hearts, with few exceptions, were far from God. It is possible to draw near to God in worship (such as in church on Sundays, singing the songs or hymns, for example) while our hearts are far from Him. It's our hearts God is after!

DAY **172**

READ
Mark 1:1–15

It is fascinating to see where each Evangelist starts his story of Jesus. Matthew begins with Abraham, Luke even further back with Adam, while John links Jesus directly to the eternal God Himself. Mark starts with the Exile – with Isaiah 40 – by identifying John the Baptist as the "voice in the wilderness preparing the way of the Lord". This bizarre prophetic figure lures the people to a barren landscape, and urges Israel to start afresh with God. To that end, John preaches national repentance and national forgiveness, inviting Israel, through baptism, to repeat, as it were, the original Jordan crossing and so to enter the new promised land of God's long-awaited Messianic kingdom!

John prepares "the way of the Lord" also by consistently pointing beyond himself to the One whose arrival will inaugurate the Messianic era of salvation characterised by the outpouring of the Holy Spirit of God. Himself prepared by the Spirit's anointing and the Father's approval, and His way prepared by John, Jesus finally enters Galilee, with God's good news. At last, God's time has come! God's age-old plans have come of age! The day Isaiah saw is here!

God's kingly rule is no longer a wistful dream but a close-up reality to be encountered head-on by repentance, and embraced whole-heartedly by faith.

A DEVOTIONAL INTERLUDE

Thought: Did you realise as you read today's reading that John the Baptist through his words effectively announces the end of the Exile? What a moment this was! The dreams of the past – forgiveness and freedom from sin and the empowering of the Spirit – were about to become reality in the appearance and ministry of the soon-coming One. The Old Testament prophets said He is coming. John announces the good news: He is here!

READ
Luke 22

In Jesus' words and actions, many threads are now being drawn together.

Held at Passover time, the Last Supper points back to the foundational event of the Exodus and God's covenant with Israel. This in turn evokes hopes of a new and greater Exodus. But, since God's redemptive promise-plan always had in view the establishing of His kingdom, so, Jesus says, the Passover will find its fulfilment through a new Exodus in the kingdom of God (vv.16–18). His cross and Resurrection establish the new covenant, just as sacrifice had attended the old covenant (Exod. 24:8).

Underlying everything is a deeper divine plan to establish his kingly rule in which the disciples of Jesus will share (vv.21,37).

As we have learned from Isaiah, new Exodus and new covenant occur under the rule of a new kind of servant-kingship (v.27) which is willing to suffer for sinners (v.37 quoting Isa. 53:12).

Marvellously and mysteriously, God's strategic plan is now coming to fruition in his Servant-King who, by His blood poured out as a sacrificial offering, inaugurates the new covenant agreement, initiates a new Exodus from sin and death, and guarantees the coming of God's kingdom!

And because our King rose from the dead, the Last Supper was turned into the Lord's Supper, not a funeral wake but a feast of good things still to come!

A DEVOTIONAL INTERLUDE

For future action: Next time you take Communion think about this – every time you take the bread and the wine you are re-iterating the start of the new covenant so long foretold and hoped for by the saints of the Old Testament. The "Passover" you participate in eclipsed the original one by the nature of the Person whose body was broken and whose blood was shed. May your next Communion service be more wonderful than ever.

DAY 174

READ
Acts 2:1–21, 36–47

To the sound of a windstorm, with flames flickering over every head, many voices erupt in a torrent of praise to God in languages they had never learned. At a stroke, the time-honoured rituals of the Feast of Pentecost are shattered!.

First question: what does this mean (v.12)?

Startling as the phenomena are, Peter links them to Joel's prophecy of the "last days": "this is what was spoken". God's story has reached a climactic stage when God exalts His Son as King, pours out His Spirit on all flesh and saves all who call upon Him!

So, it is misleading to see Acts 2 as the "birthday of the Church", as if the Church were an innovation. We do better to see here the emergence of that new covenant community of which the prophets spoke.

The tell-tale marks are evident: immediate access to God, forgiveness of sins, the gift of God's Spirit, an awesome, first-hand knowledge of God which results in sharing goods within a just society.

What this means is that Jesus is Israel's King and the world's Lord and now the way is open – as Joel had prophesied – for all to call on His Name for salvation! Only one question remains outstanding: what shall we do (v.37)? What else can anyone do but repent, believe, be filled with God's Spirit and be baptised into this God-experiencing, love-saturated, company of God's people!

A DEVOTIONAL INTERLUDE

For praise: Lift up your heart in praise right now for the fact that Jesus is the "true" (that is, final) Son of David who has ascended to David's throne by virtue of His resurrection from the dead. Praise Him also for pouring out the Spirit on all flesh – as He promised, for securing forgiveness of sins and giving us access to God, for establishing a new covenant community of which you are a part.

DAY 175

READ
2 Corinthians
3:1–6

Under pressure to produce "letters of recommendation" endorsing his ministry, Paul points to the Corinthians themselves as evidence for the work God has done in their lives through his ministry. In words which have significant Old Testament echoes, Paul says that the letters Christ has written through his ministry, are inscribed not on tablets of stone (like the law, Exod. 31:18) but on the heart of the Corinthian believers (combining new covenant terms from Ezek. 11:19–20; 36:26; Jer. 31:31).

The difference between old and new covenants could not be greater; it is the difference between life and death: "the letter kills, but the Spirit gives life" (v.6). The distinction made here is not between a literal and a spiritual reading of the text, but between the fact that the law sentences sinners to death but is powerless to do anything about it, while the gospel of the new covenant brings atonement, forgiveness of sins and actually produces real covenantal life. The ministry of the Holy Spirit is indispensable in bringing this about. Joel, Ezekiel, Isaiah, each presumed his would be the case and New Testament gospel experience bears it out. We are called to enact and commend God's saving story: only the Holy Spirit can make us "equal to such a task".

A DEVOTIONAL INTERLUDE

Prayer: Gracious and loving heavenly Father, I am so thankful for the salvation You have brought to me through Your Son. I never tire of saying thank You, for the wonder of it grows and grows upon me day by day. May my life be a "living letter" that will tell the story of a covenant-keeping God who alone has atoned for sin and has opened up for all who will receive it lasting forgiveness and everlasting life. Amen.

DAY 176

READ
2 Corinthians
3:7–18

Although that old covenant associated with Sinai was glorious, it has been eclipsed by the splendour of what the Holy Spirit achieves. Paul – and all who proclaim the same gospel – are ministers of the new covenant. Where the old covenant condemned, the new covenant brings righteousness, vindicating and securing covenant membership for repentant sinners. Where the old covenant had glory, fading though it was, how much more glorious is the new covenant which is permanent!

This is one of the densest and richest passages in Paul's writings. He is clearly utilising Exodus 34:29–35 and Ezekiel 36 in order to contrast Israelites then and now with Christian believers. Then Moses had to veil his face before the glory, fading though it was. Even today when Moses is read a veil remains, except that now the veil is not over Moses' face but over the hearts of those who hear the Torah. But, as when Moses turned to the Lord in face to face encounter and removed his veil, so now everyone who turns to the Lord by opening up to the Lordship of the Holy Spirit, has the veil removed and perceives God's glory in the face of Jesus Christ.

With unhardened hearts and unveiled faces, we enjoy and reflect His glory in our lives together as God's new covenant people!

A DEVOTIONAL INTERLUDE

Thought: Before you slip away and attend to the duties of the day think for a few moments of how fortunate we are to live in this day and age when access to God through Jesus His Son is open to us whoever and wherever we are. No need of sacrifices, ceremonies, tabernacles, temples, etc. The veil has been removed and we have seen God's glory in the face of Jesus Christ. Think – and give thanks!

DAY 177

READ
2 Corinthians 5:1–19

In this section, chapters 1–5, Paul is clearly shadowing the prophetic sequence of new covenant – new kingship – leading to new creation.

"Anointed" or "Christed" by the Spirit, and sealed as belonging to the Messiah's people (1:21–22), we are ministers of the new covenant (3:6). As servants of our King, Jesus Christ the Lord (4:6), we already share in the "new realm of reality" inaugurated "in Christ" – for "if any one is in Christ – new creation" (5:17 literal translation).

Paul's vision of "new creation" must not be limited to mean "born again" or "a Christian is a new person", true though this is. Much more than this is being said! "If any one is in Christ – new creation" means that when we come to faith in Christ we enter the realm of God's new creation. Anyone "in Christ" becomes a sample of the world's future, a prototype of what all God's created works are set to become!

To be reconciled to God – which is our deepest need – is to have the barrier caused by sin broken down and fellowship with God restored. But this means being reconciled not to things as they are, but to things as they may become in God's new order.

Peace with God does not make us passive but exposes us to the glory that transforms. New covenant Christians do not simply keep up with the times but live "ahead of the times".

A DEVOTIONAL INTERLUDE

Question: Are you trying to keep up with the times or living ahead of them? Do you understand that you are at this moment being exposed to "the glory that transforms"? You are a sample of the future. Think about these questions as you go through the day and consider whether you are living in the world or above it. Let the power of the world to come, which now you have in part, influence everything you say and everything you do.

DAY 178

READ
2 Corinthians
5:20–6:2,17–18

God's aim in reconciling us to Himself through Christ's cross is that we might become the righteousness of God. In our "great exchange" with Christ, we are saved to embody God's own world-reconciling, covenant-faithfulness and to manifest the new creation.

Paul pleads with the Corinthians to live up to this calling, "Be reconciled to God", and so to live that the "church is a sneak preview of the ultimate redemption of the world" (Richard Hays).

Isaiah's longed-for day of favour and salvation has dawned in Christ (6:2; Isa. 49:8). So, as the prophet did, Paul urges his hearers to break with "Babylonian" values by coming out of cultural compromise and coming home to true covenant living (6:17; cf. Isa. 49:9; 52:11). We are not meant to hear this call as an invitation to join an exclusive, self-righteous ghetto. We hear it as a call not to be unthinkingly conformed to the culture of violence and consumerism all around us. We hear it as the call to freedom and glory.

Those who have the courage to be a counter-cultural community, God will gladly affirm as His people, wonderfully expanding the original promise in God's covenant with David to include sons and daughters (6:18; 2 Sam. 7:14). Christians are God's royal family, dared to live differently for the sake of the new world coming!

A DEVOTIONAL INTERLUDE

Prayer: Gracious God and loving Father, help me understand what it means to be part of a counter-cultural community. May the men and women I rub shoulders with day by day and who do not know You see in me the glory of another world. I am in the world, belong to the world, but I serve another King, one Jesus. May that fact show and shine through me. In Christ's Name I pray. Amen.

DAY 179

READ
Hebrews 8:7–13; 10:11–18

The New Testament writer to the Hebrews celebrates the dawn of this new covenant era by citing Jeremiah 31:31–34 in full.

Jesus is God's unique Son, the King sharing God's throne, High Priest of heaven who, by virtue of His death and resurrection and ascension, has become the mediator of a better covenant (7:22). He eclipses Moses and the Levitical priesthood of the old order.

By His effective sacrifice, achieving what the sacrifice of animals and birds could not, Jesus is now the "mediator of a new covenant", providing for believers an "inheritance" which the writer has already linked to the promises made to Abraham (9:15; 6:12–13)

So, the writer argues, the old covenant is obsolete. There was nothing intrinsically wrong with it; it's simply past its "sell-by date". It remains as a revelation of God's will for His people: but it no longer regulates our lives, it is not the administration we are now serving under.

While the repeated sacrifices under the Old Testament system were effective for temporary forgiveness, they did not take away sins (10:11). Under the terms of the new covenant, however, Christ's one final, complete sacrifice deals finally with sin, writes the law on the heart and brings believers into a permanent state of non-condemnation (10:16–18).

A DEVOTIONAL INTERLUDE

To ponder: Consider as you go through the day what a joy and delight it is to be part of a new administration and to live in a permanent state of non-condemnation. Wesley wrote: "No condemnation now I dread, Jesus and all in Him is mine." It's easy to say, but has the meaning reached deep into your soul? Say it over and over again until its truth is fixed in your soul: In Christ I am in a permanent state of non-condemnation. Hallelujah!

DAY **180**

READ
Romans 8

Paul here waxes lyrical that what the old covenant and its Torah could not do – deal with the deep problem of sin and create genuine covenant living – God has done in the sending and dying of His Son as a sin offering and by the gift of His empowering Spirit.

So is born the new covenant community, the company of the forgiven-forgivers, the uncondemned sons of God, who live by the Spirit.

Exodus language abounds here, but in the service of a more far-reaching redemption!

With slavery behind them, marked out as God's covenant family by receiving His Spirit, the true sons of God call on God as "Abba-Father".

Led, not by a pillar of fire and cloud, but by the immediate light of God's Spirit, the covenant family marches onwards towards its God-given inheritance.

Only, in this scenario, our promised land is no partial Canaan but nothing less than a redeemed earth. We are destined to occupy a transformed creation, freed from its own bondage to decay and radiant in the glorious freedom characteristic of God's own children. We, in turn, show our true identity by our willingness to suffer for the world and Messiah's sake in fellowship with Him.

Yet, purposefully and with hope, surrounded by frustration, in a world growing old, we offer ourselves as samples of that newness for which all creation longs.

A DEVOTIONAL INTERLUDE

Dedication: We suggest making this day a day of renewed dedication in which you offer yourself once again to the Lord for Him to do in you and through you whatever He wills. Ask Him especially to make you a sample of that "newness for which all creation longs" and reveal through you to your friends and family what Christian living is all about. You supply the willingness; He will supply the power.

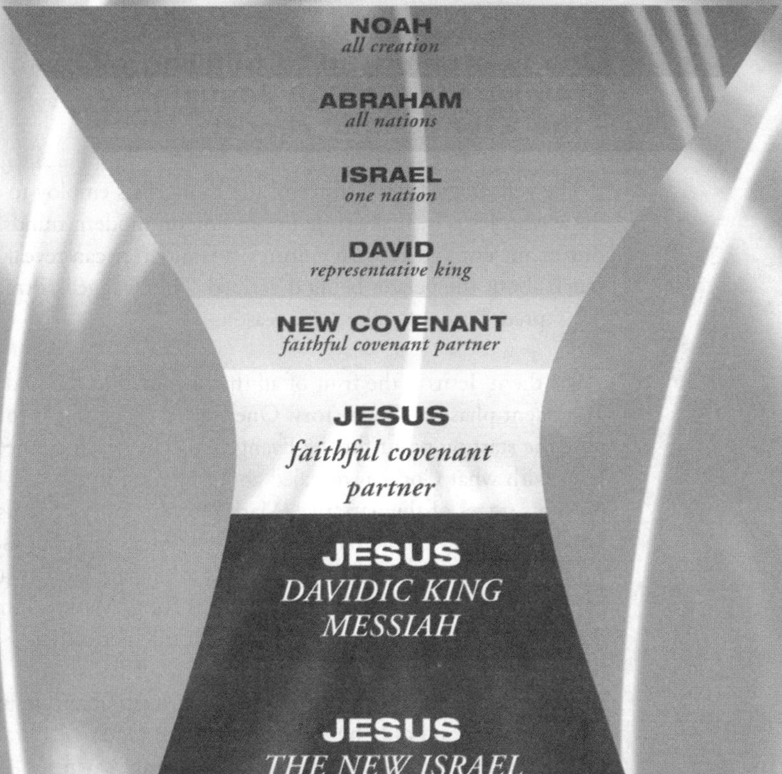

NOAH
all creation

ABRAHAM
all nations

ISRAEL
one nation

DAVID
representative king

NEW COVENANT
faithful covenant partner

JESUS
faithful covenant partner

JESUS
DAVIDIC KING MESSIAH

JESUS
THE NEW ISRAEL

JESUS
the world's Lord

JESUS
the truly Human One crowned with glory and honour

JESUS
cosmic Ruler in God's new creation new heavens and new earth

SECTION 8
THE EVANGELISTS' REPORT

God is committed to fulfilling all his promises in his Son Jesus - the Evangelists' report

The genealogies which three of the Evangelists employ to show who Jesus is, make little impression on modern minds. But in ancient and Eastern cultures, a family tree can reveal much about the person being described. The Evangelists trace Jesus' predecessors for the same reason.

For them, Jesus is the fruit of all that is rooted in the Old Testament phase of God's story. One way to gauge this is to note the starting point for the Evangelists. They each connect Jesus with what God has revealed about Himself in the previous stages of the narrative. Mark roots his story of Jesus in Isaiah's prophecy to the Babylonian exiles. Isaiah said that God would raise up a voice in the wilderness to prepare God's way back into the centre of His people's life as King. Mark is in no doubt that John the Baptist has filled that role perfectly. Matthew says, in effect, that to tell the story of Jesus adequately, you must start further back, with Abraham. Jesus can be understood only by linking Him with God's foundational promises to Abraham that envisage saving blessings for all nations.

For his part, Luke starts even further back, with Adam. Luke shows that Jesus is the true Davidic King, who brings the Israel story to its successful conclusion, and, in doing so, makes good the whole human story. John, of course, writing later, sums up what they all agree on, that Jesus can be properly understood only by rooting Him in the very eternal nature of God. In which case the story told in Jesus is the true version of the story of the One Creator God.

Matthew in particular uses the language of "fulfilment" in order to say that Jesus re-enacts and completes the whole pattern of Israel's history. Jesus is God's new and true Israel, who comes out of Egypt and successfully comes through testing in the wilderness. He is the new Moses, spelling out a new covenant charter, as in Deuteronomy, to the hearers of the new Sermon on the Mount. He is the new David, anointed to proclaim the good news of God's arriving kingdom.

All the characteristic titles of Jesus have rich Old Testament meanings. All of them have larger than individual reference which incorporate the nation's destiny.. Isaiah's "servant of the Lord", the psalmist's "son of God", and Daniel's "son of man" are all applied to Jesus as a representative figure who acts as and for His people.

If we ask: what were Jesus' aims? – the initial answer may surprise us. Jesus' top priority is to Israel, to restore the lost sheep of the house of Israel. To this end He chooses twelve new "tribal" heads, alters the rules of acceptance and non-acceptance, and proclaims that "exile is over" by forgiving sins and welcoming repentant sinners.

He challenges Israel to follow Him and take up the cross of a new way of being Israel by dying and rising with Him to the realities of a new covenant existence. He rescripts the Passover meal to focus on Himself as the one true sacrifice for sin. But alongside this grace there is a warning of judgment. Jesus looked ahead and foresaw the dreadful calamity which we now know befell Jerusalem and the Temple in AD 70–73 in the Jewish–Roman conflict. He could see it all coming. He predicted that within the lifetime of His contemporaries, foreign armies would again besiege the city so that not one stone of the Temple would be left standing. The looming shadow of AD 70 hangs over everything Jesus says and does and gives His message a terrible urgency. This was the hour of decision. His generation was the "terminal generation" from whom God was calling in the accounts. The judgment He envisaged was the judgment He was willing to bear for His people. But if His self-offering were refused then a dark fate awaited the nation. In the last week of His life, the questions about Him intensified into a loud clamour. Who was He anyway? What right did He have to redraw the lines of Israel's national life like this? Who was He to think of rewriting the story of God in so daring a way? By what authority does He do and say such things? If, as His friends, we ask the question that His enemies asked, then we might conclude with Matthew that no one could do and say the things Jesus did except Israel's God in person. In Matthew's first and final word: He is Immanuel, "God with us". In His blood the new covenant is established and sealed. In Him are realised the promises cherished in Israel that Abraham's seed would bring blessing to the world of nations. Great David's greater Son stands tall as Israel's King and the world's Lord, His resurrection from the dead the token of a new creation.

DAY **181**

READ
Matthew 1:1–17

For many modern people, genealogies are not an interesting way to begin a compelling story. But in older cultures – especially a Jewish culture – a person's family tree tells you a great deal about their significance. All the more so in Jesus' case. When Matthew wants to tell us the story of Jesus as he sees it, he plunges straight into the history of Israel. We ought not to be surprised by this move because already it has become clear that without the Old Testament phase of God's story we cannot begin to understand Jesus. Matthew offers us the genealogy of Jesus because he wants us to see straightaway that Jesus is the climax to the longer, earlier stages of God's story. The genealogy is not an exhaustive one but written up in the shape of three series of fourteen generations (v.17). In effect it is a condensed history of Israel, arranged into three main eras. Here are Jesus' roots. Matthew, first of all, connects Jesus to Abraham through whom, we recall, "all the nations of the earth will be blessed". He then links Him to the Davidic line of kings on whom the well-being and destiny of the people depended. The hopes of the whole world, the hopes of Israel, all rest on the shoulders of the One whose story Matthew is telling. So much depends on Jesus and we are glad to put all our trust in Him too.

A DEVOTIONAL INTERLUDE

Thought: Nowadays people spend large amounts of money tracing their "family tree". Sometimes they are disappointed when they discover amongst their ancestors people of ill repute. How thrilling it is that our spiritual roots, our genealogy and our family tree can be traced back to God the Father Himself. So lift up your head, throw back your shoulders. You are a child of the living God!

THE PROMISE-PLAN OF GOD

COVENANT WITH: NOAH ABRAHAM

DAY 182

READ
Matthew 1:17–21

The third move Matthew makes is to view the Jesus story as the true sequel to the Exile in Babylon five hundred years before. Nothing that had occurred in the intervening centuries had fully resolved the issue of the sin of God's people or corresponded to the prophetic hopes of salvation. Israel's continuing oppression by godless powers only seemed to reinforce the sense of still being under God's judgment. But now things are about to change. It is against this backdrop that the Evangelists highlight the significance of the Exile for Jesus. Each of them ties Jesus closely to John the Baptist whom they identify as that "voice in the wilderness" spoken of by Isaiah as heralding the return of God as King. When he appears and speaks, it will be to declare that the long "Exile" in sin and under judgment at last is over! The birth of a child will change everything. The child will bear the name of Israel's first conquering hero "Joshua" who led the people into the promised land of Canaan. But this "Yeshua" is about a bigger business. He will "save his people", Israel from her sins, and lead her – albeit through death – into the new promised land of salvation (Matt. 1:21).

Abrahamic promises, Davidic dreams, prophetic hopes at Exile – all these are coming to fruition at last in Jesus.

A DEVOTIONAL INTERLUDE

To ponder: Those who live in the Scriptures will know that time and time again whenever God's people seemed to lose hope God would remind them of His promise that a better day lay up ahead. Do you wonder as you look around just what the world is coming to? Hold on to this – all God's great promises will be fulfilled through Jesus in the glorious dawn that awaits those whose trust is in the Saviour. Better times are coming.

DAY 183

READ
Matthew
1:22–2:12

In order to show us that Jesus is the culmination of the previous phases in God's story, Matthew often uses the language of "fulfilment" (for example, v.22). By "fulfilment" he does not mean that a random selection of predictions from the Old Testament somehow land on target in Jesus.

Rather, on a larger scale, by "fulfilment", Matthew seeks to show that the whole pattern of Israel's story is being gathered up and reproduced in Jesus.

That entire story is being "filled-full" by Jesus, as Jesus is and does all that God wanted Israel to be and do. On the largest scale, the God who has always been with Israel is now with them in person to do for them – and for the world – what only God could do.

Matthew says that the birth of Jesus the "Immanuel-child" fulfils Isaiah 7:14 as a sign – "God with us" (1:22–23). This is not a simple proof-text that "proves" Jesus' divine credentials.

In its original context Isaiah's message was not a Messianic prophecy but a word to King Ahaz that the imminent defeat of his enemies would be a sure sign of "God-being-with-him".

Reflecting on who Mary's baby really is, Matthew sees in Jesus the ultimate sign of God-being-with-His-people. After all, how much more "with-His-people" can God get than to become one of them?

A DEVOTIONAL INTERLUDE

For praise: There are some who view God as a distant deity, a being high up in the heavens who stands remote from His creation. In Jesus, however, God has come close to us. Through the great act of the Incarnation we can now say God is not just for us but with us. Whatever you do today, and wherever you will go – through the Holy Spirit He will be there to love, guide, comfort, deliver and save. Give God praise for that great fact.

DAY **184**

READ
Luke 2:22–32

Simeon is an attractive figure in his own right. But for Luke, he also symbolises a faithful and expectant Israel, "waiting for the consolation of Israel" (vv.25,38). This expression was shorthand for the blessing and salvation of the Messianic era. Isaiah had captured the relief of the coming age in such phrases as: "Comfort, comfort my people" (Isa. 40:1); "the Lord will surely comfort Zion" (Isa. 51:3). The divine discontent stirring within Simeon was the work of the Holy Spirit on him. He looked for interests bigger than his own. For an old man – as he seems to be – he remains sharp and forward-looking, alive and alert in the Spirit to the next chapter in God's big story. And the Holy Spirit prompted him to discern what God was doing in this critical and climactic stage of the story, enabling him to recognise the child in his arms as the long-awaited Christ, the goal of Israel's dreams and his own desires. His song says it all. Jesus is the culmination of what God has been preparing for a very long time. He replaces the Temple as the focal point of God's glory in Israel, and becomes the One through whom Israel is now set to achieve her purpose as God's people by being a light to the Gentile nations of the world. No wonder, that seeing Jesus, Simeon knew he had seen all he needed to see to make his life worthwhile.

A DEVOTIONAL INTERLUDE

Prayer: My Father and my God, just as Simeon, when his eyes fell upon Jesus, knew that he had seen all he needed to make his life worthwhile, so this is my testimony too. The entrance of Your Son into my life has turned my life from defeat to victory, from gloom to gladness, from a life that lacked meaning to one that is now full of meaning. How I bless the day when the Saviour became *my* Saviour! Thank You my Father. Amen

DAY 185

READ
Luke 2:33–40

The day of salvation for which God has long prepared has dawned, but its coming to Israel will not be greeted with universal acclaim.

Simeon and Anna are among those who constitute a Spirit-filled "welcome committee" for Jesus, but not all would be as receptive. The cruciality of Christ is unavoidable. Nothing and no one will escape the effects of His coming. As a quite deliberate part of God's plan, this child is destined to cause great upheaval. His effect will be to turn Israel upside down. The revolution He ushers in will inevitably flush out opposition and arouse fierce antagonism. He will act as a searching light, exposing vested interest, vainglory, hidden agendas and well-disguised hypocrisy. He will force people to show their hand and to declare themselves in their true colours. Not everyone will like Him or find satisfaction in His arrival as Simeon does. Jesus brings both judgment and grace. No one will remain neutral in His presence. And His ministry, like His birth, will cause pain. The price He pays will be felt by His mother as a sword thrust through her heart. But Simeon praised God for His coming, His parents marvelled at what was said about Him, and we, with Anna, give thanks for Him and speak about Him to all who look for Israel's consolation and the world's salvation.

A DEVOTIONAL INTERLUDE

Question: Have you experienced moments when your Christian commitment has caused you to be rejected by those who reject Jesus? Most Christians have undergone such times. Whenever that happens keep in mind that though those who reject Christ may sometimes reject us, we are on the other hand gloriously accepted by God and promised a reward in heaven. The one perspective more than compensates for the other.

DAY 186

READ
Matthew 2:13–15

Matthew is showing us how Jesus, as it were, re-enacts the pattern of events in Israel's history in order to fulfil the purpose for which God chose Israel.

In this chapter Matthew refers to both Exodus and Exile – the two traumatic events that bracket the Old Testament story of Israel: Exodus – the dramatic beginning; and Exile – the effective end of her life as an independent nation under God.

Matthew describes how parents and child escape Herod's anger by fleeing to Egypt. Matthew sees their return as fulfilling words of the prophet Hosea: "Out of Egypt I called my son" (2:15b; Hosea 11:1).

Hosea is here referring to the early description of Israel as God's son (Exod. 4:22). But again we have an important insight into what Matthew means by "fulfilment" as applied to Jesus' relation to the Old Testament prophets.

For the fulfilment here is not that of fulfilling a predictive prophecy. In fact Hosea's words have no future reference at all but are a reflection on Israel's past history, recalling the Exodus from Egypt.

Once again Matthew is making the larger point that Jesus recapitulates Israel's story by beginning where she began – in Egypt. He comes up "out of Egypt" as God's "son", the true Israel of God. And immediately Matthew alerts us to the fact that a new and greater "Exodus" is under way!

A DEVOTIONAL INTERLUDE

A challenge: If there is one thing that God hates it is to see His people under the bondage of sin. The Almighty has a passion to see His people free from all that binds them. It was this passion (as we saw in earlier readings) that led Him to rescue Israel from the bondage of slavery in Egypt. Are there any bondages in your life? The Almighty is still in the "Exodus" business. Ask Him to set you free today.

DAY **187**

READ
Matthew
2:16–23

Matthew now brings the Exile into focus by quoting from Jeremiah in a passage where the prophet decribes the "new covenant" and refers to Israel as God's "dear son" (Jer. 31:20,31ff.).

Jeremiah was responding to the pain of the Babylonian Exile, by picturing Rachel, the original mother of Israel, weeping for her descendants taken into captivity in Babylon. Matthew perceives Rachel's deep grief as being felt all over again in the agony of the mothers around Bethlehem whose children have been murdered in Herod's savage purge. The "massacre of the innocents" is a violent intrusion into the Nativity story, showing the harshness of the world the Christ-child has come to redeem. Even His arrival to defeat evil brings pain before it brings consolation. Poignantly, the Bethlehem mothers are caught up in the larger story of Israel's Exile under judgment and God's act of redemption.

By drawing Exodus and Exile together, Matthew is already indicating the scale of what this child will achieve. It is clear that Jesus will gather up both ends of Israel's story – starting where she started enslaved in Egypt and again in Exile – and bringing her out in a greater Exodus, by a greater redemption, returning her not merely to the land but to her God!

Prayer: Father, how can we thank You enough for the fact that Jesus is the beginner of our story and the concluder of Your story of salvation. He sets the slaves free and brings the exiles home to You. I am so grateful that my spiritual slavery has been abolished and that I am no longer an exile but an heir of God and a joint heir with Christ. My heart is Yours forever. Amen.

A DEVOTIONAL INTERLUDE

DAY 188

READ
Matthew 3:1–15

Jesus comes to the banks of the Jordan River, where the children of Israel had once stood poised to enter the promised land, in order to submit to John's baptism, joining with all those who were repenting of their sins in doing so (v.6). John is taken aback and feels the roles should be reversed because Jesus does not seem to be a sinner (vv.11,14). But Jesus has come to "fulfil all righteousness" which in broad terms means that He has come to bring to reality God's age-old redemptive plan revealed in the Scriptures.

So, the fact that Jesus undergoes a "baptism for sinners", when by all accounts He was not one, further shows the extent to which He would identify with Israel at this climactic moment in her history. He does so in at least two ways. In being baptised, He willingly steps into Israel's shoes to fulfil her role as God's faithful covenant partner. Secondly, He shows Himself willing to bear Israel's sin and judgment by being "numbered with transgressors" as they confessed their sins and made ready for the arriving kingdom of God.

He was, in other words, being baptised for others – thus anticipating his "immersion" in the atoning death of the cross. Those willing to follow Him all the way down into the river of death would emerge with sins forgiven, stepping out into the new world of salvation.

A DEVOTIONAL INTERLUDE

Thought: Consider this before you take up the duties of the day: everything Christ did He did for us. He wore our flesh, measured its frailty, "walked in our shoes" so to speak, was baptised as our representative, immersed Himself in death so that we might live. A good response to all this would be for us to pray the words of an ancient prayer: "All this You have done for me; what have I done for Thee?"

DAY **189**

READ
Matthew 3:16–17

We linger over this crucial moment of Jesus' baptism on the banks of Jordan River.

The voice from heaven endorses Jesus as the true Davidic king whose sonship is affirmed by the anointing of the Holy Spirit as truly Messianic. The divine words are a merging of Psalm 2:7 with Isaiah 42:1 – with perhaps an echo of the offering of the only beloved son, Isaac. The words combine God's promise to the Davidic king that he would be "God's son", with Isaiah's vision of the self-effacing, servant of God who would eventually suffer in the cause of bringing salvation to others. The words from heaven, therefore, mark Jesus out as a Servant-king, set on an ambiguous and mysterious royal road which must pass through suffering and humiliation on its way to glory.

For Jesus personally, we can perhaps sense how the Father's love and approval penetrate to the depth of His heart, not only clarifying His identity and mission, but fortifying Him emotionally against the disapproval of His enemies and the misunderstanding of His friends in the three years ahead. The significance of the Holy Spirit coming in the form of a dove may derive from Genesis 8:8–12 where the dove appears as the harbinger of a new world after the Flood. The Father endorses the Son and the Spirit empowers Him to bring in the new creation!

A DEVOTIONAL INTERLUDE

To ponder: The greatest joy in the Christian life, Dr Martyn Lloyd-Jones used to say, is not just that our sins have been forgiven but that we have been made children of God and adopted into the royal family of heaven. Thus we are invited to hear the Father's voice saying to us, in similar words to those He said to his Son: "I delight in you too as my child". Read 1 John 3:1 now and ponder it throughout the day.

READ
Matthew 4:1–3

Matthew's picture of Jesus as the One who re-enacts Israel's story is further underlined by the narrative describing Jesus' temptations.

Like David confronting Goliath, the newly anointed king-in-waiting strides out to meet the evil challenger to God's rule.

His test lasts a symbolic forty days in the wilderness, re-enacting, as it were, the temptations which Israel faced and failed to resist during forty years in the wilderness and thereafter in the land. This is confirmed by the fact that Jesus quotes three times from Deuteronomy, Israel's charter of national identity and behaviour. But, whereas Israel had failed the test in the wilderness, God's "new Israel", Jesus Himself, succeeds gloriously.

Jesus is tested as "the son of God" – perhaps a faint echo of the privileged calling of Adam himself (as Luke implies in 3:38). Matthew's clear intention is to link Jesus with the covenantal "sonship" of both Israel's king (2 Sam. 7:14; Psa. 2:7), and of Israel herself whom the king represented.(Exod. 4:22–23; Hosea 11:1). It is interesting to notice that the wilderness period was seen as a "test" for Israel for, Moses says, "as a man disciplines his son, so the Lord your God disciplines you" (Deut. 8:1–5). Once again everything hangs on the obedience of one man: and He doesn't fail us!

A DEVOTIONAL INTERLUDE

For praise: Pause before going any further and allow these thoughts to lie upon your mind until they generate a stream of praise: Jesus, our new David, our great Champion, wins the victory for us over sin and Satan's forces. Thus, we are, as Scripture says, "more than conquerors". A conqueror is someone who wins by fighting. Being more than a conqueror is someone who wins without fighting.

DAY 191

READ
Matthew 4:3–4

The devil's aim, it appears, is to distort Jesus' sense of a God-given vocation by encouraging Him to adopt ungodly methods for how it might be worked out. He first challenges Jesus' faith in God's ability to provide for Him, by tempting Him to turn stones into bread to meet His own needs. This is tantamount to magic which is the desire to harness divine power to our own ends, or to bring divine forces under our control. Jesus is being tempted to abuse His power in His own self-interest. Like Israel before Him, Jesus is tempted to the sin of unbelief, that is, to live other than by faith in God's Word. Even after a forty-day fast Jesus refuses. Even though, like John, He knows God can make stones "talk", He refuses (cf. Matt 3:9). Jesus responds by declaring His intention of adhering to the covenant charter of how the true Israel should live by quoting from Deuteronomy 8:3 to the effect that "Man does not live on bread alone, but on every word that comes from the mouth of God". Jesus will wait patiently in faith for His Father to act and will not deny His call. The Holy Spirit sustains Jesus here in trust and dependency on God.

A DEVOTIONAL INTERLUDE

Prayer: My Father and my God, help me to honour You as did Your Son, with my trust and patient courage. May my reliance always be on You and on Your written Word. Produce in me, dear Father, the fruits of longsuffering and self-control so that I may be able to withstand all the wiles of the devil and rebut all his temptations in the power of the Holy Spirit. I ask this in and through the Name of Jesus. Amen.

DAY **192**

READ
Matthew 4:5-7

Secondly, Jesus is urged to throw Himself from the pinnacle of the Temple, while "naming and claiming" Psalm 91 as his protection. But such suicidal bravado is fanaticism not true faith. Intriguingly, also, Israel's original failure in the wilderness was along these lines. It was soberly immortalised in the names "Meribah" ("contention") and "Massah" ("testing") which recalled the day when the children of Israel clamoured for water, suggesting that God was out to kill them. Moses gave the place these names because the people "tested the Lord saying: Is the Lord among us or not?" (Exod. 17:1–7). The memory of this tragic event was kept alive in Israel's worship with its ringing call for an obedient response "today" (Psa. 95:7–11). As the psalmist indicates, it is tragically possible to have seen God act in mighty "works" but not to know or walk in His "ways". Jesus, for His part, would always avoid doing miracles "on demand" as proof of anything! He refuses to prove that God is with Him "on demand". He resists what He sees as presumption, as putting God to the test, by again citing the Deuteronomy command, "Do not put the Lord your God to the test". Jesus will not presume on His relationship with His Father as if God were there to serve Him rather than the reverse.

A DEVOTIONAL INTERLUDE

To ponder: Is God here to serve us or are we here to serve Him? That is a question that deserves the deepest thought and consideration. Sadly, multitudes of Christians seem to think God is under an obligation to answer their every prayer and respond to their every whim. Ask yourself today: Am I walking in the obedience of faith or do I live out my days with the assumption that God exists to serve me?

DAY 193

READ
Matthew 4:8–11

The third temptation Jesus faces is to be offered the kingdoms of the world on condition He bows down and worships Satan. We have seen from the second Psalm that God's anointed King will only have to entreat His Father for the nations to become His inheritance. Worldwide rule is His for the asking! Jesus, therefore, is quick to rebut this temptation. He repudiates the idea of idolatry, insisting, again in words from Deuteronomy: "Worship the Lord your God, and serve him only". We can see what the thrust of the temptation is.

"If you are the true Israel, God's 'son', if you are her representative king, God's 'son', then go the way of Israel and her kings before you'." But – savingly – Jesus refuses! Unbelief, presumption, idolatry – these are the sins Israel continued to be bedeviled by throughout her life in the promised land. But Jesus is saying, in effect, that where Israel failed to rise to the covenant challenge and abide by the Deuteronomic ideal, He will. His secret? Well, the Spirit led Him not only into the desert to be tested but led Him through it triumphantly.

A DEVOTIONAL INTERLUDE

Quotation: Chris Wright is one of the finest biblical scholars of our day and his remarks on today's theme form a helpful supplement to what has already been said. "On the shoulders of Jesus as the Son of God lay the responsibility of being the true son, succeeding where Israel had failed, submitting to God's will where they had rebelled, obeying where they had disobeyed." What a Saviour!

DAY 194

READ
Matthew
4:12–25

Jesus returned to Galilee, but He made His base of ministry not in Nazareth but in the more populated and influential Capernaum. He deliberately restricted His mission to the people of Israel and never embarked on a wider Gentile mission. In fact He avoided the larger, more cosmopolitan towns such as Tiberius and Sepphoris. But in returning to Galilee, Matthew sees Jesus marking out a claim, rooted in the prophecy of Isaiah, that the impact of God's Messianic King and kingdom would be felt by the nations beyond Israel. Galilee was the "way to the sea", situated on the trade routes to the Mediterranean coast and therefore to the rest of the world. However much Jesus made Israel His first priority, what happened in Galilee and Judea would eventually light up the whole world. It was here that Jesus recruited His first disciples. He called them from fishing for fish in the local lake to fishing for people in the ocean of the world. Meanwhile He launched His Messianic ministry, preaching the good news of God's kingdom. Where God's kingdom breaks into our lives in power, demons fear and fly, the sick are healed and Jesus makes news everywhere. Jesus is still the most consistently breaking news there is!

A DEVOTIONAL INTERLUDE

Thought: When Jesus said "I am the light of the world" few people realised that His message and His gospel would illuminate the centuries and make an impact on the world greater than any other individual who has ever lived. Think of it – what He did back there 2,000 years ago has reached across the centuries to impact your life in the here and now. That's worth a shout of "Hallelujah!" – is it not?

DAY **195**

READ
Luke 4:16–30

When Jesus returned to His home-town synagogue from His first preaching tour, the atmosphere was electric. Who did this carpenter's boy think he was? Jesus offers Isaiah 61 as His credentials for ministry. The "good news" heralded by Isaiah focuses on Jesus as the anointed deliverer, who proclaims the kingdom of God.

And this gospel is for the poor, for those who are economically impoverished and culturally marginalised.

Jesus' keynote is "freedom". The "release" He speaks of harks back to the unfulfilled dreams of the Jubilee year freedoms of Leviticus 25. "Today is the day", Jesus declares, for ancient scriptures to come good before your very eyes. Jesus proclaims release for the beggars in debt, for the bound in detention, for the blind in darkness, for the burdened under domination. This is the year of the Lord's favour announced in gracious words (v.22). But the gospel provokes a mixed reaction. First attentive amazement (vv.20–22), then puzzlement (v.22), then furious antagonism (v.28). The idea that the freedom is for Gentiles was too much (vv.25–27). They missed God's acceptable year because it came through God's unacceptable prophet!

A DEVOTIONAL INTERLUDE

For praise: James Montgomery wrote a verse of a hymn that captures some of the thoughts that have been presented to us today. Sing it or say it as your "sacrifice" of praise to God

Hail to the Lord's anointed, Great David's greater Son!
Hail in the time appointed, His reign on earth begun
He comes to break oppression, to set the captive free
To take away transgression and rule in equity

DAY 196

READ
Matthew 5:1–11

We call it the "Sermon on the Mount" and so make it sound like a polite homily from a pulpit. To those who first heard it must have sounded more like a manifesto for a revolutionary political party!

Those seeking the invasion of God's kingdom to restore Israel's glory, are told that it will come but only to those who are beggars in spirit and humbly dependent on God's grace. The consolation of Israel will come but it will be paid for in repentant tears. The whole earth awaits to be inherited, not by the conquering strong, but by the humble meek. Soul satisfaction is a noble quest but only those who hunger and thirst to see God's justice prevail will find it. You want mercy? Then show mercy! The sight of God is not for the elite or advantaged holders of religious office but for the pure in heart. For Israel once again to be the "sons of God" will mean making peace not war. The kingdom belongs not to those who inflict violence but to those who endure violence for the sake of this gloriously upside-down kingdom! And the blessedness is for right now! – a deeply satisfying God-given blessing that rests upon the humble poor, the meek, the mourners, the merciful and those who long for God's righteousness, peace and justice to be seen on earth.

A DEVOTIONAL INTERLUDE

Prayer: Thank You, Father, for the great "reversals of grace" that turn the world upside down and therefore right side up. Thank You too for the way your Son has impacted my life and shown me how I should live. Help me function in this upside-down kingdom the way Your Son has taught me – blessing those who persecute me and giving out love when I meet hatred. In Jesus' Name. Amen.

DAY **197**

READ
Matthew 5:13–15

Like a new Moses, Jesus issues a new Torah, not an abolition but a fulfilment of the old one, a Torah intensified and radicalised by His own presence as the fulfilment of God's promises (vv.17–20). So it was no call to return to conventional morality. Whatever its wider application, Jesus' message was originally a sharp challenge to the Israel of His day to renew their vocation as God's covenant people.

Only the "Jesus way" of being Israel has a future in it. His teaching outlines the path of true covenant loyalty to God which fulfils the intentions of the law and the prophets.

Can His disciples rise to the challenge of becoming the new people of God? Israel had been called to be a holy nation, a royal priesthood, a light to the Gentile nations. But that salty distinctiveness has been all but obliterated. A darkened people are in no position to show the way to others. Will the disciples of Jesus be the nucleus of that new people of God who will demonstrate the light of life to the world? Will they authenticate the truth they hold by the lives they live?

A DEVOTIONAL INTERLUDE

To ponder: In Christ we are called and empowered to live lives that illuminate rather than darken the world around us, to reflect and relay the love of God to everyone we meet. Ask the Lord to help you daily live and witness, whether through your words or through your life, in such a way that you impact the life of every unbeliever you relate to. "It's amazing," said Hudson Taylor, "what God can do through one life committed to him."

DAY 198

READ
Matthew 6:5–15

The Lord's Prayer has its context within the longer story we are tracing. Israel had been judged by God and sent into Exile for bringing God's Name into disrepute by her failure to live a covenant life. God's reputation has been tarnished by Israel's behaviour before the eyes of a watching world. When God moves to restore His people, says Ezekiel, it will be less for their sake than to restore the honour of His holy Name (Ezek. 36:22). Those who know the times of restoration are at hand, will have one priority in prayer: "Hallowed be your name, O Lord."

From the time of the Exile, the prophets project the hope that God would forgive His people. Isaiah says that God will blot out sins as we erase a stain, He will sweep them away like a morning mist burnt off by the sun. This longed-for forgiveness will flood an exiled people with the joy of pardon and reacceptance by God. In such a day, Jesus says, the forgiveness sinners receive from God will overflow into forgiving one another. Grace will create a community of "forgiven-forgivers". The age-old Jubilee dream (Lev. 25) may yet be realised through the gospel in a society built not on debt and vindictiveness, not on extortion or resentment but on fairness, generosity and mercy.

A DEVOTIONAL INTERLUDE

Thought: The receiving and giving of forgiveness is what the Christian life is all about. No one can call himself or herself a true believer unless he or she is willing to accept this truth and put it into practice. You have been forgiven, now if you have not yet forgiven all those who hurt or injured you then don't go any further into the day until you have done so. Only the forgiving can be forgiven.

DAY **199**

READ
Mark 2:1–12

Let's not miss the drama as Jesus pronounces forgiveness for sins (2:5). We are used to taking this personally, in the sense of having *our* sins forgiven, and we are right to do so. But it is important to remember – in the context of the ministry of Jesus – that it was God's judgment on Israel's sins which sent her into Exile in Babylon and prompted the need for national forgiveness. This hope of forgiveness for Israel was part of the prophets' promise for the future (Isa. 43:25; 44:21–22). We heard both Daniel and Ezra pleading with God to forgive an Israel "still in its sins" despite being back in the land. Isaiah offers hope to the exiles after hearing a commanding voice declaring that Israel's "sin has been paid for" (40:1–2). When Jesus heals and forgives one paralysed man, He is, in effect, proclaiming national healing and forgiveness. And His religious opponents were scandalised, not because they heard a human voice saying the words "Your sins are forgiven you" – the priests did this in the Temple every day after the right sacrifice had been offered – but because Jesus was doing it, unauthorised, and not in the Temple but on the streets. When Jesus declared the healed man "forgiven" he was, in effect, announcing that "Exile was now finally over" and that the day of salvation had arrived in and through Him!

A DEVOTIONAL INTERLUDE

For praise: In today's world psychiatrists are highly skilled in unearthing the things that trouble us. They can trace the sins once committed but long forgotten and bring them out into the light of day. But there is one thing they cannot do – they cannot forgive. Only God can do that. Jesus is God and therefore able to forgive all sin. No greater proof of His deity is needed. Praise Him for that glorious fact.

DAY **200**

READ
Mark 3:13–18

Jesus appointed twelve apostles for His own good reasons. Among them, we need not doubt, was His own human need for companionship. Mark says they were appointed to "be with him". He wanted friends on his journey who could share His exalted moments – as in transfiguration – or His darkest hours – as in Gethsemane.

His calling of the twelve was also born of His desire to see an extension of His ministry beyond Himself. He called them so that He "might send them out ...". Jesus wanted agents who would share his Messianic mission. He wanted heralds who would announce the day of judgment and favour and proclaim the nearness of God's kingdom. He wanted those who could be trusted to share His authority over personal evil. But why twelve? Why not eleven or thirteen? Well, like His Old Testament namesake, He calls twelve because they represent the twelve tribes of Israel (cf. Josh. 3–4). The choice of twelve was a powerful symbolic gesture, a political statement that, in the restored Israel, the traditional religious leaders would be replaced by fisherman and other working men. He could give no clearer sign of His intention to redefine who Israel was than by re-assigning the leadership of God's people in His way to the men of His choice.

A DEVOTIONAL INTERLUDE

Question: How much time do you spend communing with the Saviour? Not reading about Him in books such as this, but talking to Him, as a friend talks to a friend? The Christian life rises and falls at this point. Time spent in any other way may yield rewards but it must not displace time spent with Him. So once again: how much time do you spend really communing with the Saviour? A little or a lot?

DAY 201

READ
Matthew 8:5-13

Jesus had little direct contact with Gentiles during His ministry, but this was a significant meeting. Roman soldiers knew all about authority and so it shows striking humility and submission for the centurion to acknowledge the authority of Jesus. Jesus was rarely taken aback by anything: only extreme lack of faith (Mark 6:6) and, as here, sheer audacity of faith, surprise him (v.10).

For now, the scope of Jesus' mission was restricted to Israel. But the centurion's bold faith heralds the day, soon to come, when the Gentiles from every corner of the globe would come streaming in to take their places at the feast of grace with Abraham and Isaac and Jacob. A military man from Rome in the West and magi from the East would sit down together at table as equal members, in Christ, of God's one covenant family. Perhaps even Abraham will be taken aback by the crowds who follow in the footsteps of his faith! But if many are included by faith, others exclude themselves by their unbelief – a sober warning to nationalist Jews in Matthew's day and complacent Christians then and now! Let's make sure we give Jesus a joyous not a sad surprise!

A DEVOTIONAL INTERLUDE

Thought: While in a sense nothing can surprise the Lord for He sees and knows everything in advance, how pleased He must be when our love, faith and courage break out in new and delightful ways. Think of one way today you can "surprise" the Lord with an act of love, faith or courage that will bring delight and joy to His heart. And think too of making it not just today – but every day.

DAY **202**

READ
Matthew
12:15–21

Jesus Himself indicated that His own identity was shaped by the servant songs of Isaiah (42–53). Matthew develops this here, especially in regard to the way Jesus handled people and healed them. As He recalled the ministry of Jesus, Matthew sees Isaiah's vision brought to life – particularly here the glimpse we are given in Isaiah 42.

When God's servant appears He will be unpretentious, and without the need for self-justification. He is not in "show-business". He is not on an ego trip needing the impetus of spin doctors or public relations experts. He is humble and self-effacing. He is not a strident propagandist, nor an overbearing personality. He brings God's revolution, but does not advance His cause by violence or by intimidatory tactics. He fosters the tiniest flicker of faith, and deals gently with those bruised and broken by life.

When God's servant Israel fails in her mission (Isa. 42:18–19), God acts to raise up one faithful person from within Israel to restore the rest of God's people (Isa. 49:5–7). This true Israelite will be willing to suffer and die in order to bear the punishment due to the whole people (Isa. 52:13–53:12).

Through such strange and paradoxical tactics, He would in due course, as the suffering servant, "bring justice to victory".

A DEVOTIONAL INTERLUDE

Quotation: "The true way to be humble is not to stoop until you are smaller than yourself but to stand at your real height against some higher nature that will show you what the real smallness of your greatest greatness is. Stand at your very highest and then look at Christ and go away and be forever humble. Be aware that when you lose sight of Christ you yourself begin to loom large" (Philip Brooks).

DAY **203**

READ
Matthew 13:1–23

The parables are best understood in the context of Jesus' own ministry. They are not bland, timeless, abstract truths, but the cutting-edge of God's kingdom as they challenge the people of His day. Here, the seed is the "message of the kingdom" which Jesus speaks and embodies (v.19). God's kingdom comes not in a great blitz, but as a Word to be preached and believed. Jesus preaches the kingdom – like the prophets – as a two-edged sword, bringing both God's judgment and God's grace. His ministry provokes a very varied response. Resistant hearers show indifference, and remain hard and obdurate. Shallow hearers will soon fall away when the big trouble of AD 70 comes. Double-minded hearers find their new found faith in Jesus choked by the preoccupations of everyday living. The quotation from Isaiah 6 shows that this mixed result is not due to bad luck or poor evangelistic methods; it is God's intention! Jesus divides Israel by forcing a decision. Some will harden in their unbelief. But there is hope. Isaiah says of the felled tree that "the holy seed will be the stump in the land" (Isa. 6:13). So, Jesus says, in the very entity being cut back and judged there will lodge a seed (in Jesus' disciples) that will bear a disproportionate "hundred-fold" harvest (vv.8,23). Have you read Acts 2 recently?

A DEVOTIONAL INTERLUDE

For action: Open your Bible at Acts 2 and read once again the story of the great harvest of souls that were swept into the kingdom as a result of Peter's simple but Spirit-drenched preaching. Just think of it – one sermon brought 3,000 souls to Christ. Nowadays in some parts of the Church it takes 3,000 sermons to bring one soul to Christ. Suggest reasons to yourself why this may be so.

DAY **204**

READ
Matthew
13:33–35

All the Old Testament scriptures – including Psalm 78 – are considered to be "prophetic". All of them foreshadow God's future salvation in the Messianic era. Jesus quotes the opening verse of Psalm 78 (v.35) to explain what is going on in His parabolic teaching. Who better to interpret David's prophetic song than David's greater son, Jesus, to whom all these scriptures point and in whom they are all fulfilled?

Now Psalm 78 is a long recital of the turbulent history of God with Israel. That history of God's dealings with His people was with a view to the salvation of the world.

When Jesus reveals "things hidden since the creation of the world" (v.35) He is not uttering vacuous spiritual soundbites for religiously minded people, nor offering "greeting-card" clichés in vague spirituality. No! Jesus is about His Father's bigger business. He is now claiming to unveil the strategic plan of God which has been in God's heart from the beginning. This grand design is now being revealed and enacted in His ministry. These "mysteries" of the kingdom revealed in the parables are what former prophets and righteous men longed to see but can now be known because that longed-for day of salvation has at last arrived (13:11,16–17). How privileged we are as His disciples to be caught up in God's big story!

A DEVOTIONAL INTERLUDE

To ponder: In the light of today's reading this is a good opportunity to think once again of the privilege that is ours of being caught up in God's bigger story. Has this thought gripped you yet? Of course you are able to understand it intellectually, but has it gripped you in your heart? Do you thrill to the fact that you are involved in something that is not merely terrestrial but universal? If not why not?

DAY 205

READ
Matthew 13:51–52

Jesus' parables tease the mind, slipping through gaps in mental defences with the sharp thrust of God's kingdom. The kingdom's progress directly involves the disciples in whom the "seed" takes root and grows. Each disciple is given a glimpse into God's big strategy ("mystery") of bringing His rule to the world in judgment and salvation. To understand this, the "student of the kingdom" must study the previous revelation in the Old Testament and the "new" revelation brought by Jesus. The "new" things of Jesus don't cancel out but complete the "old" things. Without the Old Testament we cannot understand Jesus. But, conversely, we cannot understand the Old Testament without the newness of the gospel of Jesus. So "old" and "new" go together and interpret each other. There is continuity between them because the one God speaks and acts in both. Throughout the "old" era, God commits Himself by a series of covenant arrangements in order to further His plan of salvation. There is also discontinuity. In the "new era" all that's gone before is ransacked so as to begin to explain the revolution taking place in and through Jesus!

A DEVOTIONAL INTERLUDE

Prayer: O Father, help me understand more deeply this thought that while in Jesus there is continuity from the old, there is also discontinuity. I have tasted of His revolutionary power and I shall never be the same again. My life has been turned upside down by Him. Help me share this revolutionary message at every opportunity I am given. In His peerless Name I pray. Amen.

DAY **206**

READ
Matthew
15:21–28

At this stage in His ministry Jesus acknowledges the priority of Israel in the divine plan. The prophetic sequence of events in God's programme of salvation had always made it clear that first Israel then the Gentiles would come in. So Jesus confines His mission to Israel: "I was sent only to the lost sheep of Israel" (v.24). Moved with compassion, He seeks out those who have been cast out by the false shepherds of God's flock (cf. Matt. 9:36). Jesus presents Himself as the final restoration shepherd, foreseen by Ezekiel. This "final" shepherd would be a Prince of the house of David through whom God himself would shepherd His people (Ezek. 34). As this good shepherd, Jesus has come to regather and heal and feed the scattered, wounded, hungry sheep of God's flock.

In this light, His blunt treatment of the Canaanite woman is disturbing but just about understandable. To her credit, she remains undeterred and presses Him with admirable faith to include her in the feast of the kingdom. Already it is clear that more than enough bread is left over from feeding Israel to feed the four or five thousand and indeed the hungry multitudes across the world.

A DEVOTIONAL INTERLUDE

For thanksgiving: Some things are made to be broken. Bread is one of them. Left to itself it grows a green beard and goes bad. How grateful we ought to be that though our Lord's primary mission was to the nation of Israel, there was more than enough bread left over to include us in the redemptive plan. Give thanks for the fact that there is bread in our Father's house "and to spare".

DAY **207**

READ
Matthew
16:24–28
Daniel 7

The "son of man" (as in Daniel) is Jesus' favourite and exclusive way of referring to Himself. He comes as the truly Human One to identify with the "saints" of God fighting for their lives against evil foes. He wrestles with the wild beasts of entrenched religion and implacable political power. He emerges triumphant and is raised to a place of honour. Everything He does is for His people, as their representative. He incorporates their destiny. He defeats their enemies and is vindicated at the place of honour and judgment on their behalf. When He receives the kingdom and its authority, the saints receive it too. All that He is and does, His people are and achieve. He comes to the throne of the Ancient of Days trailing clouds of glory.

As for this future glory, it will be seen, He insists, "in this generation", within the lifetime of "some who are standing here" (v.28).

Again the earliest vision of this glory will be in transfiguration and resurrection, in ascension and the coming of the Spirit, and – as far as an unbelieving Israel was concerned – in the tragic ruin of Jerusalem and the Temple in AD 70 which would vindicate Jesus as a true prophet of God. All the more remarkable then, that this glorious and all-conquering figure will achieve God's ends by being willing to serve and in serving to suffer.

A DEVOTIONAL INTERLUDE

Thought: We have referred previously to the fact that the apostle Paul uses one term over and over again to remind us of our spiritual inheritance – "in Christ". Let this thought lie upon your mind before you go out into the day: to be "in Christ" is to share Christ's victory over sin and be a part of God's glorious plans for the future. You are a child of destiny. Never, never forget it.

DAY **208**

READ
John 1:14–17

John relates Jesus to the earlier stages of God's story with Israel by celebrating the "Word made flesh". Astonishingly, the all powerful Word of God which gave the universe life and continues to be the reason for its existence, has come enfleshed as a real human being. God's mighty Word which reverberates down through the centuries as a promise on the lips of prophets and which currently resounds throughout the world as a gospel in the mouth of apostles, is nothing less than a glorious person, Jesus of Nazareth.

All that the One Creator God has to say to His world is finally and fully summed up in Jesus! This Word, as John puts it, has "pitched his tent" or "tabernacled among us" – language reminiscent of God "dwelling" in the Tabernacle and filling it with his glory (Exod. 25:8–9; 40:34–35). Once, when God's glory passed before Moses, it turned out to be a glorious demonstration of His goodness which consists of steadfast love and faithfulness or truth (Exod. 33:19; 34:6). It is precisely this majestic combination of "grace and truth" that John believes has been gloriously concentrated and displayed in Jesus. Moses is well and truly eclipsed. The Torah was a gift from God but the ultimate grace and truth is not encoded in a book but embodied in a person.

A DEVOTIONAL INTERLUDE

Quotation: "Why is Jesus called the 'Word'? Well, one's words are the expression of the hidden thought. If you should stand before an audience without a word, hoping the audience would get your thought intuitively and immediately, it would end in futility. Only as the hidden thought is put into a word is the thought communicated. Jesus is God's hidden thought put into a Word" (E. Stanley Jones).

DAY 209

READ
John 1:1–18

The story of Jesus, John reminds us, is the key to the story of the world (vv.3–5, 9–10). Creation cannot properly be understood except from a world-view in which Jesus is the central agent of God's creative wisdom and Word, the One by whom (and for whom) the world was made (cf. Prov. 8; Col. 1:15–20). But Jesus' story is also the climax of the story of Israel (vv.6–8,11–13,17). All that Israel was meant to be as a showcase of God's glory is now focused and concentrated in Jesus. Israel's special role in bringing the light of God's truth to the nations, is now fulfilled in the one obedient "Son of God" (v.34). He does this by making His story one with our story, by taking our "flesh and blood" humanity to Himself. The humanity He assumes is the humanity He heals. Out of His fullness we have all received, grace upon grace. The "sons of God" are no longer determined by heredity or ethnicity or Torah but "to all who received him, to those who believed in his name, he gave the right to become children of God – children born not of natural descent, nor of human decision or a husband's will, but born of God" (vv.12–13). All who see His glory and believe in Him are constituted as the new covenant family of the One Creator God.

A DEVOTIONAL INTERLUDE

To ponder: Suppose the Scriptures said "full of truth and grace" rather than "grace and truth", what would be the difference? The emphasis would have been upon "truth". Truth of course is very important but the first emphasis in the Christian message is "grace". John got the order right: first grace then truth. We see truth through grace – grace is truth in glorious act.

DAY 210

READ
John 1:18

Above all, says John, the story of Jesus is the story of God. God's own glory and presence, Word and wisdom, grace and truth, are incarnated fully and uniquely in Jesus. No one has ever seen God, but the One who is at the Father's side "has made him known". Jesus perfectly "exegetes" God (v.18) – a word used elsewhere with the meaning "to tell a story". In Don Carson's words, "Jesus is the narration of God". We read God's story in the human story of Jesus because Jesus is the obedient Son who does only what He sees the Father doing and says only what He hears the Father say. Incarnation is the supreme mystery at the centre of the story. But it does not come entirely out of the blue for those who have read the clues in the story so far. There, we find a God who loves to be with His people; a God who allows Himself to be described (anthropomorphically) in human terms; a God who feels and makes Himself vulnerable. What might Israel's God look like if He emerged within the world in human flesh? If human beings bear His image, and Israel is His "son" who represents Him in the world, then the One Creator God might well appear as a Jewish human being.

But then Jesus has been in the "image of the invisible God" from the beginning!

Prayer: O Son of God, thank You for showing us the Father. We would never have known what He was like had we not looked upon Your face. Now seeing the Father in Your face we are satisfied, yet not satisfied. We are stirred to be like what we see in You. Help us become more like You in character and in attitude. For Your dear Name's sake we ask it. Amen.

A DEVOTIONAL INTERLUDE

DAY **211**

READ
John 1:19–51

John the Baptist occupies a special place in the unfolding story because he stands on the dividing line between the old and the new order. Again John the "plunger" is identified with the "voice in the wilderness" who, Isaiah had said, would prepare the way of the Lord and herald the coming rule of God. John fits the bill well. He makes a way for Jesus who is the Way. John is a lamp: Jesus is the Light. John is a voice: Jesus is the Word. John testifies that Jesus is the Lamb of God, the final Passover sacrifice for sin. John baptises in water but only with a view to a greater baptism from the One who bestows the Spirit in the Messianic age. The first tentative confessions of faith confirm this (vv.41,45,49). More is revealed in a cryptic saying of Jesus during His encounter with Nathanael (vv.50–51). Jacob, the founding father of Israel, who gave his name to the nation, once saw a ladder on which heavenly beings travelled in both directions. Later Jewish speculation posited the angels viewing Jacob at both ends of the ladder, so that he represents both an earthly and a heavenly Israel. But, says Jesus, it is not upon Jacob/Israel, but on Him, the Son of Man, that the ladder rests which bears the traffic between earth and heaven! On Him, the "New Israel" God's transactions with earth are now conducted. What a claim!

A DEVOTIONAL INTERLUDE

For thanksgiving: O God, how can we ever thank You enough for the fact that You have given us Jesus to be our Passover Lamb, to be our Mediator between heaven and earth. He is the only Ladder between heaven and earth – all other ladders are too short. I am so grateful that I have put my feet on the first rung of that ladder. I am ready for heaven and I know that through grace heaven will be ready for me. Amen.

DAY **212**

READ
John 2:1–25

If this first sign "signifies" anything, it is that the time of fulfilment has arrived. The water in the pots symbolises the old order of things, told in the earlier chapters of the story, where the Torah is often likened to water. Now that old order of preparation is giving way to the new age of Messianic fulfilment, of which wine is often a potent symbol (Isa. 55:1). Symbolically, the previous stage of the relationship has now progressed to the point of the wedding, which anticipates the description of the bridegroom (3:29). Jesus is the fully matured vintage wine, kept till last, that tops all others! In Jesus, God has saved the best revelation till last (cf. Heb. 1:1). In this sign, we behold His glory (v.11). The key to John's entire Gospel is that Jesus fulfils the meaning of the central Old Testament feasts and institutions. Nothing would more strikingly signify the "death" of the old order than the destruction of the great Temple in Jerusalem. The zeal of those who built and maintained the Temple as the house of God would prove mere tinder for the fiery zeal for God's house that burned in Jesus. That fire eventually consumed Him in the flames of sacrificial love on the cross. But, like a phoenix, from the ashes of His dying would come the triumphant Risen Life where God is met and worshipped.

A DEVOTIONAL INTERLUDE

For praise: No one has ever tasted true joy until they have tasted the joy that Jesus provides. Joy it must be remembered is different from happiness. Happiness depends upon what is happening. When what happens is happy then we are happy. But joy is that deep quality that remains even when unhappy times are upon us. And only a Christian has access to that. For that give Him praise.

DAY **213**

READ
John 2:18–25

According to the other three Evangelists, Jesus was accused by false witnesses at His trial of saying that He would destroy the Temple and in three days build another. John here records the statement made by Jesus on which such a misunderstanding might be based. Jesus did not say, "I will destroy" this building: but "[You] destroy this building and in three days I will raise it again". Of course, to claim to rebuild such an impressive sanctuary that had been forty-six years in the making – and was still unfinished – was absurd. It amounts to a gently mocking rebuff of their demand for a miraculous sign. In fact, a sign is just what they will get, one even more extraordinary than any logic could imagine. He Himself in His own body is the ultimate manifestation and location of God on earth. In this body, the ultimate sacrifice for sin will soon be made. He would be raised from the dead in three days. And His resurrection would spell the end of the old Temple as the privileged focus of the presence and worship of God. In the Risen Jesus a new Temple, a new basis for communion with God, will be established.

A DEVOTIONAL INTERLUDE

Prayer: O Father how can I ever thank You enough for the fact that my faith is not in a lifeless structure or physical building but in a resurrected and living Saviour. It was possible for Your Son to die, but not possible for Him to be held by death. Jesus is the "new Temple" in Whom I find a new basis for worship, and a new foundation for praise. All honour and glory be to His peerless Name for ever. Amen.

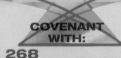

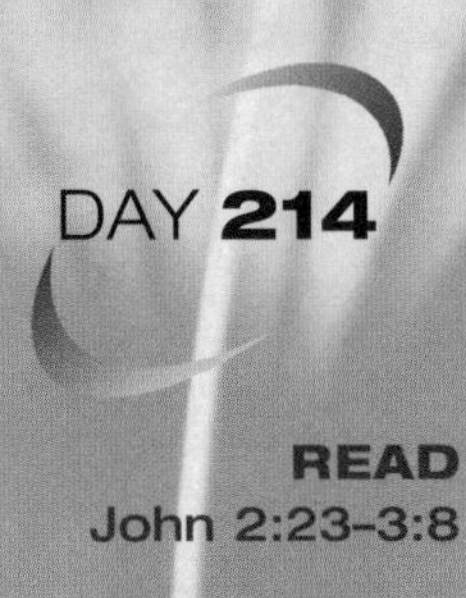

DAY **214**

READ
John 2:23–3:8

Jesus knows what is going on inside people, says John, even within a man like Nicodemus, a teacher of the law. Learned in theology and Jewish thinking, Nicodemus is curious perhaps as to how Jesus fits into the scheme of things. There is continuity between Jesus and the Old Testament revelation that explains Him. But there is also a radical discontinuity as Nicodemus abruptly discovers. Jesus does emerge out of that Old Testament truth but in doing so bursts its banks. Jesus transcends the categories to which even a sympathetic Jewish teacher might try to confine Him. Nicodemus must have a heart and mind transplant to see this! He must be born again into a whole new way of looking at things in order to grasp it. He needs a spiritual regeneration and a spiritual revolution in his mind, if he is to enter into the reality of the kingdom of God as it has come in Jesus! The "water" and "Spirit" Jesus speaks of represent the transforming work of the Holy Spirit. What Jesus describes echoes Ezekiel's prophecy about the way in which God would wash people clean, implanting a new heart and imparting a new spirit to create God's new covenant people. Will Nicodemus – will we – allow the mysterious moving of God's Spirit to outflank all our old categories and give us a new spiritual birthday?

A DEVOTIONAL INTERLUDE

For thanksgiving: If you were to say to a non-Christian that to become a follower of Jesus requires them to "have a heart and mind transplant" it might cause them to question your sanity. But that is precisely what Christianity is – a revolutionary experience that equates to a heart and mind transplant. Give thanks to God for performing that miracle on you.

DAY **215**

READ
John 3:9-21

Having used new covenant terminology – Ezekiel's "water" and "Spirit" – to describe the new birth necessary to enter God's kingdom, Jesus now utilises a strange old covenant story to make His point.

During the wilderness wanderings, the children of Israel grumble bitterly against God and under judgment succumb to deadly snake bites (Num. 21:4–9). Moses is told to make a bronze serpent and place it on top of a tall pole visible to the whole camp. Anyone who looks with faith upon this bronze snake is healed.

Now the same God who had made saving provision for a temporary bodily need, will make final provision of eternal life by lifting Jesus up on a cross. The key word is "lifted up". It implies not only physical elevation but spiritual exaltation and almost certainly reflects Isaiah's picture of the suffering servant being "lifted up" in vindication and honour (Isa. 52:13). This is characteristic of John. In a marvellous and paradoxical sense, he sees the moment when Jesus is "lifted up in glory" as occurring not at His resurrection or ascension but even earlier, at His crucifixion! Jesus' "lifting up" on the cross is not just prior to, but synonymous with, His lifting up and exaltation in glory! His throne was Calvary; He reigns from the cross. Look to Him there in faith and you will live!

A DEVOTIONAL INTERLUDE

Thought: It's interesting that a serpent is both a symbol of sin and a symbol of salvation. It is interesting also that the most effective antidote for a snakebite is the snake venom itself. The cure is that which caused the disease. When our Lord was crucified our sins were crucified in Him. He became our sin that He might be our salvation. Looking up 2 Corinthians 5:21 will enlighten you further.

DAY **216**

READ
John 4:1-42

What a teacher of Israel fails to grasp, a Samaritan woman is led to see. But the setting – Jacob's well in Sychar – intentionally evokes the era of the patriarchs, and connects Jesus again with the deep covenantal roots in Israel's story.

The old water of the Torah cannot completely satisfy, but the living water can. This inspires a change in worship. Worship no longer depends on a sacred site, be it a Samaritan mountain, nor even, more shockingly, the Temple in Jerusalem!

Some scholars detect a betrothal scene here, reminiscent of how Jacob met Rachel at a well (Gen. 29:1–10) and linking the narrative to that of the wedding in Cana (2:1–10). If Jesus is the bridegroom (3:29), who is the bride if not Israel as the Old Testament affirms?

Like the provocative parable which features an outsider, a Samaritan man who proves faithful to the Torah by caring for the wounded traveller, so here, with a Samaritan woman, Yahweh's "marriage" is not exclusively with Israel but with all who believe in His Christ. This needy woman, unsatisfied by her sexual indulgence, is now ready to meet her seventh and perfect match in Jesus. Here is the man that she, and we, have been waiting for, the perfection and wholeness of salvation for her and her family, and indeed for men and women everywhere (vv.28–29, 42).

A DEVOTIONAL INTERLUDE

Prayer: Lord Jesus, my Saviour and my God, I am so grateful that with Wesley I can say, "Thou O Christ art all I want, more than all in Thee I find". For years I tried to satisfy my soul with water that failed to quench my thirst, but one draught of the water that You give has taken away the ache and given me a new zest for life – true life. My heart is Yours for ever. Amen.

DAY **217**

READ
John 5:1–30

One of John's aims is to show how Jesus brings to full reality the major themes and events of Israel, including, here, the Sabbath. John shows us that Jesus transforms the Sabbath regulations by being, Himself, the focus of the Sabbath-rest of God. The physical (v.5) and psychological (vv.6,13) barriers to the man's healing are considerable and, in addition, the religious climate of Sabbath-keeping precluded God working in this way.

But Jesus' action shows that it is wrong to regard the Sabbath as the day when God is not at work. The Sabbath laws were not meant to curtail life but to promote it. To prevent a healing on the Sabbath is therefore to go against the whole spirit and intention of the day when says Jesus, "My Father is working still." Though His original creation work was completed to His satisfaction, God remains restless and unceasing in working for redemption in a sin-spoiled world. And where His Father works, the Son works. To believe in Jesus is to enter into God's redemptive rest and into the good of His saving achievement. This is what the lame man sampled. In Jesus the day of rest becomes the day of restoration! This does not set Jesus up in competition with God – as His accusers allege – but in fact reflects His dependence and humility, as He does only what He sees the Father doing.

A DEVOTIONAL INTERLUDE

Quotation: "We should walk through every day with eyes wide open to see what God would have us do, with ears alert to hear what he has to say, with hands ready to do the work he would have us do. This is how Jesus lived out his days when he was here on earth and this is how we should live them out too. His secret was that he did only what the Father was doing. That must be our secret too"
(Dr Cynddylan Jones).

DAY **218**

READ
John 5:31–47

With great irony, John presents Jesus to us as on trial to which witnesses are called.

This links with Isaiah 40–55 where Yahweh and pagan gods go on trial before the world to determine who is the true God. In this "trial", God looks to Israel to be His witness who will give testimony on His behalf as the one true God (Isa. 41:1–4; 41:21–29; 43:8–13; 44:6–8; 45:20–25). John puts a subtle twist on this so that Jesus becomes both the accused who is on trial, and the judge who takes on God's role of giving a verdict! The terrible irony is that Jesus' accusers are siding with the pagans in lining up against Him!

Jesus calls four witnesses in His defence: John the Baptist (vv.33–35), the work the Father has given Him to do (v.36), the Father's personal affirmation (v.37) and, above all, the Scriptures themselves (vv.39–40). Here we are on familiar ground. The entire scriptural story of God, told so far through the story of God's people, Israel, points directly to Jesus and tells His story too. Jesus is the convergence point of that earlier stage of the story. Jesus is the narrative telling of God in full and concentrated form. He gathers up all previous revelation into His own account. He is the Bible's beating heart. His is the life-story told there, and to embrace Him is to find the life that is in the story.

A DEVOTIONAL INTERLUDE

To ponder: Think about this on and off throughout the day – our faith is not a vague leap in the dark but is based on the reliable evidence of Scripture and eyewitness accounts of events that happened in history. Many in these days are seeking to overturn the Bible's veracity, but stand firm on its truth. Those who lose faith in Scripture often lose faith in Jesus. And vice versa.

READ
John 6:1-35

Echoes of the Exodus pervade this passage: the crossing of the sea (vv.1,12–21), the climbing of a mountain (v.3), the timing at Passover (v.4), the gift of bread/manna in the desert (vv.6–13; 31–33). In addition, "manna" became in later Jewish thinking a metaphor for the Torah. So the comparison being made becomes clear. Jesus is the new Moses, He Himself is the covenant provision of God's people, He is the Passover Lamb of sacrifice, He is leading God's people out in a new exodus!

The account of the walking on the water at this point strengthens the Exodus allusion and enhances the contrast being made. The stakes are high. No longer mere physical hunger needs to be assuaged. If that is all, says Jesus, you seek Me for the wrong reasons (v.26). Our energies are consumed in the search for bread but need to be exerted in the quest for what really matters, what really lasts, which is eternal life (v.27). In fact, we can do nothing to attain this except believe (v.29). Like the offer of Lady Wisdom (Prov. 9:1–6) or the invitation of the wise man (Isa. 55:1), the challenge of Jesus is to find true satisfaction in Him. Just as the woman at the well was looking for water, so now men look for bread. To drink His living water is never to thirst again; to eat His living bread is never to go hungry again (v.35).

A DEVOTIONAL INTERLUDE

Thought: One of the most powerful truths in the whole of Scripture and one which the Bible everywhere makes clear is this – there are desires in our souls which nothing on earth can satisfy. Not even the best things of earth. In some ways we have a kinship with the beasts, but so far as we can tell, earth satisfies them. However it does not satisfy us. We are made for God. He alone satisfies.

DAY **220**

READ
John 6:35–71

In the new exodus, Jesus is the living bread which comes down from heaven to feed Israel and a world which is parched and hungry in the wilderness of alienation from God. By faith He becomes the true food of the genuine "sons of God" who are vindicated by being raised up on the last day. Can a mere carpenter from Nazareth achieve this? His accusers murmur at His origins (vv.41–42) but cannot deny that, like the manna, Jesus is a fact within history. Next, His opponents question how He will feed the entire world (v.52). Here is an even greater scandal. For this bread which is Jesus to become life for others, He must offer His flesh and blood body on the cross. To receive eternal life is to appropriate by faith the reality of His incarnation and sacrificial offering of His broken body and poured out blood on the cross (v.51). If we "take Him" into our lives, He becomes our covenant provision. If we can "stomach" this truth about Him, including His ascension (v.62) – which His disciples initially found difficult to do (v.60) – then a covenant bond is forged between God and us. It is a bond we renew every time we take bread and wine. Not that the materiality of flesh or bread counts for much except as vehicles for the life-giving power of the Spirit. His very words which tell us this, are charged with life and power.

A DEVOTIONAL INTERLUDE

For praise: Prepare your heart to give God praise and thanksgiving for the fact that Christ is the bread that fully satisfies our souls. What better than to sing those words from the well-known hymn of William Williams, "Guide me, O Thou great Jehovah":

Bread of heaven; Bread of heaven
Feed me now and ever more,
Feed me now and ever more.

DAY **221**

READ
John 7:37–39

The Feast of Tabernacles was an autumn harvest festival during which people lived in makeshift shelters or booths to commemorate the departure from Egypt and the pilgrimage in the wilderness. On each of the seven days of the Feast, a laver filled with water was poured out by the priest beside the altar. This echoes Zechariah's picture of "living water flowing from Jerusalem" (Zech. 14:8) which likely merges in Jesus' mind with Ezekiel's vision of "living water flowing out from the Temple" (Ezek. 47:1–12). These deep Old Testament allusions lie behind His cry on the last day of the Feast: "If anyone is thirsty, let him come to me and drink. Whoever believes in me, as the Scripture has said, streams of living water will flow from within him." When the leaders led the returned exiles in a prayer of penitence, they linked the Feast of Tabernacles with the pillar and cloud, the water from the rock, the manna in the desert, the giving of the Torah and the outpouring of God's Spirit (Neh. 8:5–18; 9:12–20). Once more the connection with vital Old Testament traditions tells the Jesus story as one of climax and consummation. What the Feast once offered in symbol, Jesus will offer in full reality as the gift of the Holy Spirit, but only when He is glorified by death and resurrection (v.39)!

A DEVOTIONAL INTERLUDE

Prayer: Loving heavenly Father I am so grateful that You pour streams of living water into our barren lives that we may be fruitful and a source of blessing to others. I realise also that nothing can flow in unless it can get out. Grant that I will be as eager to give as much as I am to receive. I want not only my thirst to be satisfied but also to satisfy the thirst of others. Use me for that purpose I pray. Amen.

DAY **222**

READ
John 8:12–59

On the first day of the Feast of Tabernacles, the great golden candelabra were lit. Symbolism is again focused and fulfilled in Jesus. Jesus is the true and ultimate light of the whole world. He speaks and embodies that transforming revelation that saves and changes people's lives. He assumes Israel's age-long vocation of being a light to the nations (Isa. 49). He reveals God supremely. By illuminating the truth, He exposes falsehood and darkness. He is the creative energy of light. As runners carry the Olympic flame in relays to the lighting of the Olympic fire when the time for the games has come, so the lawgivers and the prophets, the sages and singers of the earlier part of the story, have relayed the flame of God's self-revelation until they plunge it into the final conflagration of truth which is Jesus. The fire that He is, gathers up what has gone before and the blaze of truth burns higher and brighter than ever before so that the whole world can see and know. But who chooses to walk in His light? So the debate rages as to who are the true sons of Abraham (a debate Paul will have with the Galatians). The natural heirs of Abraham, Jesus asserts, are in fact in slavery and need the new and greater exodus He has come to bring (v.34). Those who acknowledge Him as the truth are set free to be a true son of Abraham.

A DEVOTIONAL INTERLUDE

Thought: "Light", says one dictionary, "is the agent by which objects are made visible". How glad we are when we find ourselves enshrouded in darkness, to reach for an electric light switch or a torch. The world is a dark place, but Jesus brings light into that darkness. Just where would we be without Jesus? In darkness, stumbling from one day to another. Aren't you glad that He has lighted up your life?

DAY **223**

READ
Luke 13:10–30

The effect of Jesus' ministry is to redefine Israel so that who belongs to the true family of Abraham is determined by their response to Him.

This is why His healings are not only signs of the kingdom or acts of compassion but symbols of the healing of the nation (cf. Isa. 35).

The release of Israel from satanic oppression into the freedom of God's kingdom is embodied in the liberation of one pain-wracked woman from her crippling infirmity. The act of deliverance which heals her, at the same time rescues her from the margins of society and restores her to the full status of a true "daughter of Abraham" (v.16).

The revolution of God's reign brought by Jesus turns upside down the entrenched social order. Those who thought they were "insiders" may find themselves "outsiders" while those once considered "outside the sphere of God's grace" will, through the narrow door of repentance and faith find a way into God's kingdom feast. What Jesus says is not, of course, an anti-Jewish statement. How could it be, seeing Jesus is a Jew. But it is a prophetic indictment of the tendency on the part of God's people to become inward-looking, self-regarding, exclusive or possessive of God's truth and salvation. Through Jesus, Abraham's worldwide family of faith is coming to birth in the radical grace of the kingdom of God.

A DEVOTIONAL INTERLUDE

To ponder: What is your response to today's reading? One suggested response ought to be heartfelt gratitude to God for making you a full member of His family. Once you were an outsider, but now you are an insider. Think back to the moment (or the period) of your conversion and reflect on what God has done for you in the intervening years. Think and give thanks.

DAY **224**

READ
Luke 19:1–9

As we have seen, the upside-down kingdom of God inaugurated by Jesus is good news for the "least, the last and the lost".

The least have greatness thrust upon them by grace; the last in line come first; the lost are found. Those regarded – whether by officialdom or in popular perception – as beyond the pale through sickness or trade or poverty are now, through grace, reinstated as "sons and daughters of Abraham".

Tax-collectors like Zacchaeus were thought by many people to have disqualified themselves by collaborating with Rome either directly or, more likely, indirectly through working for Herod. Jesus targets such people.

His table-fellowship when He "eats with sinners" is His way of acting out the welcome and acceptance God offers the repentant sinner.

Eating with such a notorious "sinner" does not contaminate Jesus but "sanctifies" Zacchaeus! "Today: salvation has come to this house" – and this without recourse to Temple or sacrificial system!

God's covenant family is being reconstituted: "This man, too, is a son of Abraham" (v.9).

The only question remains: will Jerusalem, the Temple and the once-born sons of Abraham recognise this "today" as a visitation of God in judgment and grace (vv.41–44)?

A DEVOTIONAL INTERLUDE

For praise: The Gospels list three classes of people who qualify for salvation – the last, the least and the lost. In which group were you? Did you come to Christ in your later years? He promises to pay you in full. Were you deprived of education and have few talents? He gives gifts that more than compensate. Did you feel like a "missing person"? You have been found. All good reasons for exuberant praise.

DAY **225**

READ
John 10:1–18

Ezekiel had once savaged the false shepherds who mislead God's people, and pledged that God Himself would come to shepherd His flock. When Jesus says that He is the "good [or genuine] shepherd", He is making, therefore, both a highly charged political claim indicting Israel's current leaders and a bold theological claim about exactly where Israel's God is currently present and active! By comparison with Him all other leaders are thieves, perhaps, seeking false ways of being Israel (cf. 12:6). They are perhaps would-be revolutionaries advocating violence as the way to achieve God's kingdom – the word "robber" is applied elsewhere to nationalistic terrorists and guerrilla fighters like Barabbas (18:40).

Ezekiel saw God coming as shepherd only on the other side of the "death and resurrection" of the Exile. This shepherd is willing to undergo death for God's sheep that He might bring them up in resurrection to the secure pasture and abundant provision of His risen life (vv.10–11,14,18).

Like his namesake, Joshua, Jesus comes to the sheepfold of Israel (Num. 27:15–17), but now to call out his new Messianic flock. And He has other sheep scattered in all the nations whom He will bring into one fold under one shepherd, creating the one covenant family God has always desired.

A DEVOTIONAL INTERLUDE

Thought: D. L. Moody once said, "When Jesus announced that he is 'the good shepherd' he sacked all the others and made it clear that the job was now his forever." Present-day pastors and spiritual leaders are really under-shepherds, working under the direction of the good shepherd. They sometimes fail but the good shepherd never fails. His care and concern know no bounds.

DAY **226**

READ
Matthew
16:13–28

Peter's confession of Him as the Christ, draws from Jesus an amazing statement. The God-given revelation about Jesus is to form the basis of a renewed people of God. On an entirely new foundation-rock – confession of Him as the Christ – the "*ecclesia*" of God will be built. In effect, Jesus is daringly reconstituting Israel around Himself!

Extraordinary as this is, even more astounding is the way in which Jesus says it will occur – as He suffers, is killed and on the third day rises again (v.21)!

Already pre-figured by Hosea (6:3) and expanded later in Ezekiel's vision of the dry bones (Ezek. 37), the restoration of the people of God will take place when "resurrection" as a metaphor becomes resurrection as an actuality!

Jesus was throwing down the gauntlet to His contemporaries. Take up your cross and follow Me. As if to say: "Come and be Israel My way! Come down into death with Me, the suffering servant Israel and rise up with Me your anointed Messianic King as the new covenant people of God cleansed, forgiven and empowered to be the Israel God intended!"

Everything in God's purposes for His people Israel and through them for the world are converging on Jesus.

A DEVOTIONAL INTERLUDE

Prayer: O Father, the more I contemplate Your Son's commitment to living out Your story the more my heart is drawn to praise. For Him it meant death, but through that death and resurrection a new order was established. Help me understand even more clearly that I will only truly find my life in You when like Jesus I am willing to give it up here on earth. In His Name I pray. Amen.

DAY **227**

READ
Mark 9:2-32

John strangely omits the transfiguration, perhaps because, for him, the glory of Jesus is diffused right through his account. John's Jesus is not so much transfigured on one occasion as translucent throughout. Mark seizes on the incident with relish to capture in miniature the story of Jesus Who came down from glory into a sin-infested world. Jesus' story gathers up Israel's story too. Why else would Moses and Elijah appear. Do they represent the law and the prophets paying homage to Jesus? Perhaps. But even more, they represent the glorious beginning of Israel's story under Moses and the anticipated end of Israel's story when Elijah was expected to reappear. So Jesus gathers up in Himself both ends of Israel's story. Moses, who steps out of Israel's past, is eclipsed; Elijah stepping out of Israel's future is upstaged. Like them we are urged to listen and to look only to Jesus who is central to God's story.

The human story being acted out in the valley of the shadow of death below is one of misery, confusion, debate and even powerless disciples. But in a world at the mercy of evil forces, the deliverance of one deranged boy heralds the defeat of evil on the cross. And the raising up of one corpse-like child is a trailer for the raising up in His resurrection of a whole new creation.

A DEVOTIONAL INTERLUDE

Quotation: "Reflect on this fact concerning the three who saw the transfiguration. These three amazed disciples who were eyewitnesses of his majesty, who heard the voice of God ... soon backslid. Mark this: glorious manifestations of divine power in lofty mountain ranges are not in themselves any guarantee of security against deflection and failure in the spiritual life" (Leonard Ravenhill).

DAY **228**

READ
John 11:1–44

The first major section of John's Gospel (chs. 1–11) where Jesus appears to the world and to Israel is now giving way to the second half of the book where His concern is much more for the disciples and where He meets with final rejection by Israel and the world.

With chapter 11, the Book of Signs – as chapters 1–11 have been called – gives way to the so-called Book of Glory (chs. 12–21).

Some people see a pattern of six signs or miracles in chapters 1–11 which climaxes with the raising of Lazarus as the seventh and greatest sign. The Word who initiated the original creation, now, with a "loud voice", calls forth the dead as a sign of the new creation (11:43; cf. 5:25). He who had the first word on the old creation (1:1ff), now has the last word on it – resurrection. And Lazarus' resuscitation which returns him to the old world as it is – eventually to die again – turns out to be a dramatic sign of Christ's own imminent victory over death which inaugurates the new creation and releases Him into the freedom of the age to come never to die again. He is, in Himself, the resurrection and the life (v.25). But there is still to be a poignant climax to the end of the old creation. The great life-giver will give His life sacrificially in order to recreate Israel as a new covenant community and set in train the renewal of all God's creation.

A DEVOTIONAL INTERLUDE

Thought: A pastor once asked his congregation if they knew the precise moment when Jesus used the phrase "I am the resurrection and the life". Most replied that it was after He was resurrected from the dead. "No," said the pastor. "He said it before not after." He went on to say, "Jesus is not the resurrection because He rose from the dead; He rose from the dead because He is the resurrection."

DAY **229**

READ
John 11:45–12:49

Here John records a whole series of prophetic words and actions. Firstly, Caiaphas unwittingly prophesies the fruitful and effective death of Jesus. Tragically, the high priest's action would not avert the destruction of Temple and city as he hoped (11:48,51) but would seal it! Jesus would indeed die for Israel and so gather into one enlarged fold the shared Jewish–Gentile community of God (11:52)!

But where Caiaphas plots His death, Mary, in a moving prophetic action, prepares for His burial (12:7), while the foot washing done to Jesus anticipates the foot washing done by Jesus (13:1ff.). Jesus then enters Jerusalem, prophetically demonstrating what kind of king he is. He is greeted with traditional Messianic applause. But only after the resurrection did the disciples – with Holy Spirit inspired hindsight – come to put two and two scriptures together and add them up to Jesus! Then they saw – as He had already seen (12:14) that it took the whole Old Testament story to explain Him and He to fulfil it! And if "the whole world has gone after him"(12:19), what else should we expect, seeing that He is Israel's Messiah and the world's true Lord!

A DEVOTIONAL INTERLUDE

To ponder: Someone has called the story of the woman who took the precious perfume and poured it on Jesus' feet as "the sweetest story in all of the Gospels". It evoked criticism from Judas, but the woman's extravagance apparently brought great pleasure and joy to the heart of Jesus. Ask yourself now: How extravagant am I in my love for the Lord? Do you give it in thimblefuls or bucketfuls?

DAY 230

READ
John 12:20–50

The coming of the Greeks alerts Jesus to the hour of His going! But since the Son of Man will be granted rule over the nations only through suffering, John describes Jesus being in deep emotional turmoil like the waves of a stormy sea. Prophetically, Jesus discerns the voice of God from the alternative evaluations offered (vv.28–30). Like a prophet, Jesus announces that now is final judgment day for the world and the eviction of its demonic ruler (v.31). The long-running saga of God's redemptive plans which we have been tracing comes down to this crucial moment in Jesus' earthly life.

The mystery is wrapped in a parable – only the dying seed brings forth fruit. Only by plunging into the obscurity of suffering will He become visible to the Greeks! Only by being lowered into the ground will He be lifted up from the earth.

As Isaiah foretold, God's original people prove unwilling to believe and so are hardened in their unbelief (12:37–49). This is within the sovereign purpose of God (vv.39–40), but fulfils the long-range view of the prophets straining to glimpse the coming glory (v.41). And the Greeks, up for the Feast, presage a multitude of others drawn like a magnet to Jesus when He is "lifted up" in paradoxical glory on the cross (12:32).

A DEVOTIONAL INTERLUDE

Prayer: Gracious and loving heavenly Father, this message of dying to live is one that I find deeply challenging. Help me I pray to see, however, that when I am unwilling to die to self-interest and self-concern then I cannot live the life You would have me live. May I be like Jesus who aligned Himself with self-giving rather than self-saving. In His peerless and precious Name I pray. Amen.

DAY **231**

READ
John 13

This unforgettable recollection of Jesus shows the humbled disciples struggling to come to terms with His self-abasement. Jesus gives an acted parable of His coming death on the cross which reveals the full extent of His love and it is more than adequate to the full extent of our need.

The "Upper Room discourses" – as they are called – are reminiscent of Moses' farewell speeches to the children of Israel spoken on the verge of the promised land, recorded in the book of Deuteronomy. If we keep this in mind as we reflect on the words of Jesus as He takes leave of His disciples, we can trace echoes of Deuteronomy all through this moving section of Scripture. Just as Moses rehearsed the ten commandments for God's covenant people about to possess the land, so Jesus does the same for the new covenant community being created in Him as it prepares to launch out into the world. Only this time there is only one commandment and it is new (v.34). It is not new because it has never been heard of before. It is new for two reasons. Firstly, the new age of salvation is here and love's full time has come. Secondly, and above all, Jesus' unprecedented self-giving on the cross totally redefines what love really is and becomes the new measure of it.

A DEVOTIONAL INTERLUDE

Quotation: "The account says: Jesus knew ... that he had come from God and was returning to God ... took off his outer clothing, and wrapped a towel round his waist ... and began to wash his disciples' feet ..." The consciousness of greatness was the secret of His humility. The small dare not be humble. But Jesus' greatness was rooted in God. "Being in God made him great – and humble" (E. Stanley Jones).

DAY **232**

READ
John 14:1–31, 15:18–27

In these moving discourses, Jesus spells out the covenant blessings and responsibilities of the new covenant people of God as their covenant-mediator gets ready to leave them. As in Deuteronomy, a new generation stands poised to revive its covenant identity and claim its promised inheritance. So Jesus lays emphasis afresh on familiar Deuteronomic keynotes but with a revolutionary twist that places Himself at the centre. Loving God and being loved by God is worked out in obedience to what God says. This was reworked by the prophets as they envisaged the new covenant and Jesus reflects this (John 14:15–21).

Jesus' greatest prayer for His disciples is that they might receive the Holy Spirit (14:16,26; 15:26; 16:6,13–15). With their master leaving, the disciples of Jesus stand on the edge of an awesome adventure. They will need to rely utterly on the Holy Spirit to be their empowering Counsellor and Teacher who leads them into all truth and never allows them to forget what Jesus said (14:16–17; 15:26). As they confront the intimidating task of proclaiming Jesus as Lord and Christ to a sceptical world, they will be encouraged to realise that they are merely a supporting cast to the Holy Spirit: our witness is always a sub-set of His witness (15:18–27)!

A DEVOTIONAL INTERLUDE

Thought: "There are few doctrines more perplexing than the doctrine of the Holy Spirit," said a London newspaper columnist. He should have added: "The man without the Spirit does not accept the things that come from the Spirit of God, for they are foolishness to him, and he cannot understand them, because they are spiritually discerned" (1 Cor. 2:14). To the converted the Holy Spirit is not a puzzle but a power.

DAY 233

READ
John 15:1–17

The imagery of the vine is derived from the picture of Israel as God's vine which was sadly often found to be unfruitful (Psa. 80:8–9; Isa. 5). By saying "I am the vine", Jesus is assuming the identity of what Israel was meant to be so that life and fruitfulness now flow from being attached to Him.

Sometimes, too, the vine imagery is a code for "Israel-in-the-land" so that, as vine and vineyard Jesus may be indicating that He not only embodies Israel but is taking the place of the promised land itself! What if all along Jesus had displaced this contentious, blood-stained land as the place where God's people are to be rooted, the only source of abundance and fruitfulness that Israel – or anyone else – needs? Instead of a sanctified land, we have a sanctified Person. Just as Jesus has supplanted the Temple and the feasts as the focal point of God's presence and worship, so Jesus is the only holy space His people need. Our inheritance is no longer territorial except as we are heirs of the whole earth.

One thing that is clear is that remaining in the Torah by keeping the commandments is now replaced by remaining in Jesus and abiding in His Word (15:4,7,9–10). Jesus is Lord of the covenant people which is determined by His choice (15:16). Graciously, though, it's not servants He wants but friends!

A DEVOTIONAL INTERLUDE

To ponder: Let that final thought lie on your mind throughout the day: "it's not servants He wants but friends". Do you see yourself as Christ's servant – someone who does a master's bidding, or a friend – someone who has an intimate relationship? We are of course His servants, but we are more than that – we are His friends. He is a friend to you, but are you a friend to Him?

DAY **234**

READ
John 17

As if on holy ground, we watch in intimate close-up our Great High Priest at prayer.

Jesus models an integrity of heart and mind and will that is surrendered lovingly and obediently to God. Through knowing this perfect Priest, we know God (v.3). Jesus first prays for Himself that He may accomplish God's work to the Father's glory which He asks to share. He then prays for His disciples, especially for their protection and security. Finally, Jesus prays for all future believers whose faith depends on the faithful witness of His original disciples. For them He prays, above all, that they may be one in a way that reflects the unity which exists between Father and Son in the Godhead. The Trinity of love which is God has opened itself to us by an amazing grace so that believers are embraced with the same love with which the Father loves the Son! His is a prayer of consecration before the sacrificial self-giving of the cross (v.19). Our consecration takes its rise from His. Receiving us as the Father's gift to Him (v.6), and consecrating us by His own self-offering on the cross (v.19), He takes us and gives us to the world (v.18) so that – seeing the divine love and unity displayed in us – the world might come to believe (v.23) and experience that Trinity-love for itself. Surely Jesus gets His prayers answered!

A DEVOTIONAL INTERLUDE

Prayer: Gracious Father, as I see Jesus at prayer and hearken to His words I realise that He models a way of praying that leaves me feeling somewhat ashamed. How I long to echo His consecration and commitment. Dear Lord, work in me so that I might be a more consecrated person – consecrated to all that Jesus prayed for, especially the unity of His people. In Jesus' Name. Amen.

DAY **235**

READ
Matthew 21:1–21

Returning to Matthew's narrative, we note again that Jesus' entry into Jerusalem and the Temple are both symbolic actions, reflecting Zechariah's image of the royal temple builder (Zech. 6:12; 9:9). The so-called "cleansing of the Temple" spells far more than a mere spring-clean; it is an explicitly prophetic action which heralds the doom and end of the Temple (cf. Matt. 12:6,25–29). The further acted parable of the cursing of the fig tree confirms this. In the Old Testament the fig tree symbolises Israel when blessed. Withering the fig tree speaks of Israel under the covenantal curse of God's judgment! Jesus' strong words and actions are matched by what He says about the mountain cast into the sea. Though often taken as a generalised lesson in faith, His words need to be seen in context. Jesus does not say *a* mountain but *this* mountain, which must refer either to Mount Zion or the Temple Mount. Can you have the faith to see this removed and survive? The crisis for the Temple is not a crisis for God, in fact He's bringing it about. Don't put all your faith in the God-in-the-Temple-God – that current presumption on Israel's part is doomed. Faith can envisage a whole new order of things, not dependent on a material Temple in Jerusalem. Faith like this can move anything.

A DEVOTIONAL INTERLUDE

Thought: Christians can often be heard praying that God will help them cultivate a great faith that will be able to move mountains. However, mountains are not removed by a great faith, but by a small faith. Actually it is more biblical to pray for a small faith – a mustard seed faith – than a great faith. We do not need a great faith in God but a small mustard seed faith in a great God.

DAY **236**

READ
Matthew
21:23–32

The parables of Jesus, we note again, are not generalised stories about timeless truths, but powerful weapons in the conflict at hand. These stories are "Israel-specific", told in a time when Israel is being brought a final national decision. Stories which feature a "son" are especially appropriate to the occasion because, we recall, Israel was termed God's "firstborn son" (Exod. 4:22). Parables that speak of two sons are raising the issue of a divided Israel. They force the nation to face the split in its allegiance to God and the direction it is taking (cf. Luke 15:11–32). In telling them, Jesus cleverly poses the question: "Which kind of Israel is in line with God's will and which kind of Israel will the nation choose to be?"

You – the chief priest and scribes – say "yes" to doing God's will but don't actually do it! They – the sinners and outcasts – initially say "no" to God's will but repent and do it! What a challenge this story is to the leaders of God's people who are failing to recognise God's salvation as it comes in Jesus – a ministry to which outsiders and misfits are eagerly responding! The leaders couldn't see it in John the Baptist's ministry, and they can't see it now even when such dramatic change in sinners is happening right in front of their noses.

A DEVOTIONAL INTERLUDE

To ponder: One of the things that seemed often to frustrate Jesus was the fact that so many people said "Yes" to God with their lips but "No" to Him in their hearts. God does not look for lips expressing words of obedience but hearts performing acts of obedience. How about you? Are you a lip responder or a heart responder? It's an issue worth pondering.

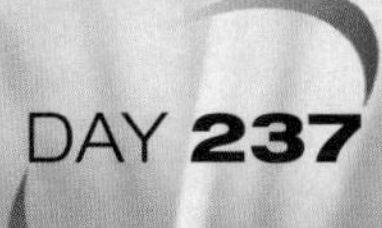

DAY **237**

READ Matthew 21:33–46.

This parable once more directly addresses Israel, previously pictured as God's vine (Psa. 80:8; Isa. 5:2; Jer. 2:21). God has sent many prophets to appeal to His people but to no avail (vv.34–36). "Last of all" He sends His own son to call in the final accounts. In killing the son, the tenants "take his inheritance" for themselves (v.38). This strongly implies that Israel's "sonship" was only held on trust, and was meant to be yielded up when the true Son and Heir appeared!

Jesus' words about the "stone the builders rejected" picks up the song of pilgrims coming up to the Temple for the Feast (Psa. 118:22–23). It echoes Isaiah where the "stone" is used of God's ultimate Temple in the Messianic age (Isa. 8:14; 28:16). There may even be a play on words here since the Hebrew word for stone (*eben*) sounds like the word for son (*ben*). The rejected Son is the chief headstone of the new Temple complex that God is building through Him. The Temple is being drastically redefined through His rejection in death and vindication in resurrection.

And no question who this powerful parable with its sting in the tail was aimed at. The religious leaders "knew he was talking about them" (v.45)! The kingdom will pass to others in judgment and grace. But this is the Lord's doing and "it is marvellous in our eyes" (v.42)!

A DEVOTIONAL INTERLUDE

For praise: A tinge of sadness lies on the spirit of all Christians when they see how our Lord was rejected by those who should have eagerly accepted Him. But it is also a cause for rejoicing that the rejected One is now the Chief Cornerstone of a new Temple complex in which we have a part. The One whom others rejected is the Rock upon which God's promises to us rest.

DAY **238**

READ
Matthew 23

Matthew here neatly mirrors Deuteronomy 27–28 so that the "blessings" (Matt. 5:3–12) are now matched by "woes" (23:13–32). The point is clear. Just as Moses brought God's people to a moment of covenantal choice, so, even more, Jesus brings Israel to its final covenantal crisis. Israel must choose: blessing or curse!

It makes sense, then, to see all the parables Jesus told in the last week of His life (21:28–46; 25:1–46), and the vision of the end (ch. 24), as primarily referring not to His second coming but to His first coming and its immediate repercussions in the imminent judgment of God during the Jewish–Roman War of AD 70–73.

That war did leave "not one stone of the Temple standing" – except, that is, for a supporting wall of the outer court which still remains sacred to Jews today as the Western or Wailing Wall.

All of Israel's previous covenantal unfaithfulness is now being laid at the door of this, the terminal generation (v.36).

But, like a hen sheltering her chicks under her wings, so God (Jesus speaks here as a prophet for God) longs to gather His people to Himself in salvation. But the "house [primarily the Temple] is left to you desolate". The only hope is to welcome Jesus by blessing Him who comes in the Name of the Lord as the ultimate pilgrim to Jerusalem!

A DEVOTIONAL INTERLUDE

Thought: In our relationship with God we are called to make a choice. Israel had to choose – blessing or curse. Though we have the freedom to choose, things will go better for us when we make a choice for freedom. Freedom is often misunderstood. One Bible teacher defines it thus: "Freedom is not the right do what we want but the power to do what we ought." It is.

DAY **239**

READ
John 19:1–22

This abused man, in the regalia of a king, seems a parody of the royal human vocation of being God's partners in ruling over the world (Gen. 1:26–28). Despite human sin and failure, this calling refuses to die (cf. Psa. 8). Created for dominion, we have rebelled against our high calling. We wear no longer a crown of honour but of shame. A "crown of thorns" is a fitting symbol of our human disgrace. The thorns are signs of God's curse on the ground on which His disobedient sons and daughters walk in rebellion (Gen. 3:17–19). Through sin, we have twisted our humanness out of shape, and misused our God-given gifts and abilities. The face in which God aimed to see His reflection, is spat upon and disfigured by blows. In all this the "Word-made-flesh" endures the universal humiliation of the victim of oppression, and the special mockery devised for Jews. Israel represents God's image-bearing humanity, and in abusing Israel, our humanness and God's image are being attacked. But Jesus atones for us all by taking our shame, bearing our sins and wearing our crown of disgrace so that He might wear again for us the crown of human honour and so bring many sons to the glory from which we fell. "Behold the Man! ... Behold your King" (vv.5,14)!

A DEVOTIONAL INTERLUDE

Prayer: Lord Jesus Christ, how can I ever put into words the gratitude my heart feels for wearing on Your brow the crown of our human shame so that we may share the crown of Your honour and glory. My heart cries out: "All this You did for me; what have I done for Thee?" I know I cannot pay you back for what You have done for me, but help me show my gratitude by living a life that honours You. Amen.

DAY **240**

READ
John 20:19–23

In a final prophetic action, Jesus "breathed on them and said, 'Receive the Holy Spirit' " (v.22). This graphic action immediately evokes the narrative of Genesis where God breathes the life of the first creation into Adam and constitutes him a living being (Gen. 2:7). It echoes the symbolic action of the prophet Elijah when he stretched out on the corpse of the widow of Zarephath's son and breathed the breath of new life into the lifeless boy (1 Kings 17:21). It connects too with Ezekiel's stunning vision of the breath or wind of God seeping down into the reassembled bodies of the slain of Israel to reanimate them and turn them into a living army again (Ezek. 37). So Jesus breathes upon the "dead" of Israel and the world and breathes new, invigorating resurrection-life into them! The covenant purposes of God have reached their climax. In the small group gathered round Jesus is a nucleus of new covenant community and a new creation humanity to whom the last Adam imparts His life. Ending as he began, John unites creation and redemption. The Word by whom the world was made took flesh and dwelt among us. The Word-made-flesh was crucified, dead and buried, but on the third day rose again with a new world in his nail-pierced hands. To as many as received Him He imparted the life of the new creation (cf. 1:12–13).

A DEVOTIONAL INTERLUDE

To ponder: When Jesus breathed upon His disciples and said "Receive the Holy Spirit", was that the moment when they were baptised in the Spirit? Or was that "breathing" the moment of their regeneration? If so what exactly happened at Pentecost? Bible teachers are divided on this issue. It is hard to think Jesus' action did not have some effect. What do you think?

DAY **241**

READ
Matthew
28:16–20

Matthew, like John at times, has presented his work as a new Deuteronomy with Israel facing a life-or-death challenge in her confrontation with Jesus. So Matthew ends his story with Jesus – Moses-like – gathering the remnant of Israel around Himself on a mountain top. But the contrast is remarkable.

What had Moses urged Israel to do? In effect, Moses had said: "Go into the promised land, observe the Torah and Yahweh will be with you always." Now Jesus stands on a mountain to commission His small disciple band: "Go, not just into a promised land but into the promised world; teach people not what Torah says but what I have commanded you" and – even more remarkably – the pledge is not, "Yahweh will go with you", but "I will be with you to the end of the age"! Matthew thus ends his Gospel where he began it, with "Immanuel, God-with-us". So if we ask again as His friends the question asked by His enemies: Who is this person?; with Matthew and with hindsight we have to say: "No one has the authority to do and say these things except Israel's God in person." Jesus both embodies Israel's mission and incarnates her God.

At His royal command a new covenant people is launched on the world with a restored Abrahamic mission to bring the blessings of God's salvation and grace to all the nations.

A DEVOTIONAL INTERLUDE

Thought: A Christian magazine once researched the favourite story that preachers like to tell. It was this: When Jesus returned to heaven after His time on earth the angels asked Him how He planned to make the gospel message known. "I have commissioned my followers for the task," He replied. "What if they fail?" asked the angels. Solemnly Jesus replied, "Then I have no other plan."

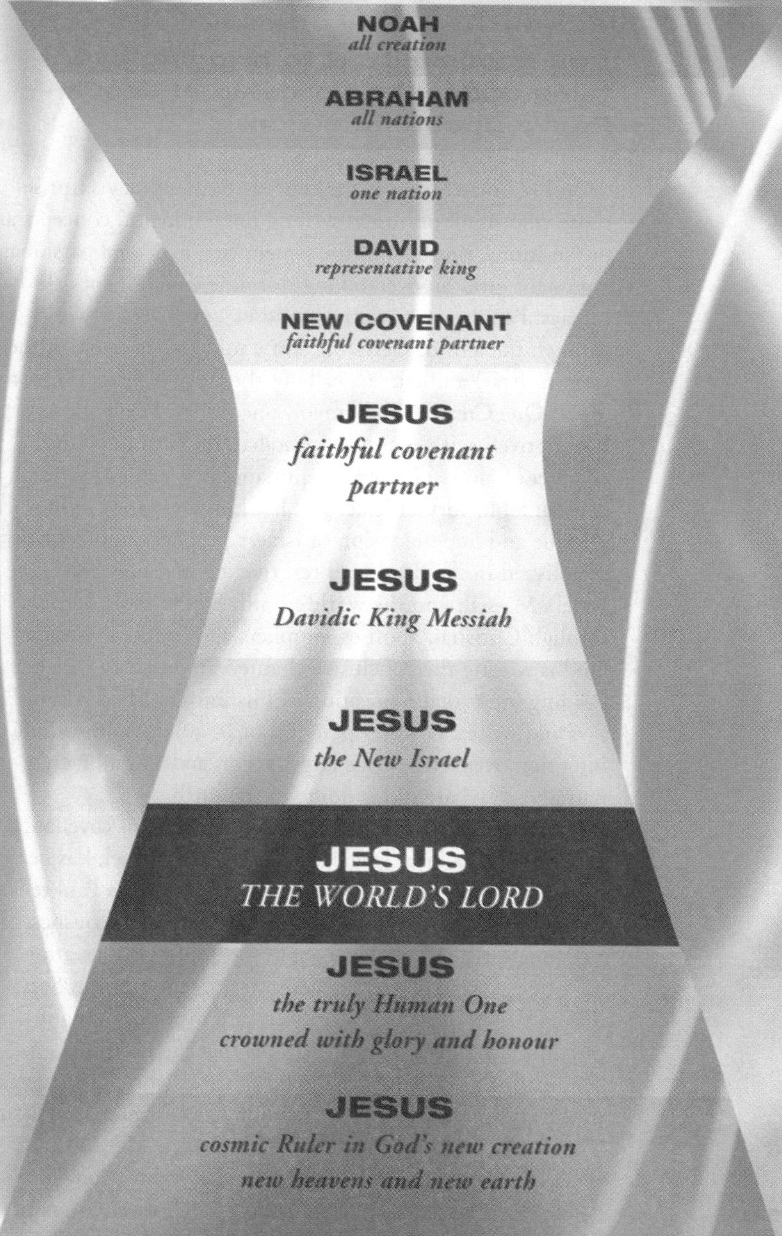

NOAH
all creation

ABRAHAM
all nations

ISRAEL
one nation

DAVID
representative king

NEW COVENANT
faithful covenant partner

JESUS
faithful covenant partner

JESUS
Davidic King Messiah

JESUS
the New Israel

JESUS
THE WORLD'S LORD

JESUS
the truly Human One crowned with glory and honour

JESUS
cosmic Ruler in God's new creation new heavens and new earth

SECTION 9

PAUL'S WORLD-VIEW PART 1

God is committed to bringing everything under the Lordship of Jesus – Paul's apostolic vision

Paul is a master storyteller. This assessment may surprise those who think of him as writing only in logical concepts and propositions. But behind the penetrating logic and passionate argument lurks an overarching storyline which shapes all that he says. Paul has a "narrative mindset". He sees the world through the lens of God's big story, told progressively in the story of Israel and climactically in the story of Jesus. This story of the One Creator God's involvement with His world, starts redemptively with the call of Abraham in faith to be the channel of God's blessings to all nations. It extends through the covenantal history of Israel and her kings, expands in the critique and hopeful vision of Israel's prophets, and is finally established in the death and resurrection of God's Son, Jesus, Israel's Messiah and the world's Lord. By the Holy Spirit, through Christian apostles, prophets and "saints in ordinary", God is writing the conclusive chapters in the story which is heading for a total renovation of His universe! Everything Paul says and writes, however practical or pastoral its immediate intention, stems from this larger vision and all-embracing narrative of what God is doing in the earth.

He views the history of Israel as a catalogue of covenantal privilege and failure. Tragically, God's "son", Israel, has been shown to share the sin of the whole world. But as Paul tells the Romans, God's covenant faithfulness – His "righteousness" – has gone forth to save His people and restore His creation. God has acted to save in the death and resurrection of His Son through whom He has began to create the one covenant family of faithful disciples from all nations that He promised Abraham. This family is made up of those who put their trust in the faithfulness of God at work in the faithfulness of Jesus! Those who believe in this way, God justifies. He vindicates them or declares them to be His own covenant people, judged before the final day to be "righteous" – that is, in covenant relationship with Him. So emerges that new covenant community, first envisaged by the prophets of the Exile. These forgiven and Spirit led "sons of God", the sample new humanity, are making their new exodus through a groaning world, heading for the new world that is coming.

Along the way, the history of Jew and Gentile mysteriously interweaves as God works out His purpose to heal the nations and restore His creation. This overarching narrative of salvation is entirely God's doing. It flows from His grace, is worked out through His power and tends to His ultimate glory. By grace, we are called to participate in this great drama by our faith, our prayers and our suffering.

It is against this storyline that Paul measures the health of the churches to which he writes. Problems arise in those he deals with when Christians lose the plot and mislocate themselves in the narrative flow of God's history. So the Galatians were under pressure to re-locate themselves in an earlier pre-Christian stage of the story and so come back under the dominion of the law. To do that, says Paul, is to fail to understand where you are in the story. Since Christ has come, the law has changed its role. It no longer lords it over us; Christ does. Know your place, then, in the story. The Corinthians' case is similar. In their charismatic enthusiasm, they were "getting above themselves", believing they were in some way superior, even to Paul! This was because they were getting ahead of themselves in the storyline. They assumed they were further down the road than it is possible to be before Jesus returns. They thought they could pre-empt the "end of the story", by-pass the normal human weakness and Christian suffering which is inevitable in this as yet unredeemed world, and so arrive at a state of perfection and completion. Paul has to remind them of their place in the story and to pull them back from their over-triumphalist "there and then" into the realistic "here and now". We do enjoy the fullness of the Spirit now, he agrees, but we have not yet arrived at final salvation. We still live by hope in what remains as the future gift of God. For their part, the Thessalonians were unsure about the way the story ends for believers in Christ and so Paul has to rehearse with them as much as knows about Christ's coming for His people whether living or dead.

Above all, the storyline calls for a radical new unity of Jew and Gentile to overcome the age-old divisions of tribe and race that stain the human story. From one angle, the whole reason for writing his letter to the Romans is to urge Jewish and Gentile Christians to be at peace with one another. He reminds them that all have sinned, that Israel's exclusive story was meant to bear fruit for the whole world, that the ground is level at the foot of the cross and that, in order to be saved, everyone, everywhere, can and must call on the Name of the same Lord, the One Lord who is over all, for salvation.

Paul admits to knowing all this only because God has revealed to him the "mystery of his will" centred in Jesus Christ. This "mystery" is the open secret of God's strategic plan to save the world through Him. It is this "mystery" Paul longs to tell and lives to implement.

DAY 242

READ
Ephesians 3:1–9

Most of us love a good mystery. Some readers relish a good crime mystery. Scientists probe the "mystery of life".

Paul obviously relishes a good mystery too: he uses the word three times in this short section. (Eph. 3:3,4,9).

The word "mystery" – "*musterion*" in Greek – was a technical term used for the secret initiation rites of the so-called "mystery-religions" of the Greco-Roman world.

The English translation "mystery" conjures up something spooky, dark, even incomprehensible.

The ancient philosophers graded "*musterion*" at the upper end of the knowledge scale attainable only by the persistent and ultra-clever disciple. But in Paul's use of the word we are not to think of the solution to a mysterious crime or entry to a mystery religion or elevation to an exclusive academy of higher knowledge. When Paul uses this term, he is drawing on Jewish and Old Testament categories. For him "*musterion*" is a secret that lies beyond the reach of human reason; a secret which could never be uncovered or known unless God Himself took the initiative and made it known to us.

And that, Paul declares, is precisely what God has done! In the gospel God has "made known" or "revealed" to us His deepest and most secret intentions. In short, "mystery" is Paul's shorthand for "God's Strategic Plan".

A DEVOTIONAL INTERLUDE

Prayer: Loving heavenly Father, how I praise You that You are not a keeper of secrets but a revealer of mysteries. How I praise You, too, that by Your Holy Spirit You have unveiled the wonder of Your Son to me and now I am Yours – saved, surrendered and satisfied. The greatest wonder to my heart is that the initiative was all Yours. You came looking for me. My heart is Yours for all eternity. Amen.

DAY **243**

READ
Ephesians
1:3–10

This "mystery" is God's single plan of salvation, born in eternity, disclosed in history.

We learn about this redemptive plan only because God has chosen to reveal it to us. God's grace has been "lavished on us" to give us a share in His own "wisdom and understanding" (v.8).

For Paul this mystery is no mystery at all: it's an open secret!

Paul has been given the inside story, been taken behind the scenes and shown a glimpse of God's secret strategy for human history!

Paul celebrates God's revelation of the "mystery of his will" at the start of this letter (1:9–10). The scope of God's strategy is breathtaking. In Eugene Peterson's stirring paraphrase: God "set it all out before us in Christ, a long-range plan in which everything would be brought together and summed up in him, everything in deepest heaven, everything on planet earth".

All believers – not just an elite – have been initiated into this "mystery". We have had a tip-off from unimpeachable sources; a leak from the highest authority has come to our notice: a file marked "Top Secret" has fallen into our possession: classified "inside information" is now in our hands – and hearts!

A DEVOTIONAL INTERLUDE

An added perspective: "So richly God has lavished upon us his grace, granting us complete insight and understanding of the open secret of his will showing us how it was the purpose of his design so to order it in the fullness of the ages that all things in heaven and alike should be gathered up in Christ – in the Christ in whom we have our inheritance allotted to us" (Eph. 1:9–11 Moffatt).

DAY **244**

READ
Ephesians
1:11–14

Paul is celebrating that there is an overall plan that God is working out. We are not at the cold mercy of the stars or in the grip of a heartless fate. There is a loving purpose behind the human story and a saving thread woven through it. Life is not meaningless. There is meaning and so there is hope. In Jesus Christ we discover God's saving plan and find out who we are and what we are here for. Our past history of sin has been cleansed at the cross. The forgiven have a future. We have been re-rooted and replanted in the grace that chose us before time began. Amid lies and distortions and fantasy, we have heard God speak His "word of truth" (v.13) to us in the gospel of Jesus. When we responded to God's grace by believing, we were "included in Christ" (v.13). "In Christ" is Paul's favourite way of describing our salvation. When we believe, our personal stories are included in the saving story of Jesus Christ.

Our current experience of the Holy Spirit confirms us in this. The Spirit is the downpayment on our future salvation, the pledge of our coming inheritance when the narrative is satisfactorily concluded.

The Holy Spirit in us guarantees that we shall participate in the successful outcome of the story which is the praise of God's glory (1:13–14).

A DEVOTIONAL INTERLUDE

For thanksgiving: Reflect further on the thought that we are not meteorites speeding across the universe to burn out on the edge of some gravitational field; we are beings made in the image of God, an important part of God's bigger story, with a destiny that will ultimately see us joined to Jesus Christ in a marriage which will last for all eternity. How wonderful! How truly wonderful!

DAY **245**

READ
Ephesians
1:15–23

Paul's prayer is our prayer for you as you travel through God's story with us. We pray that you may grow in understanding of the glorious redemptive plan of God for the world and your place in it. With Paul, we pray that you may be given "a spirit of wisdom and revelation" to know God better, to know God's plans better, to know God's future better.

Paul prays that we might have our inner eyes – the "eyes of the heart" (v.18) – opened to the heart-warming vision of God's future. Then we can live with our eyes on the end of the story. It might seem that to know how a story ends would make life tediously predictable, like knowing the punch line of a joke. But not in this case. We are in an adventure story, marching on with hope in our hearts and the Voice that calls us ringing in our ears. Hope is sure because God has invested richly in our lives (v.18). We stay confident that the God who raised Jesus from the dead has the power to bring the story of salvation to a successful conclusion. Final victory has already been won. The Name of Jesus is above every name that can be named. Jesus is the Truly Human One who already occupies the human place of dominion with all creation laid in tribute beneath His feet. Jesus is Head of the Church which shares His fullness but does not contain Him because He fills everything with His lordly presence.

A DEVOTIONAL INTERLUDE

Thought: "A small boy in Sunday School who had recently given his heart to the Lord was asked by his teacher what was his goal for the future ... what he wanted more than anything in life. His teacher was surprised when he said, 'To know God better'. The 'Spirit of wisdom and revelation' was already at work in that little boy's life. Is it at work in you, giving you that same desire – to know God better?"

DAY **246**

READ
Ephesians 1:19, 2:10, 3:20, 4:16

The more we are drawn into God's story, the more we come to realise that God is at work. In the modern world, it is difficult to conceive of a God who is the chief actor in the drama. We are so used to running our own lives, and so absorbed with what we are doing and deciding, that we find it hard to imagine a world in which God does the most important things, not just on the big occasions like Exodus and resurrection, but everyday, in every place.

In the opening burst of praise in this letter, Paul celebrates the initiatives God has taken to bless and save us. We are on the receiving end of what God has planned, decided, destined, done and made known. Because God is a relational being – Father, Son and Holy Spirit – His actions are directed to personal ends. We are in the grip, not of inexorable laws, but of a loving purpose. Philosophical speculation about how God "predestines" is best left to one side in favour of the helpful insight that such activity "frees us to do human things, leaving God to do divine things" (Eugene Peterson). God is working powerfully for us (1:19), ahead of us (2:10), in us (3:20) and through us (4:16) in order to accomplish what He has planned to do (1:19–20; 3:11). And if there is one word that describes God's *modus operandi* – His tell-tale way of working – it is "grace".

A DEVOTIONAL INTERLUDE

To ponder: Throughout time the subject of God's sovereignty and mankind's freedom is one on which there has never been any full agreement. Our reading today suggests we leave such thoughts aside in favour of seeing that the Almighty "frees us to do human things, leaving God to do divine things". You can always depend on God to do His part, can He depend on you to do yours?

DAY 247

READ
Ephesians 2:1–10

God works everything by His grace; His unsolicited gifts and unprompted initiatives. The story of God's grace in action is told by considering when it was He saved us. It was when we were dead in sins, dominated by the godless world system, drifting on the tides of fashion, driven by the sin-corrupted natural appetities and doomed under the wrath of God! But God who is rich in mercy, acted to save us by making us who were dead alive with Christ. He has raised us up and out of the dominion of darkness into the Lordship of His Son Jesus. He has seated us with Christ in the place of spiritual ascendancy over the powers that governed our lives. He is reclaiming our God-given drives and turning us into the paths of righteousness, recreating us for good works. This is God's gift to us which we receive by faith.

All of this happens to us as a result of our relationship to Jesus Christ. Our appreciation of His grace grows, when we realise that God has saved us in this way, so that we might be His showpiece in the future (2:7–9). Amazingly, God plans to put saved sinners on exhibit to show the splendour of His grace for ever. Meanwhile we are His "workmanship". He is working on us as a craftsman works on his chosen material. God even sets "traps" of good works for us to walk right into every day! What a story this is.

A DEVOTIONAL INTERLUDE

Prayer: How can I ever thank You enough, dear Father, for the fact that what I have received from You is not a reward for my effort but the result of Your undeserved love and infinite grace. You have saved me to "show me off" to the universe as an exhibit of how grace can turn a hell-deserving sinner into a saint. All glory and honour be to Your wonderful Name. Amen.

DAY **248**

READ
Ephesians 3:2–4

Paul emphasises that it was God's grace to share this secret with him (3:2–3). Paul makes no claim that he deserved to receive this privileged information. On the Damascus Road, God broke open Paul's world-view and blinded him with an amazing revelation of Jesus.

Why is he raising this here? Paul writes to the Ephesian believers in order to raise their awareness of the dimensions of their salvation and the high privileges of their Christian identity. Paul himself is evidence of a career, a ministry and a destiny passionately absorbed by this secret strategy of God.

This "mystery" – this strategic plan of God's – is Paul's magnificent obsession! If we are going to track down God's secret strategy (3:1–6), the first move we must make is to discover that it centres on Jesus Christ, on who He is, what has been achieved through Him and what is projected for Him (3:4). This is the reason why "in Christ" is Paul's instinctive way of describing the central reality of our lives as Christians.

Everything of our saving involvement in this plan occurs "in Christ".

Everything that God destines for the redemption and perfecting of His creation is "in Christ".

A DEVOTIONAL INTERLUDE

Thought: The Bible makes so much of Jesus because without Him there would be no eternal story. He is the hero of that story because He is the one who saves. A recent newspaper report told how a man saved a little boy from drowning. It said little about the boy but a lot about the one who saved him. The glory always goes to the one who saves. Isn't that how it should be?

DAY **249**

READ
Acts 9:1–20

What turned Saul, the law-enforcing Pharisee into Paul, the gospel-storytelling apostle, centred on Jesus Christ?

Well, what did Paul think of Jesus when he set out for Damascus? For Saul, Jesus was a dead and discredited Messianic pretender. His followers – following the so-called Way – were on the wrong track altogether and deserved to be persecuted as heretics. What happened on the road? Saul's companions saw light and heard sound, but to Saul the light was vision and the sound a voice!

He saw, as the dying Stephen had seen, a man about his own age, shining with transcendent glory. The voice asked him: "Saul, Saul, why do you persecute me?" (v.4). Dazzled and disorientated, Saul asks: "Who are you, Lord?" The answer is devastating: "I am Jesus whom you are persecuting." And right there, Saul made two startling discoveries about Jesus. Firstly, Jesus was alive when Saul had thought Him dead and buried and forgotten. And if Jesus was alive, then He was vindicated by God as the person He and His followers claimed Him to be! Far from being disgraced, Jesus was now honoured by sharing the very glory of the One Creator God. Stephen had been right; Saul had been wrong. Saul's slanted version of the story of God, Israel and the world, began to unravel and reform around Jesus the Christ.

A DEVOTIONAL INTERLUDE

For action: "Conversion," said someone, "is the discovery that what we thought was a theory or an illusion is actually true." Saul of Tarsus discovered that, and so no doubt have you. Just in case you haven't had your own personal moment of conversion we invite you now to accept Jesus with this simple prayer: "Lord Jesus, come into my heart, forgive my sin and make me Your child. In Jesus' Name. Amen."
If you said this prayer and meant it, write to us and we will send you a free copy of *Every Day with Jesus for New Christians*.

READ
Acts 22

Saul's second discovery came when Jesus said: "Why are you persecuting me?" It seeped into Saul's baffled mind that in hurting Christians he had in fact been hurting Jesus. Paul learned in a raw moment of experience what he later refined as a profound theology – that Jesus was as closely identified with His followers as a head is with its body! Paul was shattered to realise that he had been fighting God and opposing His Messiah! But if Jesus was the God-vindicated Christ then Paul's grasp of the biblical story was turned inside-out. Was this a conversion or a commission? Not a conversion in the sense of changing religions. Far from it. Paul now began to come to terms with the fact that the story of Jesus was the climax and centre-piece of the longer, larger story of God's dealings with the world focused in the story of Israel which he had always believed. This was a conversion to a Christ-centred view of things. It was certainly a commission, a drastic role reversal. A Rabbinic Jew, once dedicated to guarding jealously the exclusiveness of Israel, now finds himself selected to take the gospel to the Gentile world of "lesser breeds without the law".

As he did so Paul would realise that he was an agent of the one story that from Abraham onwards God had always been writing, with Jesus now at its heart.

A DEVOTIONAL INTERLUDE

Prayer: Heavenly Father, I may never have done this before but today I want to thank You for the way You brought Paul to Yourself. What an impact his conversion has made on history – and also on me. Almost half the books of the New Testament are from his pen – and what I have learned from them is beyond all telling. So thank You, dear Lord, for that most wonderful conversion. And also for mine. Amen.

DAY **251**

READ
Acts 9:20–31

When Paul arrived in Damascus it was with letters of authority from the high priest in Jerusalem to discredit Jesus and His followers. When he left the city it was as an ambassador accredited to the court of King Jesus. If this Messianic claimant, Jesus, had been resurrected, then, as a shrewd Pharisee, Paul knew that Jesus had received God's ultimate stamp of approval. Paul now proclaims Jesus as God's royal "Son" who is exalted to a place of honour and Lordship which fulfils the promises made before to the Davidic dynasty (9:20).

Jesus must be Israel's long-awaited Messiah (9:22). Much still remained to be revealed to Paul, but the Damascus Road experience was his "Copernical revolution". His sun no longer circled the earth; the earth circled the sun. No longer did eternal reality centre on the Torah and the Temple as defining Israel's unique identity, but everything to do with God, salvation and the future revolves around Jesus Christ. Paul did not change his Judaism for another religion but he changed his Judaism! Everything that Abraham had been promised and with which Israel had been entrusted, was now made good, Paul saw, in Abraham's seed and Israel's Messiah, Jesus. He came from Jerusalem to take prisoners; he returned with only one: himself – a newly captured prisoner of Jesus.

A DEVOTIONAL INTERLUDE

Thought: Contemplate the fact that after Paul met Jesus Christ everything changed. The way he thought about God was changed. How he viewed Jesus was changed. His understanding of salvation was changed. And he had a new understanding too of the concept of freedom. An old hymn puts it: "Make me a captive Lord, and then I shall be free". Has salvation changed you? How much?

DAY 252

READ
1 Corinthians 1:18–25

If Paul's view of Jesus changed as a result of his encounter on the Damascus Road, so did his view of the cross. Once, he had considered the Christians preaching of a crucified Messiah as a scandal, almost a blasphemy. For him, anyone who had hung on a cross was a law-breaker, an outcast, someone dying under the curse of God. But if Jesus had been raised from the dead, then He had been exonerated. The curse He bore must have been our curse so that blessing might come to us. Above all what had been a stumbling-block to him became the centrepiece of his message. Crucifixion had seemed the final denial that Jesus fitted into God's scheme of things. Now the cross placed Jesus at the very centre of God's saving strategy.

The all-wise power of God working out His purposes in history is explosively concentrated in the conquering weakness of the cross. The almighty wisdom of God that is fashioning the complete recovery of His creation is most convincingly demonstrated in the foolishness of the cross (1:25). No one else would have dreamt up a plan that involved saving the world through a crucified carpenter. But God did. And God did it this way quite deliberately in order to shatter the idolatrous demands of the human mind that God should act, on our terms, in ways we deem to be clever or powerful (1:19–22). What an amazing plan this is!

A DEVOTIONAL INTERLUDE

For praise: Many years ago Sir John Bowring when sailing through the South China seas saw a cross on a headland and was inspired to write this hymn:

In the Cross of Christ I glory, towering o'er the wrecks of time
All the light of sacred story, gathers round its head sublime.

In your own way and in your own words give God thanks for what one writer calls "the radiant cross".

DAY **253**

READ
1 Corinthians
2:6–16

Paul once more employs his key term "*musterion*". The words "we speak of God's secret wisdom" (2:7), more literally translated, come out as "we speak God's wisdom in a mystery". Recall that this strategic plan of God would have remained unknown unless He revealed it to us. God's plan to save the world, now focused in the cross of Jesus, baffles all godless minds. The rulers of the world certainly had no inkling when they contrived to have Jesus killed that they were crucifying the very Lord of glory. They no doubt went to bed on Good Friday satisfied with a day's work well done, having rid themselves of a troublesome prophet and Messianic pretender. But the unaided natural mind cannot understand that the world's salvation is achieved through the cross. The depths of God's wisdom are demonstrated at the cross. But only the Holy Spirit can show us this. The cross is the culmination of what God has been preparing for those who love Him. And what no eye has seen, no ear heard, no heart imagined or mind conceived, God has revealed to us by the Holy Spirit. The Holy Spirit researches the deep things in God and He comes up with nothing deeper than the cross. No higher wisdom can be found than God's redemptive plan in the cross. Those who see this are not the intellectually superior but those who love God!

A DEVOTIONAL INTERLUDE

Quotation: "If a spotlight from outer space was to be pointed at the most important place on our planet it would fall upon a hill called Calvary. But the cross that was lifted up there at a point in time was done so that we might see that really it is timeless. There was a cross in the heart of God before there was a cross uplifted at Calvary. He is the Lamb slain from 'before the foundation of the world' " (E. Stanley Jones).

DAY **254**

READ
2 Corinthians
4:4–6

However intense the visible light that dazzled him, it was the piercing inner illumination that Paul never got over. For him, that experience was like the dawn of creation when God said, "Let there be light". Paul looked into the radiant face of Jesus Christ and knew that what shone there was the very glory of God. He saw what James, and John and Peter had seen on the Mount of Transfiguration which showed that Jesus was the summary and fulfilment of all God's previous revelation. The very "*shekinah*" glory of God was no longer concentrated in the Jerusalem Temple, available only to the priests, but was streaming from the face of Jesus Christ into all believing hearts. The outshining of God's inner holiness was no longer, as the Pharisees had claimed, shining on those gathered round to study the Torah. It was to be found reflected in the eyes of those who read the open book of Jesus' life and death and resurrection. The glory Abraham glimpsed, the glory Moses longed to see, the glory that filled the tabernacle and prevented priests from ministering in the Temple – that glory which irradiated earlier phases of the story, has now "shone in our hearts to give the light of the knowledge of the glory of God in the face of Jesus Christ".

A DEVOTIONAL INTERLUDE

Prayer: Lord Jesus Christ, the Lamb slain before the foundation of the world, how glad I am that I too have looked into Your face, seen the glory of God shining through You to me, and that now I am a recipient of Your grace. Grace sought me, grace bought me, grace taught me, grace caught me – and now grace has me for ever. I am more grateful than words can convey. Amen.

DAY 255

READ
Ephesians 3:5

If God's plan centres on Christ (3:4), our next move to stay on the track of this mystery is to discover here that it was not revealed to previous generations as it has now been revealed to God's holy apostles and prophets (3:5).

And the "not" means not disclosed until now. With hindsight, the "mystery" is seen to be the actual fulfilment in a particular time and person of the Old Testament's prophetic promises. Paul is not indulging is some mystical spirituality, but is dealing with what has happened in history. There was a time when this secret was hidden: now it is out in the open!

That God's secret has been entrusted "by the Spirit to God's holy apostles and prophets" makes an important point about the divine authority of the New Testament as Scripture here.

In the Old Testament, God's "secret" was disclosed only to His prophets who stood in God's privy council or secret assembly (Amos 3:7; Jer. 23:22).

Just as, by the Spirit, their revelation became foundational Scripture so, by analogy, those who receive and transmit the "*musterion*" of God – namely the New Testament apostles and the prophetic figures associated with them – by the same Spirit, lay the foundation for the New Testament as authoritative Scripture (Eph. 2:20).

A DEVOTIONAL INTERLUDE

Thought: In giving God glory for Christ and His cross we must not forget (as we have been reminded today) the work of the Holy Spirit. He is referred to in Scripture by various terms – among others by the term, "*paraclete*". It is a Greek term made up of two words – "*para*" meaning "alongside" and "*kaleo*" meaning "to summon or call". We call and He comes alongside. Simple, but so sublime!

DAY **256**

READ
Romans 16:25–27

Paul is insistent that the revelation of the mystery is not an insight into perennial truths but a breaking open of a long-guarded secret. It does not deal in vague abstractions but is disclosed in a particular person who lived and died and rose again in a particular stage of the story. This is what gives his gospel its special shape, as a story to tell to the nations.

The prophets sowed the seeds of this mystery, but only with the coming of Jesus have these seeds sprung up into visible fruit. With the Word made flesh, the Old Testament Scriptures find their true voice. With His coming, the prophetic writings come alive and, in the gospel of Christ preached by the apostles, speak clearly as never before. In other words, once more, we see that the story of Jesus make sense of the Old Testament story of God's dealings with Israel. It was at "God's command' that all was revealed in Christ at this time. And what God aims for is what He has had in mind since He made promises to Abraham, that all nations should hear, believe and obey and so be written into the story of the One Creator God and Jesus the world's true Lord and Saviour.

A DEVOTIONAL INTERLUDE

To ponder: Once again, the issue of making this message of Christ's death and resurrection known to the whole world is before us. "Evangelism," said someone, "is not complete until the evangelised become evangelists." Has your reception of Christ's salvation stirred you to share it with others? The only way people can be saved is when they hear the message. Has anyone ever heard it from your lips?

DAY **257**

READ
Colossians
1:24–2:5

Paul reminds the Colossians that just as he has been appointed to "fill up" his quota in the sufferings associated with Christ in the Messianic age (cf. Rom. 8:22), so he is commissioned to preach the fullness of God's Word. In one sense, the Word of God, enshrined in the message of the gospel, remains incomplete and unfulfilled until it is embraced by the Gentiles. The time for this has now come.

At the heart of this "secret plan" is the revelation that in Christ the scope of God's plans is not restricted to Jews but expands to include all nations. The rich fabric of God's glory is demonstrated when God clothes the whole world in His grace and affirms the universal Lordship of Jesus Christ. The presence of Christ in and among Gentile believers is the basis of their own hope of sharing in the glory of God. To see God's glory shining in the Temple or diffused among His chosen people, Israel, was one thing; to see God's glory shimmering through previously pagan nations as the Name of Jesus is confessed, is cause for even greater wonder. God's plan, centring on Jesus, is far-reaching and aims to fill the whole earth with His glory "as the waters cover the sea" (Isa. 11:9).

We are invited to explore the central mystery which is Jesus who embodies the wisdom by which God made the world (2:2–3; cf. 1:15–20).

A DEVOTIONAL INTERLUDE

For praise: God's glory no longer shines through a temple in Jerusalem but through the lives of Christ's followers throughout the world, of which you are one. Give God thanks in your own way now for putting the glow and glory of His presence in your heart and ask Him that nothing in your life may ever prevent the light and glory of His presence shining through.

DAY **258**

READ
Ephesians 3:6

In our next move in pursuing the "mystery", we stumble right on the particular aspect of the secret Paul is relishing (3:6).

What Paul is marvelling over here is the formation of an unprecedented new community embracing the two groups who represent the bitterest divisions which tear the human race apart – Jews and Gentiles.

Throughout his apostolic career, Paul consistently fought for this aspect of the big mystery of God bringing all things under the Lordship of Christ. He warned the Galatians about the danger of Jewish Christian exclusivism and legalism: he upbraided the Roman Church for Gentile Christian arrogance.

Grace not race, faith not law, Spirit-motivated obedience from the heart not external signs like circumcision – these are the true identity-markers of the new covenant people of God.

For Paul, Israel, in line with Noah and Abraham before her, had always a larger vocation, not to be displaced but to be the nucleus of world-wide covenant family of faith!

So startling is this new unity in the Church that Paul coins three new words especially for it, each with the prefix "*sun*"– which in the Greek language means "with": "*sun-kleronoma*" ("joint heirs"), "*sussoma*" ("joint-body"), "*summetoxa*" ("joint sharers")!

A DEVOTIONAL INTERLUDE

Thought: Some Christians are thrilled that God unites them to Christ but not so thrilled that He unites them with others who may not be as likeable. But that's what grace is for. It is given to us to love those we may not naturally even like. If you are having troubles in your relationships it is not because grace is not flowing; it can only be because it is not being received.

DAY **259**

READ
Ephesians
2:11–22

In Christ and through His peace-making cross, there has come about an unprecedented unity of Jew and Gentile which Paul celebrates here.

The inclusion of "uncircumcised" Gentiles on an equal footing with Jewish believers, in the one family of God through faith in Christ, is especially notable because they were previously "excluded from citizenship in Israel and strangers to the covenants of the promise" (2:12 NRSV).

The plural "covenants" and the singular "promise" indicate again that the several covenants serve to implement the one overarching promise-plan of God. In the single strategy of God, the Gentiles have been welcomed into "the social novelty of the covenant of grace"(John Yoder).

Created by the grace of God, the cross of Jesus and the genius of the Holy Spirit, this new body is the place where pride and exclusiveness are overcome, where the ethnic hatred and religious bigotry that still bedevil our world are swallowed up in Christ. Here is revealed the down-to-earth, incarnational, relational reality and victory of God's strategic plan – here where former bitter enemies can join hands and lives in Jesus Christ. No wonder He calls it a new human race (2:15)! Through Jesus alone, we all have access to the one Father by the one Spirit. Together we make up the living temple of God.

A DEVOTIONAL INTERLUDE

To ponder: The issue of racial distinctions flares up from time to time in different parts of the world, and sometimes even in the Church. Take a moment to read John 17 focusing on our Lord's prayer for unity amongst His people. In your own words form a prayer for Christian unity and present it to the Lord. Prayer really does change things. Never let go of that important truth.

DAY **260**

READ
Ephesians 3:9

Today, we find that God's plan is a working-out of His heart-felt intention in creating the world in the first place (3:9c).

God, the Holy Father, gave us being with a view to our becoming His faithful children, in loving and obedient partnership with Him, and a perfect creaturely counterpart to his eternal Son – in short a Bride for Christ (1:4–5; 5:25ff.).

The One Creator God always intended to fulfil His creation's potential and to bring it to perfection in alliance with His mature sons. Since our Great Rebellion, under the terms our sin has set, this destiny must pass through suffering and go the way of the cross before it can again enter into its appointed glory.

It has always been His aim, undeflected by sin, to redeem His creation, not to replace it with something else.

Once again we are reminded that there is no plan-B – it's always been plan-A!

All this flows out of the Fatherly-heart of a God who took the responsibility for creating this world knowing He had the power and love to redeem it.

In Christ, the Father is set to achieve that world-wide family in a perfected creation which before the Fall, before even creation itself, He had set his heart on. Through the gospel, in the revelation of this "mystery" we are in touch with the ultimate purpose of all reality.

A DEVOTIONAL INTERLUDE

Prayer: O Father, the thought of me, a hell-deserving sinner, being close to You in heaven is almost more than my mind can take in, but to be actually joined to Jesus Christ in that mysterious union that a bride and bridegroom enjoy is even more mind-blowing. And it's not because of my merit but because of Your mercy. Eternity will be too short to express my gratitude and praise. Thank You my Father. Amen.

DAY **261**

READ
Ephesians
3:10–13

Before we know where we are, as we stay on the trail of this mystery, we find ourselves tracking down the impact of this secret plan on the cosmic forces in the heavenly realms (3:10).

And it is "through the church" that the revolution rumbles round the heavenly realms.

Did Paul really say: "through the church"! Yes, despite everything, it is by a Church in which the ability of the powers to divide and rule and destroy has been broken by the cross of Christ, that God's "multi-coloured wisdom" is flaunted before their disbelieving eyes.

As a sample of the "new human race" the Church is called to exhibit a startling new unity which overcomes the deep racial and cultural divisions in society. We defeat the "powers" of evil by this show of unity and herald to them that their division of the universe into rival wills is doomed to fail. Our unity in the relationships of family, of work and in the Church, radiates outwards from our reconciliation with God until its "peace" touches and confounds the spiritual forces of wickedness.

Our oneness demonstrates to the cosmic powers, and to the human institutions which welcome them, that God is wise enough to find ways of bringing about His ultimate purpose to unite all things in Christ (1:10–11).

A DEVOTIONAL INTERLUDE

Quotation: "I stood one evening in front of the Niagara Falls and watched with bated breath as a floodlight was turned on, slowly changing colours from blue to red, from red to yellow, from yellow to green and so on. I came away reflecting on the multi-coloured wisdom that God delights to display through His Church and thought how sad that so much of it is not seen because of our lack of unity" (Tom Rees).

DAY **262**

READ
Ephesians
3:11–21

What a breathtaking mystery story this is – God's strategic plan!

But the mystery is not mere mystification! It is a secret that can be received, grasped and communicated. Yet it remains a mystery for all that in so far as it partakes of the transcendence and infinity of God Himself.

It cannot therefore be contained. Though it can be known, it surpasses knowledge (3:19). The riches of Christ are unsearchable (3:8), as are the riches of the Father's glory (3:16). The ways and wisdom of this gracious God are multifaceted and past finding out, confounding the evil intelligence of the cosmic powers (3:10). The mysterious will of love in Christ has heights and depths and lengths and breadth which are unfathomable (3:18) and which only all the saints across all the ages can begin together to quantify. Only through prayer do we have access to this realm of mystery. The secret of the Lord is for those who love, for those who together with all the saints experience the dimensions of God's love.

The fullness to be experienced is the immeasurable fullness of God Himself (3:19b). The fullness of what this God is able to do lies beyond anything we can ask or imagine (3:20). The glory that radiates in the Church will need eternal ages for justice to be done to it (3:21).

A DEVOTIONAL INTERLUDE

Thought: "Come you surveyors and mathematicians," cried C.H. Spurgeon one evening from his pulpit in the Metropolitan Tabernacle, "bring your measuring instruments and see if you can measure the love of God." How can you measure the immeasurable, define the indefinable, limit the illimitable? It's best not to try – just simply bask in its wonder and be thankful to God that He is who He is.

DAY 263

READ
Ephesians
4:17–5:2

Everything we do as believers "in Christ" makes sense. It does so because we are connected to the big story of who God is, who we are in Christ and what we are here for. And what we are here for is to "image-forth" God's character and story. The "new self" we put on when we were made alive in Christ is "created to be like God in true righteousness and holiness" (4:23–24).

Our audaciously high calling, restored by redemption, is to "copy God" (5:1)! Why work in order to give to others, rather than steal and rob (4:28)? Because God is a working God who made the world in six days, who looked forward to the weekend and could enjoy it all the more for having achieved something worthwhile. Which is just the reason we need not only to work but to rest and take a Sabbath.

Why tell the truth? Not because it will always make people like you; they may get enraged. Not because it will guarantee your children will like you or because it will advance your career prospects with the company. We are to tell the truth because that is the kind of people we have learned to be in the school of Jesus (4:21,25).

Why forgive? Because, Paul reminds the Ephesians, it re-enacts the gracious story of how "God in Christ forgave you" (4:32).

The point is clear: if you know who you are in the big story, you know what you're here for.

A DEVOTIONAL INTERLUDE

To ponder: Is it becoming clearer why we have embarked upon this theme of God's story? We have the opportunity of being microcosms of the Godhead demonstrating to all around us on earth how God functions in heaven. He forgives, so should we. He offers unconditional love, so should we. He works, so should we. He speaks truth, so should we. That's why we are here – and that is why God keeps us here.

DAY **264**

READ
Ephesians
5:25–33

Living out the story is the Christian reason for every action and relationship. It is with this in mind that Paul views Christian marriage as a vivid sign of the greater "mystery" of Christ and Church (5:31–33)! Today, the question is not so much whether we should allow divorce and remarriage but the bigger question: why get married at all?

The final New Testament answer would appear to be: because the covenant commitment of marriage enshrines the great mystery and tells out something essential about God's big story.

To commit and to vow, to be faithful in keeping covenant, until death or desertion breaks that covenant, is to tell the story of the One Creator God who kept covenant with His creation even after the Flood. This God bonded with Israel and remained – as Hosea did – obstinately determined to redeem his love – even if it cost Him the life of His only Son on the cross.

Pretty soon it will be a definite Christian act of faith and testimony to get married. Why? Because it only makes sense to get married at all if marriage is connected to the big story of God's covenant love for His people, Christ's sacrificial passion for His bride the Church!

Husbands, then, sacrifice for their wives because Christ did: wives submit to husbands who do that – and both live to tell the tale!

A DEVOTIONAL INTERLUDE

Prayer: O God, in an age when it seems marriage is no longer seen in the light it once was, help us as Your people to show the world by our own marriages what fidelity, commitment and covenant are all about. Dear Father, You have kept Your covenant with us, help us keep our covenants with one another. Pour Your Spirit upon us that we might show the world the way to live. In Jesus' Name. Amen.

READ
Ephesians 3:7–9

Entrusted with God's plans, Paul's role in this is as God's secret agent. God's agents live by grace alone – a grace which calls and commissions and flows in and out of Paul as a mighty power (3:7–8).

Grace could carry the day with Paul because he regarded himself in humility as the "least of all the saints".

Grace has been given to me – Paul insists – to preach the unsearchable riches of Christ. No limit therefore can be put on such resources. Now that is a mystery!

And Paul receives grace in order to make plain to everyone the "administration of this mystery" (3:9).

What Paul does with God's secret is exactly the opposite of what the cults do with their murky mysteries. They hide them away in dark rites and obscure sanctuaries which only the special few can enter. But the Christian gospel which discloses the mystery of God's strategic plan is an open secret for everyone to share!

The gospel blows the lid off the stale and murky mysteries of the cults and sects and blows the bracing fresh air of freedom through every nook and cranny of our tired and musty world – even the prison cells where God's special agents are held!

The God whose eternal purpose is being worked out in Christ is a God whom we may approach "with freedom and confidence" (3:12) so that we may boldly come to, and boldly go from, God's presence.

A DEVOTIONAL INTERLUDE

For praise: What if Paul had kept to himself the secrets God revealed to him? Doubtless God would have raised up someone else, but be that as it may, let's give praise to God for the fact that the secret is out – God has a plan for the universe, a plan in which we play a part. We are now God's secret agents – not to keep His secrets but to reveal them to whoever will listen.

DAY **266**

READ
Ephesians
6:19–20

Paul's "suffering" in the course of duty alerts us to the dangers faced by a special agent inside enemy territory. We must never let down our guard or lose contact with base. We remain subversives with the "gospel of peace". The story we are caught up in is not a fantasy in virtual reality but a real battle with hostile forces. We need the whole armour of God to sustain the fight.

But we need not be discouraged by those of our agents who, operating behind enemy lines, suffer pain and imprisonment for their daring deeds, as Paul did (3:1; 6:20). To recount the noble company of apostles and martyrs is to perpetuate the memory of those of our agents who are "missing – presumed dead".

Praying in the Spirit, praying at all times, praying alertly, praying for God's special emissaries – this is the strange and paradoxical way in which God works out through us His sovereign plan. "Boldness" ("fearlessly" NIV) is a favourite attitude of Paul. Secret agent he may be, but there is nothing secret about his message. Paul asks for prayer that he might freely and publicly proclaim the "open secret" of God's redemptive plan for which he is "an ambassador in chains" (6:19–20). Strange state for an ambassador to be in! But that's part of the mystery, too; prison bars cannot stop this gospel or impede God's plan.

A DEVOTIONAL INTERLUDE

For action: In the light of today's reading, in which the power of persevering prayer has been highlighted, spend at least 15 minutes in prayer for those "operating behind enemy lines" – those special agents whose lives are often in danger as they work to share the gospel in countries where the Christian faith is opposed. It may be a cliché but it is true – prayer changes things. It really does.

DAY **267**

READ
Ephesians
1:6,12,14; 3:21

And the end of all things? "To him be glory in the church ... for ever and ever" (3:21). Every aspect of this sovereign strategy moves majestically to magnify His grace and glory (1:6,12,14).

The Father's eternal plan (1:5–6) to gather a family in love moves into our time and space worlds to pick us up in His saving hand and it's all "to the praise of his glorious grace" (1:6).

His historic action in Bethlehem and Calvary (1:6–7), redeeming us in Christ at the cost of His blood, forgiving us by grace, sharing with us His stupendous strategy for the world, fills us with unspeakable wonder so that we exist "for the praise of his glory" (1:12).

His invasion of our lives by His Holy Spirit's empowering presence, leaving the indelible stamp of His claim upon us, continues to redound "to the praise of his glory" (1:14).

The end of all things is to share in the Trinity-life of the One Creator God, to know with all the saints the four-dimensional love of this God in Christ; in the Spirit, to be embraced for ever by the same love with which the Father eternally loves the Son – this is the end of all things.

This is the eco-system of the divine life. This is the glory of God's love and will flowing out to us and back to God again in loving praise and covenant faithfulness. God's is the true love which makes the world go round!

Thought: The fact that God is working in us and through us to the praise of His glory may sometimes produce mixed emotions in us – especially when He works to rid us of those things that hinder His image being seen in us. C.S. Lewis described this as "God's intolerable compliment". As the old saying goes: God loves us as we are but too much to let us stay as we are.

A DEVOTIONAL INTERLUDE

DAY **268**

READ
Galatians
2:15–21

In Paul's view, when God justifies us, He declares on the basis of our faith in Christ's atoning death that we are acceptable to Him and that we belong to His covenant family.

"Observing the law" here probably means doing those "works of the law" – laws such as circumcision and the food laws – that played so prominent a part in distinguishing Jews in the ancient world from their Gentile neighbours. Some in the Church in Galatia were trying to impose these works of the law on newly converted Gentile Christians (cf. 6:12). And Paul is furious! No one is justified this way, it is only by faith (2:15–16). Paul personalises the issue.

If I move outside the law to go into Christ, I become technically "a sinner" (2:17). Not that Jesus encourages sin! On the contrary, says Paul, if I attempt to rebuild the bridge that I tore down back into reliance on the law, then I show that I am a transgressor (2:18), unable to keep all the law (cf. 3:10) and disloyal to Jesus! Through the law's own condemnation of me as a sinner, Paul goes on, I died to the law as lord of my life, and came alive to God. Co-crucified with Christ, I now live defined and motivated by the faithfulness of Jesus Christ who loved me and gave Himself for me. To do anything else would to give up on grace.

But Paul has burnt his bridges and is not going back!

A DEVOTIONAL INTERLUDE

Prayer: O Father, I am so thankful that through Your Holy Spirit I have come to see that the bridge of "good works" could never cross the gulf that separated You from me. You did for me what I could not do for myself and flung across the great divide the Person of Your own dear Son. Now I am reconciled, justified, and I stand in Your presence just as if I had never sinned. Blessed be Your name forever. Amen.

DAY **269**

READ
Galatians
3:10–14, 26–29

For Paul, the gospel was preached "beforehand" in the promises given to Abraham through whom God's saving blessings would reach all nations. The new covenant life enjoyed in Christ is the fulfilment of God's covenant with Abraham. Both have the same basis – faith, whether for circumcised or uncircumcised. Both involve children given by God, and a promise about the world, not just the land.

This fulfilment has been achieved through the death of Jesus and the outpouring of the Spirit. Jesus hangs on the cross under a curse (3:13 cf. Deut. 21:23). An Israel, unfaithful to her covenant vocation to be an agent of blessing for nations, would incur the curses of God culminating in exile from the land (Deut. 28:63; 29:25–28)

Jesus, "the faithful Israel", the true covenant partner of God, dies this cursed death instead of Israel. Dying as an exile and outcast, He absorbs the curse of judgment, and so the blessing promised to Abraham can now flow to the world by the gift of the Spirit (3:13–14).

By faith in Jesus Christ, the one, singular "seed" of Abraham, the one covenant people of the One God is formed (3:16, 20, 28).

Neither race, nor gender, nor social status bars anyone who believes from entering into Christ's body and therefore becoming a member of the one covenant family God promised to Abraham!

A DEVOTIONAL INTERLUDE

To ponder: How mysterious yet how amazing is this principle seen in both Testaments – the principle of faith. Let the wonder of it lie upon your mind as you move through the day. One definition of faith as we observed earlier, based on the acrostic F.A.I.T.H. is this: Forsaking All I Trust Him. Abraham believed like that, Paul believed like that and so eventually did the blundering Simon Peter. How about you?

DAY **270**

READ
Galatians
3:15–25

As a narrative thinker, Paul notes that in the big biblical storyline, Abraham received God's promises 400 years before the giving of the law. When the law came it did not nullify the previous promise of covenant. It is seen to have functioned as a temporary and parenthetical provision until Christ should come in the "fullness of time" (3:19,23–24; 4:1–4).

The law was God-given ("through angels" reflects a current Jewish belief), and mediated by Moses. But Moses' role was a divisive one ("is not of one") since Gentiles were excluded from the Sinai covenant. But God is One and ultimately seeks one people from all nations.

The law is further limited in that it cannot produce the life it demands. Paradoxically, by condemning sinners and – as it were – shutting them up as prisoners of their sin, the law drives people to trust in God's promise as the only way to be saved. The principle of faith with which Abraham sustained a covenant relationship with God has now finally come into its own with the advent of Christ. The role of the law has changed. While the law remains as a revelation of God's will for His covenant people, it no longer governs our lives as it did before Christ came to bring us under His Lordship and that of the Holy Spirit.

A DEVOTIONAL INTERLUDE

Thought: While we rejoice in the fact that the impossible demands of the law no longer rule and govern our lives as God's people, that does not mean that we can now ignore God's commands. The Ten Commandments have never been repealed. The difference between law and grace is this; the law said do this and you will live. Grace says I will do it for you.

DAY **271**

READ
Galatians 4:1–31

Paul argues fiercely throughout Galatians against those who would impose Torah-observance on Christian believers in order to guarantee their covenant membership. No, Paul asserts, only faith is necessary to be included in God's covenant family. But surely, Paul's opponents might then have argued: if law-keeping is not the way to become God's covenant people, then it is the law which governs how covenant people live? No, says Paul! Freedom is what marks God's people in Christ, not because they live "law-less" lives but because the law is fulfilled in those who live in Christ and are controlled by the Holy Spirit.

What the law can never do, Christ and the Spirit can now produce, achieving in "crucified" believers that quality of life expected of God's covenant people (cf. 5:16–26). This is gospel ethics!

Paul utilises the old story of Sarah and Hagar, Isaac and Ishmael to illustrate his point. Sarah represents the Abrahamic covenant and the Jerusalem above; Hagar is made to stand for Mount Sinai and the present Jerusalem including those who want to impose the law on Christian believers in Galatia. If Abraham is our "father in faith" so Sarah is a our "mother in faith and freedom". We are like Isaac, children born of God's promised miracle of grace and God Himself is our "Abba, Father"!

A DEVOTIONAL INTERLUDE

For praise: When we contrast our lives today with those of the Old Testament saints, we see how wonderful it is to live a life of "freedom". We defined "freedom" the other day as "not the right to do we want but the power to do what we ought". Because the Spirit lives in our hearts He motivates us to do what we ought to do. Living the life God wants us to live is not a pressure but a possibility.

DAY **272**

READ
Galatians 5:1–6; 6:12–16

Gentile believers in Galatia were, it seems, being pressurised by some zealous Jewish Christians to submit to the detailed requirements of the law, especially circumcision.

To do such a thing, Paul argues, would be to fall away from grace (5:4) and to barter your new-found freedom in Christ for a spurious sense of assurance. To go back under the law would be to lose the plot and to regress to an earlier outmoded stage of the story. It would be like turning back the spiritual clock. It would be as good as denying that Christ had come to fulfil the law by dying for us. In the glorious reality of new covenant living, it no longer matters whether or not you are circumcised (5:6; 6:15). In Christ, such signs of belonging to God are obsolete. All that matters now is faith and the Spirit expressed in us through love and humility. We are all humbled by this. Exclusive Jews have to humble themselves to accept Gentiles on an equal footing in God's covenant family. Proud Gentiles have to humble themselves to accept a Jewish Messiah as the Saviour and Lord of the world. In short, we all have to die, crucified with Christ.

But this as a price well worth paying for it ushers us into God's sparkling "new creation" life (6:15).

A DEVOTIONAL INTERLUDE

To ponder: There is a great tendency in the human heart to cling to rituals and ceremonies as these things are visible. The challenge of those who live by faith is not to rest on visual aids but to put one's trust in the unseen, in the innocent sufferings of Christ and Christ alone. How dependent are you on rituals and ceremonies? It's an issue worth pondering.

DAY **273**

READ
Romans 1:1–16

Paul carries in his mind all the time the one storyline of the Creator God's relationship with Israel and looks at every issue through that lens. So Romans is not a series of random theological topics but a coherent argument which shadows the biblical story of God and Israel. In chapters 1–4 Paul shows that in Jesus the Messiah – and especially through His cross – God has demonstrated His covenant faithfulness to Israel by dealing with Israel and the world's sin, in order to create a world-wide community of faith in line with His promises to Abraham. Chapters 5–8 show that this faith-community, undergoing a new exodus to fulfil Israel's vocation and to rewrite Adam's story by bearing the hallmarks of a new humanity, is heading now for the promised land of renewed creation.

Where Israel's traditional story fits with this is faced in chapters 9–11. There Paul is shown that Jews and Gentiles mysteriously interact as factors in God's overall saving plan for the world. Israel's vocation is enacted by Jesus and her failure borne by Him so that the way is open for Gentiles along with Jews to enjoy the blessings of salvation by trusting Christ.

This new covenant community is called – as chapters 12–16 make clear – to be a sample of what a new humanity looks like in living a life of unity and love.

A DEVOTIONAL INTERLUDE

Prayer: Loving Heavenly Father, the truth that You have been working through Israel towards a wider community – the goal that was in Your heart in the beginning – fills me with wonder and joy. As the story unfolds I find myself thrilling more and more to the fact that I am part of it. A small part perhaps, but an important part. For there is nothing unimportant in Your story. Thank You dear Father. Amen.

DAY **274**

READ
Romans 1:17–32

The gospel which tells the story of God's covenant faithfulness acting to save, also exposes the sad history of sin and God's wrathful judgment on it.

Paul's devastating analysis of how sin ruins a society is not a knee-jerk moralistic reaction to how bad things have become. Rather, Paul shows how sin turns the narrative of creation upside down, so that we humans refuse to reflect God's image but sinfully look for other options for self-fulfilment and other objects of worship. But in bowing down to self-made images, we fall victim to believing a lie. Our human story is bent cruelly out of shape.

Homosexuality is no more subject to God's wrath than the other sins mentioned. But it is a more graphic sign than most that a society has lost the plot. Perverted sexual activity is itself a sign ("God gave them over ..." v.24) that a society is under God's judgment. We are called to reflect God's image in a polar male–female relationship. To pervert this is to distort God's image and to destroy our humanness. It is as if the original creation story has been scrambled by human rebellion into a confusing code of language. The gospel re-translates our human story back into its original language of partnership with God and then re-inserts this human story into the larger narrative of a good and gracious God.

A DEVOTIONAL INTERLUDE

Thought: C.S. Lewis once used the word "bentness" to describe the core problem sin has produced in the universe. "Bentness" is when the creature is "bent" in the direction of created things rather than the Creator. We are designed to stand upright and worship the Creator. Sin has "bent" us in the direction of earth. We must decide whether we stand up straight or remain "bent".

DAY **275**

READ
Romans 2:1–29

A sad feature of the human tragedy of sin, exposed by the prophets of old and highlighted now by the gospel, is that Israel is shown to be as much part of the problem as she is part of the answer.

Not, of course, that every Jew is a robber or a murderer. The problem with Israel, as Jesus and Paul found, is a national pride in its exclusive relationship with God. But how can a nation brag of being a light to the nations when it is darkened by its own sinfulness (2:19)? Israel is still in "exile" for her sins, still bearing the reproach levelled at her by the prophet Ezekiel of "dishonouring the name of God" by her unbelief and misconduct (2:24). In such a condition, having the outward sign of being God's people – circumcision – counts for nothing. But there is a gleam of hope that a people can emerge who, while not circumcised, will truly be God's covenant people and will keep God's law (2:27). The description of people changed from the inside-out with hearts remade to love and obey God, sounds very much like Jeremiah's and Ezekiel's picture of the new covenant community. And it is. Thankfully, the story of creation gone wrong and the story of Israel falling from grace, is not the end of the story. Already we catch a glimpse of a new people of God in whose hearts the Holy Spirit has worked miracles (2:29).

A DEVOTIONAL INTERLUDE

For praise: The thrust of God's workings in the Old Testament was from the outside in (generally speaking) but in the New it is from the inside out. The Holy Spirit has come to reside and preside within us and has given us "circumcised" hearts that are free to love in the way God wants us to love. How thankful we ought to be to God that He has gone to such lengths to set us free.

DAY **276**

READ
Romans 3:1–20

Israel's privilege was to be the one nation entrusted with the very words of God. But if Israel fails, does God's Word fail? Does the faithlessness of the covenant people discredit the faithfulness of the covenant God? Does God scrap plan-A in favour of plan-B? "No," says Paul (3:4). Two things follow. Firstly, Israel is no less part of the problem of sin than the Gentile world to which Israel was meant to bring God's saving revelation. There is no one righteous. As the psalmist had foreseen, all the world is exposed as sinful and under God's judgment. In the imaginary law court where the case is presented, no one has any defence to offer. "Every mouth is silenced" (3:19). All excuses, all rationalisations, all pride, all evasions, are cut off. We sinners stand mute before a holy God with nothing left to say for ourselves.

Not even Jewish national pride in possessing the law is of any avail. In fact possessing it only serves to highlight what sin is and how guilty we all are (cf. Rom. 5:20; 7:7–8).

But if God is to remain faithful to His promise to bless the world through His covenant people, then He must find a true Israel through whom to do the job. A faithful Israel(ite) is required at this point. Step forward Jesus ("God presented him" 3:25) who is exactly what the situation demands.

A DEVOTIONAL INTERLUDE

Worship: Nothing gathers up the truth of our inability to meet God's standards like this verse from Toplady's well-known hymn, "Rock of Ages". If you know it sing it; if not, say it:

Nothing in my hands I bring,
Simply to Thy Cross I cling ...
Foul I to the fountain fly
Wash me, Saviour, or I die.

In Jesus He has cleansed us. For that give Him the worship that is due to His Name.

DAY **277**

READ
Romans 3:21–22

In the coming cross and resurrection of Jesus, God's covenant faithfulness has come to the rescue.

This salvation works "apart from law" in the sense that it is not achieved by law-keeping or in a way exclusive to Jews. At the same time it is something to which the Torah and the prophets bear witness so that it has impeccable Old Testament roots.

God's covenant faithfulness ("righteousness") has acted to save. God has achieved His own ends through the "faithfulness of Jesus Christ", the one true covenant partner. Whoever puts their faith in this faithful Jesus is "justified" in the sense of being owned by God, as belonging to God's covenant people.

What was supposed to happen at the end of history has happened in the middle of history. The verdict of the last day has been brought forward and announced in the present. God "justifies" or "vindicates" his people by finding in their favour. God declares that all those who trust in Christ for forgiveness of sins are His covenant people. The proof that God has made a "pre-emptive strike" in favour of His people is that He has raised Jesus from the dead. The ultimate sign of His own people's vindication and justification will be their own "resurrection" of which Jesus' resurrection is the guarantee (see 4:25).

A DEVOTIONAL INTERLUDE

Prayer: I am so thankful, dear Heavenly Father, for this "pre-emptive strike" I have read about today. And as You raised Jesus from the dead so, too, have I been raised from the dead to live this life that is just too wonderful to put into words. I am so glad that You have saved me and all I long for is that my life might show forth the "fruits" of Your favour. Help me, my Father. In Jesus' Name. Amen.

DAY **278**

READ
Romans 3:23–31

When God forgives sins He does it on the basis of the blood of Jesus. His gracious covenant integrity moves out in saving love to put people who believe right with Him. The cross is the crux of His action to save the world, the final demonstration of God's faithfulness to the covenant. God has dealt with the sin that spoils His creation and undermines Israel's vocation by means of the sacrificial, substitutionary death of Jesus, the Messiah. By Jesus' death for sinners, God is vindicated, because He is both seen to have dealt with sin and, at the same time, is shown to have faithfully kept His covenant commitments. There is no room then for the kind of boasting a Jew might indulge in who was proud of His exclusive relationship with God. Ethnicity is no longer an advantage card. Those works of law that marked out Israel as different are effectively sidelined when it comes to salvation and faith. God is not the God of Jews only but the One Creator God who aims to create one people for Himself out of both the "circumcised" and "uncircumcised" – Jew and Gentile. Yet though the law is marginalised as a means of marking out who God's people are, it is upheld because in it is taught the principle of faith through the foundational story of Abraham. It is to this story that Paul next turns to bolster his case.

A DEVOTIONAL INTERLUDE

Quotation: "The church ... has become increasingly accustomed to Christianity without a cross ... or at best with one hanging harmlessly in the background. We have forgotten that in the middle of this Gospel stands a cross ... the splinters of which are largely ignored by a contemporary Christian world eager to tell mostly the good part of the story" (John Fischer).

DAY 279

READ
Romans 4

Paul is mirroring the Old Testament storyline of God's promises and covenant faithfulness. Abraham, then, is not merely a random example of faith, but the key figure through whom God established that faith is the one factor which governs a right relationship with God. This occurred long before the giving of the law and even before circumcision was enjoined. This strengthens Paul's argument that it is not by law-keeping but by trust in God that a covenant people, both then and now, is born and sustained (4:3,9,22–23; Gen. 15:6). This principle applies to us ("but also for us" 4:24).

The blessedness of sins forgiven which David enjoyed comes to all who believe (4:6–9).

Abraham is the father of a universal family of faith whether Jew or Gentile (4:11–12). The scope of his inheritance is not restricted to the promised land but extends to the whole earth (4:13, anticipating 8:18–21). God gives life to the dead – including a "dead" Israel – and calls things that are not – even the "non-existent" Gentiles – as though they were. Faith in such a God honours grace (4:16), gives God glory (4:20) and engenders hope (4:18–20). We believe in God who raised Jesus from the dead who died for our sins and rose again to guarantee our vindication as God's people (4:25).

A DEVOTIONAL INTERLUDE

Thought: We just cannot get away from "faith". Wherever we turn either in the Old Testament or the New we keep bumping into this word. And why? Because without faith as the writer to the Hebrews tells us, "it is impossible to please God". A similar word to "faith" is "trust". It's one thing to "trust" God for salvation, but what about other aspects of your life? Worth thinking about!

DAY **280**

READ
Romans 5

Paul has shown that God has one covenant family, rooted in Abraham's faith, and now being created in Christ Jesus from both Jew and Gentile. Family members enjoy peace with God and rejoice in hope of once again sharing the glory of God (5:1–2, cf. 3:23).

We have been reconciled to God by the undeserved covenant love of God through the death of Jesus by which God's wrath against sin has been turned aside. Paul now stands back to see the global picture (5:12–21). Within the overall narrative of what God is doing, the stories of Adam, Israel and Jesus interact.

God's work in Jesus Christ, Israel's Messiah, finally overcomes Adam's sin and disobedience. In fact Christ has done more than merely reverse Adam's fall. Jesus has not only offered the obedience that Adam didn't offer, but He exhibits the true covenant love and faithfulness that Israel was called to show. Either way, we owe everything to the obedience of Jesus. The law served a special role in concentrating sin in Israel – and then in her representative figure of the Messiah – where it could be dealt with once and for all (5:20).

This is not just the rebranding but the remaking of the human race. Once sin reigned over us resulting in sure and certain death. Now God's grace rules our lives resulting in sure and certain life, now and in the future.

A DEVOTIONAL INTERLUDE

For praise: We have been reminded once again that "we owe everything to the obedience of Jesus". What if He had failed? The consequences of such a failure are too frightening to contemplate. But He did not fail and because of His triumph we are saved, redeemed and reconciled to God. Right now give the Lord your thanks for such perfect obedience.

DAY 281

READ
Romans 6

If anyone is tempted to presume on God's grace and persist in wilful sinning, then they have not grasped the first thing about what it means to be in Christ. We have been immersed in the drama of Jesus' dying and rising and can be expected to live a cruciform life.

You are living out of a different story now, Paul says, so don't think or behave as if you were playing a part in the unredeemed Adam story.

There are surely echoes here of the crossing of the Red Sea and the escape from slavery in Egypt (6:6–7, 16–22). In the larger story, Pharaoh's role is now played by sin. Freed from slavery to sin, we have become slaves of righteousness as servants of God. Paul celebrates the reality of living in the new covenant by speaking of an obedience from the heart to that "form of teaching to which you were entrusted" (v.17). The apostolic teaching is not just a series of beliefs we assent to but the pattern our lives are now to be conformed to and shaped by. In other words, we are placed in a new story, the story of the dying-rising Jesus.

If Paul, in telling the new exodus story of human redemption, is mirroring Israel's story, then we might expect to be brought next in the story to Mount Sinai and to the law of God. This is just what happens in chapter 7.

A DEVOTIONAL INTERLUDE

Prayer: Father, once again I come to You with praise and thanksgiving in my heart for the fact that You have taken me out of the old story – "the unredeemed Adam story" – and made me a part of the redeemed story – Your story. Grant that my behaviour and all my thinking shall be such that fits in with the thrilling story You are telling. In Jesus' Name. Amen.

READ
Romans 7

This contentious passage is also best seen in the light of the stories Paul is telling.

Paul is then not concerned here with any supposed second stage of Christian blessing or with the inner dynamics of the Christian experience. The subject throughout is the law, the Torah, given at Sinai, and how Paul now views it. Ironically, the law is part of the bondage sinners need to be freed from. And through dying with Christ, we are released from any "marriage" to the law (7:1–3). In classic new covenant language, Paul describes how we can serve God fruitfully in the Spirit (7:4–6). Where does this leave the law? Although God-given, good, holy and righteous, the law has the effect of inciting inveterate sinners to more sin which incurs more guilt and condemnation and hardens us in our sinful condition (7:12–13).

Paul speaks in the first person, not to show that his present Christian experience is an internal "civil war" between two supposed "natures" within him, no, rather, as a representative Jew, and from the standpoint of being "in Christ", he looks back with new eyes, on what it was like to be "under" God's law. Paul sees the deficiencies in his pre-Christian story but now rejoices in being part of a new story, the story of the dying-rising Jesus (7:25).

A DEVOTIONAL INTERLUDE

For thanksgiving: The controversial nature of this passage has already been noted, but do not miss the indisputable truth that the passage brings us, namely that God gives us the victory over the condemnation of the law on sinners. Keep this simple and sublime thought before you – you are not under law but under grace. Form now your own prayer of thanksgiving for this fact and offer it to God.

DAY **283**

READ
Romans 8:1–11

As we have seen, the problem is not with God's law but with the sinful people who are meant to live by it. What the "law could not do" (v.3 NKJV) was to produce the kind of covenant life it described. Sin prevented God's people living out the "righteous requirements of the law" or enjoying the life of the covenant which was the aim of the Torah. Our "flesh" (v.3) – here used in the negative sense of our disposition to disobey God – weakened the law fatally. But what the law could not do, God has done by sending His Son in the likeness of our sinful "flesh" to offer Himself as a sacrifice for sin on the cross. God condemned sin in Jesus, doing what the law also could not do, which was to deal a fatal blow to sin. God did this so that the true intention of Torah might finally be fulfilled in the creating of a new covenant people. This people no longer lives "under the law", dominated by sin, but lives under the Lordship of Jesus and is controlled by the Holy Spirit. In Christ Jesus we relish the freedom from the "law" which spelt only sin and death. Uncondemned, we live by the law of the Spirit who gives life. If the immediate sign of our being God's covenant people is that God's Spirit is in us, then the ultimate sign will be our resurrection from the dead (8:11). That Spirit of future resurrection hope reverberates within us right now!

A DEVOTIONAL INTERLUDE

Thought: Today's reading makes crystal clear just why the law, though good, brought us into bondage. We just could not live up to it. The intervention of Jesus on our behalf means that what the law could not do – deal a fatal blow to sin – has now been accomplished through Christ's death. The law rendered us helpless but the Spirit now helps us live the life God always wanted for us.

DAY 284

READ
Romans 8:12–30

Once again we catch the allusions to the first Exodus story as Paul shows how Israel's story and the human story have been taken up into the drama of God's salvation in Jesus.

Israel's bondage in Egypt was, after all, only a sign of all humanity's deeper bondage to sin and death. Both stories are redeemed by the story of Jesus.

God's sons are led by the Spirit through the present unredeemed world as the cloud and fire led God's "son", Israel, through the wilderness. On our pilgrimage, as we share His sufferings, we can cry out to "Abba, Father" at times of stress, as Jesus did.

God groans in and with His pilgrim people in a groaning world that waits for redemption as they march towards the new world coming.

Canaan was viewed in the Old Testament as a larger scale version of Eden and, in turn, points forward as a metaphor for the whole earth renewed as the scene of God's glory for which we are heading. Our freedom from slavery mysteriously interacts with the freeing of a creation bound to decay and death.

On the way to that promised future, the Holy Spirit works in every circumstance towards the "good" that God intends for us – which is to make us like Jesus. Seeing the end of the story from the beginning, our final glorification is as sure an outcome to our story as the Author's pre-set plans for us.

A DEVOTIONAL INTERLUDE

Prayer: Gracious and loving Father, it is a privilege to be a part of Your creation and an even greater privilege to be counted as one of Your servants. To be called Your child, to be considered as one of Your family, to be able to call You Abba Father is a truth that I just can't get over. Once again all I can say is "Thank You". I shall go on saying it again and again and again. Amen.

DAY **285**

READ
Romans 8:31–39

Can we sum up Paul's vision? It heralds the arrival of God's new covenant people, founded on the death of Jesus, and in which the Spirit of God is triumphantly at work. The Spirit enables believers to fulfil the just requirements of the law, to defeat the flesh and to live as God intends His covenant people to live. The Spirit joins us to the character and destiny of Jesus and so guarantees our final resurrection. The Spirit assures us of our sonship, evoking within us a heartfelt appeal to God as "Father" especially during times of crisis. The Spirit inspires hope and helps us to pray in line with God's will. The Spirit groans within us as we share a divine discontent for a better world. In every way, the Spirit sustains us in the weakness of life in the present age, and assures us of future glory.

As the Spirit floods our hearts with God's love, we know that no opposition can defeat us since Christ is our covenant protector. No deprivation can threaten us for God is our provider. No accusation can be made against us because God vindicates us. No condemnation can doom us because Christ is our advocate with the Father. And, above all, on the way to the promised future, nothing in the world as it is or in the world as it may become, can come between us and the unquenchable covenant-love of God in Jesus Christ.

A DEVOTIONAL INTERLUDE

Question: How do you feel about the fact that nothing can separate you from the love of Christ? If you have never given deep thought to this issue then do so now. Think of it – no shortcoming, no circumstance, no opposition, no person place or thing can come between us and the love which Christ has for us. Once again – how do you feel about that? Express those feelings in prayer, praise or perhaps even song.

DAY **286**

READ
Romans 9:1–13

Paul's celebration of God's enduring covenant-love leaves a question hanging in the air: Is there any place for ethnic Israel in the plot?

Paul's answer is to the effect that the story of Israel has not been written out of God's larger story but transformed and enlarged in and through her Messiah, Jesus.

Paul's own mind seems stretched to breaking point here both by the agony of the issue and by the breathtaking answers the Holy Spirit was giving him.

Israel's failure to embrace Jesus as Messiah is all the more tragic when you recall her unique God-given privileges and status (9:4) – all derived from the promises made to the patriarchs. Above all, nothing can ever take from them the privilege of being the forebears of the Messiah who is "God over all" (9:5).

But an even bigger question remains: does Israel's failure mean that God's covenant promises have fallen to the ground? Paul answers with a decisive "no". Whoever else has failed, God has not failed and nor has His Word of promise (9:6).

In fact, there has always been an ambiguity about Israel; there has always been an "Israel" within Israel (9:7–13). Genealogical descent from Abraham never did count for much, only being children of the promise. Always what matters is the promise of God which shapes the story, and what our response is to it.

A DEVOTIONAL INTERLUDE

For praise: Are you familiar with the following verse? It summarises the enduring nature of God's promises. If you know it sing it (or say it) as your response to today's reading:

Standing, standing,
Standing on the promises
of God my Saviour
Standing, standing
I'm standing on the promises of God.

DAY 287

READ
Romans 9:14–33

Paul's concern is with the fate of Israel but even more with the character and integrity of God. In the narrowing of Abraham's seed to the line of Isaac is God unjust? In the golden calf incident, (9:14–15 citing Exod. 33:19), as with God's treatment of Pharaoh, the over-riding consideration is God's glory and the honour of His Name (vv.16–18). As Israel's own prophets testify, God would be unable to affirm Israel as she stood and would need to subject her to His judgment and mercy in order to change and restore her (9:19–29). Tragically, Israel has become "objects of wrath, prepared for destruction", but God has borne with His people patiently with a view to demonstrating His mercy in the creation of an amazingly enlarged people of God – made up of both Jews and Gentiles – who respond to His call.

The greater tragedy is that more Gentiles than Jews are presently entering God's new covenant family, while Israel is preoccupied with pursuing the law in her own nationalistic and exclusive way (9:30–32). This misuse of the law has, in turn, led Israel to stumble over the Messiah (9:33). But the very fact that this "stumbling" of Israel was foreseen by the prophets holds out the tough but mysterious hope that Israel's failure, and with it her future destiny, is, somehow, incorporated into God's plan from the start!

A DEVOTIONAL INTERLUDE

Thought: One of the most intriguing truths to be found in Scripture is that God is able to take the stumbles and blunders of His people and incorporate them into His purposes. Nothing can outwit the mind of the Almighty or out-manoeuvre his strategies. As Ian Sewter puts it: "God's plans for us can never be thwarted by our failures as He includes them from the start."

DAY **288**

READ
Romans 10:1–21

Paul now further explains the strange twist in the story of redemption caused by Israel's ignorance of what God has been faithfully doing throughout her covenant history. Israel has grasped for her "own" exclusive righteousness, as if Israel said: "The covenant righteousness is ours alone". In doing this, first-century Israel lost the plot of God's big story and failed to recognise the climactic stage of the story when it dawned in Jesus.

Jesus is the "end" of the law. Negatively, He "ends" the law by bearing the judgment on sin it prescribes. He is the "end" of the law, positively, because He keeps all its covenant demands. He is the "end" of the law in that everything that the law patterns and promises Jesus fulfils. Jesus is the climax of God's covenant intention for which the law was given. The law was a good thing, fitted for a particular stage in the story. Now, its time is up. The goal of the law has arrived and it is a person, Jesus. There can now be no question of anyone hi-jacking the covenant for themselves. In Christ it is open to "everyone who believes", whatever their nationality. Wasn't this exactly what God told Abraham He wanted at the start of our story?

A DEVOTIONAL INTERLUDE

To ponder: If there is one thing Scripture emphasises again and again it is this – God delights to bless us. He gets great delight out of making His people happy. But He requires always that His blessings be shared with others, whether given to Abraham, Israel or the Church. Count your own blessings at this moment. Now consider, how much of what God has given you have you given to others?

DAY **289**

READ
Romans 10:5–21

Paul has traced the covenant purpose of God from Abraham down as far as the Exile in Babylon (9:6–33).

Then he recalls the hope offered by Moses that Israel would be restored after Exile (Deut. 30). This enables Paul to show that the Deuteronomy way of "doing the law" (10:5) is, in fact, the way of faith!

In this paradoxical way, the law can be said to be fulfilled whenever Christ is preached and people respond in faith. In what is perhaps the earliest Christian confession of faith that exists, the way to be saved is to confess that "Jesus is Lord" and to believe that God raised Him from the dead (10:9). Believing "with your heart" once again picks up the new covenant theme (Deut. 30:6; Jer. 33).

Joel's prophecy (10:13; Joel 2:32) is applied to the Jews and Gentiles who are putting their faith in Christ and acknowledging him as Lord (10:11–14). The era of restoration and salvation which Isaiah saw announced by the herald with the "beautiful feet" running over the mountain with the good news of the kingdom of God (Isa. 52:7), has well and truly come. Sadly, most Jews remain resistant to the message of the gospel, though in doing so they ironically fulfil their own Scriptures (10:16–21). But a hope remains that Israel may even be stirred to jealousy by a people of God who know Israel's Messiah as the key to God's story (10:19).

A DEVOTIONAL INTERLUDE

For action: We have been told something today that while bringing to every Christian heart a tinge of sadness should also stir us to deeper intercessory prayer, namely that most Jews remain resistant to the gospel. Notwithstanding that, many Jews come to Christ each year. Some reports say as many as half a million. Spend a few minutes today interceding for Jews who do not yet know Jesus.

DAY **290**

READ
Romans 11:1–32

In exploring further the covenant faithfulness of God in Christ, Paul here seems to be answering two implied questions.

To the question "Are any Jews being saved at all?" Paul answers with the notion, derived from the prophets, of the "remnant" who believe, Paul among them. For their part, Gentile Christians are warned against arrogantly forgetting their Jewish roots in the patriarchal promises and covenants. There is only one olive tree, one people of God to whom Gentiles have been added by grace and some Jews removed by judgment. But the one should not presume nor the other despair. Will any more Jews be saved? Though some may continue to respond, a hardening has settled over Jewish hearts until the fullness of the Gentiles has come in. In this way "all Israel" – the whole people of God – will be saved through embracing the new covenant promise of God (11:26; Isa. 27:9; 59:20–21; Jer. 31:33–34). The deliverer comes out of Zion and appeals to Zion to be forgiven and restored as a new covenant people.

This strange interaction of Jews and Gentiles is central to the "mystery" of God's strategic plan that Paul unveils (11:26).

Whether this involves the conversion of Israel on a national scale prior to the second coming of Jesus is an open question. Paul seems more concerned for what is happening "now" (11:31).

But one way or another, it's all a miracle of grace.

A DEVOTIONAL INTERLUDE

Prayer: Heavenly Father, the more I read Your Word the more I realise that everything we receive from You is all because of Your grace. The Jews with their rebellious hearts were undeserving of Your grace but then so are those of us who are Gentiles. If we had our just deserts then we would be cast into outer darkness. But grace has intervened. Glory be to Your wondrous Name for ever. Amen.

DAY **291**

READ
Romans
11:28–32

"God moves in a mysterious way his wonders to perform." This is not a puzzle to be figured out but a providence to be marvelled at.

Because they opposed the preaching of Jesus, Paul can regard his fellow Jews only as enemies of the gospel. But does God still have a special love for His ancient people? Yes, he does. God does not go back on His gifts and calling. But God has special love for Israel not because she has a specially reserved, fast-track into God's kingdom in the future that by-passes Jesus but because of His own historical commitments to the patriarchs!

Once more little is said here about the future of Israel as a nation. Paul's concern is with the wider picture of what God is doing in His world. As a result of Jewish disobedience, the Gentiles have received mercy. So now disobedient Jews may receive mercy because of God's mercy to the Gentiles! God's forgiving heart is open to all (11:32). Through a mysterious interplay between Jews and Gentiles God will achieve His breathtaking purpose.

When even Israel's failure, rejection and disobedience are woven into God's plan of salvation then we can only stand back and wonder at this strangely sovereign and covenant-keeping God. From His grace, through His power, to His glory explains it all. All that's left is our worship.

A DEVOTIONAL INTERLUDE

Thought: "From His grace, through His power, to His glory." That pregnant phrase sums up the whole of Scripture. The consideration of that stupendous fact leaves us with just one thing to do – fall to our knees in worship. Nothing in us gave rise to God's love and grace, and nothing in us can extinguish it. Never forget – His love for us is based not on our faultless character, but on His forgiving nature.

DAY **292**

READ
Romans 12:1–2

When our whole beings are gripped by God's grace (as in 11:33–36), we can only respond by the offering of our whole selves to God in worship. Our sacrifice, of course, is living, not dead like animals; holy, as we dedicate our entire life to God; and spiritual or reasonable, in that we make an intelligent and fitting response to grace.

This covers all of life. How is this done? First, Paul says, refuse to let the "world squeeze you into its own mould" (J.B. Phillips). We become non-conformist in our thinking and behaving, by rejecting the story told by this present evil age. Being "transformed" by the "renewing of our minds" once again describes authentic new covenant living with a new heart, and God's law implanted in our minds. It is an affront to proud intellectuals to learn that sin has affected our minds, distorting our thinking and darkening our understanding, so that when the things of God are first presented to us as sinners, we "just don't get it". And this re-programming of our minds is a life-long process which starts when we humble them before God. It continues as we bend every mental and intellectual power we possess to the joyous task of loving God with our minds and growing in understanding of His plan of salvation! This *Cover to Cover* journey you are on is designed to help you do just that!

A DEVOTIONAL INTERLUDE

To ponder: There is a great deal of anti-intellectualism in some parts of today's Church. One Christian put it like this: "Sometimes when I go to church I might as well unscrew my head and put it under the seat. The emphasis is on feeling good and there is no attempt to engage with my brain." Remember we are commanded to love God not just with all our hearts but also with all our minds.

READ
Romans 14:9–12

Paul here discusses the vexed question of what Christians can legitimately disagree about and how they can live together in unity when they do! The "strong" have a robust sense of their freedom in Christ and so have few scruples about what they eat or do. The "weak" are those who do have scruples about many things and feel some areas of life are "off limits". Such matters as feast days and food laws are matters on which Christians may rightly differ. What must not happen is for the "weak" to judge and condemn the "strong" or for the "strong" to look down patronisingly on the "weak".

Both parties are called to realise that they are in God's story which rolls inexorably on towards final resolution.

No one is in a position to judge another because we shall all stand before God's judgment seat (14:10–11).

Above all, the story of Jesus stands at the heart of God's big story and ours. Crucial to our grasp of that story is the recognition that Jesus died and rose again to become Lord of the dead and the living, Lord of our present and our future. The onus is on the "strong" Christians to make the story of the cross their central dynamic by acting sensitively towards a brother "for whom Christ died" (14:15). Living out the story together in this way honours its Author and commends it to outsiders (14:18).

A DEVOTIONAL INTERLUDE

For action: In the light of the fact that Scripture calls us to "maintain the unity of the Spirit in the bonds of peace" and live in harmony with one another, this issue must be treated seriously. Is there anyone in your circle of friends or relationships with whom you have a difference of opinion that has caused a rift to come between you? If so, before the sun goes down determine to seek a reconciliation.

DAY **294**

READ
Romans 15:4–13

Christian hope derives from the Scriptures (15:4) and from the Holy Spirit (15:13).

We are enriched by seeing that the Old Testament is not a static book but has a powerful momentum that presses towards God's future. Dark as some passages may seem, the narrative points forward to find its final meaning in Jesus. In other words, the ancient Scriptures generate enormous hope.

Reading the Old Testament in this way should give us hope that, despite appearances to the contrary, history is going God's way. This especially encourages those non-Jewish participants in the story who were originally not addressed by the hopeful visions offered by the Old Testament prophets. Only when Jesus Christ comes to make good those promises do Gentile believers find a new history for themselves. While Jews rejoice, therefore, that God is a truthful God who keeps His word, Gentile believers glorify God for the mercy that includes them in His saving plans on an equal footing. Through Jesus, God has kept his age-old promise to Abraham to bring blessing to all nations. And Gentile believers can't thank Him enough!

Jew and Gentile hope knows no bounds, fed as it is by prophetic scriptures, fixed as it is on Jesus the Messiah (15:12) and overflowing as it does by the Spirit's power in one united chorus of praise.

A DEVOTIONAL INTERLUDE

For praise: Join in praise to God right now along with the many thousands who will be reading these lines, people from all nationalities, who have been saved by grace and washed in the blood of Christ. Praise Him for the fact that from all nations, with all their differences and cultures, He has formed, through Jesus, one family who is to the praise of His glory.

DAY 295

READ
Romans
15:14–16:27

In Romans, the gospel is the good news that God's covenant faithfulness ("his righteousness") is revealed in the preaching of Jesus. As Messiah, Jesus has dealt a death blow to the sin which ruins God's good creation and holds both Jew and Gentile in its thrall. God's covenant faithfulness has acted to save by overcoming in His Son's death and resurrection all the negative factors that oppose the truly human life – namely, sin, death, the flesh and, surprisingly, the law of God itself. But through Christ, God reverses Adam's plight and offers the prospect of a new humanity in Christ. This newly human, new covenant community, is leading the way through a groaning world to the new creation God. God's plan mysteriously interweaves the stories of Israel and the world and wraps them up in the story of Jesus.

God's covenant-love writes a new chapter in the human story, with new characters, forgiven and empowered by the Spirit, who are learning their parts in the new drama of being human. Whether Jew or Gentile, these new covenant people sing from the same songsheet of love and worship with one voice. The ordinary saints Paul greets at the end of this letter are the real heroes in the story. In the end, the mystery of God's strategic plan evokes astonished praise of the One and "only wise God".

A DEVOTIONAL INTERLUDE

Prayer: O Father, the more I understand Your ways and purposes in the past, and the more I learn of Your plans for the future, the more confident I am of living in the present. Help me realise even more fully that when I feel as if there is not much happening in my life You are at work nevertheless. Often You do Your greatest work in secret. Blessed be Your Name for ever. Amen.

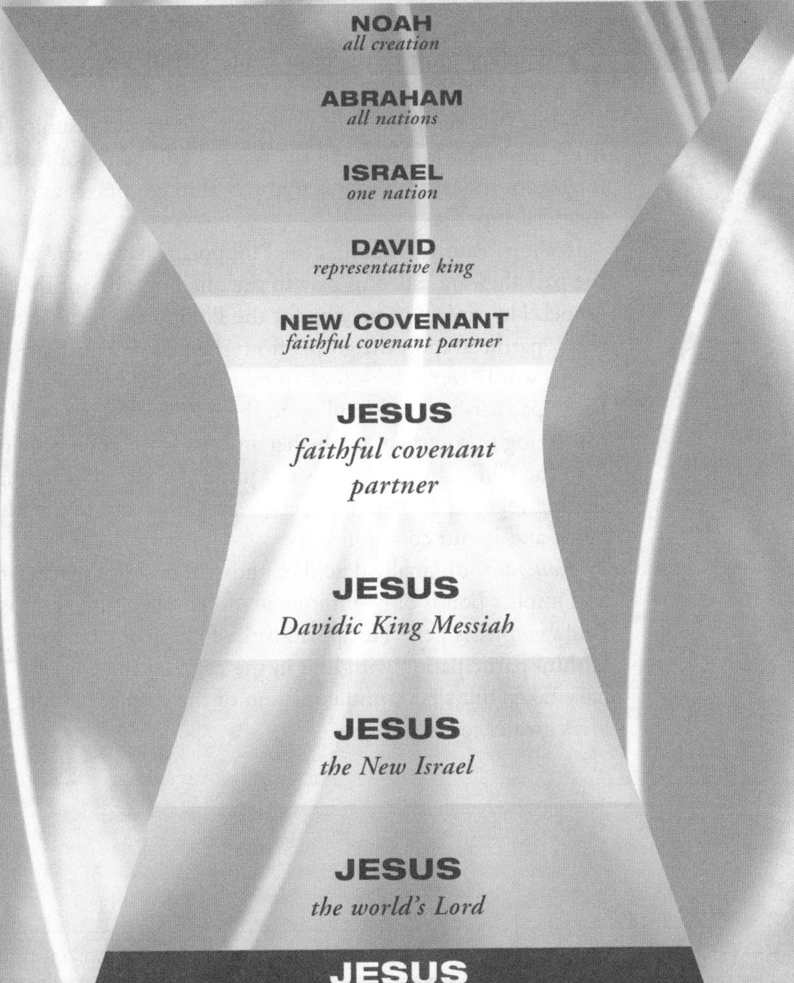

NOAH
all creation

ABRAHAM
all nations

ISRAEL
one nation

DAVID
representative king

NEW COVENANT
faithful covenant partner

JESUS
faithful covenant partner

JESUS
Davidic King Messiah

JESUS
the New Israel

JESUS
the world's Lord

JESUS
THE TRULY HUMAN ONE CROWNED WITH GLORY AND HONOUR

JESUS
cosmic Ruler in God's new creation new heavens and new earth

SECTION 10

PAUL'S WORLD-VIEW PART 2

DAY 296

READ
Philippians 1:1–5

Philippians must be the most famous thank-you note in history!

While Paul does warn against false teachers and disunity, his main reason for writing is to thank the Philippians for their long-term sponsorship of his ministry through prayer and financial support.

In short, Paul rejoices that the Philippians have come alive to the part they are called to play in the ongoing story of the gospel. He rejoices in praying for the Philippians because of their "partnership in the gospel from the first day until now".

The word "*koinonia*" – is often translated "fellowship" or, as here, "partnership" and implies "to share in" something, to "hold something in common" – whether an experience or an activity.

In the Christian case, this is not just a sharing together but a sharing together in something else – in Christ and in the Holy Spirit and in our common story.

"*Koinonia*" originally described those in business partnership and implies bonds of commitment and co-operation. This is Paul's emphasis here. He applauds the Philippians for their faithful participation with him in the cause of the gospel. They have taken out shares in the mission of the gospel. Nothing gives greater joy.

A DEVOTIONAL INTERLUDE

For action: A devotional moment consists of more than just focusing on God and His goodness; it also means being thankful to those whom God has used to bring blessing into our lives. Philippians, we are told, is the most famous thank-you note in history. When did you last write a thank-you note to someone who was a "minister of the Lord" to you? If you have not done so, sit down and write one today.

DAY **297**

READ
Philippians 1:6

The Author of the story has the stamina to see it through to a satisfactory ending. The "good work" which God began might refer to the Philippians' support for Paul's ministry. But the mention of the "day of Christ" makes it more likely that it refers to the saving work of grace begun in their lives at conversion – of which their backing for Paul is, of course, evidence.

What God begins He completes. You may feel you are in the middle of a slow movement right now but God composes no "unfinished symphonies". What He starts, He continues. God never grows weary in well-doing, or downs tools. He does not repent of His sacrifices. His purposes for our lives cannot be thwarted. What a comfort this is. Jesus laid a sure foundation on the cross and God is committed to completing what is built on it. Tracing God's big story has shown that God's covenant commitments are permanent. We are saved in three tenses – we have been saved, we are being saved, we will be saved. God's good work covers all three – from commencement through continuation to completion! What grace!

"All's well that starts well!"

A DEVOTIONAL INTERLUDE

Thought: You cannot be sure of many things in this world. Projects are started and then laid aside. People make promises and then forget them. However, when it comes to God, you can bank on this – whatever He starts He finishes. The Almighty "never downs tools". Let this thought be your anchor – what God has started in your life He is committed to finishing. Yes "all's well that starts well".

DAY **298**

READ
Philippians 1:6

Today we stand back, to see the end of the story from the beginning.

God has set alight in the heart of every true believer an "inextinguishable blaze" which is God's own burning passion to see His story succeed.

Knowing that God always takes the initiative in salvation makes us confident that the "good work" begun in our lives cannot be thwarted. Where our human decisions might prove unreliable, God's unshakeable resolutions give hope.

When Christian saw water being poured on the fire in *Pilgrim's Progress*, he feared that the devil was quenching God's work of grace. Wondering why the flames burned "higher and hotter", he was shown the "backside of the wall where a man was pouring oil secretly into the fire. This it was explained to him, was Christ who continually with the oil of grace maintains the work already begun in the heart".

I have a tight deadline to meet for this book in the *Cover to Cover* series – *God's Story*. And there is a day of completion for the big story itself, a "deadline" if we can call it that when it is so full of life! The "day of Christ" will be not just a judgment day of quality control on our lives, but a glorious day of completion and consummation, a splendid coming-out parade of these to whom God has applied the finishing touches, a proud curtain call at the end of this act of the drama.

A DEVOTIONAL INTERLUDE

For praise: How grateful we ought to be for the fact that the fire God lights in our hearts can never be put out by the devil's cold water. Remember this verse from Wesley's great hymn?

There let it burn with holy fire
And inextinguishable blaze
And trembling to its source aspire
In humble prayer and fervent praise.

Sing it with joy and praise in your heart remembering thousands of others will be singing it too.

DAY **299**

READ
Philippians 1:12–18

This remarkable passage again speaks volumes for the way in which being in God's story transforms our view of reality.

Paul would argue that even prison looks different if you can see it as providing strange opportunities for the furtherance of the gospel. He's not in prison for crime but for Christ!

Providence is a dull word for such a sparkling truth. God's overarching strategy is very flexible in its tactics. God is infinitely adaptable and can work out His sovereign will in the most unfavourable conditions. Knowing this makes Paul remarkably resilient. Trying to tame him is like trying to take a tiger by the tail! What an irrepressible prisoner Paul is!

Paul mentions three effects of his imprisonment: it evangelises his enemies; it encourages his friends; it is being exploited by his rivals.

But as long as Christ is preached, Paul is content that the true story is being told of what the One Creator God has done for His world.

Paul is spiritually buoyant. Suppressing this man is like trying to sink a cork in a bath! But Paul would only say, it's all Christ's doing and He can do the same for any believer in Him. The Holy Spirit can make you irrepressible whatever your circumstances. Whatever has happened to you, can you believe with Paul that it might somehow tend to the furtherance of the gospel?

A DEVOTIONAL INTERLUDE

Question: Do you believe God can make you "irrepressible" whatever your circumstances? It's easy to say but not so easy to put into practice. Paul's secret lay in the fact he believed, as he put it in Romans 8, that all things were working together for good to him because he loved God. When you believe (really believe) that nothing can work successfully against you then you too will be irrepressible. Try it and see.

DAY 300

READ
Philippians 1:19–20

These words are a veritable tapestry of grace woven from strange threads.

Although imprisoned, Paul believes that whatever happens to him is in God's hands, and can only work for his ultimate good.

We may recall the similar attitude of Joseph (Gen. 45:5–8; 50:19–20) or Job whose very words – "this will turn out for my deliverance" – Paul quotes (Job 13:16).

This is the poise of the Christ-centred life. After all when Paul was first imprisoned in Philippi the walls fell down; but not this time.

Paul believes this will turn out for his vindication so that he will "not be put to shame" in the sense of being let down by God. Whether in the short term or in the longer eternal sense, deliverance will come. Like Job he knows that his redeemer lives and that he will stand in that day! Paul is sustained by the prayers of others and by his own experience of the Holy Spirit. God "choreographs" the drama to supply the needed resources of the Spirit to Paul.

God sovereignly and mysteriously interweaves our intercession and His interventions into the final tapestry of His strategic purpose.

Our prayers count for something in God's big scheme of things, usually in ways beyond our knowing. We are not puppets on a divine string, but free and willing partners in the story God is enacting.

A DEVOTIONAL INTERLUDE

To ponder: Some time ago research amongst a group of Christians showed that 99% believed the most important discipline was prayer, and the same number claimed it formed the greatest challenge in their lives in terms of time, inclination etc. Consider this as you go through your day – if God weaves His interventions with our intercessions how many deliverances will not take place today?

DAY 301

READ
Philippians 1:21

Nothing is more remarkable than the way God's story brings perspective to the Christian's confrontation with death.

Here the question is raised: Is death a plus or a minus?

Paul looks death in the face and confronts the ultimate question: "Will death add to you or only take away?" Paul's answer is clear: "To me to live is Christ, to die is gain." For those for whom living means Christ, death will only gain us more of Him.

Paul expresses a new valuation of death, asserts a victory over death and expects vindication after death.

With similar confidence, our Christian forebears looked death in the face. Imminence of death concentrates the mind wonderfully on what is vital. As the old adage goes: we must deal with death or it will kill us! Paul's deliberations about whether to stay or go sound as if he's negotiating with God. But he is not bargaining with God here. Rather he is exercising the unique freedom of someone who, long ago, handed over complete control of his life and reputation to the Lord Jesus and is not now about to take it back!

To use business jargon, Paul is in a "win-win" situation. He can't lose because he is totally committed to Christ being magnified in his body whether by life or death. Death is not the last chapter in the story we are in, for its author is the Author of life!

A DEVOTIONAL INTERLUDE

Quotation: "The best man who ever lived went down through death and came back, and the first thing He said was, 'Fear not' there is nothing here to fear. He who was so right in everything else, the ages being witness, is He wrong here? He who never lets us down in one single area of life, will He let us down in this central area? It is impossible" (E.S. Jones).

DAY 302

READ
Philippians
1:27–30

Just as Paul read his circumstances in the perspective of the story of the gospel, so now he urges the Philippians to make the same gospel the narrative pattern on which to base their lives. The imperative "Live your lives ..." or "Let your conduct be ..." uses a unique political verb which means "live as citizens of a kingdom".

Anticipating 3:20, Paul gives here the Christian Citizens Charter. The gospel of Jesus is not only good news to be received and believed but has the power to shape our behaviour and lifestyle.

Conduct "worthy of the gospel" is characterised especially by a serious commitment to Christian unity: "standing firm in one spirit" as if in warfare; "striving together for the faith of the gospel" as if in an athletic contest. Disunity in the Church still mars our witness to the gospel. If only we could remember that we are committed to a common cause as citizens of the same city, athletes playing in the same team, soldiers fighting on the same side. Unity would make us fearless in the face of any opposition. The increasing conflict that is coming to the Church will surely test how united we are but will expose the difference between those who are perishing and those who are being saved. We shall count it as a privilege to be found worthy to suffer for the sake of the gospel as Paul did.

A DEVOTIONAL INTERLUDE

Thought: The New Testament fairly bulges with the importance of Christian unity. Our Lord in John 17 prayed that His people might be one in order that the world might believe. "We appear to suffer from a pathological inability to get on with one another," says John Stott, "or to co-operate in the cause of the Kingdom of God. We ought not to make light of this grievous situation."

DAY **303**

READ
Philippians
2:5–11

We invite you to spend a number of days reflecting on this one rich passage of Scripture.

In what may be an early Christian "hymn to Christ", Paul dwells on the mindset of Jesus "who, though he was in the form of God, did not regard equality with God as something to be exploited, but emptied himself, taking the form of a slave, being born in human likeness. And being found in human form, he humbled himself and became obedient to the point of death – even death on a cross.

Therefore God also highly exalted him and gave him the name that is above every name, so that at the name of Jesus every knee should bend in heaven and on earth and under the earth, and every tongue should confess that Jesus Christ is Lord to the glory of God the Father" (NRSV).

This memorable passage tells a number of stories as one story. It will help you if you refer back to Day 12 to refresh your memory on how the whole Bible works this way. Now let's consider how the five circles apply here.

At one level it is of course the story of Jesus.

But then again this story is told, by way of contrast, as the true story of Adam.

The story told here is also telling of the strange but climactic fulfilment of the story of Israel.

And then again what is truly remarkable is that Paul is telling this story as the story of God!

What is being told finally is the story of the world.

A DEVOTIONAL INTERLUDE

Prayer: Gracious Father, once again I give You thanks for allowing me to be one of the characters in Your story. I see today that one of the purposes of my involvement in Your story is to be part of the great hymn of worship to Your Son. Today, as all over the world men and women give You praise I gladly add my own. Blessed Trinity I give You my heartfelt worship. In Jesus' Name. Amen.

DAY **304**

READ
Philippians 2:5–11

The first story this passage tells is, of course, the story of Jesus.

Jesus is described as "being equal with God" and "being in the form of God" which both express full-scale divinity.

But does Paul imply of Jesus that this is something He "does not yet have but is seeking to grasp or snatch" (as in the NIV)?

Or should it be taken as referring to "what someone already has but chooses not to exploit or take advantage of" (as in NRSV)?

The latter is undoubtedly the best way of reading the text and has considerable implications. Christ "did not regard equality with God as something to be exploited ..."

In other words, Christ refused to exploit to His own advantage the position of equality with God which He already had.

Christ never stops "being equal with God" or "in the form of God". What happens is that such states are dramatically re-interpreted in unexpected ways.

Without ceasing to be what He was, the Lord Jesus did not take advantage of His exalted position, He did not exploit it for His own selfish purposes. When He came among us He did not dazzle us with displays of overwhelming divine power nor did He intimidate us with bullying tactics. He never acted in possessive or exploitative ways. He was secure enough and humble enough to look us in the eye and meet us at our own level.

A DEVOTIONAL INTERLUDE

To ponder: Did God have to become human in order to save us? The answer of course must be "Yes". We see something of God in nature, but we do not see Him fully, except in the life of Jesus. "Jesus," said a little boy in Sunday School "is the best photograph God ever had taken." "Jesus," said one theologian, "puts a face on God." We would never know what God is truly like had we not seen Him in the Son.

DAY **305**

READ
Philippians 2:5–11

In some translations, Jesus is said to have "emptied himself" (e.g. NRSV). This may mislead us into asking, "emptied of what?"

The answer usually supplied is that Jesus laid aside divine attributes such as omnipotence and omniscience. But Paul is almost certainly using the word "emptied" in the sense of "rendering something powerless", or "emptying it of apparent significance" (cf. Rom. 4:14; 1 Cor. 1:17).

The translations "but made Himself of no reputation" (NKJV) or "made himself nothing" (NIV) are not far short of the mark. Even better, perhaps, to say "he poured himself out".

Paul is celebrating the stunning story of God's utter self-giving of Himself in Jesus Christ. When he looks at Jesus from manger to cross, Paul sees a life poured out in lavish self-expenditure for the sake of others. The one glorious pre-incarnate life of God poured itself into a human life at Bethlehem and poured out in sacrificial death at Easter. We can perhaps hear an echo of Isaiah 53:12 where the servant of the Lord "poured out his soul unto death" (KJV). His life and death taxed his deepest inner resources. For the sake of us prodigals our Eldest Brother entered the far country of rebellion and death and squandered His life in righteous living and redemptive dying. Thank God He did.

A DEVOTIONAL INTERLUDE

For praise: Does it not evoke within you the deepest praise when you consider that Jesus was born not in a mansion but in a manger, that He lived the life not of a celebrity, but a carpenter? Think of it also in this way – He forsook the glory of heaven that you and I might have a part in God's story. Dwell on that thought before you move away and do other things. And give Him praise.

DAY **306**

READ
Philippians
2:5–11

The story of Jesus being told here, is also, by way of contrast, the true story of Adam, our human story.

Adam – made in the image of God – grasped at being equal with God, a status which was not his to have. But Jesus, the Last Adam, refused to cling on to His divine status, voluntarily renouncing what He had every right to.

Where Adam in pride sought to become like God, Christ in humility becomes human.

This is the truly human life. In Jesus, the Truly Human One achieved that destiny which was always envisaged for Adam's sons – sharing with God's dominion as "Lord" over the world (v.10).

It is usually assumed that being God and being human are inherently incompatible states. God is, of course, the Creator and we are mere creatures, but they are essentially compatible (Gen. 1:26–28). It is then, strangely appropriate for God to come in into His world in human form in Jesus.

It is wonderful to realise that our human nature is a vehicle designed by God as a means through which He can express Himself! God called humans to be the sovereign wise rulers of this world so that He might be the sovereign-wise ruler of the world by becoming human Himself!

This is the only authentic and truly human story, which fulfils every human potential to the glory of the Father.

A DEVOTIONAL INTERLUDE

Prayer: O God, the more I think of the stoop made by Your Son from heaven to earth, the more my soul is filled with unutterable joy. I do not have to knock at the gates of heaven, Jesus has come knocking at the door of my heart. What grace, what humility, what love. What I dare not dream of – that Jesus the Son of God should come to me – has happened. And I am more grateful than words can convey. Amen.

DAY 307

READ
Philippians 2:5–11

The third story embedded in this profound "hymn" is the strange but climactic fulfilment of the story of Israel.

Called out of slavery to be God's servant partner for the salvation of the world, Israel refused the way of humility and obedience.

As a result Israel plunged down into the "ignominious death" of exile, ending up ironically enslaved again in the very place from which Abraham had first come at the beginning of her story!

As Israel's Messiah, Jesus re-runs the Israel story successfully.

Jesus particularly moulds Himself to that concentrated version of the story which is told in Isaiah 40–55. There, God's agent brings God's salvation through humble servanthood and willing obedience to death. How differently might Israel's story have unfolded if Israel had gone the way of God's servant Jesus; how Israel's story might look if it passed through the prism of Christ's humble death and triumphant vindication told in the parallel story of Paul in 3:1–21.

It involves not being obsessed with acquiring status and glory. It means not acting in self-regarding or exploitative ways. It means exhibiting the self-less, other-regarding humility, born in those who have been immersed in baptism into the story of this dying and rising Jesus.

A DEVOTIONAL INTERLUDE

Thought: "Everyone's life is a story," said Eugene Peterson, "whether God is in it or not." However, what a different story we have to tell when God is in it. Imagine recounting the story of your life if Jesus had not saved you. Doubtless there have been good times and bad times, light and shade – but without Jesus there is no sense of destiny. Destiny is what makes the difference.

READ
Philippians 2:5–11

What is truly remarkable is that Paul is telling this story as the story of God!

What does it feel like to be a god and to behave like one?

Telling the story of Jesus like this is a way of telling the story of the One True God! The astonishing thing about the humility with which Jesus stooped to conquer us is that the person who never stopped being equal with God, chose to walk such a path of lowliness.

The narrative of Jesus from manger to cross is therefore the definitive revelation of God! This story throws totally fresh light on God.

The climax which quotes Isaiah (v.11; Isa. 45:23) applies to Jesus the name "Lord" which was reserved in the Old Testament exclusively for the One Creator God, Yahweh. This is not only God's stamp of approval on Jesus as sharing the very "Godness" of God. It is God's way of telling us what "being equal with God" really looks like – it looks like this!

God is shown to be selfless, pouring out His life for the sake of others. In Christ God has told His real autobiographical story. God is not a being gripped with the lust to exploit His advantages; He is motivated not by the love of power but the power of love.

Here is the truth about Christ, about God, and about universal humanity, all wrapped up in a very particular Jewish story.

A DEVOTIONAL INTERLUDE

To ponder: Some children in a Christian school were asked to write on the subject: What is God like? Their answers included words like – power, majesty, authority, greatness and so on. Astonishingly no one used words like humility, gentleness, graciousness, love. It is these latter words however that endear Him to us. Perhaps this might be a good time to ask yourself: what is my picture of God?

DAY **309**

READ
Philippians 2:5–11

One last reflection on the stories being told here in Paul's celebration of Jesus Christ.

Finally what is being told, by contrast, is the world's story – in particular the story of the world Paul knew, of Roman imperial power and might. And that world is being subverted because Jesus Christ is the Last Emperor!

For the early Christians, Jesus was the Jewish "Messiah", "the Christ". Psalm 2 had declared God's intention to make His king in Jerusalem the Lord of the whole world. As a result of His obedience unto the death of the cross, Jesus has been exalted and given the name above every name. This name, in context, can only be "Lord" – the very name applied in the Greek Old Testament to God Himself (Isa. 45:21)! When Jesus is announced then all must bow the knee and confess that "He is Lord".

Caesar's empire, like every subsequent imitation, is a parody of the real thing!

While Paul wrote, the Caesars were annexing for themselves the title "*kurios*" or "Lord". Nowhere outside of Rome would this have been felt more keenly than in the Roman Colony of Philippi. But the Christians there had heard and believed a different script in which Jesus, not Caesar, is Lord of the world. No wonder so many of the first apostles ended up in prison or that so many Christians now as then give their lives for Jesus.

A DEVOTIONAL INTERLUDE

Question: What does the Lordship of Christ mean to you? Is it merely a biblical doctrine or does it relate to the way you live, the way you think, everything you do? "You call me Lord, Lord," said Jesus to the people of His day, "but you do not do what I say." Someone has put it like this; If we do not crown Him Lord of all, we do not crown Him Lord at all". Is Jesus Lord of all that goes on in your life?

DAY **310**

READ
Philippians 2:12–13

Paul's unforgettable telling of the Jesus story comes with a "therefore" attached, calling us to respond. We do so not simply by drawing a logical conclusion or even by following an example, but by being connected to a power which changes our life.

Of course, there is no hint that we can achieve our own salvation. Salvation is God's gift. But we are urged to "work out our salvation" in the sense of living out the life we possess in Christ.

No passive "let go and let God" attitude will do. We are participants in the drama not spectators of it.

We must co-operate with the power of God working in us.

Deep within the springs of each Christian's personality, God is at work re-directing our wills and rejuvenating our motivation to do His will!

This is the glorious reality of the new covenant life once promised by Jeremiah and made good by the Holy Spirit.

Do you hear your inner self saying: "I can't do God's will, I'm too weak, I keep failing"? God says, "I am working actively inside you to will and to work what pleases Me. I am continuing the good work I began in you and will bring it to completion."

How awesome! "Danger – God at work!" No wonder Paul reacts with "fear and trembling", not because he has a nervous disposition, but at the thought that the mighty Creator God is working in and through him!

A DEVOTIONAL INTERLUDE

Thought: Someone has said, "Whenever you see the word 'therefore' in the Bible always ask yourself what it is there for". The "therefore" in this passage, as the writer has pointed out, calls us to respond by connecting to the power which operated in the life of Jesus. The Christian life it has often been said is not our responsibility but our response to His ability. How well connected are you?

READ
Philippians
2:14–16

In today's world celebrities are famous merely for being famous. But to be a star in God's eyes demands no heroic exploits except the major feats of not grumbling or complaining, both of which cast a slur on the reputation of God! God's new covenant people are called to avoid the mistakes of the earlier phase of the story.

Paul recalls the tiresome attitude of the children of Israel in the wilderness which so severely put God to the test. But, as Daniel hoped, one day the "righteous will shine like the stars".

Darkness is defined as the "crooked and perverse generation" – a term once applied to a rebellious Israel (Deut. 32:5).

Christians are one with God's Old Testament people and are now challenged to live with uncomplaining patience and to hold firm the Word of Life by believing and testifying to its truth.

Paul often describes in sacrificial terms Christian ministry which exhausts our energies and entails suffering. But this "sacrifice" is not dragged from him reluctantly but is part of his joyful self-offering in the cause of the gospel. Yet his outpouring of life is a drink offering that climaxes their sacrifice, not his! Amazingly, the self-offering of apostles and martyrs is only the crowning seal of value placed on your faith as Christ's people.

A DEVOTIONAL INTERLUDE

Prayer: O Father, living as I am in a darkened society, help me I pray to shine out as a bright light reflecting the glory of Your presence and the power of Your love. Help me also to have complete confidence in Your Word and to live uncomplainingly, sacrificially, counting it all joy to suffer for You if and when necessary and pouring out my life as did the apostle Paul as a "drink offering" to You. Amen.

DAY 312

READ
Philippians 2:19–29

How do ancient travel plans end up in Holy Writ? Because even our small-scale domestic stories are vital to God's big story. The genius of the gospel is that it sanctifies the mundane and makes the ordinary sublime. Timothy will arrive at Philippi soon, while Epaphroditus is coming later; of such is the kingdom of heaven. God's story is not all about headline names and incredible feats. It's curiously heartening that some of the apostles rate only half a line of Scripture while these two "saints in ordinary" rate half a chapter!

Timothy and Epaphroditus are Paul's friends as well as his co-workers, and two of the gospel's countless "unsung heroes".

Timothy was a role-model in seeking the interests of others rather than his own and was as near to a son as Paul ever had.

Epaphroditus was evidently missing home and worrying how the Philippians might be reacting to news of his illness. How very human!

Welcome him back, says Paul, without thinking he has let you down by returning when in fact he risked his neck for me. All in all this is a wonderful sample of how redemption transfigures everyday events and the Holy Spirit inspires a practical down-to-earth spirituality. Who you are, what you are doing and even where you are going today, matters to the Lord and contributes crucially to His story.

A DEVOTIONAL INTERLUDE

For thanksgiving: A man said to a preacher after he had heard him preach on the theme "Giving Thanks": "I have nothing to be thankful for." Nothing to be thankful for? What about our five senses, reason unimpaired, the gift of God's own Son and so on. Then of course there's this drawn from our reading today – everyone matters to God be they pensioner or preacher, accountant or apostle, child or king! Give thanks.

DAY 313

READ
Philippians 3:1–2

Paul derisively denounces those he calls "dogs" who if you let them cut your body, will mutilate your faith! Who is this fierce talk aimed at and why?

Like the Galatians, the Philippians are being troubled by some Jewish Christians who want to impose on Gentile Christians the specific marks of Jewishness – particularly circumcision.

We recall that circumcision was the outward sign, in males at least, of being in God's covenant family, especially important for Jews living outside the promised land, and a contentious issue in the apostolic mission.

"Circumcision" stands here for "covenant people" or status.

But circumcision was always meant to signify a deeper "circumcision of the heart" (Deut. 10:16; 30:6; Jer. 4:4; 9:25 cf. Rom. 2:28–29). And, since Christ has come, it no longer counts for anything in a believer's relationship with God. To say otherwise is to threaten the freedom of the gospel of grace. So, when so much is at stake, Paul does not mince his words.

For Paul, faith in Christ is now the only indelible sign of being in God's covenant family. He reacts strongly to anything that says knowing Jesus is not enough and seeks to drag believers back to an earlier outmoded stage of the story. God's story is now an open book and freedom is the chapter we are in.

A DEVOTIONAL INTERLUDE

To ponder: One of the greatest temptations we Christians face, said C.S. Lewis is, "Christianity and ..." What did he mean? Christianity and something else. Christianity and psychology; Christianity and good works; Christianity and human effort. Some Jewish Christians in Paul's day said Christianity and circumcision. Faith in Christ is all that is needed for salvation. Make sure there are no "ands" in your life.

DAY **314**

READ
Philippians 3:3

Paul celebrates the fact that the Philippian Christians – whether Jewish or Gentile – are bone fide members of God's new covenant community. The trademark of physical circumcision operative from Abraham's day has become obsolete and the real "circumcised ones" can now be defined as those who enjoy the privileges of the new covenant relationship promised by the prophets long ago.

Christians now serve or worship God "in the Spirit". To live "in the flesh" is to live centred on oneself and without God. In this case "in the flesh" is particularly apt since the problem people are those who are trusting to a literal cut in the flesh! On the other hand, to live "in the Spirit" is to live a human life in all its aspects controlled and empowered by the Spirit of God.

Our worship, too, is characterised by the way "we boast in Christ Jesus".

Trusting Christ and experiencing the Spirit are the only genuine signs of being in God's covenant family. Our trademark is that we exuberantly exult in the glory of the person of Jesus Christ, totally repudiating any confidence in the flesh. Our status before God does not depend on any inherited patterns of privilege or achievements of our own piety but solely on Christ and the Spirit. We are in God's covenant family through grace. This is our story, this is our song!

A DEVOTIONAL INTERLUDE

For praise: You will no doubt know the following song that Billy Graham made famous. To sing it seems an appropriate response to today's reading

This is my story, this is my song
Praising my Saviour all the day long
This is my story, this is my song,
Praising my Saviour all the day long

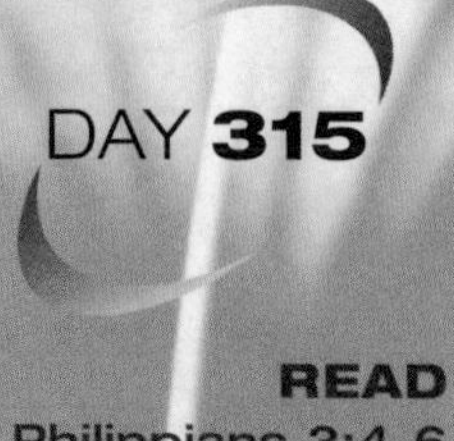

DAY **315**

READ
Philippians 3:4–6

Personal stories are transformed when they are caught up in God's larger drama of salvation. Paul's autobiography is especially instructive because it mirrors that of Jesus (Phil. 2:5–11) and, as the story of a representative Jew, shows what Israel might be if it followed his example.

Paul never denigrates his Jewish heritage, only the false confidence he had once placed in it. By his own account, he loved the patriarchs, honoured the Torah, worshipped at Temple and synagogue, and soaked himself in the Hebrew Scriptures as the living oracles of the One Creator God. He never denigrates these things in themselves, only the false confidence he had once placed in them.

His zeal for the law, he sadly recalls, had led him to persecute the Church, but in other respects he could claim to be "blameless", not in the sense of being "faultless" but in scrupulously using the law's prescribed remedies when he sinned. But his law-keeping has become distorted into his "own righteousness".

Paul's past was fine but had no future in it!

Of course, there should have been because that previous narrative was meant to lead somewhere, in fact to the feet of Christ. Paul for one has found the rainbow of salvation at the end of the trail and sees absolutely no need to retrace his steps.

A DEVOTIONAL INTERLUDE

For prayer: Father, help me to appreciate and value all that Christians owe to the Jews in giving us our Bible and their Messiah. But help me, too, to value Jesus above everything else as the gold at the end of every rainbow.

DAY **316**

READ
Philippians 3:7–8

Paul's immersion in the saving story of Jesus has led him to draw up his profit and loss account. In his "revised balance-sheet", the apostle reveals that his old status and privileges did not, in any way, add up to the joys of salvation in Christ. In fact all that was previously profitable to him he has decisively written off, consigning them to the "rubbish dump"!

This is tough talk again from Paul especially about things that were once so precious to him. But knowing Jesus surpasses everything else.

Note again how closely Paul's testimony mirrors the story told of Jesus in 2:5–11. Like his Lord, Paul too has renounced a privileged status, suffered loss, undergone humiliation. In other words this is the cruciform, Christ-pattern worked out in the history of one Jewish man.

As such Paul exemplifies the way all his fellow-Jews might go to fulfil their destiny and achieve their true identity. And if we were to ask Paul, "Was it worth it?", he would surely reply with a resounding "Yes!" Right now he has gained a relationship with Christ; in that decisive future he is sure he will be "found in Christ" with covenant membership not guaranteed by law but given by God to those who believe in Jesus. How much richer can anyone be?

A DEVOTIONAL INTERLUDE

For action: Have you ever drawn up a spiritual profit and loss account? Do so now. Think of all your achievements, credits, degrees, wealth, your status in society – everything that the world regards as important. Then think of the fact that you are an heir of God and a joint heir with Jesus Christ. Would you be willing to count all you possess as loss in order to win Christ? If the answer is "Yes" then you are growing.

DAY 317

READ
Philippians 3:9

In the new script being written of his life-story, Paul rejoices that he has discovered a new way of "righteousness" which here means something like "vindication".

God vindicates those who take their stand with the crucified Messiah, Jesus.

For Jews, like Paul, it means that they are no longer taking their stand with Torah or any of its works, like circumcision, but wholly and finally casting in their lot with God's crucified and exalted servant, Jesus, who has Himself been vindicated in resurrection and exaltation to the place of supreme Lordship.

As a result, they too are vindicated and declared to be His covenant people.

But the move cost Paul everything. Like his Lord, Paul has stepped down into disgrace in order to step up into God's life and glory. Like his Lord, Paul found that his privileges advantaged him nothing, nor could he exploit his privileged status for any gain that accrued to him.

This humbled him and recalled him to Israel's original servant vocation.

In embracing this, Paul obediently submitted to immersion in his Messiah's humiliating death. But because Christ was raised and exalted to final vindication, Paul too looks forward to ultimate vindication in final resurrection through Christ. His story becomes our future!

A DEVOTIONAL INTERLUDE

Thought: Clearly there is a reproach in the gospel. The writer to the Hebrews bears down on this point: "Let us, then, go to him outside the camp, bearing the disgrace he bore" (Heb. 13:13). There is a shame at the heart of the cross and it must be borne. Paul experienced it and so must we. Our commitment to Christ may immerse us in His "shame" but we shall be immersed also in His "glory".

DAY **318**

READ
Philippians
3:10–11

Paul has a completely new ambition: he wants above all to "know Jesus" more and more. But notice that knowing Jesus involves entering more and more deeply into an experience both of His risen power and His suffering death!

Paul looked back on the price of knowing Jesus as a cost infinitely worth counting. He wrote in his journal: "All my intellectual and moral achievements gasped their final breath when I had that breathtaking encounter with Jesus, crucified and risen; the old me died and a new Paul arose as if from the dead."

So when Paul speaks of knowing Christ more he is speaking out of an already profound and firsthand experience.

He already knows Christ as a moral power penetrating to the depths of his personality. He knows Christ as the living Lord who gives him the surge of courage to face an angry mob. He knows Christ as the captivating Saviour turning the moral effort of a legal past into a life-stretching adventure with the Holy Spirit. He knows how Christ fills the wings of his abilities and ambitions. No wonder he still wants "to know him"!

Having been enrolled in the curriculum of Christ's sufferings, Paul is willing, for the further joy set before him, to be a graduate of the "school of Calvary" whatever it costs.

A DEVOTIONAL INTERLUDE

To ponder: One of the exciting aspects of the Christian life is that there is always "more". However well we know Christ, there is always more to know of Him. It may be an arguable point but perhaps Paul knew Jesus better if not better than anyone who has ever lived. Yet he wanted to know more. Are you satisfied with what you know of the Saviour or do you, like Paul, long to know more?

DAY 319

READ
Philippians
3:10–11

The deepest inside knowledge of the story of Jesus comes through "holding shares in His sufferings".

Paul has made a re-investment of his life. Having written off all his previous assets as a Pharisee, he has declared himself bankrupt, gone into voluntary liquidation and is now resolved to invest his life's capital in the ongoing sufferings of Christ!

The resurrection does not cancel out the cross, so that Jesus did all the dying while we do all the triumphing. No! By raising Jesus from the dead God endorsed the whole self-giving, servant lifestyle that had taken Him to the cross. Consequently, if we enjoy the power of His resurrection operating in us – and by the Spirit we certainly do – then we must realise it is meant to empower us precisely to enter into the fellowship of His sufferings in the real world. This is what knowing Jesus means.

Note again how the language of 2:5–11 is echoed here as Paul talks of being "conformed" to the cruciform pattern of the way Jesus died. Finally, as with Jesus, Paul hopes to "attain to the resurrection of the dead" which, as the prophets knew, is the way God ultimately vindicates His people and shows they are really His. In this strange but true love story, the way of the cross leads home; the way of death leads to life; the way down is the way up.

A DEVOTIONAL INTERLUDE

Quotation: "When we shrink from suffering we deprive ourselves of the joy of knowing God more deeply. Suffering produces pain (I am not referring necessarily to physical pain) but we emerge through the pain to be a new person. The apostle Paul knew the brokenness that came from suffering for Christ and it was this that made him the great man he was. Only broken people truly know God" (Evan Roberts; Welsh Revivalist).

DAY **320**

READ
Philippians 3:12

One feature of being caught up in an ongoing story is that we never stand still.

To encourage us to keep pace with God, Paul gives us a vivid insight into his own spiritual progress. He makes two virtually parallel statements built around the metaphor of a race in which the central message, emphasised twice, is: "I press on". Paul brackets this intense sense of purpose with three disclaimers which give a realistic context for his aspirations: he has not yet obtained; he has not yet been made complete; he does not consider himself to have taken hold of his final destiny.

Paul is under no illusions about the present life. He is "betwixt and between". He has gained Christ but there is so much more to know and his eye is on the well-stocked future of God's story as a goal to be reached.

Paul was apprehended at the crime scene by Jesus on the Damascus Road and now he presses on to "take hold of that for which Christ took hold of him". Paul's career was turned around. Jesus now sets the agenda for what is important to Paul; God's purposes not Paul's plans matter most. The goal and the prize that await at the finishing tape – whatever way you look at them – can only be that ultimate experience of "knowing Jesus" which he has already told us is his over-riding ambition. May God help us to live at "full stretch" for Him.

A DEVOTIONAL INTERLUDE

Thought: We do not all travel along the road of Christian discipleship at the same rate. We grow old at the same rate. A year is as long for a lad in his teens as a man in his seventies, but progress in the things of God is not made at a fixed rate. Paul has been described by one writer as "a pace-maker". He sped along the path of discipleship at speed. And why? Read Romans 5:17 for the answer.

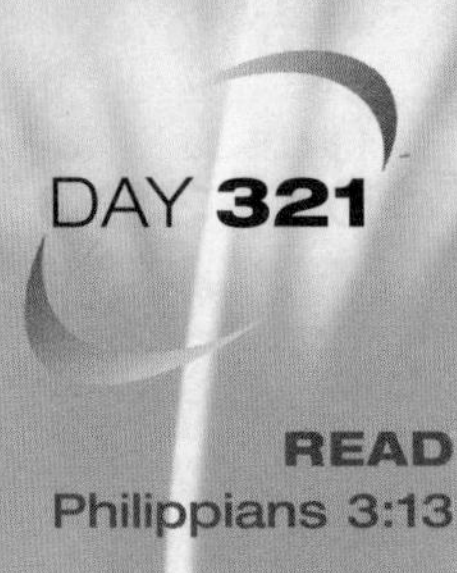

DAY **321**

READ
Philippians 3:13

We live life forwards and understand life backwards. In God's fast-moving narrative, we are swept up in a momentum not of our own.

Inevitably we must leave some things behind, even cherished landmarks.

Contrary to common practice, it is perhaps wise not to put too much of a psychological slant on Paul's "forgetting what lies behind".

It's certainly true that we must never allow needless regrets or memories or failures or limited education or handicaps of birth to stop us pressing forwards with Jesus. But when Paul uses the athletic imagery to refer to his apostolic ministry, the likely point at issue here is that he refuses to rest on past successes but concentrates on pressing on towards the goal. He wants to do this without distractions. So we need to keep the race metaphor simple. Whatever else you do, don't look back over your shoulder.

"Keep on keeping on" as the saying goes. As the great nineteenth-century scholar, J.B. Lightfoot, paraphrases: "Do not mistake me, I hold the language of hope not of assurance ... forgetting the landmarks already passed and straining every nerve and muscle in the onward race, I press forward toward the goal."

In this way we are invited to turn the landmarks into signposts to the future.

A DEVOTIONAL INTERLUDE

Prayer: Lord Jesus Christ, help me keep keeping on I pray. Don't let me look back over my shoulder to focus on the things of the past or to see who is coming up behind me. Help me to keep my eyes on You and to run the race with no distractions – past or present. You are my goal Lord Jesus and I want to grow more and more like You until that day when I shall see You and be transformed into Your Image. Amen

DAY 322

READ
Philippians
3:17–18

Although Paul uses strong language to warn of the twisted truth these "enemies of the cross" exemplify, he weeps for them at the same time. These are the only tears in the letter of joy, showing that Paul is torn apart by the thought of Christians living like pagans and "idolising their bellies" in the process! What they delight in, is what Paul considers they should be ashamed of.

As before in this letter, Paul targets the "mindset" behind such behaviour. Their failure is that "their minds are set on earthly things" (NRSV). "Earthly things" in this context are not the practical affairs of everyday life but things that characterise a worldly outlook which is in opposition to God. An "earthbound mindset" will involve both personal sins and those social sins which destroy unity and community in the Church. This is the tragic outcome of lowering our sights and forgetting the over-arching and transcendent narrative that defines who we are as Christians.

Paul has commended the mindset of Jesus as the only authentic criterion of a godly and truly human life. To live by any other story than the cross-shaped one is to court destruction. To abandon the cross is to forfeit the future inheritance. The narrow way of following Jesus leads to life. Anything else is a dead end.

To ponder: Not all are willing to admit that their minds need to be transformed. "What's wrong with my mind?" they say. "I am a perfectly normal person." But there is an enormous difference between what the world thinks of as normal and what the Bible teaches as normal. The Christian mind (or mindset) is a mind set on God and His purposes. Do you have a "mind" like this?

A DEVOTIONAL INTERLUDE

DAY **323**

READ
Philippians 3:20

In stark contrast to those whose horizon is limited by this world, Paul now affirms that a true Christian's "citizenship is in heaven". James Moffatt's famous version of this, "you are a colony of heaven", though strictly not an accurate translation, brilliantly catches the flavour of what Paul is saying.

This was apt language to employ in this letter because Philippi was a military colony of Rome. Nowhere outside Italy was there any city more thoroughly Roman. Its motto might well have been: "When in Philippi do as the Romans do"! But the Christians in Philippi know they owe allegiance to a different Emperor and another kingdom. Their rule of conduct is: "When in Philippi do as Christ did"!

New followers of Jesus become citizens of another kingdom, called to a wholly new politics of thinking and behaving. Sadly this has often been misconstrued, by us as much as by our critics, as if we exist in a time-warp, intent only on preserving old values and permanently behind the times. But a colony of heaven is not backward-looking, representing only "the forces of conservatism".

On the contrary we represent the future as citizens of the coming kingdom. Christians ought more often to be taken for revolutionaries than traditionalists!

A DEVOTIONAL INTERLUDE

Quotation: "A quaint old Yorkshire Christian, whenever anyone would ask him where his home was, would reply, 'My home is in heaven, but my residence is in the city of Leeds.' What do you see as 'home'? Heaven or the place of your residence here on earth? If some discerning soul called at your residence would they say to themselves: 'This is a colony of Jesus Christ'? If not why not?" (taken from a church newsletter).

DAY **324**

READ
Philippians 3:20

We remind ourselves that the genuinely Christian mindset is not one which is "set on earthly things".

Enemies of the cross cannot be friends of the resurrection!

But because our "citizenship is in heaven" our hopes and horizons, destiny and dreams are bound up with heaven and "we eagerly await a Saviour from there, the Lord Jesus Christ". The Caesars and other significant benefactors in the ancient world were, at this very time, expropriating the title "saviour" for their own self-glory. When they visited a provincial town, on their arrival (know as a "*parousia*"), they were accorded VIP treatment. But believers are awaiting the arrival of the MIP (Most Important Person)!

Our place in the bigger story reminds us that our salvation is predominantly a future event and experience. Our life in Christ however vibrant now is but a tiny foretaste of what is yet to come!

And this future hope is a decidedly earthly hope. Salvation is ultimately not about our going to heaven when we die; rather, heaven is coming here in the person of the Saviour bent on reclaiming and renewing His entire creation.

That's why we'll need – and will assuredly receive – brand new, resurrection bodies. But to say that is to take a sneak look at the last page of the exciting final chapter in the different story we are enacting.

A DEVOTIONAL INTERLUDE

Thought: Many Christians think that the final hope of the Christian is to be with Jesus in heaven. That of course is quite true, but there is to be a new earth we are told in Scripture, for God is going to renew the whole of His creation. However, as the writer says, "that's taking a sneak look at the last page of the story". See it just as a taster. The banquet will come later.

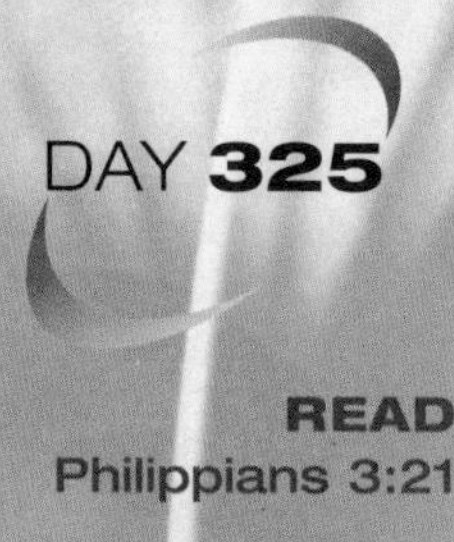

DAY **325**

READ
Philippians 3:21

At times in its history the Church has sadly downplayed the value of the material creation, and in particular, of our physical bodies. But we do not become more spiritual by denigrating the physical which God saw as good and our Saviour saw fit to assume at Bethlehem.

Paul is not contrasting our "lowly" body with something "higher" or "more spiritual". He is contrasting our present "body of humiliation" with our future "body of glory".

For sin, disease and ageing do humiliate us. Anyone who has stood by the hospital bed of a loved one whose body was shrivelled up by cancer, or watched a beloved parent's dignity reduced by Alzheimer's, knows this only too well.

Yet it was such physicality that the Son of God honoured in His Incarnation, and offered on the cross for our salvation.

By His bodily resurrection from the dead, He majestically affirmed the goodness of God's original creation even as He magnificently inaugurated the new creation.

This is our sure and certain hope for all who die "in Christ". Again the match with 2:5–11 assures us that the Father's glory which Jesus went through death to share, He will share with us in resurrection.

Our first creation body may be ravaged by age and disease and succumb to death, but our new creation body is guaranteed to be resplendent with glory. Praise the Lord!

A DEVOTIONAL INTERLUDE

Prayer: Thank You, dear Lord, for reminding me of the fact that this body of humiliation which now enwraps me is to be changed into a glorious body – one that will never age, never run out of energy, and never die. No more headaches, or aches and pains. The prospect of this make me feel like shouting: O day of joy and delight, delay not your dawning. Let the angels be sent forth to gather the elect. Even so come Lord Jesus.

DAY 326

READ
Philippians 4:19–23

The thought of God's lavish giving moves Paul to a characteristic burst of praise as if he were punching the air as winners do today.

Like all Paul's letters, Philippians ends, as it began, on the note of grace. It is God's grace which begins a good work in our lives and is pledged to complete it at the day of Christ.

God's providential grace can turn prisons into preaching centres, and enable His people to face death with extraordinary equanimity.

Above all, recall the amazing grace of our Lord Jesus Christ in not exploiting His advantages, in humbling Himself to be a servant and becoming obedient unto death.

And only grace could break a proud Pharisee and make a Christ-obsessed apostle.

Celebrate the grace that makes us citizens of heaven's kingdom and raises our sights to a coming Saviour. Hope for transforming grace by which He changes our despised, death-ridden earthly bodies into radiant, resurrection bodies modelled on His.

Grace begins and sustains the story; resilient grace that makes us ready for anything: gracious supply that means we lack for nothing!

Grace flows from start to finish. Grace in the end is "The grace of our Lord Jesus Christ be with you all. Yes!"

A DEVOTIONAL INTERLUDE

To ponder: How interesting that Paul in prison should end not with "grace to me", but "grace be with you". That shows how other-centred the great apostle was. He could say this because grace was not just a theory to him but a living fact. He was saved by grace, he lived by grace and he dispensed grace to everyone he met. As you go through the day may grace be with you from start to finish.

NOAH
all creation

ABRAHAM
all nations

ISRAEL
one nation

DAVID
representative king

NEW COVENANT
faithful covenant partner

JESUS
faithful covenant partner

JESUS
Davidic King Messiah

JESUS
the New Israel

JESUS
the world's Lord

JESUS
the truly Human One crowned with glory and honour

JESUS
COSMIC RULER IN GOD'S NEW CREATION NEW HEAVENS AND NEW EARTH

SECTION 11
JOHN'S FINAL VISION

God is committed to renewing the whole of His creation – John's final vision on Patmos

Our curiosity about the future is insatiable.

Eagerly, if somewhat sheepishly, we read our horoscopes, gaze into our crystal balls and try to sneak a look into what lies ahead. More pretentiously, big business hires expensive trend-analysts or futurologists in an attempt to predict the market. It's all a bit of a lottery; and we don't always get the weather forecast right!

This is where John shouts his good news to us of what he has glimpsed of the final state of affairs. Swept up by the prophetic inspiration of God's Spirit, he is taken to a high-mountain vantage-point and shown a stunning vision of the future (Rev. 21:10). They say "on a clear day, you can see for ever" and this is an exceptionally clear day!

As if from far below, we shout up to John on his lonely pinnacle of vision: "What can you see from there, John?"

John replies: "I can see a sparkling new world, a whole new creation."

"What does it look like?" we enquire.

"It looks like a city! But a city which is stretched out in all directions! It's like a new kind of Jerusalem teeming with people from every nation as if up for an international festival, enjoying the presence of God".

"What else can you see?"

"I can see that no one is crying, there are no cemeteries, no prisons; I can see no one in pain or suffering any disease; and I think I can see God's face! And yet everything is radiating such a glorious light that I am not sure what I see; when I stare at the face of God, more often than not, I see the human face of Jesus."

This is John's seventh and final vision; this is the ultimate vision. We might shout to him to be more specific but we'll shout ourselves hoarse.

Once again we are reminded that "people are not changed by moral exhortation but by transformed imagination". Nowhere is this insight more necessary than when approaching John's Revelation. Otherwise, crassly literal minds will be blinded to the truth.

Intriguing images, dazzling visions, majestic metaphors, stunning symbols – these are the currency of trade here. These images sharpen and fade, merge and separate before our very eyes as if on a giant computer screen. These visions dazzle us at the same time as they enlighten us. Yet what they portray is not less real but even more real for being given to us in this way; because it is these intensely poetic words that, we are assured, are trustworthy and true (21:5) and can be submitted to as conveying divine authority and disclosure.

John celebrates the ultimate victory of the Lamb and His martyrs, together with all His faithful followers who have not loved "their lives so much as to shrink from death" (12:11). He visualises the ultimate environment for redeemed people, a new heaven and new earth, and holds out the prospect of attaining the ultimate prize of looking on God's face.

DAY 327

READ
Revelation 21:1

When John peers into the future he sees in one dazzling vision an entirely new creation: "I saw a new heaven and a new earth" (21:1).

All of God's strategic covenant commitments and dramatic redemptive intrusions; the continuous energising of His creative Spirit and the never-ceasing flow of His Word – it has all been leading to this – both Hebrew prophets and Jewish Christian apostles agree.

Isaiah hears God say: "Behold, I will create new heavens and a new earth. The former things will not be remembered" (Isa. 65:17 cf. 66:22). Creation and redemption are held together (Isa. 40–55); it is the Creator who redeems and in redeeming creates again.

The Apostle Peter has seen in the cross and resurrection of Jesus the death and rebirth of the world.

Answering critics of God's slowness in keeping His promises, Peter re-affirms Isaiah's vision. Even though the cosmos is melted down to its constituent elements, in judgment and resolution, "in keeping with his promise we are looking forward to a new heaven and a new earth, the home of righteousness" (2 Pet. 3:11–13). Paul, too, sees this present world released into the freedom God's sons already enjoy (Rom. 8:18–22). God has not written off His good creation. The Christian's future environment is not heaven in an ethereal sense but a redeemed earth.

A DEVOTIONAL INTERLUDE

Prayer: Gracious and loving Lord, I see that this glorious new life You have given me here on earth is only a precursor to a glorious new world, a new heaven and a new earth. Help me never forget that in that new world You are going to create I have a part to play – a part that was predestined for me before the foundation of the world. My gratitude knows no bounds. Thank You my Father. Amen.

DAY **328**

READ
Revelation 21:1,4.

John sums up the whole biblical vision of what lies ahead as not some merely spiritual salvation but the ultimate reconciliation of spirit and matter, the reclaiming and restoring of God's own good creation.

John's "no mores" say it well. He reports that in the final new creation there will be "no more sea" (21:1). This could sound disappointing to sailors and lovers of oceans. But the "sea" in Scripture represents the forces of chaos brought under control at the first creation. John is shown a resplendent landscape from which the untamed restlessness of evil and disorder has been banished for ever.

It follows, as the greatest miracle of all, that there is "no more death" (21:4). And no more death means no mourning, no crying, no pain, no disease, no cot-deaths, no cancer, no Alzheimer's, no widows and orphans. The God who stooped once to wash the dust from tired feet, will wipe away every tear from every grief-stricken eye – the "old order passing away".

But this will not just be "paradise regained" as if all will be returned to how it was before – everything will be transformed and enhanced: better than before, with every potential fulfilled and every seed bearing fruit.

This is the Christian hope – a redeemed earth for which you and I will need, and receive, brand-new resurrection bodies.

A DEVOTIONAL INTERLUDE

Quotation: "A little girl who had been born blind, received through the miracle of modern-day surgery her sight. She clapped her hands with delight and said 'Mummy why didn't you tell me it was so beautiful?' 'I tried my darling,' said her mother, 'but I just didn't have the words.' That's John's predicament in Revelation 21: he tries to tell us of heaven's beauty but . . . [it] will be more wonderful than words can convey" (David Evans).

DAY 329

READ Revelation 21:2,9–10.

It is a fundamental feature of our Christian hope that, ultimately, we are not going to heaven: heaven is coming here!

This is reinforced by the second great image John sees in which the new creation is viewed as a city. Note again that this is flexible imagery. There are not two entities: a city within a creation; but the new creation is viewed as a city.

"I saw the Holy City, the new Jerusalem, coming down out of heaven from God" (21:2).

It comes to a mountain top (21:10). Here are echoes of the ancient myth of the mountain of the gods merged with Mount Zion in the vision of the Hebrew psalmist when he sang: "Great is the Lord, and most worthy of praise, in the city of our God, his holy mountain" (Psa. 48:1). According to Ezekiel, the Garden of Eden was set also on a mountain (Ezek. 28:12–16) so that what we have is a fusion of images, Jerusalem with Paradise restored!

The Jerusalem John sees is a city which "comes down out of heaven from God" (21:2,10).

Again it is emphasised, heaven is coming here – "from God" for this is a God-designed and God-made city.

It was to see this that Abraham left Ur, the epitome of Babylonian civilisation, turning his back on the city man was building, setting out on the great faith adventure, "looking forward to the city with foundations, whose architect and builder is God" (Heb. 11:10).

A DEVOTIONAL INTERLUDE

Thought: The heavenly city described in Revelation 21 is clearly a place without fault or flaw. Imagine living in a world where all is perfect. Here there is something wrong with everything; there nothing is wrong with anything. The grand reason for that of course is because God is its Architect. Whatever the Almighty builds is faultless. It is sin that spoils things and there no sin will ever be found.

DAY **330**

READ
Revelation 21:11

The new Jerusalem is a holy city – the dwelling place of the holy God (21:2,10). This is the significance of its remarkable shape – as wide and high as it is long (21:16). The symbolism of the shape derives from the Holy of Holies in the Temple which was a perfect cube (1 Kings 6:20). There, on one sacred spot on earth, God was manifest in concentrated form. But what was once compressed into one place, now pervades the whole. In other words, in this new world, everything is holy space, everywhere is filled to the same intensity with the holy presence of God. No wonder a temple is redundant there (21:22).

The city John sees is a glorious city – brilliant with the radiant glory of God Himself (21:11). This is in stark contrast to the city of Babylon, which represents all that humankind has built without God. Babylon was built for self-glorification. Its idolatry made it vulnerable to demonic infiltration so that it became the home or "the dwelling-place of demons" (18:2). But God's new Jerusalem is the dwelling-place of God and shines to His glory.

The Bible is a "tale of two cities" – Babylon and Jerusalem: salvation rests on coming out of the one culture and becoming a citizen in the other, so that your name is enrolled in the "Lamb's book of life" (21:27). A place in the new city is not to be missed.

Prayer: O God my Father, how can I tell out the feeling that surges within me when I realise that my name has been enrolled in the Lamb's book of life? There is a place in that new city just for me. And I have it not because of my merit but because of Your mercy. Blessed be Your Name forever. How I long that my unsaved friends and loved ones will be there also. Save them dear Lord. In Jesus' Name. Amen.

A DEVOTIONAL INTERLUDE

DAY **331**

READ
Revelation 22:
12–27

The New Jerusalem is an inclusive city, which welcomes true believers from before and after Christ's coming, Old and New Testament believers who trust God for the coming of the Christ. The city's gates are inscribed with the twelve tribes of Israel and its foundation stones with the names of the twelve apostles (21:12,14). John has heard the songs of Moses and the Lamb (15:3).

This is an international city, fulfilling and far exceeding what Abraham was promised – descendants as innumerable as the stars in the night sky, as the grains of sand on the seashore – in whom all the nations of the earth would be blessed.

John hears that there are 144,000 in this company (7:4) – in other words, that God's covenant family is complete, no one in who shouldn't be there, no one out who should be in. But when he looks, he sees a multitude which no one could number from every nation, tribe, people and language group!

And to this city the nations and their kings bring tribute. Again this, symbolically, contrasts with Babylon. A man-made culture is ultimately self-defeating. It consumes all in its quest for self-glory and self-gratification. But in the new Jerusalem, every human potential will be realised, all seeds will bear fruit, all history and culture will be redeemed and made good to the glory of the Creator.

A DEVOTIONAL INTERLUDE

To ponder: Today you will step out into a world that is consumed with self-glory and self-gratification. Doubtless at some point you will meet with frustration or difficulty that will cause you to realise that though the world is beautiful there are evidences that it has been spoilt by sin. The world you are heading for in the future however is different. No frustration, no difficulties, no sin. Keep hope alive!

DAY **332**

READ
Revelation
22:1–3

John is finally shown the new Jerusalem as a garden-city. Its flowering completes the movement from first creation to new creation. There is, in effect, a restoring of the Garden of Eden without going back to it (22:1–2).

Here is development and expansion from a mere garden to a garden-city – one with all the benefits of urban living and all the joys of country life. There may be no more sea, but the river of true life runs sparkling through the city-centre. To this city, by the Spirit, we have already come as worshippers (Heb. 12:22f.); towards this city, by faith, we continue to march as pilgrims.

"No longer will there will be any curse" says it all (22:3). God's judgmental curse, once pronounced over the whole earth because of Adam's disobedience, is now rescinded. A thornless world appears. Creation is finally released into the liberty and blessing already tasted by the redeemed children of the One Creator God (Rom. 8:19ff.).

This is the new environment prepared for this new covenant people. And it is this company, purified and redeemed, which is the bride of the Lamb; the people who are in every way the perfect complement to Jesus. For this reason the city is portrayed as a beautiful bridal city (21:2,9).

But how can a city be a bride? The answer to that, John sees, is in those who live there.

A DEVOTIONAL INTERLUDE

Thought: Though metaphors seem to clash with each other in John's description of the Holy City this again shows how language is inadequate to describe the glory that awaits us. A beautiful environment awaits a beautiful people. And the beauty of the people of God arises not from their own efforts but rather because they have been made beautiful through the grace and power of Jesus Christ.

DAY **333**

READ
Revelation 21:3–7

John is shown the inhabitants of the city, God's new covenant community: "Now the dwelling of God is with men, and he will live with them. They will be his people, and God himself . . . will be their God." God finally has the people He always set His heart on.

This is the God we should have known about throughout the biblical story – who loves people and longs to be with them and who had quiet walks and conversation with Adam and Eve in the garden in the cool of the afternoon. This is a God who camped and decamped all those years with Israel in the wilderness, marking His presence with a pillar of cloud by day and fire by night, who showed up in the sanctuary built for Him with the golden mist of His Shekinah glory and who gave Himself an earthly address in the Temple in Jerusalem.

And here is the great summary covenant statement: "I will be their God and they will be my people" which runs like a recurring thread through all His dealings in history (cf. Lev. 26:11–12). Here are those who have slaked their eternal thirst at his fountain (21:6).

Verse 7, "I will be his God and he will be my son" takes the amazing covenantal promise made to David that he and his descendants could enjoy a unique Father–son relationship with God, and extends it to all! So at last, God's people reign with Him on the earth (22:5).

A DEVOTIONAL INTERLUDE

Prayer: Father, the more I contemplate the glory that lies ahead the more wondrous it seems. I have read today that You are a God who loves people and longs to be with them. I am so glad that I am one of the people You long to be with. I long to be with You too, my Father. My thirst has been slaked at Your fountain and my heart rejoices to know that I will never thirst again. Thank You dear Lord. In Jesus' Name. Amen.

DAY **334**

READ
Revelation 21:5-6

The last word on human history is spoken by the voice of Him who sits on the throne: "I am making all things new" (21:5 NRSV). It seems as if the One Creator God is so brim-full of vitality that He cannot do anything else but create. His final word declares that "it is done" (21:6). This declaration introduces the splendid sight given next of the new Jerusalem (21:9–22:11), just as it had closed the account of the downfall of the unholy city, Babylon (16:17–21). When it comes to judgment or salvation, only God can say "it is done". The old creation is wrapped up, the old order of things is passing away; the new creation, the new city, are ready and waiting to be unveiled (21:6). The joy of tracing the biblical story is to realise that God is the beginning and end of it. Our God had the first and last word on the old creation and the first word on the new creation. We may live ambiguously and sometimes anxiously "between the times". How near the end we are we do not know for sure. Is there meaning to be found? Meaning is to be found in God who is not only the A and the Z but the whole alphabet in between; in the One who, standing in the middle of history, proclaimed its end – "It is finished" – and then breathed the Spirit of a new beginning into those who staked their future and eternal destiny on his cross and resurrection.

A DEVOTIONAL INTERLUDE

For praise: Some psychologists claim that what is wrong with the human soul is that it lacks a sense of identity and meaning. We don't know who we are (as we said earlier) because we don't know whose we are. Our meaning and identity as children of God lies in knowing whose we are – we belong to Jesus. We may not know everything the future holds but we know Jesus. And that is enough.

DAY 335

READ
Revelation 21:7–8

It is the "overcomers" who inherit all these things (21:7); who are they?

If the rest of the book of Revelation is anything to go by, they are very definitely not some spiritual equivalent of the Marine Corps, not the few super-powered macho Christians.

The overcomers are all who fight the fight of faith and win on a daily basis some minute victory; those who have put all their faith in the blood of the Lamb to save them, who faithfully confess the Lordship of this Jesus, and who do not love their lives so much they "shrink from death" (12:11)!

The followers of the Lamb through their own suffering and self-giving love share in the implementation of His victory over evil and death. They have glimpsed the coming glory and been captivated by John's vision. They live as heralds of the new day, harbingers of a new world, samples of the world's future.

For this you keep fighting the fight of faith, achieve minor victories of integrity and patience and prayer. And this is your inheritance. Soberly, John allows himself a terrible glance over his shoulder into the abyss (21:8) at the fate of those who have debarred themselves from being part of this!

But the angels who have supervised the judgmental destruction of Babylon and the old order of things want to show him something better. Who in their right minds would want to miss that?

A DEVOTIONAL INTERLUDE

Thought: Amongst the most penetrating and exciting words Jesus ever gave us were these: "In the world you will have tribulation; but be of good cheer, I have overcome the world" (John 16:33 NKJV). One preacher suggests that we are so one with Christ that when we see the Lord we might say: "Why Lord, did I overcome the world or did you?" We will hear Him answer gently: "Why we both did, for my victory is Your victory."

DAY **336**

READ
Revelation
22:1–16

What stirs John most of all is the prospect held out to us all of a new vision of God Himself: "They will see his face ..." (22:4). This surely is the ultimate prize, the final vision. Yet if one thing is clear throughout John's Patmos experience it is that whenever he looks to see the One Creator God, it is the Lamb who comes into focus!

The Lamb receives the bride, the Lamb lays the foundations of the city, the Lamb is the temple and the light in it, the Lamb shares the throne of God. The slain Lamb who now stands to rule keeps coming into view.

To see the very face of God surely would be heaven on earth: the "beatific vision" as the medieval mystics called it. But John gives the distinct impression throughout his "revelation" that whenever he peered closer to look into the face of God, what came into focus was the human face of Jesus – so much do they have in common. So Jesus shares with the One God the fullness of deity as Alpha and Omega, the Beginning and the End (22:13 cf.1:8). As the final fruit from David's root, the king of kings, Jesus is the Morning Star of the eternal day of God's kingdom, one empire, at least, on which the sun never sets.

With his own visionary experience dazzling his eyes and the sublime heavenly voice ringing in his ears, John falls down to worship (22:8).

A DEVOTIONAL INTERLUDE

For worship: I wonder do you know the words of this old but famous hymn. You might sing it (or say it) as your response to today's reading:

Face to face with Christ my Saviour. Face to face what will it be,
When with rapture I behold Him, Jesus Christ who died for me
Face to face will I behold Him, Far beyond the starry skies
Face to face in all His glory, I shall see Him by and by.

DAY 337

READ
Revelation 22:17–21

John's closing exhortations are a fitting lesson in how to respond to God's big story.

John's instinctive response of worship is surely right, even if he over-estimated the value of his angelic vision-bearer (22:8)!

He urges the Church not to lose its distinctive edge (22:14–15) or to lose hope that the story ends well, fixing our hopes and eyes not on dates or world events but on Jesus and His coming (22:7,12,17,20).

He warns against adding to or subtracting from the revelation he has passed on to us – the vision he has shared with us is too true to tamper with and too good to miss.

For this Noah overcame fear and stepped into the ark and with even more faith stepped out of it again.

For this Abraham launched into the great unknown trusting the Word of God.

For this Israel was chosen, loved, delivered and covenanted with.

For this David left his father's flock, and was anointed king.

For this the prophets were persecuted as they pictured God's future in stunning pictures and powerful words.

For this the Lamb came and lived among us. For this He chose 12 apostles, entered Jerusalem and laid down His life to displace the Temple. For this He died and rose again with a new world in His nail-pierced hands. For this He shares God's throne and intercedes, and for this He is coming again.

A DEVOTIONAL INTERLUDE

To ponder: "Everyone", it has been said, "needs a guiding vision, something to aim at, something to live for". What guides you? Is it climbing to the top of your career, ensuring you have enough in your old age? There's nothing wrong with those things of course but a Christian has something to aim for beyond those aspirations – seeing Jesus. Is that your "guiding vision"?

12

SECTION 12
RESPONDING TO GOD'S BIG STORY

Responding to God's big story

This is the challenge and invitation then: to discover your place in God's strategic plan and redemptive story.

What is your place in Noah's story?
As part of the new creation "in Christ", you are called to keep your feet firmly on this old ground, respecting the earth but travelling through it as a pilgrim, walking keenly towards the future new heavens and new earth "all landscaped with righteousness" (*The Message*).

Where are you in Abraham's adventure?
Following in the footsteps of faith, you are challenged to live counter-culturally, not wedded to the society man is building, but to the city God is building, living daringly by faith not sight, confident in trusting Jesus "the seed of Abraham" and serving Hs mission to bring blessing to an accursed world.

Where are you in Israel's vocation?
By grace, grafted onto the stock of the Old Testament people of God, revering your Jewish roots but living free from the burden of Torah, you are enabled to keep covenant with God through the death of Christ and the indwelling power of the Holy Spirit as members of a "chosen race, and royal priesthood", called to praise before the world the God who has brought you out of darkness into His marvellous light.

Where are you in David's destiny?
By redemptive transfer from the kingdom of darkness, you now find yourself in Messiah's kingdom and community, confessing Jesus as Lord of the world, learning with others how to be "kings and priests" unto God for the sake of the world.

Where are you in the prophetic hope?
Enjoying the blessing of the new covenant in Christ's blood, you relish being forgiven, your heart responsive to God, His will your growing delight, His Spirit within you as God's empowering presence, among the new people who serve one another as the true temple of the Living God.

Where are you, above all, in the Jesus story?

This for all of us is the crucial question.

Have I repented and embraced Him as the Master-story of my life?

Will I be His disciple? Am I a follower of Jesus Christ?

In order to become one, we must first "repossess" our own stories repentantly, by acknowledging our past as our responsibility. We have to learn to say, "I did that". Then we must bow the knee to Jesus, and "immerse ourselves in His story", dying with Him and rising with Him to a new life. This is what faith and baptism involve. As for the future, we stay honest by continuing to "own" our own stories. We own the successes and failures, the trophies and the scars, the glorious pages and the sad or bad chapters. All the while, it is helpful to realise that "my" story is now "our" story. I didn't begin the story and, in all likelihood, will not be asked to finish it, but only to take my part in it faithfully, joyfully, wholeheartedly and with others.

When the day comes, then – as it surely will – when the red book is handed to you which says, "This is your life", what will it add up to?

What story, or better whose story, will it tell?

In the words of St Columba: "Since all the world is but a story, it were well for thee to buy the more enduring story, rather than the story that is less enduring."

Fame is a fleeting phenomenon in our celebrity-conscious media-driven, modern world. The writer to the Hebrews celebrates the heroes of faith. But none of them achieved fame merely by being celebrities. They are famous for being faithful.

Noah and Abraham and Moses, David, the prophets and all the unsung heroes of the faith, were often insignificant players on the world stage. They were made famous by God's story. And so are we all. Yet, "Not one of these people, even though their lives of faith were exemplary, got their hands on what was promised. God had a better plan for us: that their faith and our faith would come together to make one completed whole, their lives of faith not complete apart from ours" (Heb. 11:39–40 *The Message*).

DAY 338

READ
Acts 13:13–25

For over 200 years in the modern Western world we have been sold a story other than God's story, with a script written by philosophers, scientists and evolutionary thinkers, and in which the leading role is played by human reason. Nothing can be treated as true that cannot be proved by reason.

Now, in our so-called "post-modern" world, these confident overarching narratives have broken down so that many people now assume that there is no story, no overall plot-line, that makes sense of anything. "Life is a string of pearls whose thread is broken." We are cast back on our own self-made stories.

Is there a bigger, better story that will show us who we are? Paul says "yes, there is" and he proceeds to tell it at Antioch: This story is told in the Bible: it is God's story and it is God who is the chief actor in it.

Notice how Paul emphasises God's actions and initiatives. God chose our fathers; He made the people prosper in Egypt. He led them out; He endured for forty years; He overthrew seven nations; He conquered Canaan; He gave Israel judges; He installed and removed Saul; He raised up King David – "a man after my own heart"; He brought to Israel, from this man's descendants, a Saviour ... (vv.16–23).

A DEVOTIONAL INTERLUDE

Thought: At no other time in history has the need for "story" been more necessary. As you observed in today's reading "people now assume there is no story, no overall plot-line that makes sense of anything". How refreshing it is to realise that against the background of pessimism and gloom a cosmic story is being worked out – one in which God plays the lead part. What a thought to begin a day!

READ
Acts 13:26-31

Paul reminds us that the story of Jesus (13:26–37), though not the end of the ongoing story, is the climax of the earlier stage of the story of God's covenant relationship with His people Israel (v.23).

Like Matthew, Paul employs the idea of "fulfilment" to say this (vv.27,29,33). "To fulfil", we recall, is "to bring something to its intended goal" – in other words, to complete, or to fill full with meaning. The gospel Paul proclaims is the fulfilment of God's plan in a Person who fulfils the promise of God.

It is the fulfilment of a plan (vv.26–27) which the first-born "sons of Abraham" should have known about since it began with him. God's ground plan is, as we have seen, to bring blessing to the whole world through one family, one nation and its King.

The deep irony is that the religious leaders in Jerusalem unwittingly fulfilled this previously stated plan of God by rejecting Jesus. Mysteriously, we see hinted at again, that even the failure of Israel seems to have been accommodated in God's plan from the beginning. This plan was fulfilled in a Person for all that was written was "written about him" (v.29).

This whole saving narrative pivots on the dramatic events of Jesus' death and resurrection from the dead – viewed by Paul as a mighty creative act of God (v.30).

A DEVOTIONAL INTERLUDE

Prayer: Gracious and loving Father, I see again even more clearly that the pivotal point of Your story is the death and resurrection of Your Son. Help me not to take this for granted, but with gratitude. Had Jesus not come to this world, died for my sins and risen again I would still be in my sins – condemned to a lost eternity. I am grateful to the very core of my being. Thank You my Father. In Jesus' Name. Amen

DAY **340**

READ
Acts 13:32–37

The Easter events, Paul proclaims, were the fulfilment of a promise (v.32). Paul sums up the gospel as the "good news of the promise" which God originally made to the fathers, Abraham, Isaac and Jacob, and especially confirmed to David.

He recalls God's promise to David – recorded in 2 Samuel 7:14 – of a throne, a dynasty, a kingdom which will last for ever and, above all, of a special Father–son relationship with God. This was further spelt out in the coronation psalm (Psa. 2), confessional song (Psa. 16) and prophetic testimony (Isa. 55).

But it was not King David himself who fulfilled God's dreams; he's dead and buried. It was Jesus, the Anointed One, who is no longer dead and buried: He did die but is very much alive and ruling.

Paul now presses home his case, issuing a challenge and an invitation. It is, he urges, through this Person that you can be written into the story of salvation. The challenge of God's story is that it offers everyone of us a bigger, better, story to be part of, to be drawn into what He has been doing, is doing and will do in human history and on this earth!

Why stay in amateur dramatics in the school hall when we are summoned to appear on Broadway or in the West End?

A DEVOTIONAL INTERLUDE

For praise: It might sound repetitive to keep reminding ourselves that we have been invited to be a part of God's big story and to be drawn into what He is doing, but is there in earth or heaven anything bigger and better than this? This is a promise – the more you dwell on this thought the more it will grip you. And the more it grips you the more you will want to praise the Lord. So once again – think and give thanks.

DAY **341**

READ
Acts 13:38–39

The gospel declares that we can be freed from our own self-made stories whatever their failure. On the basis of Christ's death on the cross, God offers us forgiveness for our sins. He invites us to trade in the old, dog-eared, much corrected script of our own life for a brand new one He'll help us write. God is seemingly more interested in setting people free than in controlling them!

Yet, the invitation, however personal, is not to embark on a solo career but to join the rest of the cast as they seek to live out this story together (vv.39–48). Come and join the cast of thousands who are repentantly, enthusiastically, sometimes blunderingly, but always hopefully, learning their parts in this greatest story ever told.

Paul is here test-driving his characteristic term which derives from the Old Testament concept of righteousness. There God is "righteous" because He is faithful to the covenant, and people are "righteous" who live faithfully within the covenant. When God "justifies" then, He "re-righteous them" by restoring them to covenant membership.

In this gospel "everyone who believes", is justified by faith and joins the community of faith (v.39) and so makes the story their own.

A DEVOTIONAL INTERLUDE

To ponder: Have things gone wrong in your life? Does it seem like the story of your past is a battered script, unworthy to be read. Then consider this – now you are a Christian you have a new role and a new part to play in a story that will go on playing throughout all eternity. So shoulders back, lift up your head, you are a player in the greatest production the world has and can ever know. "Rejoice. And again I say rejoice!"

DAY **342**

READ
Acts 13:40–52

God is faithful and utterly to be depended on but He is not predictable. He can do startlingly new things which even His people, used to His normal ways of working, may find disconcerting or even unacceptable. The dramatic story of Jesus explodes in the middle of history to shatter preconceived ideas about God. As the prophet warned, God's people who should know better, can find themselves on the same cynical side as sneering unbelievers (13:41; cf. 17:32).

Some opponents will make life difficult for those who respond to the story, and verbal abuse may intensify into open hostility (vv.45,50). But others are enthralled by the story, and can't wait to hear more (13:42).

As for the newly recruited "actors", they can't disguise their joy in the undeserved "grace" of God (13:43c).

The servant's mission to bring light to the Gentiles (13:47 cf. Isa. 49:6; Luke 2:32) strengthens the apostles' resolve to take the gospel to the pagan world, where they find a ready response. New believers buzz with the vitality of life with an eternal quality (v.48), and share exuberantly in the divine energy that has been let loose in the world as they are "filled with joy and with the Holy Spirit" (v.52).

These disciples relish the fact that the story is an on-going story and that the cast list grows by the day (v.48)!

A DEVOTIONAL INTERLUDE

Thought: One of the issues which trouble some Christians is the unpredictability of God. They want a God who is "safe", one who acts and behaves in ways that can be anticipated. Lindsey Glegg, a famous Christian who rose to prominence in the early twentieth century used to say: "God is a God of surprises. Just when you think you have figured Him out you will find you haven't." Perhaps He has a surprise waiting for you today.

DAY **343**

READ
Hebrews 1:1

Nowhere in the New Testament is there a better summary of the relationship between Old and New Testaments than here.

In the earlier stage of the story, God spoke in fragmentary and varied ways. Now in these "last days" He has spoken His final Word in Jesus. Once more we see that Jesus is the summation of all that God has previously said about Himself and His people in the Old Testament Scriptures.

Note, too, that while no one can be sure whether we are approaching history's final day or hour, the New Testament is clear that we have been in the "last days" ever since Jesus came.

We see elements of both continuity and discontinuity here. There is continuity because it is the same God who speaks then and now. And those who respond to His Word form one continuous story of faith, as chapter 11 especially highlights. Throughout his letter, the writer assumes that what was said then to God's people in the earlier part of the story continues to apply to us now.

But there is a sharp discontinuity too, in the unfolding story of God's self-revelation. What was partial ("fragmentary"), is now full. What was provisional ("in the past"), is now final ("in these last days"). Above all, what was spoken through God's servants ("through the prophets"), has now been uttered in His Son.

A DEVOTIONAL INTERLUDE

Quotation: People unread in comparative religions like to say, "One religion is as good as another". It sounds broad-minded. Actually it is a judgment of ignorance. "Christianity is in a category by itself. We claim for the religion of Jesus Christ that it is unique, unsurpassed and unparalleled, the word not of a prophet but the Son Himself. Jesus is God's last word to his people." (W.E. Sangster)

DAY 344

READ
Hebrews 1:2–3

The inheritance rights of "sonship", once partially and provisionally attached to Israel and her kings (cf. Exod. 4:22–23; 2 Sam. 7:14), now pass to their intended recipient, the eternal Son, Jesus. The eternal Son who radiates God's glory became the embodied Son who exactly represents God's being and thereafter exists as the exalted Son who sits enthroned as God's right-hand man.

This rich language is mined from various parts of the Old Testament and Jewish writings, where it is applied to the eternal wisdom of God by which He made and sustains His creation.

The third Old Testament category which the writer uses here, and fully develops throughout the letter, is that of priesthood. The writer skilfully blends Old Testament prophecies and psalms to make the link between "Son" and "King" and "priest" (2 Sam. 7; Psa. 2; Psa. 110 cf. 1:5,13).

We may well marvel that there is a God who has broken the seemingly eternal silence and spoken to us His life-giving Word. And Jesus, the Son of God is God's central message. In reviewing creation's origins and ultimate destiny – Jesus is the wise agent and trusted heir.

And in the cleansing that is indispensable if a sin-spoiled world is to be restored to its full potential – Jesus is the one effective sacrifice and ever-efficient priest of God's salvation.

A DEVOTIONAL INTERLUDE

Prayer: Lord Jesus Christ, how perfectly You fulfil all the Old Testament prophecies and roles of Son, King, Priest and Sacrificial Lamb. What a destiny I have and what a story to tell – all the roles You fitted into were in order to save me, sanctify me and make me fit for heaven. And if I were the only one to receive salvation You would have done it just for me. Thank You dear Saviour. Amen.

DAY **345**

READ
Hebrews 1:5–19

Here several Old Testament threads are woven into a chorus of praise in honour of Jesus. Varied voices from the earlier stage of the story are heard singing from the same songsheet the glory of God's plan now unveiled as the glorious Person, Jesus.

Notice once again, how crucial in the outworking of God's saving plan was His covenant commitment to David (2 Sam. 7; Psa. 2). Again we see that scriptures are drawn together because the writers discern the underlying connections between them that form a coherent pattern and promise. This particular interweaving of quotations has been described as a "coronation liturgy" in which God declares that the King is His Son (1:5). It heralds His acclamation, as the King is presented to His people (1:6–12) and His anointing and enthronement (1:9,13).

Notice too how the quotations match the statements of verses 1–3: verses 5–9 mirror verse 2; verse 10 mirrors verse 2; verses 11–12 mirror verse 3a; and verse 13 mirrors verse 3c.

Amid first-century fascination with angels, the writer places Jesus far above the angels, with a greater name (v.5 "Son"), a loftier dignity (v.6 "worthy of worship"), a higher status (vv.7–12 as the unchanging One), and a superior function (vv.13–14, He reigns at God's right hand, while they serve).

A DEVOTIONAL INTERLUDE

For action: Of all the descriptions given to Jesus none is greater than the fact He is King. How are we to proclaim His Kingship? The words of an old hymn provide an answer:

Rise up O men of God, have done with lesser things
Give heart and soul and mind and strength
To serve the King of Kings!

JESUS

ISRAEL / MOSES

DAVID

NEW COVENANT

DAY 346

READ
Hebrews 2:5–9

That God brings his "firstborn into the world" (1:6) is not a reference to the incarnation but to the ascension. Just as God brought His first-born people, Israel, into the promised land, so He has brought His eternal "Son" made flesh through death up into the realm of eternal salvation. He has entered ahead of us the "world to come" (2:5).

The one Son's humiliation is set to achieve glory for God's many "sons". Psalm 8 is itself a lyrical expansion of Genesis 1:26–28. The writer now expounds it to show that the eternal Son of God assumed the human condition, with its vulnerability to death, in order to bring humanity through to its intended glory. Once more, the original and overarching plan of God is revealed as made good in and through Jesus. The eternal Son was willing in His incarnation to be made temporarily "lower than the angels" and so was crowned with the honour due to a victorious humanity to whom all things in creation are subject. In a rebellious and sin-torn world, we do not yet, of course, see the final outcome of God's plan to subject the world to a redeemed human race. But we do see Jesus, the truly Human One, who has gone ahead of us and who guarantees our ultimate inclusion in the triumph of God's design. Jesus shares our humanity, dies our death, bears our sins, and now wears our crown!

A DEVOTIONAL INTERLUDE

Thought: Have you ever thought about the vulnerability of Jesus and what that meant for Him? Then think about it for a few moments now. Vulnerability means "open to emotional or physical attack". The Saviour voluntarily put Himself in a position where He could be attacked by both human and devilish forces and be subject to pain and death. And He did it all for you.

DAY **347**

READ
Hebrews 2:10

God's purpose is to redeem His original creation. He aims to "bring many sons" in a new exodus, not just to the promised land but to the glory of shared dominion with Him. That God is achieving this through the incarnation and suffering of Jesus, in identification with sinful humanity, is thus described as strangely "fitting" to God (2:10)

Doing it this way, fits God's nature as the source and agent of all things in creation and salvation. Only such a God could have initiated such a staggering plan and carried it through. So the whole execution of the plan is consistent with His character as a God of "grace" (2:9).

Its outcome, too, is entirely appropriate to Him, in being not some panic-driven emergency which He might be embarrassed to acknowledge as His own but, in fact, the very pre-determined way in which He intended to maximise His glory.

And if it was "fitting" to God, then it was "necessary" for Jesus to suffer in our humanness for us, if He were to be the "author of our salvation". This vivid word "author" can be variously translated "leader" or "pioneer" which suits the pilgrimage theme so favoured by the writer (3:7–4:11). Even better, perhaps, it means "champion" so that it highlights the heroic struggle Jesus fought in order to bring our human story through to God's intended conclusion.

A DEVOTIONAL INTERLUDE

Quotation: "A pioneer is someone who goes ahead of others, opens up new territory, makes a path along which others can follow. This is precisely what Jesus has done for us; he went through the darkest regions of death which was a most trackless area, and fought with adversaries which we will never have to fight. He is the Champion of champions; the Pioneer of all pioneers. Blessed be His wonderful name." (David Thomas)

DAY **348**

READ
Hebrews 2:11–13

When the story of Jesus was grafted onto our sinful, rebellious story, suffering was a inevitable outcome for Him. His sufferings were the means by which He was "made perfect", not in a moral but in a functional sense. In other words, His willingness to endure sufferings fully equipped Him for the task of being our champion and priestly Saviour. To be so closely identified with us qualified Him to be our Priest.

The One who consecrates is, in the Old Testament, God (Exod. 31:13; Lev. 20:8), but here it is a role assigned to Jesus (cf. Heb. 13:12). He makes His perfection ours. Consecration has a necessary corollary in cleansing from sin and defilement for those set apart for God must first be purified from sin.

So even though Jesus shares deep solidarity with us, He remains distinct from us as the "one who consecrates" (cf. Heb. 4:15; 7:26–28).

Yet, we are said to share a common origin with Him. This may be read as from "one stock" or one "family" or one "ancestor" like Adam or Abraham. It may mean simply that we both derive from the One God!

Christ and His covenant people share the same family, the same Father, which is why He is not ashamed to call them brothers!

A DEVOTIONAL INTERLUDE

To ponder: Wouldn't you think that Jesus, being who He is, perfect, unsullied by sin and the delight of His Father's heart, would be more tentative in relating to us as "brothers"? Not so, however. We are told that He is not ashamed to call us "brothers". Not ashamed? What amazing grace! What astonishing acceptance! Nothing in heaven or earth can equal this.

DAY **349**

READ
Hebrews 2:12–13

With Jesus, God's final Word, the prophetic hopes are an "idea whose time has come". This convergence of the Jesus story and the human story can be told through three Old Testament references.

The prophetic assertion; "I will declare your name to my brothers" (Psa. 22:22) is put in the mouth of the singing Jesus who leads us in praising God. In this way, we find our voice in His voice. We praise in and through His praise. We join in worship that Jesus is already leading.

The prophetic vow: "I will put my trust in him" (Isa. 8:17) becomes His pledge of total reliance on God, so that He leads us in confident trust in God. We put our faith in His faithfulness, we trust in His trust. We believe in God through Him.

The prophetic willingness in dark days to stand up and be counted as God's servant: "Here am I, and the children the Lord has given me" (Isa. 8:18) becomes His rallying call to us, His spiritual "offspring", to bravely make ourselves available with Him for what ever God wants us to be and do.

He lived these words. He sang this psalm on the cross from its opening minor key of God-forsakenness to its major key of praise. On the cross, He entrusted His spirit to His Father's tender hands and said to Mary, "Here is your son" and to John, "Here is your mother".

In this way He qualified to be the head of the whole family of faith.

A DEVOTIONAL INTERLUDE

For praise: As you open your heart in praise and worship to God right now keep in mind that Jesus is the leader of all the praise and worship that ascends to the Father. "We praise in and through His praise." Whatever words you use as you praise Him are merged into the stream of praise that Christ co-ordinates. Multitudes all over the world are praising God through Jesus at this moment. Let's join them.

DAY **350**

READ
Hebrews
2:14–18

Although Jesus is the chief actor in God's story and ours, His humanity is no actor's mask! He is not a god dressed up as a man. He bleeds real blood and tears real flesh. He feels and suffers as truly one of us even to the point of death.

By doing this, He aims to destroy, or nullify, the power of the devil. This is not the power to kill us indiscriminately but the devil's cunning in making death his ally against sinful men and women, both to consign them to final judgment and damnation and to hold them in perpetual fear.

But we have a champion whose death was not a sentence of death on His own rebellion but the consecration of an obedient life to God's will to save sinners (cf. 10:5–7).

The "second Adam to the fight and rescue came" as our "David", defeating our ultimate "Goliath".

The nature which He assumed in order to achieve this was not angelic but human, and especially Jewish. He stood in line as Abraham's "seed" to fulfil the faith story Abraham began. Being made like His human brothers in every respect save sin was essential to Him – that He might qualify to be a High Priest – and was vital to us – in order to bear God's wrath upon our sin and so propitiate it.

He is "merciful" enough to come to the aid of the tempted because He resisted temptation, remaining "faithful" to God despite suffering.

Prayer: How thankful I am, dear Father, that when I come to You through Jesus I am coming to One who knows my every feeling, One who has worn my flesh, measured its frailty and can sympathise with my every emotion. And He did all this without sin. He knows my condition because He has been in my condition. My gratitude will just not go into words. Blessed Trinity. Thank You. Amen.

A DEVOTIONAL INTERLUDE

DAY 351

READ
Hebrews 3:1–6

The writer tells his readers: "You have a champion, Jesus. He is the faithful son over God's house". Jesus is contrasted with Moses.

As God's "apostle", sent with God's final message (cf. 1:1; 2:1–4), and as "high priest" (cf.1:4; 2:17), He eclipses Moses who was called the "sent one" (Exod. 3:10) and was associated with priestly functions (Psa. 99:6). Yet again we see how Jesus gathers up, expands and enriches all that went before in the Old Testament.

Hebrews is a sustained exposition of the superiority of Jesus over all previous revelation and institutions. In the writer's eyes, Jesus is "better" than the prophets, "better" than angels, "better" than Moses, Joshua and Aaron. He establishes a "better" priesthood, based on a "better" sacrifice which inaugurates a "better" covenant and introduces a "better" hope of a "better" resurrection!

He is superior to Moses – the faithful founder of the nation – and has greater glory because He is not merely a servant "in" the house but the Son "over" God's house – in same way that the builder of the house has greater honour than the house itself.

In the flow of God's story, everything is owed to the faithfulness of Christ. Our challenge is to play our part in the story as members of God's house by staying faithful.

A DEVOTIONAL INTERLUDE

Thought: A man looked at some pictures in a famous gallery and said to the attendant; "I don't think much of these pictures." The attendant replied, "Excuse me, sir, but the pictures are not on trial." It was the people who viewed them who were. It is the same with Jesus, when we look at Him He is not on trial – we are. We judge ourselves by our judgement of Him. He is the best character in God's story, the One who brings it to life.

DAY **352**

READ
Hebrews 3:7–19

The writer to the Hebrews has a dynamic view of Scripture. Unlike Paul, he never introduces an Old Testament quotation with "It is written" but prefers "It says" or " He is speaking".

Like Paul, he believes there is one continuous story unfolded in Scripture, so that what the Holy Spirit said then is said now. This enables him to recall the crisis of faith which Israel had in the wilderness, in order to challenge his readers to reaffirm their own commitment to Jesus.

The original story told in the book of Numbers (chs. 12–14) shows both the unfaithfulness of Israel and the faithfulness of God. The story is recorded as a prophetic warning in Psalm 95 which was in regular use as an introit to the liturgy in the synagogue liturgy. Those who rebelled were privileged to be have been led out of Egypt and had seen God's works but had not embraced His ways. God was angry with that whole generation and they never made it to the "rest" of the promised land.

Don't share their unbelief, says the writer, or doubt, as they did, that God is with you. Encourage one another as long as "today" lasts. And don't throw away your confidence.

Between past redemption and future rest there is much ground to cover. The story is not over yet. Heed "today's" voice and keep moving on in faith.

A DEVOTIONAL INTERLUDE

For action: Consider this: Scripture bids us encourage one another not every year, every month or every week, but every day. Many of your fellow Christians are dying on the vine simply because of a lack of encouragement. People don't despair because so many bad things happen to them; they despair because so few good things happen to them. Go out of your way to encourage someone this very hour.

DAY 353

READ
Hebrews 4:1–14

The story of the people of God is bracketed by an original promised "rest" and an ultimate future "rest".

Entering the "rest" of God has both a literal and metaphorical reference. There is rest that is already assured which is the creation-rest God enjoys since completing His first creation work (Heb. 4:3–5; Gen. 2:2) and which is the goal of all His creation.

There was a "rest" which Israel achieved through conquering and entering into the "rest" of the land of Canaan (Heb. 3:18–19 but cf. Heb. 4:8; Josh. 1:13; 21:44). But, in a figurative way, this Canaan-rest anticipates the "rest" of consummation (4:9–11) when as believers we will have completed our work and will enjoy the festivity of final salvation in the heavenly realm.

There remains a "rest" available now to those who put their total confidence and trust in the completed work of God in Christ. The Holy Spirit contemporises this, offering us a satisfying foretaste of that future "rest" if "today" we will hear His voice and obey.

If heaven overflows with joy at one sinner who repents, how much more over a whole world restored? That will be a party to beat all parties and God will be the life and soul of it! To be outside of this would be hell; to be inside it will be the very heaven of heavens.

A DEVOTIONAL INTERLUDE

To ponder: Many Christians are puzzled by the concept of "God's rest" which is referred to several times in Scripture. To be "in Christ" is to be in rest. No more struggling to come up to standard, no more striving to be good. The Spirit within us empowers us for that purpose. Our souls find a place of rest through faith "today" that is merely a foretaste of things to come. A taster now, the full banquet later.

DAY **354**

READ
Hebrews
9:23–10:10

Hebrews can intimidate us with all its talk of priests, sanctuaries and sacrificial ritual, so much of which seems remote to us. We may ask – what does all this religious language have to do with reality? Hebrews answers: in one sense, nothing at all.

That's just the point – Christ is the only Priest, altar and sacrifice we need for a lasting relationship with God. But apart from Israel's story and God-given worship we would lack this rich vision of who Jesus is and what He has achieved.

The writer sums up his vision by noting the impact of the three "appearings" of Jesus (9:23–28).

Jesus has "appeared once . . . to do away with sin" – this is an unrepeatable historically based fact (9:25–26). Jesus now "appears" after His ascension in the heavenly sanctuary to represent us in God's very presence (9:24).

He will "appear a second time, not to bear sin, but to bring salvation to those who are waiting for him" (9:28).

What gives His ministry saving power – past, present and future – is that it is not the unwilling sacrifice of a dumb animal but a man's willing and conscious self-sacrifice in service to God's will (10:5–10). This carries God's story forward into a wholly new phase of fulfilment and establishes us on a wholly new covenant basis with God (10:8–10).

A DEVOTIONAL INTERLUDE

Prayer: O Father, how wonderful it is to be living in a day and age when an animal sacrifice is no longer needed. The best those sacrifices could do was to cover sin, but the sacrifice of Jesus my Saviour not only covers it, but cleanses it and makes my conscience clean. I am so grateful for this, my Father. Accept my praise and worship – worship that comes from a heart made clean. Amen.

DAY **355**

READ
Hebrews
10:32–34

Where do we fit in "God's honours list", "God's roll-call of fame"?

Note that the writer starts not with the Old Testament heroes but with his readers' own vigorous faith (10:32). In other words, you are in the same story, the same arena as them (12:1). Their witness is not meant to intimidate you but to inspire you.

In uncertain times we need encouragement to keep our nerve. The writer addresses such a time and need.

For Jewish Christians far away from the impending disaster about to strike Jerusalem, these were deeply disturbing days. Their old securities were literally being swept away as much of their Jewish heritage was threatened with extinction by the pagan Romans. Nearer to home was even more uncertainty. Living in the capital of the Roman Empire, they were also threatened with persecution for their new-found faith.

With every foundation, outside of Christ, being shaken, this great pastoral writer offers them his word of exhortation and encouragement (13:20–22). He does it by reminding them and us of what gives significance to our lives. And what gives deep and lasting significance to our lives is to be an active participant in the on-going story of faith.

A DEVOTIONAL INTERLUDE

Quotation: "Hebrews 11 has been described by someone as 'The Westminster Abbey of the Bible' as it honours the names of some of the illustrious men and women of Scripture. And remember, they were there not simply because of their exploits, but because they acted in faith. Nothing delights God more than trust and confidence in Him. Nothing. Remember that the next time you worry that you are an 'unknown'." (Wendell Smith)

READ Hebrews 10:35–11:1

Hebrews 11 is, in fact, a special re-reading of the story of Israel and her ancestors. The writer could have listed the long catalogue of unbelief – as in chapter 4 – but here he lights on the gripping examples of radical obedience and passionate trust that are also true of the same story.

The closest parallel to Hebrews 11 is the list of heroes in the Jewish Book of Sirach (Ecclesiasticus).

Sirach, written about 180 BC, celebrates Israel's famous – from Enoch, and Noah, right down to the kings.

Interestingly the story climaxes with a glowing portrait of a contemporary of the writer – Simeon II, son of Jonathan – who held office as high priest from 219–196 BC, emerging from the splendid and ordered worship of the Temple (Ecc. 50:5–7, 12–21).

Hebrews, however, re-writes the story to show that its true climax is Jesus, the splendid and glorious and ultimate High Priest who, having made the final effective sacrifice, officiates in the heavenly sanctuary where He lives to bless His people, and from where He will re-appear at history's end. Hebrews 11 then is not an isolated message about faith but serves to reinforce its whole message that Jesus is the final Word and fulfilment of every Old Testament office and institution.

A DEVOTIONAL INTERLUDE

For praise: Hebrews, as you have gathered by now, was written to show the supremacy of Jesus over every other person in the universe. He is the hero of God's story. As you survey the great list of heroes and personages, remember that He is out there ahead of them all – leading the procession because of His outstanding faith and confidence in His Heavenly Father. Give Him glory and praise.

DAY **357**

READ
Hebrews 11:1–5

So what, briefly, are the implications for our faith? That faith is essentially a future-orientated assurance of things hoped for (11:1)!

Faith is not fuelled by gratitude for past mercies. Gratitude is good and natural but even the godless can be grateful. The faith talked about here reaches forward for the power of God because we trust Him to keep His Word and promises.

It is – in the title of John Piper's memorable book – "faith in future grace". You can believe in future grace because it is its own evidence. Faith opens our closed eyes to understand creation. It does so intuitively, as we recognise God's power behind the world (cf. Rom. 1:19–20). And faith responds to God's revelation that He is the One Creator whose Word brought the world into being (Gen. 1:1f.). The creational scale of God's big story is vital if our faith is to stretch beyond our domestic concerns to embrace the God who creates worlds.

Faith is the only difference – so far as we can tell – between Cain and Abel. Cain's lack of it, led him to silence his brother. Abel's faith enables his blood still to speak. By faith Enoch walked with God right out of this world and into the next. But then Enoch's faith was not self-serving but expressed his desire to please God. Such faith will always write new chapters in faith's story.

A DEVOTIONAL INTERLUDE

Thought: New chapters similar to Hebrews 11 are being written every day by people like you who go out into the day trusting in the Holy Spirit to hold them, and living out their lives in response to divine grace. Don't just look back to great people of the past, look forward to the day that is ahead and determine by God's grace to draw by faith from the great resources of God. Today you can write a new chapter in faith's story.

DAY **358**

READ
Hebrews 11:6–7

If you have travelled with us through the year thus far, I trust your faith has enjoyed firsthand experience of the trustworthiness of God's character.

Faith believes in God not as a vague backdrop to life but as an active responder to the appetite for Him which He Himself whets in our hearts. God is a rewarder not a refuser. God is not a God who has "off days" or gets moody. This is no lottery. God is a covenant-making, covenant-keeping God. For this reason, true faith-people are God-orientated, God-obsessed, passionate pleasers of God. The current self-absorption of much popular Christianity compares poorly with such radically counter-cultural faith. We want to be able to control our own destiny, and to reduce everything to manageable proportions. Our pride is hurt by the realisation that we don't know all the answers.

We want to plan our schedules, and feel insecure when we are told that the life of was Jesus was "plan-less".

No wonder Noah condemned the world by faith. His foolish obedience was a standing contradiction to a culture that was taken up with eating, drinking and family-making and which was not in the least bit concerned with saving anything up for what turned out to be an exceptionally rainy day!

A DEVOTIONAL INTERLUDE

To ponder: Where is your life's focus? On yourself or on Christ? We bring great pleasure to our Lord when we focus on Him in a response of faith and obedience rather than focusing upon ourselves in self-absorption. It should be noted that self-absorption is different from self-consideration. There is nothing wrong with considering yourself; just don't be absorbed by it. Be absorbed by Him.

DAY **359**

READ
Hebrews 11:8–12

If you have some confidence that God's bigger story gives perspective to your own personal drama then you can put your faith in God even without knowing where you're going (v.8). We walk as children of the light but sometimes in the dark for we walk by faith not sight. It was in the deep and dreadful darkness of a God-induced trance-like sleep that Abraham received a prophetic vision of the troubled centuries ahead.

He lived in the promised land as if he were a stranger in it, feeling rootless and unsettled and incomplete. He erected his tents every night, no doubt wondering as he did so if there was anything permanent! His faith was stretched – as ours is – by living in "transition".

And knowing you are part of God's big story stirs you to believe God even without knowing how (vv.11–12)! Abraham and Sarah confronted the reality of their own bodies and faced the impossible. But from what was considered "as good as dead" new life sprung.

The seed grows, said Jesus, secretly, and even the experienced farmer "does not know how" it happens (Mark 4:27). Of such is the kingdom of God.

A DEVOTIONAL INTERLUDE

Prayer: Heavenly Father I do not know quite where You will lead me in the future, but my faith is not in a planned destination but in a faithful companion and guide – the Lord Jesus Christ Himself. Loving Father, Your reign in my life is my realisation, Your rule my release. Knowing You will be there in my future gives me a confidence and joy that nothing can take away. I am so deeply grateful. Amen.

DAY 360

READ
Hebrews
11:13–15

You can enjoy faith in future grace without knowing "when" (11:13).

Abraham's faith was stretched to breaking point before Isaac arrived. But the city never did arrive.

Abraham was the first of a line of heroes of faith of which it is said: "These all died in faith" (11:13 NKJV). What a wonderful epitaph: not "died disillusioned, embittered, nostalgic for the glories of the past" but died still believing. Isaac, of whom we know so little and even Jacob, a mixed character if ever there was one, are famed for this. And noble Joseph spoke believingly about the future grace coming to his people (11:20–22)

When faith is harnessed to God's larger, long-term redemptive story, it is no longer motivated by short-term goals or fixed on short-term gains. Faith looks beyond the visible and the immediate, creating waves beyond its own life-span which influence the future. Without seeking to control the future, or manipulate God, faith makes a difference to those following on in the continuing story.

Such faith reaches up and beyond the kitsch glitter of contemporary culture to the mountain peaks of a more abiding city (v.10), an alternative homeland (v.14), a better country (v.16), a more lasting reward, solid joys and lasting treasure (v.26), a better resurrection in a superior kingdom.

A DEVOTIONAL INTERLUDE

Quotation: "There is a grave in the Swiss Alps in which the body of a climber who fell to his death whilst attempting to climb the Matterhorn lies. His grave is marked with these three simple words: 'He died climbing'. When you die will the same be said of you – in a spiritual sense I mean? Reach continually for the skies, in the true sense of that word. Always look up, never down." (R.B. Jones)

DAY **361**

READ
Hebrews 11:17–22

The mystery in the story of faith, which believes "not knowing how", deepens into "not knowing why" (11:12–19).

Does it make sense to sacrifice Isaac the child of promise on whom the whole promise-plan hinged? Did Abraham wonder how he would return with Isaac?

The writer here construes it – perceptively – as Abraham's faith in a God who can raise the dead! This God defies the odds, surmounts the arguments, does wonders to faith. Faith is tested most when God seems mysterious or even contradictory in His purpose. Then we are tempted to elevate principles or dogma above a relationship with the living God and to say: this can't happen or this can't be true when it is.

If Abraham had been a slave to his own logical consistency he would have rejected the angel's veto as wishful thinking and Isaac would have died right there and then. But fanaticism isn't faith. And Abraham trusted enough to listen.

It was George Muller who said: "Save me from pride in my own consistency" (i.e. always wanting to be proved right).

Hebrews speaks compellingly to Christians tempted by a hostile society to blunt the cutting edge of commitment to the uniqueness of Jesus Christ. Faith is the gift to trust God as the Author of the story, whatever the turbulence and contradictions on the way.

A DEVOTIONAL INTERLUDE

Thought: Nothing tests faith more than confusion. Confusion erodes our sense of competence and of being in control. But it is also the context in which we can develop the muscles of our faith. Faith in God when everything is clear is one thing, but faith in Him when all around is utter confusion is another. Remember when you are struggling to hold on to God He is holding on to you. Trust.

DAY **362**

READ
Hebrews
11:23–27

Moses was born into a faithful family who saved his infant life because they believed the story of God's people which gave them a different view of the world to the one offered by Egypt's power.

Moses early on refuses in faith to let that Egypt define who he is. His later choices are just as socially provocative. He prefers partnership in suffering with God's people to the usual pleasure-seeking lifestyle promoted by Pharaoh's media. Moses opts for disgrace in the will of God which he regards as a better bet that all the accumulated wealth and wisdom, kudos and perks of a high-flying career in the Egyptian diplomatic service!

His faith made him more sure of the invisible than the visible, and incited him to forego short-term satisfaction for God's long-term reward. Faith emboldened him to defy a tyrant. Faith made him obediently implement the details of God's saving plan for Israel.

No doubt Moses' example of faith inspired a normally reluctant people's willingness to cross the Red Sea. And Moses, no doubt, shared the people's surprise at their own faith which saw Jericho's walls fall and, even more, the faith of the foreign whore, Rahab! These remarkable testimonies bear witness to the way in which our lives are transformed by being taken up into God's saving story.

A DEVOTIONAL INTERLUDE

To ponder: Here's something to chew on, so to speak, throughout the day: are you as sure of the invisible as you are of the visible? Ian Sewter, one of the background contributors to this edition of *God's Story* says: "Faith is the catalyst that transforms our lives to reject visible worldly pleasures in order to embrace the invisible rewards of being taken up into God's story." How sure are you of that?

DAY **363**

READ
Hebrews
11:32–40

Gideon, Barak, Samson, Jephthah, David and Samuel – unlikely heroes, flawed heroes, but all famous because they played their part in the story at crucial moments in the drama. The writer claims to have run out of time to tell all the stories he has to hand! But his summary gives us vivid glimpses of extraordinary, death-defying, risk-taking audacity.

No wonder the writer says "the world was not worthy of" such believers (v.38). The world doesn't deserve them! How could it? The world has no standard of measurement that can assess such people's true worth; they go right off the top of the scale! But what matters is "God is not ashamed to be called their God" (11:16b).

For our part, we may not know where or how or even why or when, but, like them, we know who. He dazzles us, we seek; He calls, we answer; He leads, we follow; He challenges, we obey; He dares, we risk; He invests all in us, we stake all on Him.

Our story of faith is the same as theirs: without us they are not part of a complete story (11:40).

Ecclesiasticus gave its roll-call of honour by inviting us: "Let us now praise famous men." Hebrews says the heroes of the Old Testament stage of the story were famous not for being celebrities but for being faithful. Hebrews wants us, like them, to be "made famous" by the story.

A DEVOTIONAL INTERLUDE

For action: What are your thoughts and feelings now as you come to the closing days of our meditations? We said earlier that expression deepens impression. Take a sheet of paper and in approximately 50 words write down what these daily meditations have done for you. You will be surprised how a summarised statement will clarify what has been happening in your soul over these last 12 months.

DAY **364**

READ
Hebrews 12:1-3

One enormous consolation as we come to the close of this *Cover to Cover* survey of God's strategic plan is that we did not start this story and we aren't expected to finish it.

Only one person has ever been able to say with total sincerity: "I have accomplished all that you gave me to do"; only one person could, in death, say, "It is totally finished". But then of course He is the author and finisher of your faith and mine. He also began the race and finishes it as we run it with Him.

Faith is therefore supremely demonstrated in the story of Jesus Himself, our champion who fought the good fight of faith and brought faith to its full and complete expression. He brought the whole dimension of faith to a new level of completion in His death and resurrection.

Jesus brings the story of Israel's faith to its destined climax by His own faith and endurance, leading those who believe from all nations into the abiding presence and worship of the One True God. He did this "for the sake" of the joy before Him or – if we read the preposition another way – "instead of" the joy set before Him. That is, Jesus forwent the joy of being spared death but went through the terrible and shameful death by crucifixion.

So faith rises in our hearts when we consider His story. Because He fought the good fight, and finished His race, so we can we.

A DEVOTIONAL INTERLUDE

For praise: Let your thoughts dwell for a moment on the fact that our faith is not a product of our own intellect or disposition – Jesus is both its author and perfector. This means, does it not, that we are what we are because Jesus is who He is. It's all because of Jesus that we have a part in His story. Once more open your heart in praise and gratitude to Him for that most glorious fact

DAY **365**

READ
Romans
11:33–35

Having traced God's story during the past 12 months, what should be our settled response to God's story?

Firstly, Paul marvels at God's "depth" of resources and that He is especially "rich in mercy" (11:12,30–32; Eph. 2:4).

Paul marvels at God's wisdom, though, like Job, it is often only when unjust suffering disrupts our normal story, that we connect with the deeper story an all-wise God is working out.

Paul recognises God's infinite knowledge and asks: "Who has ever given to God, that God should repay him?" (v.35).

Secondly, Paul ponders how unsearchable are God's judgments, and asks, "who has been his counsellor?"(v.34).

Thirdly, Paul exclaims, that God's paths are past finding out! God's plan was often a hidden stream flowing beneath the surface of events, not always obvious to the participants themselves.(e.g. Joseph Gen. 45:4–5; 50:19–20). Who knows His mind except Jesus and the Spirit given to us (1 Cor. 2:16)? We cannot find God's ways, but they find us!

It is this paradoxical wisdom which Paul celebrates as he tries to grasp the breathtaking strategy of God in history.

This is the story of this strange, angular God; an untameable God; a tough-loving and tender-talking, compassionate and unquenchable God. This God's redemptive love is alone adequate to the great tragedies of the world. Let's worship Him and never lose the "Oh!".

A DEVOTIONAL INTERLUDE

Prayer: My Father and my God, how can I thank You enough for what You have revealed to me through Your Word as I have meditated upon it day by day? May the wisdom of Your Word that has been pouring into my soul now translate itself into my witness, my work and my worship. And from now on may I indeed never lose the "Oh!". In Jesus' Name I ask it. Amen and Amen!

NATIONAL DISTRIBUTORS

UK: (and countries not listed below)
CWR, PO Box 230, Farnham, Surrey GU9 8XG.
Tel: (01252) 784710 Outside UK (44) 1252 784710

AUSTRALIA:
CMC Australasia, PO Box 519, Belmont, Victoria 3216.
Tel: (03) 5241 3288

CANADA:
CMC Distribution Ltd, PO Box 7000, Niagara on the Lake,
Ontario L0S 1JO.
Tel: (0800) 325 1297

GHANA:
Challenge Enterprises of Ghana, PO Box 5723, Accra.
Tel: (021) 222437/223249 Fax: (021) 226227

HONG KONG:
Cross Communications Ltd, 1/F, 562A Nathan Road, Kowloon.
Tel: 2780 1188 Fax: 2770 6229

INDIA:
Crystal Communications, 10-3-18/4/1, East Marredpally,
Secunderabad – 500 026.
Tel/Fax: (040) 7732801

KENYA:
Keswick Bookshop, PO Box 10242, Nairobi.
Tel: (02) 331692/226047

MALAYSIA:
Salvation Book Centre (M) Sdn Bhd, 23 Jalan SS 2/64, 47300 Petaling
Jaya, Selangor.
Tel: (03) 78766411/78766797 Fax: (03) 78757066/78756360

NEW ZEALAND:
CMC New Zealand Ltd, Private Bag, 17910 Green Lane, Auckland.
Tel: (09) 5249393 Fax: (09) 5222137

NIGERIA:
FBFM, Helen Baugh House, 96 St Finbarr's College Road, Akoka, Lagos.
Tel: (01) 7747429/4700218/825775/827264

PHILIPPINES:
OMF Literature Inc, 776 Boni Avenue, Mandaluyong City.
Tel: (02) 531 2183 Fax: (02) 531 1960

REPUBLIC OF IRELAND:
Scripture Union, 40 Talbot Street, Dublin 1.
Tel: (01) 8363764

SINGAPORE:
Campus Crusade Asia Ltd, 315 Outram Road,
06–08 Tan Boon Liat Building, Singapore 169074.
Tel: (065) 222 3640

SOUTH AFRICA:
Struik Christian Books, 80 MacKenzie Street, PO Box 1144,
Cape Town 8000.
Tel: (021) 462 4360 Fax: (021) 461 3612

SRI LANKA:
Christombu Books, 27 Hospital Street, Colombo 1.
Tel: (01) 433142/328909

TANZANIA:
CLC Christian Book Centre, PO Box 1384, Mkwepu Street,
Dar es Salaam.
Tel: (051) 2119439

UGANDA:
New Day Bookshop, PO Box 2021, Kampala.
Tel: (041) 255377

ZIMBABWE:
Word of Life Books, Shop 4, Memorial Building, 35 S Machel Avenue,
Harare.
Tel: (04) 781305 Fax: (04) 774739

For e-mail addresses, visit the CWR web site: www.cwr.org.uk

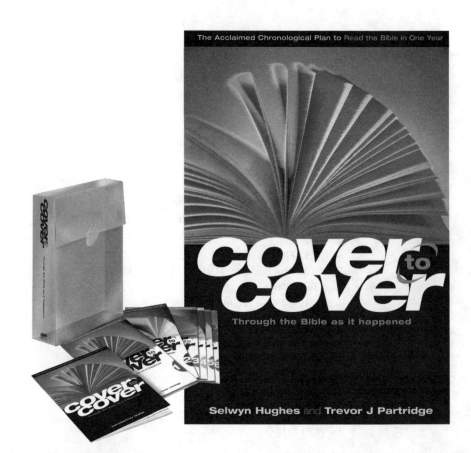